The Cultural Politics of Art in Iran

Modernist Iranian art represents a highly diverse field of cultural production deeply involved in discussing questions of modernity and modernization as practiced in Iran. This book investigates how artistic production and art criticism reflected upon the discourse about *gharbzadegi* (westoxification), the most substantial critique of Iran's adaptation of Western modernity, and ultimately proved to be a laboratory for the negotiation of an anti-colonial concept of an Iranian artistic modernity, which artists and critics envisioned as a significant other to Western colonial modernity. In this book, Katrin Nahidi revisits Iranian modernist art, aiming to explore a political and contextualized interpretation of modernism. Based on extensive fieldwork, interviews, and archival research, Nahidi provides a history of modernist art production since the 1950s and reveals the complex political agency underlying art-historiographical processes. Offering a key contribution to postcolonial art history, Nahidi shows how Iranian artistic modernity was used to flesh out anti-colonial concepts and ideas around Iranian national identity.

KATRIN NAHIDI is a postdoctoral researcher at the University of Graz. She has taught at the University of Graz, the University of Osnabrück, and the Ludwig Maximilian University of Munich. Her articles on Iranian modernism have been published in academic journals, including *kritische berichte*, *Stedelijk Studies*, and *Artl@s Bulletin*.

The Global Middle East

General Editors

Arshin Adib-Moghaddam, *SOAS, University of London*
Ali Mirsepassi, *New York University*

Editorial Advisory Board

Faisal Devji, *University of Oxford*
John Hobson, *University of Sheffield*
Firoozeh Kashani-Sabet, *University of Pennsylvania*
Madawi Al-Rasheed, *London School of Economics and Political Science*
David Ryan, *University College Cork, Ireland*

The Global Middle East series seeks to broaden and deconstruct the geographical boundaries of the "Middle East" as a concept to include North Africa, Central and South Asia, and diaspora communities in Western Europe and North America. The series features fresh scholarship that employs theoretically rigorous and innovative methodological frameworks resonating across relevant disciplines in the humanities and the social sciences. In particular, the general editors welcome approaches that focus on mobility, the erosion of nation-state structures, travelling ideas and theories, transcendental techno-politics, the decentralization of grand narratives, and the dislocation of ideologies inspired by popular movements. The series will also consider translations of works by authors in these regions whose ideas are salient to global scholarly trends but have yet to be introduced to the Anglophone academy.

Other books in the series:

1. *Transnationalism in Iranian Political Thought: The Life and Times of Ahmad Fardid*, Ali Mirsepassi
2. *Psycho-nationalism: Global Thought, Iranian Imaginations*, Arshin Adib-Moghaddam
3. *Iranian Cosmopolitanism: A Cinematic History*, Golbarg Rekabtalaei
4. *Money, Markets and Monarchies: The Gulf Cooperation Council and the Political Economy of the Contemporary Middle East*, Adam Hanieh
5. *Iran's Troubled Modernity: Debating Ahmad Fardid's Legacy*, Ali Mirsepassi

6. *Foreign Policy as Nation Making: Turkey and Egypt in the Cold War*, Reem Abou-El-Fadl
7. *Revolution and Its Discontents: Political Thought and Reform in Iran*, Eskandar Sadeghi-Boroujerdi
8. *Creating the Modern Iranian Woman: Popular Culture between Two Revolutions*, Liora Hendelman-Baavur
9. *Iran's Quiet Revolution: The Downfall of the Pahlavi State*, Ali Mirsepassi
10. *Reversing the Colonial Gaze: Persian Travelers Abroad*, Hamid Dabashi
11. *Israel's Jewish Identity Crisis: State and Politics in the Middle East*, Yaacov Yadgar
12. *Temporary Marriage in Iran: Gender and Body Politics in Modern Persian Film and Literature*, Claudia Yaghoobi
13. *Cosmopolitan Radicalism: The Visual Politics of Beirut's Global Sixties*, Zeina Maasri
14. *Anticolonial Afterlives in Egypt: The Politics of Hegemony*, Sara Salem
15. *What is Iran? Domestic Politics and International Relations*, Arshin Adib-Moghaddam
16. *Art and the Arab Spring: Aesthetics of Revolution and Resistance in Tunisia and Beyond*, Siobhán Shilton
17. *Tunisia's Modern Woman: Nation-Building and State Feminism in the Global 1960s*, Amy Aisen Kallander
18. *Global 1979: Geographies and Histories of the Iranian Revolution*, Arang Keshavarzian and Ali Mirsepassi
19. *Fixing Stories: Local Newsmaking and International Media in Turkey and Syria*, Noah Amir Arjomand
20. *Schooling the Nation: Education and Everyday Politics in Egypt*, Hania Sobhy
21. *Violence and Representation in the Arab Uprisings*, Benoît Challand
22. *A Social History of Modern Tehran: Space, Power, and the City*, Ashkan Rezvani Naraghi
23. *An Iranian Childhood: Rethinking History and Memory*, Hamid Dabashi
24. *Heroes to Hostages: America and Iran, 1800–1988*, Firoozeh Kashani-Sabet
25. *The Making of Persianate Modernity: Language and Literary History between Iran and India*, Alexander Jabbari
26. *Schooling the Nation*, Hania Sobhy

The Cultural Politics of Art in Iran

Modernism, Exhibitions, and Art Production

KATRIN NAHIDI
University of Graz

Shaftesbury Road, Cambridge CB2 8EA, United Kingdom

One Liberty Plaza, 20th Floor, New York, NY 10006, USA

477 Williamstown Road, Port Melbourne, VIC 3207, Australia

314–321, 3rd Floor, Plot 3, Splendor Forum, Jasola District Centre, New Delhi – 110025, India

103 Penang Road, #05-06/07, Visioncrest Commercial, Singapore 238467

Cambridge University Press is part of Cambridge University Press & Assessment, a department of the University of Cambridge.

We share the University's mission to contribute to society through the pursuit of education, learning and research at the highest international levels of excellence.

www.cambridge.org
Information on this title: www.cambridge.org/9781009361408

DOI: 10.1017/9781009361392

© Katrin Nahidi 2023

This publication is in copyright. Subject to statutory exception and to the provisions of relevant collective licensing agreements, no reproduction of any part may take place without the written permission of Cambridge University Press & Assessment.

First published 2023

A catalogue record for this publication is available from the British Library.

Library of Congress Cataloging-in-Publication Data
Names: Nahidi, Katrin, author.
Title: The cultural politics of art in Iran : modernism, exhibitions, and art production / Katrin Nahidi, Université de Genève.
Description: Cambridge ; New York, NY : Cambridge University Press, 2023. | Series: The global Middle East
Identifiers: LCCN 2023012068 (print) | LCCN 2023012069 (ebook) | ISBN 9781009361408 (hardback) | ISBN 9781009361378 (paperback) | ISBN 9781009361392 (epub)
Subjects: LCSH: Modernism (Art)–Iran. | Art–Political aspects–Iran.
Classification: LCC N7285.5.M63 N34 2024 (print) | LCC N7285.5.M63 (ebook) | DDC 709.55/0904–dc23/eng/20230515
LC record available at https://lccn.loc.gov/2023012068
LC ebook record available at https://lccn.loc.gov/2023012069

ISBN 978-1-009-36140-8 Hardback

Cambridge University Press & Assessment has no responsibility for the persistence or accuracy of URLs for external or third-party internet websites referred to in this publication and does not guarantee that any content on such websites is, or will remain, accurate or appropriate.

In loving memory of my father Essi, and Amoo Behrooz, whose respective absence and presence have been the motor for this research

Contents

List of Figures		*page* xi
Acknowledgments		xiii
	Introduction	1
1	Exhibitions of Modernist Iranian Art: The Construction of a Secular Heritage	19
	Iran Modern and the Iranian Diaspora	20
	The Tehran Modern: The Cancellation of an Exhibition	46
	Tehran Museum of Contemporary Art: *The Tehran Modern* in Iran	67
2	Cultural Politics in Pahlavi Iran: The TMoCA'S Architecture and the Evolution of *Gharbzadegi* in Arts and Politics	91
	Westoxification: The Discourse of *Gharbzadegi*	92
	Queen Farah Diba and Her Support of Arts and Culture	107
	The Architecture of Tehran Museum of Contemporary Art	113
	Iranian Modernist Art and Jalal al-e Ahmad's Concept of *Gharbzadegi*	131
3	"*Saqqakhaneh* Revisited": The Art-Historiographical Construction of a Local Modernism	146
	Shi'ite Material Culture in Modernist Iranian Art	148
	Politics of the Period	162
	The Naming of *Saqqakhaneh*	167
	Saqqakhaneh's Existence as a Group	176
	The State's Recognition of *Saqqakhaneh* as an Expression of a State-Sponsored Modernism	189
	Saqqakhaneh's Discursive Afterlife	193

4 Jalil Ziapour and the *Fighting Rooster Association*
(*K̲orūs-e Jangī*) 208
   Cubist Aesthetics in Iran 208
   The *Fighting Rooster Association* 229

   Conclusion 256

Select Bibliography 265

Index 283

Figures

1.1 Mohammad Ehsai, *Gerehaye Khayam*, 1968	page 33
1.2 Bahman Mohassess, *Fifi Sings of Joy*, 1964	37
1.3 Nahid Hagigat, *Escape*, 1975	41
1.4 Ardeshir Mohassess, *Untitled*, 1978	43
1.5 Frank-Walter Steinmeier standing in front of the painting *Mural on Indian Red Ground* (1950) by Jackson Pollock at Tehran Museum of Contemporary Art	47
1.6 Afshin Parvaresh, *Khabar Furi (Breaking News)*, June 15, 2017	85
1.7 Afshin Parvaresh, *Emrooz Ekhtetamiyeh, Fardah Sham-e Akheir (Today is the closing day, tomorrow the last supper)*, June 15, 2017	85
2.1 Exterior view of the TMoCA	115
2.2 Noriyuki Haraguchi installing *Matter and Mind* (1971) at the TMoCA, 1977	117
2.3 Interior view of the TMoCA with Haraguchi's oil pool	118
2.4 The monument *Shahyad Aryamehr*	122
2.5 Interior view of the TMoCA with view of the rotunda	124
2.6 Andy Warhol and Iran's Empress Farah Diba, in front of a screen print portrait by Warhol during a reception at the Waldorf Astoria Hotel	130
3.1 Parviz Tanavoli, *Heech and Chair II*, 1973	187
3.2 Parviz Tanavoli, *Heech and Table I*, 1973	187
3.3 *Saqqakhaneh* Exhibition Catalog, 1977	191
3.4 *Saqqakhaneh* Exhibition Catalog, 2013	203
4.1 Jalil Ziapour, *Zaynab Khatoun*, 1953, repainted in 1962	210

4.2 Jalil Ziapour, cover of *Fighting Rooster* magazine
    [*Korūs-e Jangī* magazine], vol. 1, Tehran, 1948   236
4.3 *In the name of the merciful*, calligraphy in the form of a
    hoopoe, Iran, seventeenth/eighteenth century   237
5.1 Koorosh Shishegaran, *For Today*.   257

Acknowledgments

I am very thankful to Ali Mirsepassi and Arshin Adib-Moghaddam for publishing my manuscript in the Global Middle East Series and to the editor Maria Marsh and her assistant Rachel Imrie of Cambridge University Press for their terrific support during the publication process.

This book is an outcome of my doctoral dissertation. The field research was made possible by the generous support of the Swiss National Science Foundation (SNSF) within the Sinergia Project "Other Modernities – Practices and Patrimony of Visual Expression Outside the West" (2013–2017), for which I would like to express my gratitude.

I would like to thank Wendy Shaw, my *Doktormutter*, for supervising my dissertation and for her invaluable support and unconditional trust in this project.

I would also like to thank Burcu Dogramaci, my second supervisor, and Sussan Babaie, who encouraged me at the very beginning to turn this topic into a doctoral thesis. My thanks also go to Silvia Naef and Irene Maffi for their help and advice during the "Other Modernities" SNSF project.

Besides the professional support, it is, above all, the help and acceptance of friends and family that make such a mammoth project possible. I deeply thank my mom Heidi, my brother Michel and my sister Susi, and their families, who have been taking care of my emotional, physical, and culinary well-being throughout my life, particularly during the COVID-19–related lockdowns. To Vici, my dearest friend, for her constant motivation and encouragement. To Sandra, my dissertation comrade in Switzerland, for her relentless willingness to give me feedback on any writing and her unbridled optimism. Also, a big thank you to Tina and all our students in Baumschulenweg for showing me my privileges and their worldly wisdom. And to Kathrin, Anna, Charlotte, Yanna, Alireza, Haleh, Fati, and Evelina for their friendship during this period.

The field research for this study was not only a journey into the art of Iran but also a journey to my Iranian family, who welcomed me with open arms during my research trips and gave me a home in Tehran. I am forever grateful to Mahin and my cousins Elnaz and Roozbeh. Endless thanks also to my favorite travel group, Negar, Sanam, and Ali, with a special thanks to Leili, who have made my stay in Iran an unforgettable memory.

Without the active support of Hadi Abdollahi, Helia Darabi, Hamide Atashpah, and Ava Serjouie, I would never have found my way around the libraries and archives in Tehran.

Last but not least, I am immensely grateful to the artists and art critics who so generously and willingly allowed me access to their thinking and works.

Introduction

Through the mist of time, I think back to the semi-dark interiors and spotlighted walls of Tehran's art galleries. I go back five years, ten years, fifteen years, and I stop around that period. I try to remember the names of the galleries. Gallery Borghese, Gallery Saba, Gallery Iran, Farhang Hall, and the Abyaz Palace, where four of Tehran's five biennial art exhibitions were held. Good old names and good old days![1]

Inspired by art critic Karim Emami's 1977 article "Saqqakhaneh Revisited," which was highly influential in shaping Iran's art history, this study seeks to revisit modernist Iranian art production to explore a more political and contextualized interpretation of modernism in Iran. A theoretical framework rooted in postcolonial critique and interwoven with iconographic analysis will help dismantle imperial notions of modernity and has the potential to decolonize modernist Iranian art history. This approach will allow us to see that Iranian modernist art was not simply a local implementation of universal modernist practices but a highly diverse field of cultural production that negotiated and reflected upon questions of modernity and modernization as practiced in Iran. Modernist artistic expression was closely tied to both a critique of the adaptation of Western modernity, articulated using the term "westoxification" (*gharbzadegi*), and the country's political struggles for liberalization and democracy.

In recent decades, art historians have established an accepted canon and trajectory for modernist Iranian art. Modeled after stylistic categorization and terminology of European art history, this canon has established a hierarchical order of modernist art and narrates a story of modernism's evolution in Iran based on the idea of linear artistic progress. However, a methodology dominated by biographical study and formalism largely detaches Iranian modernist production from its

---

[1] Karim Emami, 'Saqqakhaneh School Revisited', *Saqqakhaneh* Exh.-Cat (Tehran: Tehran Museum of Contemporary Art, 1977).

sociopolitical and sociocultural context of origin and places this art in a political vacuum. In this context, formalist art criticism and its focus on stylistic development became a decisive means of categorizing Iranian art as modern and secular and, thus, interacting with modernist art from Iran in the broader discourse of global modernity. This is reflected in the established canon of modernist art in Iran, which takes as its underlying and organizing principle the idea of artistic progress in the form of a common narrative about the evolution of modernism in Iran. It is, however, important to note the canon of modernist Iranian art does not simply represent a hierarchical order of formal and aesthetic qualities. Instead, as Elizabeth C. Mansfield points out, "the canon serves as a means to demark cultural and social boundaries." As a "realization of a culture's self-conception," the art-historical canon "allows a society to visualize itself" and "gives material form to a society's fantasy of collective identity."[2]

How have these boundaries become so widely accepted? What does it mean to write the history of modernist art in Iran? Whom and what interests does the depoliticized history of formalist progress serve? What are the contexts and purposes of a continuing formalist Iranian art historiography today? What is the artists' agency in this discourse? What ideological significance did and do modernist artworks still possess?

Art historians typically identify the foundation of the Art Academy at Tehran University in 1941 as the beginning of modernist art in Iran. This is seen as the first indication of modernist artistic production because the foundation of universities happened in the broader discourse of Iran's modernization programs and was an essential strategy for implementing Western modernity in Iran. This modernization becomes evident in the case of the art academy, which replaced earlier systems of artistic training with Western models of education. The director of Tehran's art academy, the French architect and archeologist André Godard, developed the curriculum for artist education in Iran based on the teaching methods of the French École-des-Beaux-Arts system. Thus, students became familiar with Western art not only at the academy but also during their state-sponsored stays in European

---

[2] Elisabeth Mansfield, 'Border Patrols. Art History as Identity,' in E. C. Mansfield (ed.), *Making Art History: A Changing Discipline and Its Institutions* (London: Routledge, 2007), 14.

capitals, where they had the opportunity to deepen their studies and expand their knowledge about European contemporary artistic trends. After their return to Iran, the first generation of modernist artists experimented with techniques of Western modernism and adopted European artistic styles, such as Impressionism, Expressionism, Cubism, and abstract art.

Various art-historical accounts classify the period of the 1940s and 1950s as a time of asynchronous and often belated attempts to translate European artistic discourses into the Iranian context. For art history, however, this era of formalist imitation and experiments with Western modernity created the necessary technical foundations, which paved the way for the evolution of a local modernism. The resulting emergence of a specific Iranian modernism in the 1960s and 1970s, which is often seen as a skillful symbiosis of Iranian visual traditions and Western means of modernist expression, has often been interpreted as the pinnacle of Iran's modernist art history. In these historiographical accounts, merging Iran's visual traditions with the expression of modern Western forms signals the country's successful modernization while preserving a specific national identity. After a short period during which modernism flourished, however, the linear art-historical narrative of Iran's adaptation and appropriation of modernity comes to a sudden end with the rise of political Islam and the growing dissemination of revolutionary ideology, eventually leading to the Iranian Revolution in 1978/79.

The predominantly formalist methodological approach of Iranian art historiography, which often focuses on the aesthetic adaptation of modern European modes of expression, produces an art history based on stylistic divisions. This idea of Iranian modernism as a sign of the successful visual implementation of Western modernity played into the hands of official cultural politics. Under the monarchy of Mohammad Reza Shah Pahlavi (1941–1979), cultural politics and the promotion of art and culture played a crucial role in communicating Iran's successful modernization and secularization both domestically and abroad. In particular, modernist art became an important signifier for the efficiency of the state's modernization programs. For their nationalist and westernizing ideology, Pahlavi cultural programs often used Iranian modernism as part of a power-political strategy to prove Iran was on its way to becoming a westernized nation-state. This became even more important after the events of Iran's oil nationalization leading to the coup d'état in 1953, which shattered the country's unstable political structures of secular democracy. Backed by British and US secret services, the coup overthrew the democratically elected Prime Minister Mohammad Mosaddeq. After the coup and the reinstatement of Mohammad Reza Shah's royal dictatorship, the government established national surveillance systems to prevent a further "politicisation of the society," as Ali Ansari explains.[3] After the political events of 1953, the monarchy became the most important patron for the promotion and exhibition of modernist art in Iran and institutionalized all fields of cultural production. In this regard, the institutionalization of critical voices against the monarchy became a power-political strategy for defusing any kind of oppositional criticism.

This instrumentalization of Iranian modernist art helped to strengthen the ideological bond with Iran's Western allies during the Cold War. During this period, Cold War capitalist ideology promoted abstract art as a symbol of an allegedly universal culture. Peter Weibel explains, "The concept of a neutral universal culture, which the ruling cadres of the respective countries all tended to deploy, functioned as the pillar of the global system." Based on the ideas of modernization and progress, "universal culture, a knowledge of the same languages, literary and visual works all became the fraternal signs by which the capital accumulators of the world recognized one another."[4] In this context, modern and, in particular, abstract art played a crucial role in presenting this idea of universality. Modern abstract art was often seen as a symbol of freedom of expression and as a means of fighting totalitarianism. Thus, modern art helped propagate abstraction's superiority over socialist realism in the field of art and Western capitalist superiority over Soviet Socialism in the political realm. In this way, abstraction was turned into an ideological weapon to construct a common Western identity that traversed countries and national borders and to communicate allegedly universal ideals of freedom and liberalism.[5] In this context, Iran's appreciation of modernist art

---

[3] Ali M. Ansari, *Modern Iran: The Pahlavis and After: Reform and Revolution* (London and New York: Routledge, 2007), 162.
[4] Peter Weibel, 'Globalization: The End of Modern Art?' *ZKM Magazine*, 2013. https://zkm.de/en/magazine/2013/02/globalization-the-end-of-modern-art
[5] See Frances Saunders Stonor, *Who Paid the Piper? CIA and the Cultural Cold War* (London: Granta, 1999), 1–7; Eva Cockcroft, 'Abstract Expressionism: Weapon of the Cold War,' *Artforum*, vol. 15 (1974), 39–41; Serge Guilbaut,

served as confirmation that it had the symbolic capital of "taste" necessary to recognize the universal language of Western modernism. Pierre Bourdieu explains that "material or symbolic consumption of works of art constitutes one of the supreme manifestations of ease, in a sense both of objective leisure and subjective facility."[6] In the case of Iran, Bourdieu's sociological analysis illustrates that culture not only functions in the realm of class distinction within a national society but can also be applied as political currency on a higher level to emulate Western nation-states and to move up in the global world order. Looking at modernist art, visiting museum exhibitions, and the general appreciation of modernism by the royal family in Iran thus helped to demonstrate that the monarchy and its royal members had "a relation of immediate familiarity with things of taste."[7] This image was also deployed globally in foreign policy as a vital sign of the Pahlavi monarchy's modernity and its "unconscious unity of class" with Western nation-states.[8]

The institutionalization and instrumentalization of modernist art by the Pahlavi state established a powerful historiographical paradigm, which places modernist artistic expression from Iran in the service of the monarchy. In particular, both recent exhibition projects outside Iran and the exhibition activities of the Tehran Museum of Contemporary Art (TMoCA) repeat this paradigm. In these contexts, modernist Iranian art plays a key role as a visual manifestation in memorializing prerevolutionary Iran as a westernized and secularized country. During this time, the Ministry of Fine Arts and Culture in Iran also supported the publication of art-historical overviews about the evolution of Iranian modernist art. In these books, contemporary art critics and art historians shared their first-hand findings and decisively shaped the field of formalist modern art history in Iran. This generation of writers tried to establish a different narrative, which reached further back and paid more attention to the intellectual underpinnings of cultural exchange, which has been forgotten in more recent approaches. One example of these formalist stylistic overviews is *L'art moderne en Iran* (1967) by the painter and critic Akbar

---

How New York Stole the Idea of Modern Art: Abstract Expressionism, Freedom, and the Cold War (Chicago: University of Chicago Press, 1983).
[6] Pierre Bourdieu, *Distinction: A Social Critique of the Judgement of Taste* (Cambridge, MA: Harvard University Press, 1984), 55.
[7] Ibid., 77.   [8] Ibid.

Tajvidi, who locates the beginning of modernist art in Iran around 1890 when Iranian artists became familiar with Western arts during their travels to Europe. According to Tajvidi, from this point on, artistic experiences in the "contact zones" altered Iranian artistic production tremendously and introduced Western artistic means into the Iranian context.[9] According to Tajvidi, a short period of imitation allowed Iranian artists to catch up with developments in painting in European art history. After that, Iranian artists began merging Persian visual traditions, such as calligraphy and ornamentation, with modern Western art, achieving in this manner, according to the author, an unprecedented manifestation of artistic innovation and creativity in Iran.[10]

In 1974, art historian Ruyin Pakbaz provides a more critical approach to the adaptation of Western modernism in Iran. He points out that the integration of Western artistic means dates back to Safavid times and significantly influenced Qajar painting. Despite earlier adaptations of Western aesthetics, Pakbaz considers only Iranian art after World War II modern because it marks a radical break with earlier artistic traditions, symbolizing "a battle of ideas ... between the old generation and the new."[11] Throughout his book, Pakbaz follows the idea of a formalist evolution and categorization of Iranian art while also emphasizing the significance of nationalizing tendencies in visual art. For him, the artistic turn to Iran's traditions was intended to create a specific version of Iranian modernism,

> The richest feature in the style and character of contemporary art in Iran over the last few decades is the artist [sic] search for a definite identity, their effort to create a genuine Iranian school of contemporary art with a distinctive national character. These artists took advantage of novel technical possibilities of expression in Western art to evolve an original Iranian personal style.[12]

It is interesting to note that Pakbaz characterizes the incorporation of Iranian elements as "personal," which implies the ideas of subjectivity

---

[9] See Marie Louise Pratt, 'Arts of the Contact Zone,' *Profession* (1991), 33–40.
[10] Akbar Tadjvidi, *L'art moderne en Iran* (Tehran: Ministry of Fine Arts and Culture, 1967). 5.
[11] Ruyin Pakbaz, *Contemporary Iranian Painting and Sculpture* (Tehran: Ministry of Fine Arts and Culture, 1974), 8.
[12] Ibid., 9.

and genius. "Subjecting influences from abroad" in combination with "painstaking critical analysis" of the universal European modern represent, for Pakbaz, a way to make the "latent national genius and creativeness" visible.[13] Despite his initial openness toward modernism, Pakbaz remains critical of the practice of modernist expression in Iran. For him, Iranian modernist art "lacks historical continuity" and could not fulfill its "declared objective of founding an 'Iranian' style."[14] This is because "only a handful of contemporary Iranian artists have really understood their culture."[15] For Pakbaz, the majority of Iranian artists produced only formalist artworks while ignoring the sociocultural and sociopolitical discourses of their time. In his numerous writings over the years, Pakbaz further elaborated his critical assessment of the practice of modernism in Iran, which was influenced by a Marxist approach and has shaped the field of modernist art historiography in Iran.[16] In particular, a younger generation of artists and art historians have critically questioned the adaptation and implementation of Western modernity in Iran, the monarchy's ideological instrumentalization of modernist art, and the artists' agency during this time. For many critics, such as the artist and writer Iman Afsarian, the discursive constitution of Western modernity and its claim to universalism were by no means applicable to the Iranian context. For Afsarian, Iranian artists tried to catch up with Western modernity in the art field due to a general inferiority complex surrounding the West. This catching-up, however, only took place on a visual and formalist level, without a "historical awareness" of the history of Western modernity or the Iranian sociopolitical context.[17]

As will be shown in this book, opinions on modernist Iranian art vary greatly. For art historians, Hamid Keshmirshekan and Fereshteh Daftari, who have contributed tremendously to global scholarship on modernist Iranian modernism, the incorporation of traditional elements from Iran's visual heritage represents a principal expression of

---

[13] Ibid.   [14] Ibid., 39.   [15] Ibid., 40.
[16] See Ruyin Pakbaz, 'Dar jostiju-ye hoviyat' [Seeking Identity], *Herfeh: Honarmand* (Tehran, 2007), 18; Ruyin Pakbaz, *Encyclopedia of Art* (Tehran, 1999); Ruyin Pakbaz, *Naqashi-ye Iran. Az diruz ta emruz* [*Iranian Painting. From Yesterday to Today*] (Tehran: B Nashr-e Naristan, 2000).
[17] Iman Afsarian, 'Chera ma nemitavanim honar-e moaser dashte bashim?' [Why Can't We Have Contemporary Art]. *Herfeh: Honarmand* (Autumn 2015), 101–103.

identity politics. In these accounts, merging modernist expression with local Iranian traditions represents an artistic strategy for exploring a possible modern Iranian identity in the broader discourse of global modernity based on cultural difference.[18] However, this conceptualization of modernist art in terms of hybridity is also based on the dominance of formalism. It operates with the idea of merging universal elements of Western modernity with local traditional expression. Consequently, Iranian creativity and artistic innovation originate within Western modernity's framework, which in turn reaffirms Western hierarchies.

A closer look at various contributions to Iranian art historiography reveals that these accounts operate with varying concepts of modernity and modernist art production. In this regard, two major views on the adaptation and appropriation of modernity in the Iranian context can be extracted from the existing historiography. The first concept is based on the idea that Iranian artists fully adapted modernist expression by means of assimilation and mimicry. The second model suggests that the search for an Iranian version of modernism was achieved on an aesthetic level through cultural mixing. Yet, as different as the positions may be, whether they support or oppose the government of Mohammad Reza Shah and whether they promote the idea of Western modernity's completion or its failure in Iran, it is a politically motivated formalist understanding of modernist art from Iran that prevails. The dominant perception of artistic production from this period is that it was secular, westernized, and modernist. According to art historian Shiva Balaghi, a formalist methodology leads, in this regard, to the concealment of the artists' political engagement and their struggle for liberalization. Balaghi explains,

Iranian artists in the 1960s and 1970s were engaged in the search for a solution to "the problem of culture" under capitalism. In the cultural lexicon

---

[18] See, for example, Fereshteh Daftari, *Persia Reframed: Iranian Visions of Modern and Contemporary Art* (London and New York: I. B. Tauris, 2019); Hamid Keshmirshekan (ed.), *Amidst Shadow and Light: Contemporary Iranian Art and Artists* (Hong Kong: Liaoning Creative Press, 2005); Hamid Keshmirshekan, *Contemporary Iranian Art: New Perspectives* (London: Saqi Books, 2013).

of Iran, the "West" did not simply represent a higher civilizational model to be emulated, but an imposing presence on its national autonomy.[19]

This points to a third model of modernity in Iranian visual art, in which the merging of Western elements with Iranian visual traditions was not a formal but an analytical artistic strategy. Due to formalism's dominance, the analytical and critical deployment of a simultaneously intellectual and aesthetic language has been widely neglected in Iranian art historiography. This study tries to alter the general perception of modernist Iranian art as mere visual experiments with Western means of expression and to situate it within the social and political context of its origin by means of a contextual approach to art history and a critique of formalism.

In the years after World War II, the formalist approach flourished as the leading methodology in the reception and analysis of modernist arts. Art critics such as Clement Greenberg contributed significantly to formalism's success in establishing itself as the dominant method in modern art history. Focusing solely on formal-aesthetic qualities of modernist artworks, formalist criticism conceals the interdependent correlation between art and its social and historical frameworks. For Greenberg, art's sociopolitical contexts compromise the ideals of modernisms' aesthetic autonomy and pureness. Due to the continued dominance of formalism, nonformalist approaches began sprouting up in the 1950s, and a countermovement started in reaction to the formalist agenda. The proponents of nonformalist art history followed a more contextual and synthetic approach by taking the historical circumstances of artistic productions into account. The debate about formalism and politics in art history reached new heights in the 1990s when advocates of nonformalism criticized formalist art history as a means of depoliticizing artistic practice and neutralizing art's critical implications.[20] For instance, the art historian Deniz Tekiner argued that the formalist methodology and its concealment of art's social

---

[19] Shiva Balaghi, 'Iranian Visual Arts in "The Century of Machinery, Speed, And the Atom": Rethinking Modernity,' in Shiva Balaghi and Lynn Gumpert (eds.), *Picturing Iran: Art, Society and Revolution* (London and New York: I. B. Tauris, 2002), 24.

[20] For a further discussion and summary of the debates about formalism in art history, see Deniz Tekiner, 'Formalist Art Criticism and the Politics of Meaning,' *Social Justice*, vol. 33, no. 2 (2006), 31–44; Johanna Drucker, 'Formalism's Other History,' *The Art Bulletin*, vol. 78, no. 4 (1996), 750–751.

implications serve capitalist market interests. For Tekiner, the focus on art's aesthetic qualities confirms "the prevailing system of art commodity exchange and its ideology" and transforms artworks into "objects in commodity relations."[21]

In the case of Iranian modernist art, the close ties between formalist criticism and the state's instrumentalization of modernist art led to its interpretation in a political vacuum. The idea of art as a symbol of Iran's successful modernization has shaped the reception of this artistic production to this day. This, in turn, shows that modernist Iranian art has evolved out of a complex discursive construction of Iranian modernity and points, in fact, to art and politics' close relationship with and interdependence on one another. Chantal Mouffe writes,

There is an aesthetic dimension in the political and there is a political dimension in art. From the point of view of the theory of hegemony, artistic practices play a role in the constitution and maintenance of a given symbolic order, or in its challenging, and this is why they necessarily have a political dimension.[22]

The French philosopher Jacques Rancière holds a similar view of the relationship between art and politics. Rancière writes, "art is not, in the first instance, political because of the messages and sentiments it conveys concerning the state of the world" but rather because "the specificity of art consists in bringing about a reframing of material and symbolic space."[23] With this in mind, the depoliticization of modernist art and its interpretation as aesthetic evidence of art's autonomy indicate a questionable concept of modernity. The underlying idea of modernity "tries to retain the forms of rupture, the iconoclastic gestures, etc., by separating them from the context that allows for their existence: history, interpretation, patrimony, the museum, the pervasiveness of reproduction."[24] Rancière strongly criticizes the modernist narrative and its obsession with the "new" and art's alleged radical break with representational styles. He even states that these notions of modernity "have been deliberately invented to prevent a clear

---

[21] Tekiner, 'Formalist Art Criticism and the Politics of Meaning,' 40.
[22] Chantal Mouffe, *Agonistics: Thinking the World Politically* (London: Verso, 2013), 91.
[23] Jacques Rancière, *Aesthetics and Its Discontents* (Cambridge: Polity, 2009), 23.
[24] Jacques Rancière, *Dissensus: On Politics and Aesthetics* (London: Bloomsbury Academic, 2010), 21.

Introduction 11

understanding of the transformations of art and its relationships with the other spheres of collective experience" and help to stage modernist art as a symbol of artistic autonomy and universality.[25]

This is reflected, especially in the case of Iran, in the way the institutionalized discourse of modernist art took hold of and materialized artistic expression as visual evidence of the state's successful modernization, westernization, and secularization. The concept of secularism is closely tied to Western modernity and denotes an assumed neutral separation between religion and politics. It encompasses multiple historical, cultural, and regional conceptions but was mainly developed in Christian contexts.[26] This poses the question of secularity's applicability to non-Western societies. In most cases, colonialism and imperialism formed the relationship between secular and religious realms in non-Western countries.[27] This is also the case for Iran, where modernist Iranian art shows us the limits of Eurocentric concepts of secularity and modernity.

Both for the Pahlavi regime, as well as for contemporary art historiography, Iran's discourse on artistic modernity evolved from an ideological closeness to the West. As we have seen, Iran's modernist art history rests on similar pillars, such as canon, styles, and linear history of progress, which support the idea of the autonomy of Western modern art. According to the curator and writer Okwui Enwezor, "the very notion of proximity to the West," which was a result of global power politics, represents the interpretation and reception of non-Western modernities "a double-edged sword."[28] For Enwezor, this idea comes into play because the "sword cuts a swath between the revolutionary and emancipatory portents of the postcolonial critique of master narratives and the nationalist rhetoric of tradition and authenticity."[29] For this reason, Enwezor suggests a "postcolonial

---

[25] Ibid.
[26] See Charles Taylor, *A Secular Age* (Cambridge, MA: Belknap Press of Harvard University Press, 2007).
[27] For further investigation on the topic, see Mirjam Künkler, John T. S Madeley and Shylashri Shankar, *A Secular Age beyond the West: Religion, Law and the State in Asia, the Middle East and North Africa* (Cambridge: Cambridge University Press, 2019).
[28] Enwezor Okwui, 'Mega-Exhibitions and the Antinomies of a Transnational Global Form,' *Manifesta Journal: Journal of Contemporary Curatorship*, no. 2 (2003), 113.
[29] Ibid.

response" to the new emerging interest in the field of non-Western modernities based on the idea that, "in its discursive proximity to Western modes of thought, postcolonial theory transforms this dissent into an enabling agent of historical transformation and thus is able to expose certain Western epistemological limits and contradictions."[30]

This observation leads to a broader question: How can we even study modernist Iranian art? How can one write the history of Iran's artistic modernity while being aware of the "darker side of modernity," such as colonialism, imperialism, and universality?[31] To avoid these ideological pitfalls of Western modernity when studying Middle Eastern modernities, the art historian Prita Meier suggests that rather than "simply include the non-Western into the modernist canon," art historiography should try to "disrupt the foundational assumption of modernist art history that Western production is the universal norm."[32] This assumption of Western universality rests on the problematic and paradigmatic presupposition that "the modern is just a synonym for the West" and that modernity is often staged as the intellectual property of enlightened Europe.[33] This means that, for non-Western countries, "to become modern, it is still said, or today to become postmodern, is to act like the West," as Timothy Mitchell explains.[34]

This demonstrates that the "classical" and static conceptualization of Western modernity is insufficient for more in-depth study of art histories outside the West. Therefore, it is necessary to reflect on theoretical concepts of modernity, which may help us consider the complexity and multitude of non-Western modernist art and liberate its artistic expression from constant comparison and tropes of imitation and belatedness.[35] In particular, in the face of globalization, we

[30] Ibid.
[31] See Walter D. Mignolo, *The Darker Side of Western Modernity: Global Future, Decolonial Options* (Durham, NC: Duke University Press, 2011).
[32] Prita Meier, 'Authenticity and Its Modernist Discontents: The Colonial Encounter and African and Middle Eastern Art History,' *The Arab Studies Journal*, vol. 18, no. 1 (2010), 29.
[33] Timothy Mitchell, 'The Stage of Modernity,' in Timothy Mitchell (ed.), *Questions of Modernity* (Minneapolis: University of Minnesota Press, 2000), 1.
[34] Ibid.
[35] For a further investigation of the topic of "Other Modernites," see, for example, Silvia Naef, Irene Maffi, and Wendy Shaw, '"Other Modernities": Art, Visual Culture and Patrimony outside the West: An Introduction,' *Artl@s Bulletin 9*, no. 1 (2020), Article 1.

must rethink concepts of modernity. Shmuel N. Eisenstadt, for instance, introduced his concept of "multiple modernities," a term that criticizes the universal claim of European modernity and argues that "Western patterns of modernity are not the only 'authentic' modernities."[36] For Eisenstadt, modernity's history represents "a story of continual constitution and reconstitution of a multiplicity of cultural programs."[37] Eisenstadt's understanding of modernity as a form of culture allows different views on what makes a society modern. This theoretical premise opens up a critical perspective on Iran's history and responds to the uncanny question: Is Iran modern? It explains that modernity in Iran was a continually evolving process, and the country's search for its national traditions was not a break with modernity but instead, in its very ideological core, a product of the same modernity, which would also give rise to political Islam. Iran's modern turn to "the invention of tradition" happened primarily within the Western episteme and is evidence of the transcultural moment of modernity in general and, in particular, of the transculturality of modernity in Iran.[38]

Transcultural modernity is reflected in Iranian modernist art, where processes of encounter, local translations, and adaptations decisively shaped vernacular artistic production. A transcultural perspective on modernist Iranian arts helps to challenge not only nationalist art historiographies but also binary divisions between the local and the global. In recent years, scholarship on global art history has discussed and explored theoretical concepts and possible ways the discipline might expand.[39] For example, with James Elkins's famous question, *Is Art History Global?*, art history started to reflect upon its limits as a field rooted in a Eurocentric framework.[40] From the early 2000s, various art historians laid the theoretical foundations to establish theoretical tools for research on non-Western modernist and contemporary art. Most of these historiographical considerations are based on

---

[36] Shmuel Eisenstadt, 'Multiple Modernities,' *Daedalus*, vol. 129, no. 1 (2000), 3.
[37] Ibid., 2.
[38] See Eric Hobsbawm and Terence Ranger, *The Invention of Tradition* (Cambridge: Cambridge University Press, 2012).
[39] See Monica Juneja, 'Alternative, Peripheral or Cosmopolitan? Modernism as a Global Process,' in Juli Allerstorfer and M. Leisch-Kiesl (eds.), *»Global Art History«: Transkulturelle Verortungen von Kunst und Kunstwissenschaft* (Bielefeld: Transcript, 2018), 79–108.
[40] James Elkins, *Is Art History Global?* (New York: Routledge, 2007).

a global concept of modernity and follow a transcultural approach. The "more" global endeavors in art history often focus on the transnational transfer of knowledge, the migration of forms and discourses, and their interaction with local conditions during decolonization.[41]

Global art theory and reconceptualizations of modernity build an essential framework for this study of modernist Iranian art and its aim of revisiting modernist Iranian art production. Nevertheless, analyzing Iranian modernism remains challenging for several reasons, including that modernist Iranian art does not yet have the specific scholarly framework of a scientific discipline. It is important to note that Iranian artists from the 1940s to the 1970s did not call their art "modern." In their own and art-historiographical accounts, it is often called *mo'aser*, which means contemporary. In particular, the first generation of Iranian artists marked their radical break with past artistic traditions by naming their production "new art." Art from this era, however, emerged in the broader discourse of Iran's modernization. Thus, this kind of modernist Iranian art gained importance as a microcosm negotiating the complex question of how to be modern while also being Iranian in a newly established nation-state seeking its definition and recognition from Europe. For this reason, this study employs "modernist" as a general organizing term for artistic production, which uses modernist expression on an aesthetic level while dealing with the discursive constitution of "being modern" in Iran.

From a regional point of view, modernist art from Iran could be part of Islamic art history as a discipline that studies artistic and cultural productions in the broader Middle East.[42] Islamic art history, however, has neglected twentieth-century art produced in Middle Eastern countries. Having evolved from Orientalist and colonialist strategies of

---

[41] For a transcultural approach toward global art history, see the following selected titles: Hans Belting and Andrea Buddensieg, *The Global Art World: Audiences, Markets, and Museums* (Ostfildern: Hatje Cantz, 2009); Smith Terry, Okwui Enwezor, and Nancy Condee (eds.), *Antinomies of Art and Culture: Modernity, Postmodernity, Contemporaneity* (Durham, NC: Duke University Press, 2008); Grenier Catherine (ed.), *Modernités Plurielles 1905–1970 Dans Les Collections Du Musée National D'art Moderne* (Paris: Centre Pompidou, 2013); Okwui Enwezor, Katy Siegel, and Ulrich Wilmes (eds.), *Postwar: Art between the Pacific and the Atlantic, 1945–1965* (London: Prestel Publishing, 2016).

[42] See Wendy M. K Shaw, *What Is 'Islamic' Art? Between Religion and Perception* (Cambridge: Cambridge University Press, 2019).

Introduction

knowledge production about the West's significant "other," the discipline of Islamic art history instead created a canon that starts with the birth of Islam and ends around 1800, excluding the modern age. In his famous critique, Finbarr Barry Flood exemplified how "the ideological implications of the production of Islamic art" produced an imagined "golden age" of Islamic art before modernization.[43] Flood points out that the exclusion of modern cultural production follows "the rise of neoconservative discourses emphasizing the failure of Muslims to make the transition to Euro-American modernity" while neglecting the enduring political repercussions of Western colonialism and imperialism on the region.[44] Consequently, as Sussan Babaie writes, this "scarcity of scholarship on the period between the eighteenth and the end of the twentieth century and the absence of a sustained interrogation of the emergent modernities of the Islamic world" leaves modernist Iranian art production in a sociopolitical and sociocultural vacuum.[45]

This book tries to shed light on modernist art production from Iran and to illustrate the political challenges and artistic complexities of the period and is divided into four chapters. This study concentrates on Tehran as main site of Iranian art production. The capital became the center of artist networks, cultural-political debates, and exhibitions that shaped modernist Iranian art under the Pahlavi monarchy. A closer look at Iranian art historiography in Chapters 1 and 2 reveals how Iran's modern history is remembered and reiterated. Chapters 3 and 4 attempt to retrace the histories ignored in contemporary exhibitions and overviews while focusing on modernist Iranian art production and its employment of modernist artistic formal language to address changing social and political conditions. Close analyses of selected artworks will help to establish a less formalist and more contextualized approach toward modernist art. It will be shown that these artists used modernist modes of expression not only for formal innovation but also as an essential means of responding to the political discourses of their time.

---

[43] Barry Flood Finbarr, 'From Prophet to Postmodernism? New World Orders and the End of Islamic Art,' in Mansfield, *Making Art History*, 31–53, 39.
[44] Ibid.
[45] Sussan Babaie, 'Voices of Authority: Locating the "Modern" in "Islamic" Arts,' *Getty Research Journal*, no. 3 (2011), 133–149, 140.

The first chapter examines contemporary exhibitions inside and outside Iran as historiographical sites of knowledge production about modernist Iranian art. A comparative perspective will show how these exhibitions repeated and strengthened the historiographical paradigm that modernist Iranian art production symbolizes the country's successful modernization and secularization during Pahlavi rule. A close analysis will demonstrate that the depoliticized reading of Iranian modernist art in the respective exhibition contexts serves different contemporary political interests. With its focus on the formalist qualities of Iranian art, the exhibition *Iran Modern*, held in 2013 at the Asia Society in New York, represents a significant attempt to inscribe Iranian modernist art in the new emerging canon of global modernities. Evolved from the Iranian diaspora discourse in the United States, the exhibition addressed both the diasporic *self* and the *other*, that is, the host country. By celebrating Iran's modernist art as a golden age of secularism, the exhibition functioned for the diaspora community as a metaphorical return to Iran's prerevolutionary era.

The second case study looks at the canceled exhibition project *The Tehran Modern*, which was supposed to present artworks from Tehran Museum of Contemporary Art's collection at the National Gallery in Berlin and the Museum MAXXI in Rome, as an example of the political instrumentalization of modernist art as a means of soft power. After many years of negotiations, the exhibition was supposed to be the crowning jewel of the successful nuclear negotiations with Iran in 2015. German officials, however, canceled the exhibition in December 2016 after several postponements of the artworks' departure and delays in obtaining permission from the Iranian side for their export. German media suspected Iran's troubled relationship with its modernity as the cause for the delays and, in the act of cultural politics, thus intentionally boycotted the exhibition. For this reason, the third part of this chapter will investigate the details of Iran's refusal to send parts of its modernist collection abroad. Above all, it was Tehran's art scene that mobilized opposition against the export of the works and the opaque preparations for the exhibition. Hence, the protests against *The Tehran Modern* exhibition can be seen as an expression of democratic culture in Iran, in which the art scene demanded transparency and a say in the country's cultural policy and that the institutions of the Islamic Republic preserve Iran's modern heritage.

The second chapter will delve deeper into the museum's history and foundation under the rule of Mohammad Reza Shah. During the Pahlavi's reign, royal patronage of the arts became an effective response to the growing critique of the Shah's radical reformation programs, which materialized under the umbrella term *gharbzadegi* (westoxification). The critique formulated with westoxification contributed decisively to the politicization of Islam, which eventually led to the Islamic Revolution. In this context, it is important to note that Iranian intellectuals developed the concept of *gharbzadegi* through the lens of Western anti-Enlightenment philosophy. *Gharbzadegi* both denotes an anticolonial critique of repeated imperial interferences in Iran's modern history and represents the most substantial criticism of Iran's monarchy as overly westernized. The term came into full swing after the intellectual Jalal al-Ahmad published his essay, *Gharbzadegi*, in 1962.

For a deeper insight into Pahlavi cultural policy, this section will analyze the architectural design of the Tehran Museum of Contemporary Art, showing that the instrumentalization of art and architecture helped to communicate the new ideology established by the Pahlavis. To alter the perception of modernist art in Iran as a mere illustration of Pahlavi modernization, the last part of the chapter will introduce al-e Ahmad's art criticism. These texts demonstrate that his attempt to establish a significantly different version of Western monarchy also included the field of modernist art. As important source material, his texts reveal that modernism was less a kind of formalist experimentation with Western modernity and more a new artistic language that provided Iranian artists with new means of expression to address social and political themes of their time.

The idea of *Saqqakhaneh* plays a key role in Iranian art historiography because the artistic group represents the first successful translation of global modernism into the Iranian context. *Saqqakhaneh* is considered the first movement that moved beyond the belated imitation of Western artistic styles and established a local modernism rooted in Iranian visual traditions. To shed light on a possible definition of *Saqqakhaneh*, Chapter 3 will examine artworks and various written sources associated with *Saqqakhaneh*. *Saqqakhaneh* was not a self-styled art movement, nor did the artists share a common aesthetic program. The multiple designations of *Saqqakhaneh* as a school of modernism, an artistic group, or even an independent art movement reveal no uniform definition of the term. This leads to the conclusion that art historiographical processes were more influential on the evolution of *Saqqakhaneh* as a category than the artists' actual collaboration. Recognizing this distinction gives an important insight into the complex and shifting politics that prepared the ground for the reception of artworks connected to *Saqqakhaneh*. As a celebration of the Pahlavi monarchy's liberal sponsorship of art and culture, these works play a crucial role in the memorialization of prerevolutionary Iran.

The fourth and last chapter introduces the *Fighting Rooster Association*, which was founded in 1948 by the painter Jalil Ziapour (1920–1999), the writer Gholam Hossein Gharib (1923–2003), the playwright Hassan Shirvani, and the composer Mortezza Hannaneh (1922–1989). A closer look at the *Fighting Rooster's* artistic productions reveals that the first generation of modernist artists was already deeply invested in creating a specifically Iranian modernism. Until recently, art historiography considered Jalil Ziapour's works as belated imitations of European modernist art resulting from an artistic immaturity concerning Western modernism. The artistic adaptation of French Cubism enabled Ziapour and the *Fighting Rooster Association* to elaborate a suitable visual vocabulary for creating an artistic subjectivity rooted in Iranian cultural heritage. In addition, it helped foster the Fighting Rooster's political hopes and ambitions for Iran's democratization and to proclaim an alternative national identity rooted in the country's spiritual heritage to counter Iran's adoption of modern Western rationality.

As a student at André Lhote's private art school in Paris, Ziapour became familiar with the body of cubist thought, which was highly influenced by the antirationalist and antipositivist thought of the philosopher Henri Bergson. Bergson's antirationalist philosophy would become highly influential for these Iranian artists. The members of the *Fighting Rooster* translated Bergson's metaphysical ideas through Sufi tropes into the Iranian context. In light of Orphic Cubist theory, this chapter traces the transcultural moments of Iranian modernist art and the global interrelations of modernism. As will be shown, far from mere imitation, the Iranian translation of Cubism represents the search for Iranian art beyond Orientalism and exoticism.

1 | *Exhibitions of Modernist Iranian Art*
The Construction of a Secular Heritage

Since the 2000s, repeated exhibitions of modernist arts from Iran have established a paradigmatic historiography for the modernist era in Iran. Yet, by ignoring the initial context of production, exhibition, and discussion, this historiography serves contemporary interests to stage Iran's modernist art as a sign of modernization and secularization.

To expose the symbolic and political value of modernist Iranian art, this chapter will focus on two case studies, the exhibition *Iran Modern* (2013–2014) and the canceled exhibition project *The Tehran Modern*. In light of these exhibitions outside Iran, it will also be necessary to investigate the history, legacy, and exhibition activities of the Tehran Museum of Contemporary Art (TMoCA) as the official institution for modern art in Iran.

The exhibition *Iran Modern* at the Asia Society in New York, evolved within the Iranian diaspora discourse in the United States and tried to construct a genuine nationalistic approach toward Iranian modernist art. The exhibition raises significant questions about the hegemonic interpretation of what and who defines Iranian art as Iranian, especially when it is exhibited outside Iran. This becomes evident in the artworks selected for the exhibitions. The curators Fereshteh Daftari and Layla S. Diba narrated their story of Iranian modernism with a selection of one hundred artworks by Iranian artists produced between 1953 and 1979. Due to the US sanctions against Iran, there was only one piece on loan from Iran, Ahmad Aalis's *Self-Portrait*. Thus, ninety-nine of the selected artworks belonged to public or private collections outside Iran. This meant that essential works from the TMoCA and other public and private institutions and collections in Iran were not included in the exhibition and, thus, not part of this story of Iranian modernism.

An analysis of the canceled exhibition *The Tehran Modern*, which was scheduled to be held at the National Gallery in Berlin and the

Museum MAXXI in Rome in 2016 and was to feature artworks from the collection of the TMoCA, will shed light on the political instrumentalization of modernist art and highlight how Iranian modernist art often functions as a means of soft power and a signifier of secular modernity and successful modernization based on rationality and progress. Although modernist Iranian arts, as visible relics of Pahlavi culture, have not yet been fully integrated into the cultural politics of the Islamic Republic of Iran, in today's Iran, modernism is also understood as a practice of secularism.

A comparative perspective will show how the different exhibition projects in Tehran, Berlin, and New York conceptualize Iranian modernist art as a general expression of secularism and freedom of expression while using it for their respective political ends.

Iran Modern and the Iranian Diaspora

The exhibition *Iran Modern*, held at the Asia Society in New York from September 2013 until January 2014, is one of the many examples of cultural productions by the Iranian diaspora community that effectively communicate "Iranian" culture to English-speaking communities across the globe. On the one hand, the exhibition tried to establish an art-historiographical approach based on an interpretation that differed from the dominant narration of Western modernism. On the other hand, it attempted to establish a similarity between Western and Iranian modernist artistic movements. A discussion of their similarity could be observed in Iranian diaspora politics in the aftermath of the September 11 attacks, when the diaspora community tried to preserve their image as "good" and successful migrants. This was done by celebrating Iran's modernist art as representing a golden age of secularism and constructing a diasporic concept of Iranian modernity. The exhibition functions on two levels, that of the diasporic *self* and that of the *other* – the country in which they live. For the community, *Iran Modern* becomes the nostalgic trope of a metaphorical return to a prerevolutionary Iran. The intense focus on art as an expression of secularity and promotion of the idea that, before the revolution, Iran had been on its way to becoming a "Westernized" country not only addresses the diaspora community but also was intended to alter the perception of Iran and Iranians in the United States. Yet, this overarching narrative, which is deeply rooted in the discourse of the Iranian diaspora, creates conflicting stories regarding the exhibition's hypothesis and the selected artworks.

An Outline of Iranian Migration in the United States

The exact number of Iranians living outside Iran's territorial borders is unknown. It is estimated that about five million Iranians, including children and grandchildren of Iranian immigrants, live outside Iran.[1] These Iranian immigrants or their ancestors mainly left their homeland during two phases of Iran's history in the twentieth century. The first phase of emigration occurred between 1950 and 1977. There were two main types of immigrant. Members of both groups emigrated temporarily as well as permanently. On the one hand, some students participated in state-sponsored programs in other countries to foster the Pahlavi's modernization program but eventually took up permanent residence there. On the other hand, we find political opponents of the Pahlavi regime, who orchestrated their political resistance from abroad but may also have nonetheless found themselves opposed to the political outcomes of the revolution.[2]

The second and most significant wave of Iranian emigration was caused by the conditions and events of the Iranian Revolution (1978/79). Political supporters of the monarch, Mohammad Reza Shah, formed the first major group that left Iran during the revolutionary upheavals. Well-educated and wealthy members of an urban upper and middle classes left Iran to escape prosecution under the new regime.[3] These emigrants tried to preserve their class status in their new lives abroad. As a westernized urban elite, many Iranian emigrants had the cultural capital "to establish themselves as members of the bourgeoisie" in their new places of residence.[4]

However, in the aftermath of the revolution, many political activists who had supported the overthrow of the monarchy left the country but were later prosecuted in the newly established Islamic Republic. Alongside political opponents, religious and ethnic minorities also

---

[1] See Nader Vahabi, *ATLAS de la diaspora Iranienne* (Paris: Ed. Karthala, 2012).
[2] Hamid Naficy, *The Making of Exile Cultures: Iranian Television in Los Angeles* (Minneapolis: University of Minnesota Press, 1993), 27.
[3] Ibid.
[4] Manuchehr Sandijian, 'Temporality of "Home" and Spatiality of Market in Exile: Iranians in Germany,' *New German Critique*, no. 64 (1995), 3–36, 18.

feared prosecution. The flow of Iranian emigrants increased again during the Iran–Iraq war (1980–1988) when young Iranian males tried to escape military service.[5]

Due to the many immigrants, "an alternative Iranian map began to emerge, one that lies beyond the boundaries of the Islamic Republic of Iran."[6] The most significant number of Iranian expatriates can be found in the United States, primarily in California and Los Angeles, which is sometimes called "Tehrangeles" or "Irangeles."

Iranian emigrants are a highly heterogeneous and diverse group in terms of ethnicity, language, education, religion, and political affiliations. Iran is a multiethnic and multireligious state that comprises different ethnic groups, including Turkish, Kurdish, Bakhtiari, Armenian, and Qashqa'i populations. Religiously, the Iranian diaspora community includes Shiites, Jews, Baha'is, Zoroastrians, and Assyrian and Armenian Christians. Although these groups use different languages at home, there is one unifying element that ties these diverse ethnic and religious communities together, inside and outside Iran: their shared mother tongue, Persian.[7]

Although Iranian emigrants are a highly diverse group, their joint opposition toward the Iranian Revolution and the Islamic Republic of Iran functions as a means of unification: "The totalising narrative of the 'Revolution' as a marker of shared communal identity plays an important role in presenting a bounded and comprehensible Iranian migrant experience."[8] The opposition toward the new regime in Iran – which called itself Islamic and patronized Islamic belief to maintain political power – is another reason for the general absence of religiosity and high levels of secularism among Muslim Iranian migrants. Being Islamic is not a significant point of identity for diaspora Iranians.[9]

---

[5] Naficy, *The Making of Exile Cultures*, 27.
[6] Resa Mohabbat-Kar, 'Introduction,' in Heinrich Böll Foundation in cooperation with Transparency for Iran (eds.), *Identity and Exile: The Iranian Diaspora between Solidarity and Difference*, volume 40 of the Publication Series on Democracy (Berlin: Heinrich Böll Foundation, 2016), 9–25, 12 (hereafter *Identity and Exile*).
[7] Naficy, *The Making of Exile Cultures*, 27.
[8] Cameron Mcauliffe, 'Unsettling the Iranian Diaspora: Nation, Religion and the Conditions of Exile,' in *Identity and Exile*, 36.
[9] Naficy, *The Making of Exile Cultures*, 26.

Iranian Exile and Diaspora

Due to political reasons, for many Iranians living in exile, a return to their homeland is impossible, nor is life in today's Iran even remotely imaginable. Living in exile, however, has many consequences, as Hamid Naficy states,

> On the one hand, they refuse to become totally assimilated into the host society; on the other hand, they do not return to their homeland – while they continue to keep aflame a burning desire for return. In the meantime, they construct an imaginary nation both of the homeland and of their own presence in exile.[10]

The forced separation from one's home country is often a traumatic and painful experience for exiles. In the case of Iranian exiles who had left Iran due to the revolutionary upheavals, the separation correlated with a loss of status, family ties, and property in Iran. Official media in Iran harshly criticized the exiles for deserting the country.[11] The eight-year war between Iran and Iraq was another traumatic event for Iranians living in Iran, as well as for Iranian emigrants, due to the "inability to affect its course from a distance, and the guilt of living in safety," Naficy explains.[12]

As a remedy for trauma, displacement, and the loss of their roots, exiles often join diaspora communities to participate in an imagined nation beyond national territories and to collectively demonstrate how one is different from the host society. In his classical definition of diaspora, William Safran emphasizes the centrality of a specific geographic homeland for the exiles.[13] Safran's definition of diaspora corresponds well to the context of the *Iran Modern* exhibition in this chapter; the historian of anthropology James Clifford has criticized it, emphasizing that the real or symbolic homeland does not play as central a role as that asserted by Safran:

> Decentered, lateral connections may be as important as those formed around a teleology of origin/return. And a shared, ongoing history of displacement, suffering, adaptation, or resistance may be as important as the projection of a specific origin.[14]

---

[10] Ibid., 16.   [11] Ibid., 130.   [12] Ibid.

[13] William Safran, 'Diasporas in Modern Societies: Myths of Homeland and Return,' *Diaspora: A Journal of Transnational Studies*, vol. 1, no. 1 (1991), 83–99, 89.

[14] James Clifford, *Routes: Travel and Translation in the Late Twentieth Century* (Cambridge, MA: Harvard University Press, 1997), 249–250.

The shared imagination of a return from exile may also take place on a metaphorical level as the return to a symbolic homeland, as in the case of Iranian emigrants. Many emigrants left Iran before or during the revolution, and many of their children consider themselves part of the Iranian diaspora. However, they have never lived in the Islamic Republic of Iran. Since the Iran of the Pahlavi era they reference no longer exists, their return can only happen in a symbolic realm.

According to Clifford, while the homeland is an important point of reference for exiles, the host country plays an equally significant, if not a larger, role in the context of living in diaspora. Iranian emigrants, in particular, were strongly affected by the domestic politics of the country where they were in exile. When students occupied the US embassy in Tehran and took fifty Americans hostage in 1979 after the Iranian Revolution, the perception of Iran and Iranians in the United States deteriorated. During the so-called hostage crisis, the Iranian students tried to coerce the extradition of Mohammad Reza Shah, who had already left Iran in January 1979. Domestically, the hostage crisis strengthened the revolutionary ideology. As Stephanie Cronin writes,

> The coup allowed the Khomeini faction to place itself at the head of yet another anti-imperialist mass mobilization, outflank the Left, silence all opposition and push through a new constitutional proposal based on clerical domination.[15]

On an international level, as a "gross breach of international law," the hostage crisis alienated the rest of the world from Iran and the Iranian Revolution. Although the Shah died in the summer of 1980 – and with him, the reason for the hostage-taking – the occupation of the embassy did not end until January 1981.[16]

The hostage crisis strongly affected Iranians living in the United States. The media often depicted the hostage-takers and average Iranians as criminals and terrorists. Iranians in the United States faced legal and financial difficulties. As Naficy explains, "President Carter canceled the visas of all Iranian students, forcing them to reregister,

---

[15] Afshin Matin-Asgari, 'From Social Democracy to Social Democracy: The Twentieth Century Odyssey of the Iranian Left,' in Stephanie Cronin (ed.), *Reformers and Revolutionaries in Modern Iran: New Perspectives on the Iranian Left* (London: Routledge, 2004), 37–64, 47.

[16] Ali M. Ansari, *Modern Iran: The Pahlavis and After* (London: Routledge, 2007), 290.

and deported those found in violation. The severing of all diplomatic and economic ties between the two countries made the transfer of funds and legal documents, travel, and communication into ordeals."[17] The hostility toward Iranians led to harassment and discrimination, resulting in many Iranians trying to hide their Iranian identity and denying their Iranian roots.[18]

Despite the negative image of Iran in the United States during the 1980s, "Iranians are considered a very successful group of immigrants and have been praised for their activities by various US officials."[19] This image of success relies on status, education, and income and becomes a shared identity among Iranian migrants. By celebrating festivities such as the Persian New Year, which has its roots in pre-Islamic history, the diaspora community connects itself to the time of the Persian Empire. It thus alludes to Pahlavi nationalism while distancing itself from the Islamic government in Tehran. As Donya Alinejad and Halleh Ghorashi explain, "it also promotes a positive image of Iranian culture by relating it to the pre-Islamic era, the era of fame and power." They established a secular image of Iranian identity based on "a non-Islamic discourse on strength, wealth, and power."[20] In this context, Iranian culture functioned as a symbol for the economic and cultural value of Iranian immigrants in the United States and promoted "identity politics through difference."[21]

It was only in the aftermath of September 11, when President George Bush and his administration called Iran part of the "axis of evil," that Iranian identity politics in the United States moved from a discourse of difference to one of sameness to avoid anti-Muslim sentiments and discrimination.[22] The background of Iranian migratory experiences in the United States shows that both voluntary and involuntary emigrants often join diaspora societies to remedy displacement, fragmentation, and rootlessness. As Naficy explains, "when social structures are threatened, communitas emerges and helps the exiles maintain similarity through elaborations of differences based on ethnicity and

---

[17] Naficy, *The Making of Exile Cultures*, 131.
[18] Judith Albrecht, '"How to Be an Iranian Woman in the 21st Century?" Female Identities in the Diaspora,' in *Identity and Exile*, 51–67, 56.
[19] Donya Alinejad and Halleh Ghorashi, 'From Bridging to Building: Discourses of Organizing Iranian Americans across Generations,' in *Identity and Exile*, 62–75, 62.
[20] Ibid., 64.   [21] Ibid., 65.   [22] Ibid., 66.

locality."[23] But, as this example of the Iranian diaspora has shown, identity formations in the diaspora communities are also fluid and the subject of constant negotiations. As Stuart Hall explains,

The diaspora experience as I intend it here is defined, not by essence or purity, but by the recognition of a necessary heterogeneity and diversity: by a conception of "identity" which lives with and through, not despite, difference; by *hybridity*. Diaspora identities are those which are constantly producing and reproducing themselves anew, through transformation and difference.[24]

The Narrative of the Exhibition Iran Modern

The exhibition *Iran Modern* evolved from the Iranian diaspora discourse in the United States and tried to construct a national history of modern Iranian art. Held not in Tehran but rather at the Asia Society in New York, the exhibition's location reflects the diaspora's deterritorialized state. The curators, Layla S. Diba and Fereshteh Daftari, created their art-historiographical narrative with artworks belonging to private and public collections outside Iran. This means that the exhibited artworks have their history of migration, transfer, circulation, and translation processes and may also have a migratory identity.

On a substantive level, the exhibition *Iran Modern* constructs a linear narrative of the development of Iranian art, which is also deeply rooted in the specific discourse of the diaspora. According to the curators, after formalist experiments with modernity, which can, for example, be observed in Jalil Ziapour's adaptation of cubism, modernism culminated in the artistic movement of *Saqqakhaneh*, whose members merged folkloristic elements with the European discourse of modernist art.[25] *Saqqakhaneh* was "the first major tendency to turn the gaze inward" and became "a mold for Iranian identity, which had been the subject of concern looming over the entire history of Iranian

---

[23] Naficy, *The Making of Exile Cultures*, 91.
[24] Stuart Hall, 'Cultural Identity and Diaspora,' in Patrick Williams and Laura Chrisman (eds.), *Colonial Discourse and Post-colonial Theory: A Reader* (London: Routledge, 1994), 227–237, 235.
[25] Layla S. Diba, 'The Formation of Modern Iranian Art: From Kamal-al-Molk to Zenderoudi,' in Fereshteh Daftari and Layla S. Diba (eds.), *Iran Modern*. Exh. Cat. Asia Society Museum (New York: Asia Society Museum in association with Yale University Press, New Haven, CT, 2013), 45–65, 54.

civilization."[26] The exhibition's strong focus on *Saqqakhaneh* seeks to emphasize *Saqqakhaneh* as an innovative and national example of a local modernism and to prove that Iranian modernism is not an imitation of Western modernist arts. The other parts of the exhibition try to demonstrate that Iranian modernism should be seen as equal to Western modernism because it, too, relies on paradigms of universalism, secularism, radical subjectivity, and abstract expression of forms. It is not surprising, therefore, that, in the exhibition's narrative, the history of modernist art in Iran ends in the late 1970s, when the revolution took over and many Iranians fled the country. For the curators, modernist artistic expression was closely tied to the Pahlavi monarchy. Layla Diba states, "The Queen and her advisors became a locus for innovative ideas, which spurred the surge of local modernism."[27] Critical voices against royal cultural politics were, for the curators, not politically motivated but lacked an understanding of modernist art: "Daneshvar and Al-e Ahmad's taste in art appears to have been quite conventional and tended to favour traditional and Expressionist art."[28] This statement shows that the curators see modernist art and the discourse of the revolution as entirely separate units or even in opposition to one another. As Diba goes on to explain, "Iranian artists were absorbing fifty years of European and American modernism in the space of a few years, and this engagement was cut off at its height in 1979."[29]

The assumption that the revolution ended the blossoming of modernism in Iran is also observable in the selection of artworks. *Iran Modern* did not present revolutionary artworks, such as paintings, posters, and visual ephemera. However, these forms contributed decisively to the revolution's success and were partly designed by modernist artists.[30] Revolutionary propaganda art does not correspond with the exhibition's concept of modernism because this artistic production relies on naturalistic expression and promotes Islamic belief in the service of the revolution.

The exhibition presents works in different artistic media to mark the sharp break in the art-historiographical narrative of progress. Whereas

---

[26] Fereshteh Daftari, 'Redefining Modernism: Pluralist Art before the 1979 Revolution,' in *Iran Modern*, 25–43, 29.
[27] Diba, 'The Formation of Modern Iranian Art,' 55.   [28] Ibid.   [29] Ibid., 56.
[30] See Peter Chelkowski and Hamid Dabashi, *Staging a Revolution: The Art of Persuasion in the Islamic Republic of Iran* (London: Booth-Clibborn, 1993).

"true" modernism was presented using mainly paintings and sculptures, documentary photography illustrates the anti-Shah demonstrations and the revolutionary turmoil in 1978 and 1979, with works by Abbas, Bahman Jalali, Rana Javadi, and Kaveh Golestan. The black-and-white press photographs function less as artworks and more as documentation of the revolution and historical witnesses that prove the exhibition's hypothesis that "the flourishing pluralism temporarily lost momentum."[31]

In this context, the project raises important questions that not only are limited to Iranian art historiography but also relate to the larger field of non-Western modernities. Which ideas and conceptions of modernity does the project promote? Who speaks, and how do they legitimize the position they are speaking from? With the exhibition organized in a cultural institution in New York, Iranians living in Iran were hardly the target audience since visiting it was nearly impossible for them due to visa restrictions and the length of the journey. Who, then, was the target audience?

Tradition as Visual Resource

The exhibition *Iran Modern* had a strong focus on the formalist aspects of modernist art production that endeavored to alter the perception of Iranian modernism and present it as a more global endeavor. Proceeding from a formal-aesthetic appreciation of Iranian modernism, it promoted a view beyond mere imitation and belatedness. In doing so, the exhibition project tried to demonstrate that Iranian art was a pluralistic enterprise fully equivalent to Western modernism in its artistic innovation. With their exhibition project, the curators, Daftari and Diba, aimed to redefine modernism and to reinscribe Iranian arts into the global modernist canon. Iranian art, according to Daftari, "belongs to the larger landscape of world heritage, to global modernism."[32] In line with major Western art-historiographical practices, such as Alfred Barr's famous chart of artistic expression in the twentieth century, which was designed as the cover for the *Cubism and Abstract Art* exhibition catalog in 1936, *Iran Modern* constructed rigid divisions to classify Iranian modernist arts.

[31] Daftari, 'Redefining Modernism,' 40.   [32] Ibid., 26.

Together, the exhibition's promotion of a strong focus on formal-aesthetic principles and the simultaneous exclusion of the social and political circumstances of artistic production function as an important means of staging Iranian modernist art as a symbol of secularity and emphasizing the autonomy of modernist arts. This strategy has also helped to establish a similarity between Western and Iranian artistic discourses as part of an attempt to communicate that Iran was already on its way to becoming a "westernized" country before the revolution.

The exhibition catalog's opening essay by the curator Daftari is an attempt to redefine modernism and to reinscribe Iranian arts into the modernist canon. It seeks to demonstrate that "the Western monologue has been interrupted" and that Iranian modernism is a part of the new emerging art histories shaped by postcolonial thought.[33] Daftari's argument relies strongly on Barr's definition of modernism, which he conceptualized as a visual language characterized by abstract tendencies and nonnaturalistic means of expression. According to Daftari, Iranian art can be easily integrated into the larger narrative of modernism because "Iranian art would have been modern long before the West turned away from nature."[34] Layla Diba also understands modernist expression as a formal-aesthetic practice oriented toward abstraction:

Modernity is defined here as the global socioeconomic transformations in the wake of the industrial revolution and the subsequent emergence of democracies and the spread of worldwide capitalism. The term 'art of the modern era' primarily means figurative and narrative art of the twentieth century; 'modernism' as used herein refers to abstract and semi-abstract avant-garde art of the twentieth century.[35]

To illustrate that Iranian modernism was also a pluralistic enterprise, both exhibitions set up rigid categories of modernist expression based on formal-aesthetic principles. The exhibition is divided into four chapters: *Saqqakhaneh*, calligraphic modernism, abstraction, and political art. While affirming the paradigm set by Barr, the retroactive categorization of modernist expression in Iran is intended to demonstrate that Iranian modernism is evidence of the country's past modernity. Each of these art-historiographical categories expresses characteristics of modernity. The first category, *Saqqakhaneh*, defines

[33] Ibid.   [34] Ibid.   [35] Diba, 'The Formation of Modern Iranian Art,' 49.

the exhibition's focus and is intended to show that Iranian artists successfully liberated themselves from past traditions of Persian crafts, such as calligraphy and textiles. In the narrative of *Iran Modern*, the incorporation of traditional motifs represents merely a visual resource to achieve artistic innovation.

The term *Saqqakhaneh* was first used by the art critic Karim Emami in 1963 to describe the artistic practice of a group of artists such as Parviz Tanavoli, Charles Hossein Zenderoudi, Faramarz Pilaram, Mansour Ghandriz, and Massoud Arabshahi, who all experimented with tropes and techniques associated with local and folk aesthetic traditions at that time. While working within the European modernist discourses at the time, such as abstraction and Lettrism, they also consciously included traditional techniques such as calligraphy, metalwork, and textiles.

In the proper sense, *Saqqakhaneh* refers to public water fountains commemorating the Shiite martyrs of the battle of Karbala who were denied water in the desert.[36] Thanks to Emami's art criticism, the idea of *Saqqakhaneh* as a group or school of art became an essential concept in general Iranian art historiography, which will be further investigated in Chapter 3. Yet, *Saqqakhaneh* acquired a major significance for the curators of the exhibition *Iran Modern*, particularly as a "culturally specific modernism." Both curators characterize the first period of modernist arts in Iran in the 1940s and 1950s as a time in which Western paradigms of modernism were imitated. After this period of immature experiments with modernity, *Saqqakhaneh*'s turn to local traditions became the motor of their creativity. Layla Diba moves entirely within the established patterns of Iranian art historiography when she explains,

> The rediscovery of popular art forms – every day utensils, printing blocks, votive objects, and stamps, which conveyed powerful universal and local messages – both empowered and exhilarated Saqqakhaneh artists and provided the inspiration needed to liberate them from the conventions of academic painting and traditional art, much as the cubists had used African art or the abstract expressionists had used Native American art.[37]

The curators thus identify the locus of *Saqqakhaneh*'s significance as one of the formal innovations that led to a specifically Iranian modernist

---

[36] Peter Lamborn Wilson, '"The Saqqa-Khaneh" from Saqqakhaneh, 1977,' *Iran Modern*, 231–233.

[37] Diba, 'The Formation of Modern Iranian Art,' 57.

expression. As Daftari explains, "with the Saqqakhaneh school, Iranian painting finally found its national style and authentic visual language."[38] But, in their relationship to nationalist concerns, the artists echoed the sociohistorical discourse of their time. Cultural critics such as Jalal al-e Ahmad criticized the blind imitation of the West and demanded a modernization that preserved an Iranian national identity. In Daftari's view, *Saqqakhaneh* "provided a comfortable mold for the Iranian identity, which had been the subject of concern looming over the entire history of Iranian civilization – a culture often threatened by outsiders."[39] While al-e Ahmad and other theorists searched for an Iranian identity rooted in Shi'ism, Daftari and Diba maintain that, in retrospect, *Saqqakhaneh* and other Iranian styles of modernism were detached from an Islamic context and should rather be seen as secular practices rooted in the modernist paradigm of formal innovation.

Despite the religious associations of the movement's name, the artists were not proselytizing Shi'ism. The term Saqqakhaneh is a misnomer because it does not easily accommodate the pluralist composition of the movement, whose members were interested in a variety of sources, from the pre-Islamic era to secular or even subversive subject matter.[40]

With this line of argumentation, the curators try to downplay the incorporation of Islamic visual elements, presenting it as a strategy to combine "low" and "high" art. As Diba writes, the inclusion of "traditional" elements in the *Saqqakhaneh* artists' visual expressions articulated their modernity. "Saqqakhaneh artists delved deeply into popular culture to form individual styles in a dazzling display of creativity and vitality. It appeared as if the waters of modernism broke the dam of tradition."[41]

Secularity

The exhibition's leitmotif is the idea of modernist expression as a sign of successful secularization during Pahlavi rule. Chapter two of the exhibition, which focuses on calligraphic modernism, offers a good example to illustrate this claim. Calligraphic modernism is a widespread practice in modernist Islamic arts and can be found as an aesthetic practice in the works of many Middle Eastern artists.

---

[38] Ibid. [39] Daftari, 'Redefining Modernism,' 29. [40] Ibid., 30.
[41] Diba, 'The Formation of Modern Iranian Art,' 57.

Although one might locate calligraphic experiments in the broader discourse of Islamic modern art, Daftari maintains that Iranian calligraphy occupies a secular position.

In Iran, or even in diaspora (Zenderoudi has lived in France since 1961), this calligraphic modernism, complex and diverse in its references, at times incorporates irreverent text in sloppy handwriting, antithetical to a pan-Islamic impulse, or asserts an identity that is secular and Iranian, not to be misconstrued as Arab or Islamic.[42]

However, the curators' selection of Mohammad Ehsai and Reza Mafi clearly undermines this assumption. As a traditionally trained calligrapher, Ehsai employs calligraphy as his main artistic medium in his modernist explorations. This kind of calligraphic painting is often called *Naqqashi-khatt*, which is characterized by its being composed of abstract and calligraphic gestures. In Ehsai's calligraphies, entangled letters create fascinating ornaments and independent patterns. Though his abstract compositions look very modernist, they are deeply rooted in Persian and Islamic calligraphic traditions. As Sussan Babaie argues,

Ehsai's work has an underlying emphasis on the metaphysical traditions of *erfan*, which draw upon the rich cache of mystical notions deeply rooted in Persian poetry, painting, music, and other arts. Clearly his not only is a locally situated tradition but also is deeply personal and spiritual.[43]

Contrary to how he is portrayed in the context of the exhibition *Iran Modern*, Ehsai's calligraphic paintings were not even considered part of the modernist discourse in Iran before the revolution due to their religious content. Instead, as Hengameh Fouladvand explains, "For years, an 'elite' mentality looked at calligraphic painting as substandard to modern international works and made it clear that modernism and its evolution in art translated only to avant-garde art, and it could not be 'sacred'."[44] One example of Ehsai's artistic practice at the *Iran Modern* exhibition is the painting *Gerehaye Khayam* (1968). The artwork consists of bold black letters in Persian script against a bright orange-golden background.

---

[42] Daftari, 'Redefining Modernism,' 33.   [43] Babaie, 'Voices of Authority,' 141.
[44] Hengameh Fouladvand, 'Mohammed Ehsai's Modernist Explorations in Calligraphic Form and Content,' *Arte East*. https://arteeast.org/quarterly/mohammed-ehsais-modernist-explorations-in-calligraphic-form-and-content/?issues_season=summer&issues_year=2008, accessed 11 June 2018.

Figure 1.1 Mohammad Ehsai, *Gerehaye Khayam*, 1968. Acrylic and oil on canvas. 99.1 × 137 cm. Collection of Mohammad Ehsai.

The letters are illegible, and it seems like they have fallen apart while still being inseparably interlocked. The title, *Gerehaye Khayam*, translates to "Khayyam's weeping." It refers to Omar Khayyam, a poet, mathematician, astronomer, scientist, and Sufi. During his life in Nishapur, in eleventh-century Persia, Khayyam was widely known as a mathematician and scientist. As an esteemed religious scholar, Khayyam also published several treatises on Islamic faith. It was only after his death that Khayyam became famous for his collection of poems, *Rubaiyat* (Quatrains), for which he is mainly remembered today. Khayyam integrated central concepts of Sufism into his poems, such as divine transcendence, love and the beloved, the spiritual path, and the idea of unity. Rubaiyat is an example of Persian Sufi poetry.[45] With his work, Ehsai creates a solid visual correspondence to religious iconography, which can be found, for example, in folios of the Qur'an,

---

[45] Mehdi Aminrazavi, *The Wine of Wisdom: The Life, Poetry and Philosophy of Omar Khayyam* (Oxford: Oneworld Publications, 2005), 137.

in which the use of black letters against a golden background is a common way of adorning sacred texts.

Mafi's works are other examples of calligraphic modernism in the exhibition. Mafi was like Ehsai, a traditionally trained calligrapher. Coming from a religious background, Mafi did not employ calligraphy as a means of modernist expression but as a form of critical resistance toward the propagated politics of modernization. Yet, as a politically engaged artist, Mafi created illustrations for leftist publications.[46] Included in the exhibition was his painting *Untitled* (1973), which represents his political agenda.[47] In this work, Mafi draws on the political iconography of raised fists, an international symbol of leftist solidarity with oppressed people, which became a significant element in the visual propaganda of the revolution. Darting flames of blood-red letters reading *Allahu Akbar* (God is the greatest) take possession of the foreground of the canvas. With this calligraphy painting, Reza Mafi illustrates the revolutionary fight of a radical fusion of leftist and Islamic ideologies, which would later be called "red Shiism."

Abstraction

Though the artists Nasser Oveissi, Jazeh Tabatabaie, and Sadegh Tabrizi have often been associated with the *Saqqakhaneh* movement in the past, they were omitted from the exhibition.[48] This is because Oveissi, Tabatabaie, and Tabrizi employ motives from eighteenth- and nineteenth-century Qajar art in their visual artistic language and maintained a more figurative style, which did not correspond to the curators' understanding of modernist art. On the other hand, abstract artworks were staged as evidence of a universal language of modernism. Thus, for the curators, abstract art was a "true" expression of modernism, while figuration seemed to be merely decorative. This rhetoric of abstract art as a sign of progress and universalism, as proclaimed by the exhibition's curators, is very similar to Western cultural politics during the Cold War, when abstraction was used to

---

[46] Diba, 'The Formation of Modern Iranian Art,' 58.
[47] Reza Mafi, Untitled, 1973. Oil on cardboard. Collection of The Farjam Foundation.
[48] Hamid Keshmirshekan, 'SAQQĀ-KĀNA SCHOOL OF ART,' *Encyclopedia Iranica*, Online edition (2009), www.iranicaonline.org/articles/saqqa-kana-ii-school-of-art, accessed 4 July 2018.

stage the alleged superiority of Western art over socialist art. The celebration of abstraction in the exhibition helps to herald Iran's Pahlavi past as a sign of progressiveness and to frame its presumed superiority over the Islamic Republic, which was portrayed as an opponent of progress and modernity. Abstract art was highly appreciated during the Pahlavi rule because it served as a sign of the country's modernity and its closeness to its Western allies, yet, as Daftari explains, "After the 1979 Revolution, abstraction was pursued as an antidote to the ideologically dogmatic figurative art practiced by leftists and Islamists alike."[49]

In the 1950s and 1960s, many Iranian artists left Iran to study modernist art in European countries. The painter Behjat Sadr began studying in Italy in 1956, where she became a student at the Roberto Melli Academy in Rome and later enrolled at the Academy of Fine Arts in Naples. Sadr's works were exhibited internationally and were shown at the Venice Biennial, Sao Paolo Biennial, in the United States, and numerous exhibitions in Iran. At first glance, Sadr's artworks can be understood as gestural abstractions. Sadr's characteristic artistic language appears in her black paintings, where she applies black paint with a palette knife or brush to different materials. The very process of painting becomes visibly comprehensible as a gesture on the black surfaces of her works. The movements of the palette knife and the brush stroke leave structural patterns on the painting's surface and create scriptural or even calligraphic impressions, as one can see in the paintings *Untitled* from 1974 and 1977, which were displayed at the exhibition.[50] With her black paintings, she commented on the social-political discourses of her time. The strong presence of smudged shades of black in her artistic works alludes to Iran's most important resource: crude oil. As stated by the curator, Morad Montazami, during the Pahlavi era, the oil business promised not only wealth and modernization,

The frustrations and resentments were far more complex than the simple desire for utopia of the 1960s and 1970s that grew out of the nationalist

---

[49] Daftari, 'Redefining Modernism,' 35.
[50] Behjat Sadr, Untitled, 1974, Oil on cardboard, 92 × 140 cm, Collection of Mitra Goberville Hananeh; Behjat Sadr, Untitled, 1977, Oil on cardboard, 149 × 80 cm, Collection of Mitra Goberville Hananeh.

struggle of oil-producing countries for their autonomy, a struggle that had started in the 1950s.[51]

In this context, Sadr's paintings "displayed an anxious vigilance with regard to this economic globalization, its influence on the integrity of artistic work and its capacity to conceal a profound cultural crisis under the guise of humanistic progress," as Montazami explains.[52]

With an eye to Sadr's first-hand familiarity with international art discourses, however, Daftari concludes that it "comes as no surprise that she opted for the progressive language of abstraction, a universal option, and language of her cosmopolitan time."[53] Yet, reading Sadr's works as a mere expression of universalism leads to a depoliticization of her art, which is very similar to the exhibition's depoliticized interpretation of Reza Mafi's works. As a central figure in Tehran's art scene who also taught at the College of Fine Arts, Sadr joined the group surrounding the cultural critics Ebrahim Golestan, Jalal al-e Ahmad, and Simin Daneshvar, all of whom reflected critically upon the role and function of modernist art in Pahlavi Iran.[54]

Originality and Radical Subjectivity

Modernist art production in Iran often functioned as a critical means of expression to illustrate the social conditions of its time. Many artists in Iran responded to the pressing questions of the Shah's modernization and secularization programs, which were part of the so-called *White Revolution* and aimed to transform Iran into a Western industrialized country. Many artists and intellectuals took a critical stance against the radical modernization programs. The resistance to and critique of the Shah's implementation of his modernization program grew under the political umbrella term *gharbzadegi* (westoxification), which came into full swing after the intellectual Jalal al-e Ahmad published his eponymous essay in 1962. In his essay, al-e Ahmad likened westernization as he saw it in Iran's adaptation of Western modernity to being infected with a highly contagious disease.

---

[51] Morad Montazami, 'Cosmogonic Modernism,' in Morad Montazami and Narmine Sadeg (eds.), *Behdjat Sadr: Traces* (Paris: Zaman Books, 2014), 12–32, 20.
[52] Ibid.   [53] Daftari, 'Redefining Modernism,' 35.
[54] Montazami, 'Cosmogonic Modernism,' 20.

Iran Modern *and the Iranian Diaspora*

The metaphor of illness, exclusion, and isolation finds visual expression in the works of the painter and sculptor Bahman Mohassess (1931–2010), which were also shown at the exhibition *Iran Modern*. In his paintings, drawings, collages, and sculptures, Mohassess uses figurative language, depicting hybrid beings, part human and part animal. Irrespective of their external appearance, Mohassess's creatures, always isolated and alone, are set against a monochromatic background. One painting exemplary of his oeuvre is *Fifi Sings of Joy* (1964). The title and the contents of the painting diverge severely while retaining a bitter irony. The portrait shows Fifi, a female figure, completely isolated on a white-yellowish surface. Fifi is depicted as consisting of a rectangular red torso with broad shoulders and a female bust. A very skinny neck connects the head to the torso. The figure's

Figure 1.2 Bahman Mohassess, *Fifi Sings of Joy*, 1964. Oil on canvas. 70 × 50 cm. Collection of Ramin Haerizadeh, Rokni Haerizadeh, and Hesam Rahmanian. Photo by Ramin Haerizadeh.

head has been replaced with a huge, open, and screaming mouth. The figure beats its chest with its hand, reinforcing the scream. Although the lack of eyes and the abstract language of forms impede the viewer's identification with the figure, in its combination of content and forms, the painting generates an emotional involvement on the part of the spectator. The pastose application of the paint creates a tactile and sculptural dimension that brings Fifi to life. *Fifi Sings of Joy* is a striking example of Mohassess's works as a painter. In it, the aesthetic execution of amorphous and isolated creatures reveals visual parallels to the pictorial worlds of European modernist artists, such as Francis Bacon and Pablo Picasso.

The visual proximity of his works to modernist European artistic discourses also explains why Mohassess's works function in the context of *Iran Modern* as a further expression of the concept of modernity promoted by the exhibition. As we have seen with regard to Mafi and Sadr, in the context of this exhibition, modernist Iranian art serves not only as a sign of secularism, universalism, and abstraction but also as a mark of modernist discourses like "originality" and "radical subjectivity." The curators employ works by Mohassess to make this case.

Yet, looking at the artist's biography, one can see that migratory experiences and movements deeply influence Iranian art history. The painter and sculptor, who studied in Rome and took up residence in Italy after the political events of 1953 in Iran, remained in Italy until he died in 2010. After the revolution, Mohassess, in particular, was almost forgotten and not part of artistic discourses in Iran. He was rediscovered in the early 2000s through the global turn of art history and thanks to the initiative of a younger generation, such as the filmmaker Mitra Farahani, who made a documentary about Mohassess and the collectors and artists Ramin and Rokni Haerizadeh, who commissioned a new piece of work from the artist.[55] Ignoring the transcultural moment in his career, the exhibition reduces Mohassess's work to a merely subjective expression. By doing so, the exhibition foregoes an opportunity to reflect on its standpoint critically. This is particularly regrettable since Mohassess's work harbors the potential to ask what constitutes Iranian art or artists as Iranian.

---

[55] In recent years Bahman Mohassess became more known through the award-winning documentary film *Fifi Howls From Happiness* by Mitra Farahani (2013), 96 min.

However, the exhibition did reduce Mohassess's work to a mere expression of artistic subjectivity, as demonstrated by the following statement by curator Daftari, "A misfit in art historical narratives and intolerant of all political systems, Mohassess found refuge in his private mythology and in Rome."[56] To Daftari, Mohassess's "private mythology" is the reason for his artistic independence: "Not inclined to create a national idiom nor interested in progressive western or Italian movements such as Arte Povera, he lived his life as a fish out of water."[57] *Iran Modern's* curator presents Mohassess's works as an example of radical subjectivity and presses them into the mold of the mythical male genius. This obsolete narrative disregards the social embeddedness of artistic practice. Contemporary art critics, however, emphasized "the bitter protest and eloquent satirical metaphors" in his works and compared his artistic approach to the muralism of the Mexican Revolution.[58]

In the 1950s, Bahman Mohassess joined Jalal al-e Ahmad and other political activists in actively fighting to nationalize Iran's oil.[59] During this time, artists and intellectuals joined the protests on the streets, filled with high hopes for the nationalization of Iran's oil and the resulting democratization of the country.[60] The coup against Mosaddeq, sponsored by foreign intelligence services, and the reinstallment of Mohammad Reza Pahlavi as Shah of Iran were the cause of trauma, disappointment, and political retreat for many activists. For many Iranians, the coup d'état of 1953 represented a tragic event. For Bahman Mohassess, it was why he turned his back on Iran and emigrated to Italy, where he had previously studied art. As an openly homosexual artist, Bahman Mohassess was not part of the heteronormative society created by secularizing laws concerning family and sexuality during Pahlavi rule. The Shah's bio-political reforms aimed at a "heterosexualization of the public space and diffused the

---

[56] Daftari, 'Redefining Modernism,' 34.   [57] Ibid.
[58] Ehsan Yarshater, 'Contemporary Persian Painting,' in Richard Ettinghausen and Ehsan Yarshater (eds.), *Highlights of Persian Art* (Boulder: Wittenborn Art Books, 1979), 363–377, 364.
[59] Jalal Al-e Ahmad, 'For Mohassess and the Wall [Be Mohassess va baray-e divar],' in Mustafa Zamaninya (ed.), *Adab wa hunar-i imruz-i Īrān: Mağmū'a-i maqālāt-I* (Tehran: Nashr-e Mitra, 1994), 1341–1355, 1344.
[60] Ervand Abrahamian, *A History of Modern Iran* (Cambridge: University Press, 2008), 116.

repudiation of same-sex love and sexuality among the lower classes."[61] Although he had collectors and commissions from Iran, Mohassess chose self-imposed exile in Italy, where he would spend nearly the last six decades of his life.

Political Art and the End of Modernism

The last chapter of the exhibition covers political Iranian art and presents works by the artists Nicky Nodjoumy and Nahid Hagigat, satirical drawings by the caricaturist Ardeshir Mohassess, and photographs by Bahman Jalali documenting the revolutionary demonstrations in 1979. In his paintings, the painter Nodjoumi depicts the brutal actions of SAVAK and their treatment of political dissidents and opponents. SAVAK was Mohammad Reza Shah's secret service, founded in 1957. The scholar Ali Ansari calls it a "tool of oppressive dictatorship" that was intended to circumvent any further politicization of Iranian society in the aftermath of the 1953 coup against Mosaddeq. Thus, SAVAK was meant to oppress any political opposition against the monarchy and to secure royal power.[62] The bleak atmosphere of state monitoring and censorship, which dominated all spheres of cultural expressions, are also thematic issues referred to by another artist discussed in this chapter, Nahid Hagigat, in her black-and-white aquatints *Surveillance* (1977) and *Escape* (1975). The images' grainy black-and-white surfaces bear visual similarities to photos of surveillance cameras. *Surveillance* harmlessly depicts three people in a public space standing in front of a balustrade. Yet, it also addresses the habitual spying and the monitoring of private life in the public sphere, instilling an uneasy feeling in the viewer without overtly expressing criticism. The etching *Escape* goes one important step further toward overt political commentary and shows a fleeing woman running from the darkness over the mountains toward a liberating light.

In this exhibition's context, the inclusion of politically committed artists in the narrative of Iranian modernism is rather problematic because it seeks to normalize and glorify the Pahlavi monarchy as a period in which citizens allegedly had democratic rights that included pluralistic artistic expression and freedom of speech. Presenting works

---

[61] Katarzyna Korycki and Abouzar Nasirzade, 'Desire Recast: The Production of Gay Identity in Iran,' *Journal of Gender Studies*, vol. 25, no. 1 (2016), 50–65, 57.
[62] Ansari, *Modern Iran*, 171.

Iran Modern *and the Iranian Diaspora*

Figure 1.3 Nahid Hagigat, *Escape*, 1975. Aquatint, Paper. 37.5 × 30.5 cm. The British Museum London. © The Trustees of the British Museum.

by Nodjoumi and Ardeshir Mohassess within the narrative of the golden age of the Pahlavi past, however, is a rather ironic act, given that, due to the political content of their artworks, these artists had to leave Iran and live abroad in exile.

The satirical drawings by the internationally acclaimed caricaturist Ardeshir Mohassess were also shown in the exhibition without any further contextualization of his life and work. Ardeshir offended the king and state authorities with his political cartoons, which had been published in Iranian magazines and newspapers since the early 1950s. From 1976, until his death in 2008, Ardeshir lived in exile in the United States.[63] Yet, despite his biting comments and his efforts to document political events he deemed important, Ardeshir did not conceive of himself as being an activist-cum-artist, as he explains in an interview: "One can never change anything by art. The only thing that one can say is that artists in each period of history leave a record so that people in the future will know about their time."[64] Deeply influenced by anticolonial politics and bolstered by a degree in political studies from Tehran University, Ardeshir Mohassess dedicated his artistic practice to the fight against tyranny and oppression, publishing his cartoons as illustrations of Iran's modern history.

He had the active historical memory of constitutional revolution, the colonial dominations of his homeland by the British and the Russians, a change of dynasty, a military occupation by the Allied forces, and a massive social uprising for political liberty, all dashed out by a vicious military coup engineered by American and British intelligence forces.[65]

Even after the Iranian Revolution, Ardeshir Mohassess continued to comment on politics in the newly established Islamic Republic and criticize the imperial politics of his new home country.

The exhibition showcased Ardeshir's drawing *Untitled* (1972), a striking example of his artistic practice and an expression of his harsh criticism of Pahlavi politics. The drawing illustrates how Pahlavi politics harnessed the *zurkhaneh* wrestler Shaban Jafari to maintain political power. In its visual execution, the drawing combines press photographs (with Qajar motives) and miniature painting as a commentary on current political events. The visual coalescence in Ardeshir's drawing of the political figure Shaban Jafari and iconographic allusions to the white demon of Ferdowsi's *Shahnameh* function as a political metaphor for contemporary political events in Iran. Jafari, depicted here as a hybrid creature, part political agent and part demon, practiced the ancient sport *zurkhaneh* and was well known in

---

[63] Nicky Nodjoumi and Shirin Neshat, 'Introduction,' in *Ardeshir Mohassess: Art and Satire in Iran*. Exh.-Cat. Asia Society (New York: Asia Society Antique Collectors' Club, 2008), 11–15, 11.

[64] Ardeshir Mohassess, 'A Conversation with Ardeshir,' *Ardeshir Mohassess*, 31–37, 35.

[65] Hamid Dabashi, 'Ardeshir Mohassess, Etcetera,' *Ardeshir Mohassess*, 17–29, 18–19.

Iran Modern *and the Iranian Diaspora*

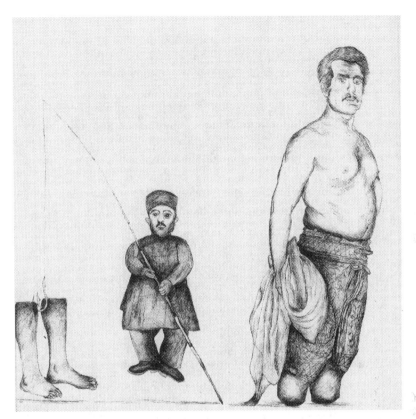

Figure 1.4 Ardeshir Mohassess, *Untitled*, 1978. Ink on paper. 48.3 × 48.3 cm. Collection of Massoud Nader.

Iran as a right-wing political agent who led the pro-Shah demonstrations during the power struggle between Mohammad Reza Shah and Mohammad Mosaddeq. In return for his support, the Shah supported Jafari's founding of a modern sports complex after the fall of Mosaddeq. Jafari had a close relationship with the Shah and organized public mass performances of *zurkhaneh* trainings for royal celebrations. Due to his constant, aggressive efforts against critics of the Pahlavi regime, Jafari fell out of grace with the monarchy, which distanced itself from the wrestler.[66] In particular, as Hushang

---

[66] Hushang Chehabi, 'JA'FARI, ŠA'BĀN,' *Encyclopedia Iranica*, Online edition. www.iranicaonline.org/articles/jafari-saban, accessed 4 July 2018.

Chehabi explains, the opposition saw Jafari as a major enemy, "For Mohammad Reza Shah's opponents, be they leftists, Moṣaddeqists, or Islamists, Šaʿbān Jaʿfari is one of the most hateful figures of 20th-century Iran, a man who served reactionary causes."[67]

In Ardeshir's rendition, Jafari is not depicted as an enemy but as a marionette whose strings are pulled by the monarch. Bare-chested and dressed in patterned or embroidered shorts, in *Untitled* (1972), Shaban Jafari stares at the viewer from the right side of the drawing. The naked torso, the shorts, and the cloth in the man's hand characterize the figure as a *zurkhaneh* wrestler. *Zurkhaneh* means house of strength and refers to where this ancient form of wrestling is practiced. As an ancient sport with origins in pre-Islamic times, *zurkhaneh* performances were highly welcomed under the Pahlavi dynasty, and the "symbolism contained within each *zūrkhāna* ranges from Shi'ite to nationalist and Sufi elements."[68]

Visually, Ardeshir often used Qajar officials to depict representatives of the Pahlavi monarchy. On the left side, we see a man in Qajar clothing holding a fishing pole in his hands with the naked man's feet hanging at the hook. Compared to the detailed depiction of Jafari, the Qajar official moves in the background. In combination with the fishing pole, however, his background position allows him to appear as the puppeteer, who pulls the strings of his puppet in the foreground, thus, actually giving the Qajar official a more powerful position.

Even though the wrestler's legs are cut off at his knees and seem ready to tumble any moment, he stands with great pride. Iconographically, Jafari's amputated legs refer to the hero Rostam's slaying of the white demon in the Iranian national epic, *Shahnameh* (The Book of Kings), by the ninth-century poet Ferdowsi, a book highly valorized under the Pahlavi regime. This scene is very popular in Persian images and can be found in miniatures and coffeehouse paintings. In this story, King Kay Kavus went on an expedition to conquer the country Mazandaran, which was ruled by demons and wizards. After beating the wizards, the king and the army could not defeat the demons. The white demon took King Kay Kavus and his men prisoner. Rostam, as a faithful companion of the king,

---

[67] Ibid.
[68] Lloyd Ridgeon, *Morals and Mysticism in Persian Sufism: A History of Sufi-futuwwat in Iran* (London: Routledge, 2014), 173.

immediately set off on a journey to liberate the king. On his journey, Rostam had to complete seven trials (*Haft khan-e Rostam*). Rostam's seventh trial was to defeat the white demon, which Rostam killed during a bloody fight, in which he also cuts off the demon's legs.[69]

Ardeshir transforms various well-known visual and literary motifs in his artistic rendition to express his political criticism. Ironically, Ardeshir used famous figures from Ferdowsi's *Shahnameh* in particular, given that, as the "poet of the fatherland," Ferdowsi became immensely important in the construction of a specific Pahlavi nationalism and his "Shahnameh came to represent the canonical heritage of ancient Iran" and "developed into a cultural tool used by Iranians to imagine their civilization as old, unique, and foundational."[70]

A close analysis of *Iran Modern* shows how the exhibition tries to compare Iranian modernist expression to Western modernism by constructing rigid divisions and categories of modern art. In the context of this exhibition, modernism functions as a symbol to prove that Iranian modernist art production was mainly based on formalist experiments to achieve a visual language based on idioms of Western modern art. For this purpose, the exhibition operates with specific markers that define Iranian modernity. The strong focus on *Saqqakhaneh* helps to support the idea that "real" Iranian modernism started with a sharp break with artistic traditions. The so-called *Saqqakhaneh* movement is staged as an emancipatory artistic movement that freed Iranian artistic practice from earlier traditions of handicraft while at the same time preserving Persian traditions as a visual resource for artistic innovation. According to the exhibition's narrative, the sharp break with past Persian traditions led to abstract experiments with visual forms and colors, culminating in the artistic practice of the male genius seeking to express his subjectivity in the artworks displayed. The preceding analysis of selected artworks has demonstrated, however, that this depoliticized understanding of modernist expression ignores the initial context in which the artworks were produced and discussed. By doing so, the exhibition clings and renarrates Pahlavi nationalism using modernist art as an overarching narrative that operates with a specific understanding of modernism based on paradigms of

---

[69] Abolqasem Ferdowsi, *Shahnameh: The Persian Book of Kings*, Dick Davis (tr.) (New York: Mage, 1997), 406–410.

[70] Talinn Grigor, *Building Iran: Modernism, Architecture, and National Heritage under the Pahlavi Monarchs* (New York: Periscope, 2009), 54.

universalism, secularism, and abstraction. Modernity in Iran is not only conceptualized as a sign of secularism but also historically identified with the second reign of Mohammad Reza Shah, which came to an allegedly sudden end with the Iranian Revolution in 1978/79. However, this analysis of the displayed artworks at *Iran Modern* demonstrates that the tight framework of the exhibition's narrative creates conflicting stories between the exhibition's thesis and the selected artworks.

The understanding of modernist artistic expression as an achievement of the Pahlavi monarchy can be attributed to the discourse of the Iranian diaspora and its exiles, who fled their country in the course of the Iranian Revolution. The exhibition creates the narrative of a golden age of modernist art in the Pahlavi past from its specific perspective on the diaspora. By doing so, the Iranian diaspora community generates its own version of Iranian history and promotes a concept of modernity shaped by Pahlavi ideology and reiterated in the diaspora discourse. As Alex Shams explains, however, the diasporic standpoint brings with it pitfalls, as "This nostalgia is dangerous because it erases the very real material and social inequalities that existed in the past and that need our attention in the present."[71] These kinds of representation also "present a misleading view of the past that takes elite history as if it represented the nation as a whole, thus obscuring the reality of most people's memories of the past."[72] Iranian history, however, demonstrates that the Pahlavi era was only a golden age of modernization for a small elite.

The Tehran Modern: The Cancellation of an Exhibition

Frank-Walter Steinmeier and Jackson Pollock's Mural on Indian Red Ground

In October 2015, Frank-Walter Steinmeier, then German foreign minister, traveled with a delegation to Tehran. A press photograph shows the minister during his visit to the Tehran Museum of Contemporary

---

[71] Alex Shams, 'The Weaponization of Nostalgia: How Afghan Miniskirts Became the Latest Salvo in the War on Terror,' *Ajam Media Collective*, vol. 6 (2017). https://ajammc.com/2017/09/06/weaponization-nostalgia-afghan-miniskirts/, accessed 4 July 2018.
[72] Ibid.

The Tehran Modern 47

Figure 1.5 Frank-Walter Steinmeier standing in front of the painting *Mural on Indian Red Ground* (1950) by Jackson Pollock at Tehran Museum of Contemporary Art. (© picture-alliance / dpa / Bernd von Jutrczenka).

Art standing in front of the painting *Mural on Indian Red Ground* (1950) by Jackson Pollock (Fig. 1.5).[73] This photograph has been circulated widely in different media. But what makes its depiction so significant?

The particular importance of this image lies in the visual interaction of place and object. Steinmeier's astonishment illustrates his surprise at seeing Jackson Pollock in Tehran. In the course of art-historiographical developments, Jackson Pollock and his artworks came to embody modernist artistic expression. As a result, modernist art and particularly American art, took on an important ideological role during the Cold War years. At that time, the field of art history was strongly involved in promoting abstract art as an expression of Western cultural freedom in opposition to the socialist East.[74]

For Steinmeier, as a representative of the German state, the work by Pollock not only epitomizes a specific idea of modernity but also has a

---

[73] The picture circulated widely in German media, for example, www.monopol-magazin.de/kunst-aus-schah-sammlung-kommt-nach-berlin

[74] See Greg Barnhisel, *Cold War Modernists: Art, Literature, and American Cultural Diplomacy* (New York: Columbia University Press, 2015).

mirror-like function. According to the French psychoanalyst Jacques Lacan and his concept of the mirror stage, the *I* comes into being in the moment when the infant creates and identifies with the image of its reflection in the mirror.[75] Lacan's mirror stage is an essential model of thought in postcolonial theory and constitutes, according to Homi Bhabha, "the dominant strategy of colonial power." As Bhabha goes on to explain, it is closely connected to the act of stereotyping that creates the imaginary picture of the colonial other:

> The Imaginary is the transformation that takes place in the subject at the formative mirror phase, when it assumes a discrete image which allows it to postulate a series of equivalences, samenesses, identities, between the objects of the surrounding world.[76]

However, identifying the self in the mirror stage is highly problematic because the image is "simultaneously alienating and hence potentially confrontational" while also forming "the basis of the close relationship between the two forms of identification complicit with the Imaginary – narcissism and aggressivity."[77] For Bhabha, these two terms encapsulate the exercise of colonial power "in relation to the stereotype which, as a form of multiple and contradictory belief, gives knowledge of difference and simultaneously disavows or masks it."[78] This observation, however, leads Bhabha to the conclusion that "[l]ike the mirror phase, 'the fullness' of the stereotype – its image as identity – is always threatened by 'lack'."[79]

Steinmeier looking at Pollock in Tehran can be interpreted as a reflection and recognition of Germany's modernity, a modernity that Steinmeier not only found in Germany but also rediscovered in Tehran. In this context, Pollock's work functions as a reference to Iran's secular heritage and a time when the Pahlavi monarchy highly appreciated modernist art as a symbol of the country's modernity. By recovering parts of Iran's heritage from modern times, similarities could be constructed between Iran and the West. At the same time, in terms of Bhabha's theorization of the mirror stage, this photograph

---

[75] Jacques Lacan, 'The Mirror Stage as Formative of the Function of the I as Revealed in Psychoanalytic Experience,' in Vincent B. Leitch et al. (eds.), *The Norton Anthology of Theory and Criticism* (New York: W. W. Norton, 2001), 1163–1169.
[76] Homi Bhabha, *The Location of Culture* (London: Routledge, 1994), 110.
[77] Ibid.   [78] Ibid.   [79] Ibid.

demonstrates that the discourse of similarity is deeply rooted in the exercise of colonial power and serves, in this case, as a statement of Germany's successful and superior development as a modern nation.

The construction of similarities on the common ground of the idea of a secular modernity was fundamental in nuclear negotiations with Iran. The strong emphasis on Western powers and Iran's shared modern heritage was a significant factor in justifying the nuclear deal with Iran. After the rise of political Islam, the Iranian Revolution in 1978/79, and the country's religious Islamic political leadership, Iran turned, in the eyes of the West, from a close ally during Pahlavi times into an alleged enemy of Western powers with ambitions of nuclear proliferation.

After many years of negotiations, the successful diplomatic resolution of the nuclear conflict with Iran in April 2015 constituted the exhibition's political background. Only shortly after Steinmeier's trip, Majid Mollanoroozi, director of the TMoCA, and Günther Schauerte, vice president of the Foundation of Prussian Cultural Heritage in Berlin (*Stiftung Preußischer Kulturbesitz*), signed the so-called "memorandum of understanding," an agreement to present works from the collection of the TMoCA at the National Gallery in Berlin. Sixty works from the museum's collection were supposed to travel to Berlin and later to Rome. Among the pieces selected were works by Western modernist artists such as Pablo Picasso, Max Ernst, Jackson Pollock, Mark Rothko, and Francis Bacon. It also included paintings and sculptures by modern Iranian artists such as Jalil Ziapour, Parviz Tanavoli, Hossein Zenderoudi, and Behjat Sadr, which form an integral part of the museum collection in Tehran.

The planned exhibition was intended to celebrate the diplomatic resolution of the nuclear dispute in 2015. However, after Iran delayed granting permission for the artworks to be exported, German officials canceled the exhibition in December 2016. An analysis of the project shows that the exhibition was deeply rooted in a patronizing discourse of nuclear politics and soft power and that the rhetoric of the German exhibition makers was marked by colonial and Orientalist stereotypes. During the planning of the exhibition, German cultural politics neglected the role of modernist art in Iran in general and the function of the TMoCA in particular. This poses the question of the museum's relevance in today's Iran. Is it justified to celebrate the nuclear deal with a collection of artworks, once a symbol of Pahlavi modernization, almost forty years after the foundation of the Islamic Republic?

Contrary to the media coverage in Germany, the exhibition was not canceled because of Iran's troubled relationship with its modernist heritage, but rather, first and foremost, because the art scene in Iran orchestrated a protest against the clandestine preparations made for the exhibition and the opaque museum politics of the Islamic Republic of Iran.

Nuclear Politics in Iran

In Germany, the exhibition and its rediscovery of Iran's allegedly secular and modern past before the Islamic Revolution were supposed to help justify the resumption of business relationships with the former enemy, Iran. The exhibition project was supposed to reflect a turning point in international relations and politics with Iran marked by the nuclear deal. In this respect, the planned exhibition and the TMoCA's modernist collection had an enormous political significance, which becomes clear when one looks at the major issues in the nuclear dispute with Iran and its implications on a global scale. After the successful overthrow of Prime Minister Mosaddeq in 1953 and during the Cold War, Mohammad Reza Shah became a close ally of Western states in their fight against Soviet socialism. But, with the Iranian Revolution in 1979 and the overthrow of the Shah, Iran lost this status. As a secular monarchy, Iran had been a possible political partner of the West, but after the revolution, when the country declared Islam its state doctrine, it was disqualified as a reliable partner of Western powers. Led by Islamic clerics, the country was often depicted as an angry theocracy and enemy of Western modernity.[80] This shift in the West's perception of Iranian politics is particularly visible in the history of Iran's nuclear program. The Iranian nuclear program dates back to the Shah's modernization program when nuclear energy promised an endless supply of energy for Iran's transformation into a modern industrial state. The Eisenhower administration initiated atomic development in Iran with the "Atoms for Peace" program. With the support of German, French and US companies, Iran installed more than twenty nuclear power reactors during the Shah's reign.[81]

---

[80] President George Bush called Iran a country of the "axis of evil" in his State of the Union Address in 2009 to represent Iran, Iraq, and North Korea.

[81] Saira Khan, *Iran and Nuclear Weapons: Protracted Conflict and Proliferation* (London: Routledge, 2005), 48.

After the Iranian Revolution, the nuclear program was put on hold because of Ayatollah Khomeini's skepticism toward nuclear energy. Khomeini did not merely condemn atomic power plants because they were a remnant of the monarchy but rather because, for Khomeini, nuclear energy was not compatible with Islamic theology. With the war between Iran and Iraq, atomic power gained a new relevance for military defense in the 1980s, and subsequent leaders of Iran resumed the development of Iran's nuclear program.[82] Iran's nuclear program and its ambitions to proliferate nuclear weapons became a major subject matter of world politics from the early 2000s. The reasons for the nuclear conflict with Iran are manifold and complex, but the main charges against Iran were those of clandestine uranium enrichment and the refusal to cooperate with the International Association for Energy Economics. During the years of negotiations, Iran always stressed that it was only interested in using nuclear energy for civil purposes. Nevertheless, "the members of the P-5 plus one and Israel insist that Iran intends to weaponize."[83] As a signatory of the Nuclear-Non-Proliferation Treaty (NPT), Iran always stressed the treaty's legally binding nature during these negotiations. Iran was among the first signatories after the establishment of the NPT in 1968. This international treaty has clearly defined goals, as stated by the United Nations Office for Disarmament Affairs.

The NPT is a landmark international treaty whose objective is to prevent the spread of nuclear weapons and weapons technology, to promote cooperation in the peaceful uses of nuclear energy and to further the goal of achieving nuclear disarmament and general and complete disarmament.[84]

This document understands nuclear energy's critical and destructive potential and its tremendous dangers, not only in the form of atomic weapons but also in unpredictable nuclear accidents. In Fukushima and Chornobyl, the utopian promise of atomic energy became a terrible nightmare.

The NPT was established to contain a global nuclear threat. As Shampa Biswas points out, "NPT was among many efforts to craft a

---

[82] Ibid., 51.
[83] Shampa Biswas, *Nuclear Desire: Power and the Postcolonial Nuclear Order* (Minneapolis: University of Minnesota Press, 2014), 21.
[84] See United Nations. Office for Disarmament Affair, 'Nuclear Non-Proliferation Treaty.' www.un.org/disarmament/wmd/nuclear/npt/, accessed 23 October 2017.

global nuclear order to restrain the dangers of nuclear power while liberating its 'peaceful' possibilities for the larger collective good."[85]

The countries that participated in the nuclear negotiations with Iran were the so-called P-5 plus 1, namely, the five states with a permanent veto power in the United Nations Security Council (the United States of America, China, France, Russia, and the United Kingdom), plus Germany. The Nuclear Non-Proliferation Treaty allows these nations to possess nuclear weapons legally. But, it also creates a nuclear hierarchy, as Shampa Biswas elaborates,

> The hierarchical global nuclear order that the NNP constitutes also helps produce and sustain nuclear weapons as objects available only to those who have the requisite credentials (the institutional apparatus, adequate maturity) and legitimate access (to fissile materials, technological know-how) to possess – making them luxury goods that confer status and ranking.[86]

Surprisingly, this broader issue of the global nuclear order has received little critical attention. One can even observe a form of depoliticization in this debate, as "questions of inequality, powerlessness, and exploitation are seen as marginal to the more serious dangers of nuclear security."[87]

Iran's alleged aspirations to possess atomic weapons and its lack of cooperation with the international community had severe consequences in the form of sanctions, which paralyzed Iran's national economy and threats of military interventions. Iran was hardly treated as an equal signatory of the treaty. The fear of the horrific potential of an Iranian nuclear bomb and the rhetoric of the controversial president, Mahmoud Ahmadinejad (2005–2013), stoked the dispute during his years in office.[88]

In 2013, Hassan Rouhani was elected as the president of Iran. With the nomination of Mohammad Javad Zarif as foreign minister, the president chose an experienced diplomat who had received his education as a lawyer in the United States. Rouhani and Zarif, representatives of more moderate politics, were on the Iranian side responsible for the success of the nuclear negotiations with the P5+1 group. In April 2015, Iran accepted a comprehensive agreement regarding its nuclear program, which forbids the proliferation of uranium and requires that Iran cooperate with international inspectors for the next

---

[85] Biswas, *Nuclear Desire*, 1.   [86] Ibid., 23.   [87] Ibid., 15.   [88] Ibid., 3.

decade. This diplomatic solution was reached under President Barack Obama, who oriented US foreign policy toward preventing a war with Iran and stabilizing the region with Iran as a strategic partner.[89] The nuclear deal with Iran marked a significant geopolitical shift. In 2015, after a long period of isolation, the international perception of Iran changed, and Iran was, for a brief historical moment, invited back to the table of the nuclear world order.

Modernist Art in Germany

The exhibition of works from the TMoCA in Berlin was supposed to celebrate Iran's return to international politics. Presenting parts of a modernist collection of the TMoCA in Berlin had particular relevance for Germany. Although Iran has thousands of years of artistic patrimony, German officials deliberately chose to represent Iran's modern Western heritage. This extraordinary interest in Tehran's modern art collection was also generated by Germany's experience after World War II, and the considerable role modern art played in rehabilitating Germany and allowing it to distance itself from National Socialism and reconnect with European states.

With the seizure of power by the National Socialists in 1933, art and culture were used to promote Nazi ideology. Modern art, in particular, became a public enemy because of its incompatibility with the racial and national worldview of the National Socialists. Modern art was considered *entartet* (degenerate) and widely prohibited. The defamation of modernist art characterized artistic and cultural politics during the Third Reich. They resulted in the flight, emigration, and persecution of artists and those working in cultural fields; the shutting down of institutions; the destruction of artworks; and many other cruelties. The distressing climax of these politics was the exhibition *Entartete Kunst* (Degenerate Art), held in Munich in 1937. The exhibition presented confiscated artworks from German museums to pillory modernity and modernist artistic expression. The hanging of the images was chaotic, and the walls were filled with defamatory statements and caricatures.

---

[89] For further investigation of the diplomatic negotiations, see Trita Parsi, *Losing an Enemy: Obama, Iran, and the Triumph of Diplomacy* (Yale: Yale University Press, 2017), 354.

The style in which the artworks were presented was meant to underscore assumptions about the hazards and dangers of modern art.[90]

To reclaim its place in the international community after World War II, Germany tried to demonstrate its economic progress and cultural transformation. The first exhibition of *documenta* in Kassel in 1955 was an attempt to respond to the crimes committed by Germany before and during the war.[91] Moreover, it was a conscious response to the trauma of the *Degenerate Art* exhibition held in 1937. The first *documenta* exhibition did not present contemporary art but displayed artworks that had been labeled *degenerated art* by National-Socialist propaganda. The curators Arnold Bode and Werner Haftmann tried to establish the continuity of German modernism. Exhibiting prewar modernist artists and their references to archaic art was supposed to construct a modern tradition, which had always existed and was only interrupted by the antimodern politics of the Nazis.[92] Andreas Huyssen argues that "the rediscovery of modernism and abstraction (…) helped West German culture move beyond the muck of nationalist and fascist image traditions and reestablish links with international developments."[93] Furthermore, he explains, "the reconstruction of modernism combined with the embrace of French and American trends clearly denationalized the culture of the Federal Republic of Germany."[94] One major challenge in postwar Germany was getting rid of the "radical nationalism that led to Nazism,"[95] on the one hand, while building a *Wirtschaftswunder* (economic miracle) nation-state with a redefined national identity and economic ties with the United States, on the other hand.[96]

---

[90] Katrin Engelhardt, 'Die Ausstellung "Entartete Kunst" in Berlin 1938,' in Uwe Fleckner (ed.), *Angriff auf die Avantgarde: Kunst und Kunstpolitik im Nationalsozialismus* (Berlin: Akad. Verl., 2007), 94–98.

[91] Gregor Wedekind, 'Abstraktion und Abendland: Die Erfindung der documenta als Antwort auf "unsere deutsche Lage",' in Nikola Doll (ed.), *Kunstgeschichte nach 1945: Kontinuität und Neubeginn in Deutschland* (Köln: Böhlau, 2006), 165–182, 174.

[92] Walter Grasskamp, *Die unbewältigte Moderne: Kunst und Öffentlichkeit* (München: Beck, 1994), 76.

[93] Andreas Huyssen, 'German Painting in the Cold War,' *New German Critique*, no. 110 (2010), 209–227, 215.

[94] Ibid.

[95] Nuit Banai, 'From Nation State to Border State,' *Third Text*, vol. 27, no. 4 (2013), 456–469, 457.

[96] Ibid., 459.

The Tehran Modern

The state's protection of modern art became evidence of Germany's successful democratization and its sharp break from its National-Socialist past. The *documenta* exhibitions promoted the idea of a shared Western cultural identity in artistic fields, where abstraction was seen as a new universal language that stood beyond national disparities. The idea of art as a universal language also led to the depoliticization of modern art and the exclusion of the "politically charged and fervently anti-capitalist avant-gardes."[97]

"Soft Power"

During the postwar reconstruction of Germany, modernist art became an ideological means to reconnect with Western powers and to demonstrate that Germany had broken with its National-Socialist past. This instrumentalization of art, as manifested in the first *documenta* exhibitions in Germany, is an essential component of the political strategy of soft power. The Oxford English Dictionary defines soft power as "power (of a nation, state, alliance, etc.) deriving from economic and cultural influence, rather than coercion or military strength."[98] The political scientist Joseph S. Nye coined the term in the 1980s and explains his concept as follows,

> We know that military and economic might often get others to change their position … But sometimes you can get the outcomes you want without tangible threats or payoffs. The indirect way to get what you want has sometimes been called "the second face of power."[99]

Soft power has become a crucial political strategy in foreign policy, as seen in the nuclear negotiations with Iran. One of the cornerstones for "getting others to want the outcomes that you want" lies in the field of culture because it "is the set of values and practices that create meaning for a society."[100]

---

[97] Ibid.
[98] 'Soft Power,' *Oxford English Dictionary* (Oxford, 2020). www.oed.com/view/Entry/183898?redirectedFrom=soft+power#eid94504988, accessed 12 August 2017.
[99] Joseph S. Nye, *Soft Power: The Means to Success in World Politics* (New York: Public Affairs, 2004), 5.
[100] Ibid., 5.

When a country's culture includes universal values and its policies promote values and interests that others share, it increases the probability of obtaining its desired outcomes because of the relationships of attraction and duty that it creates.[101]

Modernist artistic production, particularly, often functions as a sign of universalism. This is due to the evolution of the artistic avant-garde's visual experiments with the abandonment of naturalistic representational conventions at the beginning of the twentieth century. The sharp break with past, national aesthetics, and local pictorial traditions helped establish modernist art as a universal symbol of cosmopolitanism and internationalism. However, the eurocentric idea of universalism belongs to "the technologies of colonial and imperialist governance" and can turn into an ideological means to erase cultural difference.[102]

The Idea of Cultural Exchange: Berlin and the TMoCA Exhibition

A close analysis of the exhibition's project demonstrates that the display of Tehran's modernist art collection in Berlin was deeply rooted in the discourse of soft power. In this context, modernist art attained a tremendous symbolical value, which German officials utilized as a sign of Iran's modern heritage. The museum's collection was used to create a common ground between Western states and the Islamic Republic of Iran. Iran's modernist heritage was staged as evidence of the country's potential for cooperation with Western countries concerning nuclear negotiations.

The official proclamations of museum representatives in Berlin demonstrate that the exhibition's planning and conceptual organization were motivated by art as a means of soft power. Hermann Parzinger, president of the *Foundation of Prussian Cultural Heritage* in Berlin, praised the signing of the exhibition agreement as a "symbolic bridge in a time rife with conflict."[103] He further states that the exhibition "underlines the power of art to civilize and to bring nations together.

---

[101] Ibid., 11.   [102] Bhabha, *Location of Culture*, 280.
[103] See Press Release of Stiftung Preußischer Kulturbesitz, 21 October 2016, www.preussischerkulturbesitz.de/fileadmin/user_upload/documents/presse/pressemitteilungen/2015/151021_Iran_ENG.pdf, accessed 15 August 2017.

In holding this exhibition, we also deliberately want to help strengthen civil society in Iran."[104]

The concept of soft power is closely tied to the ideas of cultural exchange and culture as a bridge between different partners. The primary motivation behind this project lies in the concept of cultural dialogue and exchange between Iran and the West. Cultural dialog is an integral part of the self-image of the *Foundation of Prussian Cultural Heritage*.

As one can observe in Parzinger's foreword to the exhibition's catalog, *The Tehran Modern* conceives of cultures as fixed entities. To establish the idea of the necessity of dialogue and bridge building, the author operates with irreconcilable divisions between "Us" and "Them," "East" and "West," modernity, and Islam. The precious currency in this model of cultural exchange is modernist art in its function as a universal value of shared humanity. This frequent instrumentalization of contemporary and modernist art from the Middle East often follows political aspirations because, as Jessica Winegar explains, "art is a uniquely valuable and uncompromised agent of cross-cultural understanding," adding "that art constitutes the supreme evidence of a people's humanity."[105]

These quotes demonstrate that the project understands cultures as self-contained units and not as products of hybridity, although the concept of hybridity became a major paradigm in critical theory in the twentieth century. Homi Bhabha's terminology of hybridity radically questions the idea of purity and originality of cultures:

This interstitial passage between fixed identifications opens up the possibility of a cultural hybridity that entertains difference without an assumed or imposed hierarchy.[106]

The concept of hybridity also influences and changes the idea of the boundary because, as Bhabha explains, "the boundary becomes the place from which *something begins its presencing* in a movement not dissimilar to the ambulant, ambivalent articulation of the beyond."[107] To emphasize and illustrate his idea of interstitial passage, Bhabha refers to Martin Heidegger's metaphor of the bridge. The philosopher

---

[104] Ibid.
[105] Jessica Winegar, 'The Humanity Game: Art, Islam, and the War on Terror,' *Anthropological Quarterly*, vol. 81, no. 3 (2008), 651–681, 652.
[106] Bhabha, *Location of Culture*, 4.   [107] Ibid.

Byung-Chul Han, however, has pointed out that Bhabha employs only a fragmented citation, which does not capture Heidegger's theological conception of the bridge. Heidegger's bridge is, according to Han, a theological figure that illustrates an interstitial passage on the one hand, but at the same time also ensures the actual emergence of the riverbanks, as Heidegger writes: "Always and ever differently the bridge escorts the lingering and hastening ways of men to and from, so that they may get to other banks and in the end, as mortals, to the other side."[108] Thus, Heidegger's bridge functions foremost as a connection that gathers the mortals "before the divinities,"

> The bridge gathers, as a passage that crosses, before the divinities – whether we explicitly think of, and visibly give thanks for, their presence, as in the figure of the saint of the bridge, or whether that divine presence is obstructed or even pushed wholly aside. The bridge gathers to itself in its own way earth and sky, divinities and mortals.[109]

Considering Heidegger's conception of the bridge, Han states that this image does not illustrate cultures' hybridity because the term's theology does not permit any mixing. Heidegger's bridge does not connect existing spaces but instead generates these separated places. As Heidegger wrote: "It does not just connect banks that are already there. The banks emerge as banks only as the bridge crosses the stream."[110] "Here and there," "inside and outside," and "self and other" relate to each other in a dialectical tension. Heidegger's dialectic, according to Han, does not leave any space for hybrid creations based on difference.[111] As a result, Heidegger's bridge is ultimately very narrow and does not provide the space for playful multiplicity that is an essential part of the concept of hybridity.

This discussion illustrates the underlying idea of cultural exchange, also reflected in *The Tehran Modern* project in Berlin. Here, cultural exchange functioned in the sense of Heidegger's bridge, generating separate places, the self and the other, and presenting German cultural politics as the significant other to Iranian cultural politics.

---

[108] Martin Heidegger, 'Building Dwelling Thinking,' in Heidegger, *Poetry, Language, Thought* (New York: Harper Colophon, 1976), 152–153.
[109] Ibid.   [110] Ibid.
[111] Byung-Chul Han, *Hyperkulturalität. Kultur und Globalisierung* (Berlin: Merve Verlag, 2005), 27.

The dialogue between Iran and Germany was not only supposed to establish a connection among Western states, as Parzinger states, "but also with countries beyond our understanding. Our value measures with regard to their perspective on freedom, democracy, and rule of law are not universally shared."[112] Iran is defined here as an ultimately foreign negotiation partner. Referencing Willy Brandt's political doctrine of "change through reapproachement," Parzinger emphasizes the enormous significance of culture as a means of soft power when "West and East encountered one another in the middle of the Cold War."[113] As the author further maintains, cultural fields lend themselves exceptionally well to successful encounters between two parties, and "[a]rt and culture can build bridges, particularly also in dialogue with difficult nations."[114] These statements construct an image of Iran as a "difficult nation" and an irrational and lawless other to the rationally minded liberal West. Parzinger's substantial distinction is attributed to the failure of modernization in Iran. For him, the TMoCA was established in the course of modernization during Pahlavi rule, when "Persia was supposed to achieve the modernity and living standard that the English, French, and Germans had developed for themselves over many generations," but, as Parzinger adds, "this was an illusion based on the unimaginable wealth from the oil business."[115] Yet, this failure of modernization was not unique to Iran but could also be observed in other Muslim countries in form of an alleged "truculent repudiation of Western politics," as the author states.[116]

Without any historical references to the global anticolonial struggles of Third World countries, which strongly shaped the decades of the 1960s and 1970s, the author states that cultural backwardness led to Western modernity's rejection. The West epitomizes, for him, the achievements of modernity, whereas the East catapulted itself into cultural backwardness by adhering to the religion of Islam. This statement neglects postcolonial history and demonstrates a disappointment with the failure and rejection of the West's colonial efforts. Modernity, in this context, is understood as a purely Western achievement. The author completely ignores the dark side of European modernity built on

[112] Helmut Parzinger, 'On the Unifying Power of Art and an Unrealised Exhibition,' in Dorothée Brill, Joachim Jäger, and Gabriel Montua (eds.), *The Tehran Modern: A Reader about Art in Iran since 1960* (Berlin: Nationalgalerie, Staatliche Museen zu Berlin, 2017), 6–13, 6.
[113] Ibid., 6.   [114] Ibid., 13.   [115] Ibid., 7.   [116] Ibid., 8.

colonialism and exploitation[117] when he emphasizes the work ethic that led to the "modernity and living standard that the English, French, and Germans had developed for themselves over many generations."[118]

The author's reductionist view on Iran's modernity refers to the broader discourse of Western modernity's failure in the Middle East. This classic orientalist rhetoric reached new heights in the 1990s when Bernard Lewis and Samuel L. Huntington popularized the idea of "the clash of civilizations" in their writings. In the post-Cold-War period, Lewis's essay "The Roots of Muslim Rage" (1990) and Huntington's book *The Clash of Civilization and the Remaking of World Order* (1996) set the stage for an alleged rivalry between the secular and rational West and its essentially other and irrational counterpart, the Islamic East.[119] These assertions egregiously ignore the role of Western interventionism and colonialism in the political realities of Middle Eastern countries. Instead, these authors promote the idea that "the political failures of modernity in the Middle East occurred in a sealed vacuum, where well-intentioned reformers strived to bring democracy."[120] These assertions consolidate and reaffirm ideological boundaries between the East and West and serve as justification for Western interventionism in the Middle East.

Huntington and Lewis's visions present only reductionist views of non-Western modernities and propagate the idea that the adaptation of Western modernity in the Middle East was marked by failure and deficiency, which Islamic societies brought upon themselves due to their inherent irrationality.

In the case of Iran, the definite failure of the Shah's modernization project was sealed by the Iranian Revolution in 1979 and manifested in how the government dealt with modern art, according to Parzinger,

---

[117] See Frantz Fanon, *The Wretched of the Earth* (New York: Grove Press, 1963), 79; Mignolo, *The Darker Side of Western Modernity*.
[118] Parzinger, 'On the Unifying Power of Art,' 6.
[119] See Bernard Lewis, 'The Roots of Muslim Rage,' *The Atlantic*, September 1990. www.theatlantic.com/magazine/archive/1990/09/the-roots-of-muslim-rage/304643/, accessed 8 April 2020; Samuel P. Huntington, *The Clash of Civilizations and the Remaking of World Order* (London: Penguin Books, 1996).
[120] Ali Mirsepassi, *Intellectual Discourse and the Politics of Modernization: Negotiating Modernity in Iran* (Cambridge: Cambridge University Press, 2004), 44.

Western art, which, previously, had been supposed to illustrate the modernity of the Shah regime, as well, was suddenly considered poison; the cultural opening up became a symbol of degeneration, and the TMoCA's splendid collection disappeared into storage.[121]

This neglecting of Iran's modern artistic heritage had devastating consequences, as Parzinger further explains, because the "clerics' ban on all non-Islamic forms of art after the Revolution, reinforced by decades of isolation, propelled this alienation of Iranians from Western art even further."[122] For the Foundation of Prussian Cultural Heritage, this so-called alienation was merely the expression of the selfless motivation to reconnect with an "artistic-cultural dialogue" that had been established under Pahlavi monarchy and the art politics of queen Farah Diba. This cultural bridging reached a "milestone" with the foundation of the TMoCA and its "most important collection of Western art of the twentieth century outside of Europa and North America." The cultural partnership to an end with the revolution, when "all principles of dialogue were militantly rejected."[123]

Iran and Germany: Transcultural Moments of Exchange

Despite its emphasis on cultural exchange, the project ignores the historical relationship between Germany and Iran. Not only did Germany import the majority of its oil from Iran, but the Pahlavi monarchy was also very popular in the German yellow press, especially after Mohammad Reza Pahlavi's marriage to Soraya Esfandiari-Bakhtiari, whose mother was German. In a book, Richard Blank presents a collection of press reports, which shows Germany's identification with the Iranian monarchy. While trying to distance themselves from the Third Reich, in particular in the years immediately following World War II, the Germans tried to reconnect to a glorious past, which they associated with an image of the German Empire. The Persian monarchy offered a suitable foil for their historical illusions.[124]

The German yellow press intensely celebrated the Shah's power and splendor while completely ignoring the political realities in Iran. This is

---

[121] Parzinger, 'On the Unifying Power of Art,' 8.   [122] Ibid.   [123] Ibid.
[124] Richard Blank, *Schah Reza – der letzte deutsche Kaiser. Dokumente aus der Regenbogenpresse.* Shah Reza – Germany's last emperor. Yellow Press Reports (Reinbek bei Hamburg: Rowohlt, 1979).

also reflected in the project of *The Tehran Modern*. The project presents modernist arts as purported symbols of freedom and democratic rights during the times of the Pahlavi monarchy. However, the representation of the monarchy as Western and enlightened neglects an integral part of German history. West Germany was an important center for Iranian dissident students to orchestrate their resistance against the Pahlavi regime and their politics in Iran. In West Berlin and other German cities during the 1960s, Iranian dissidents played a significant role in the evolution of the German student movement and the formation of the radical left.[125] In particular, with his 1967 publication, *Persien, Modell eines Entwicklungslandes* (*Persia, Model Developing Country*), the Iranian intellectual Bahman Nirumand, a fervent critic of the Pahlavi monarchy living in West Berlin, had a strong influence on the politicization of German students. In his book, Nirumand strongly criticized the Shah's modernization programs, known as the White Revolution, and denounced the Shah's autocratic dictatorship. Nirumand tried to draw international attention to Iran's antidemocratic totalitarianism and human rights violations. In this manner, Nirumand painted a very different picture of Iran, which, at the time, was a highly appreciated, close associate and ally of Western powers in the Cold War.[126] His book was very successful and sold many copies in leftist political groups because Nirumand outlined "a global context that linked the struggles in Iran, Vietnam, and the rest of the Third World."[127] Thus, Nirumand depicted Iran's fight against injustice and oppression as one example of global antiimperialist resistance.

Due to Nirumand's book and the Iranian students' protests, Mohammad Reza Pahlavi, the Shah of Iran, became a major enemy of the German student movement. Nirumand's open critique of the Shah's politics strongly contributed to the mobilization of the masses that protested against the Shah during his state visit to Germany in 1967. On June 2, 1967, thousands of anti-Shah protestors filled the streets in Berlin. Pro-Shah demonstrators and agents of SAVAK, the Shah's secret police, attacked the anti-Shah protestors. The violence

---

[125] For a detailed account of the role of Iranian dissidents for the radicalization of the German Left, see Quinn Slobodian, *Foreign Front: Third World Politics in Sixties West Germany* (Durham: Duke University Press, 2012).
[126] Bahman Nirumand, *Persien, Modell eines Entwicklungslandes* (Reinbek b. Hamburg: Rowohlt, 1967).
[127] Slobodian, *Foreign Front*, 108.

escalated further when German police officers also attacked the anti-Shah protestors. During the police attack, one officer shot the student Benno Ohnesorg, who had participated in the demonstration. Ohnesorg's death became an important event in German history, changing postwar Germany's sociopolitical discourse enormously. For the German leftists, the murder of Ohnesorg served as alarming evidence of the state's police violence and uninterrupted fascism. Subsequently, Ohnesorg's death became the foundational myth behind the student movement's politicization and a significant reference point for the Red Army Fraction's terrorist acts.[128]

However, this part of German-Iranian history is not at all reflected in the exhibition's conception. Instead, it seems, the exhibition's organizers fall back into the old patterns of the German yellow press when celebrating the achievements of the Pahlavi state. The exhibition promised to bridge the seemingly irreconcilable differences which Parzinger presented in his text. The author refers to a tradition of cultural exchange between Iran and the West and argues that dialog between the countries can be reactivated.[129]

An Uneven Cultural Dialog

Even though dialog and opening up are the keywords in this discussion, the question arises of which concept of dialog is being promoted. The process of opening up seems to be rather one-sided. It promotes a hierarchical imbalance since only Iran is supposed to open up and send parts of its museum collection abroad, while the West remains free of political obligations. For instance, the idea was never considered to send artworks from German museums to Iran to establish an artistic and institutional exchange. The Iranian resistance toward the exhibition in Berlin responded to the patronizingly clandestine preparations for the exhibition and the nondisclosure of which artworks from the collection of Tehran Museum had been selected. According to Joachim Jäger, director of Berlin's New National Gallery, the secrecy surrounding selecting artworks to be presented in Berlin was only a marketing strategy. Due to institution's dependence on visitor numbers, the

---

[128] See Eckard Michels, *Schahbesuch 1967: Fanal für die Studentenbewegung* (Berlin: Ch. Links Verlag, 2017).
[129] Parzinger, 'On the Unifying Power of Art,' 9.

organizers of the exhibitions concealed the names of the artists and artworks to attract more visitors and to turn the exhibition into a financially marketable art event.[130]

For Parzinger, however, the reason for the exhibition's cancellation lies once more in Iran's allegedly troubled relationship with modernity. The author accuses the clerics of being enemies of Western modernity, fighting an "intra-Iranian conflict" against the process of international openness initiated by Rouhani's moderate government.[131] Despite the failure of the common project, Parzinger finds positive words because

> It continues to be a tremendously powerfully signal when, after four decades, those responsible in Tehran have undertaken serious efforts to retrieve a collection of Western art from storage, including works with homoerotic content, while, elsewhere in the Near East, radical forces irretrievably destroy the cultural heritage of humankind in a particularly barbaric way.[132]

Upon closer inspection, Parzinger's "tremendously powerful signal" becomes rather problematic. In his statement, Parzinger tries to distinguish Iran as a positive example in direct contrast to the Taliban in Afghanistan or the Islamic State in Syria and Iraq and their destruction of cultural sites as medially staged acts of iconoclasm. The Islamic State's destruction of cultural heritage at archaeological sites and museums in Syria and Iraq was seen globally as the "most iconic representations of contemporary violence against humanity."[133] Although ISIS has staged its demolition of antiquities "as a re-enactment of the 7th century c.e. destruction of idols in the Ka'aba," it is important to note, as Ömür Harmanşah has pointed out, that ISIS's destruction of cultural heritage is not so much an expression of Islamic iconoclasm but instead served the "enrichment of ISIS's ultramodern imagery-machine."[134]

The organizers of the German institutions comport themselves with a colonial and patronizing attitude when they describe Iran as allegedly Muslim exceptionalism by emphasizing that Iran's appreciation of its modernist heritage stands out against other Islamic societies. Iran's

---

[130] Joachim Jäger, Interview by the author, Hamburger Bahnhof, Berlin, 6 September 2017.
[131] Parzinger, 'On the Unifying Power of Art,' 12.   [132] Ibid.
[133] Ömür Harmanşah, 'ISIS, Heritage, and the Spectacles of Destruction in the Global Media,' *Near Eastern Archaeology*, vol. 78, no. 3 (2015), 170–177.
[134] Ibid.

The Tehran Modern

collection of modern art, however, plays no significant role in Iranian public discourse, but the German side claims a prerogative to interpret Iranian heritage. This is due not only to Germany's interest in these works' preservation but also to the symbolic value of modernist art as an expression of Western freedom. Furthermore, it also poses a question of cultural ownership. In this context, modern art production and modernity per se were seen as products of the West, which belong in Western institutions, well equipped and trained to preserve modern masterpieces for coming generations. Western art institutions thus regard Iranian museum politics and their preservation work with a certain unease. This discomfort draws on the stereotype of an Islamic prohibition of the image and leads to false conclusions, such as what Jessica Winegar has called the "widely held erroneous assumptions that Muslims reject image-making" and "proof of Muslim provinciality or even backwardness."[135] The idea of the Islamic prohibition of the image serves in Parzinger's context as a sign of Iran's unique position in the Middle East. Iran's appreciation of modernist art shows its civilization in contrast to "barbaric forces" destroying "humankind's earliest cultural heritage."[136]

The accompanying publication, *The Tehran Modern – A Reader about Art in Iran since 1960*, supports the idea that Iran was almost a westernized country before the revolution, while the revolution and the years following it were characterized by angry citizens occupying the streets of Tehran and demonstrating side by side with antimodern clerics. This reader, which functions as a substitute for an exhibition catalog, is at the same time a reminder of the exhibition project's failure, as the selected artworks from the museum's collection in Tehran are not presented.[137] Two artists it does feature are the photographers Bahman Jalali and Rana Javadi. Jalali achieved great fame for his photo series *Days of Blood – Days of Fire*, which documented the Iranian Revolution with its demonstrations and the revolutionary upheavals on the streets of Tehran.[138] The majority of the photographs in *The Tehran Modern* publication, however, depict the protests in 1979 and show Khomeini's supporters holding placards with his face

---

[135] Winegar, 'The Humanity Game,' 652.
[136] Parzinger, 'On the Unifying Power of Art,' 9.
[137] See Brill et al., *The Tehran Modern*.
[138] Bahman Jalali, *Days of Blood – Days of Fire, 1978–1979* (Tehran: Zamineh, 1979).

and front pages of newspapers with the headline "The Shah has left" as signs of the revolution's success. Female portraits from before the revolution are contrasted with the revolutionary photographs. The first images in the catalog present portraits of different Iranian women: *A girl playing violin* (1977) and *Female musicians at a wedding* (1973). Another photograph depicts a woman buying cooked beetroots on the streets of Tehran, and the last prerevolutionary picture depicts a bar scene in which a woman sits at the counter in a café with a modernist interior architecture smoking a cigarette. These images of women wearing fashionable Western outfits precede the revolutionary images depicting women wearing black *chadors* veiling their whole bodies. These images suggest to the German public that Iranian women had been living in freedom in Iran in the 1960s and 1970s when they had the right to perform music in public, not to wear a veil, and to smoke cigarettes. Yet, this conclusion is misleading. In reality, Jalali and Javadi depicted only a small urban elite who could afford to eat in restaurants and buy the latest trends in Western fashion. Most of Iran's population did not live in urban but rather rural areas. While today, 55 percent of Iranian women attend university, in the 1970s, less than 1 percent of women went to college in Iran.[139] Using these pictures in the exhibition's discourse provides a distorted view of Iran's history. It glorifies the Pahlavi past by representing "elite history" and "obscuring the reality of most people's memories." These images produce "a narrative that equates freedom with clothing," as Alex Shams explains.[140]

The strategic employment of these images in the catalog suggests that Iran has a modern past, which can be traced through the TMoCA's collection and the excavation of its works. This rhetoric, full of archaeological metaphors, was formative for Hermann Parzinger's statements and German media coverage, which drew on orientalist concepts. The assumption that the museum collection had been invisible for almost forty years is wrong and contributes "to the TMoCA legend, moving beyond Aladdin's simple cave to add a hint of Tutankhamon's tomb to its aura," as David Galloway, former curator of the TMoCA, explained.[141]

This image of a trove of modern art decaying in the TMoCA's cellar was spread by the media with the help of archeological metaphors and

---

[139] Shams, 'The Weaponization of Nostalgia.' [140] Ibid.
[141] David Galloway, 'Remembering TMoCA,' in Brill et al., *The Tehran Modern*, 38–49, 40.

the imagery of excavations. In turn, the idea was promoted that Iran's secular past was only covered with the dust of the Islamic Republic and that, once they were brought out of the cellar and the dust brushed off of them, traces of modernity would become visible. The archaeological imagery of excavations emphasizes the project's colonialist approach. Under Pahlavi rule, archaeology actively contributed to the formation of an Iranian national identity dating back to the ancient Persian Empire and meant to erase Iran's Islamic history.[142]

German media coverage concentrated mainly on Farah Diba, with the German art magazine *Monopol* publishing a whole issue dedicated to the Tehran collection. The magazine cover showed Andy Warhol's screen-print portrait of Farah Diba with a headline reading "The Treasure of the Queen and Berlin's Museums."[143] On the one hand, the strong focus on Farah Diba is based on her engagement in Iranian art politics of the time. On the other hand, classifying artworks according to royal dynasties follows principles of classification, which can be found in archaeology and Islamic art history. This classification leads to the misleading conclusion that Iranian modernist art was primarily produced in the service of the monarchy. This assumption illustrates the project's generally Eurocentric approach toward Iranian art, which largely neglects the role and function of modernist art in the discourse of the Islamic Republic.

Tehran Museum of Contemporary Art: *The Tehran Modern* in Iran

After Berlin canceled the exhibition due to delays in issuing transportation permits for the artworks, German officials suspected this was the work of conservative forces in Iran rallying against President Rouhani's politics of opening up and his cooperation with the West.[144] German media held Iran's anti-Western politics responsible for the cancellation of *the Tehran Modern* exhibition in Berlin. *Die Zeit*, for example, a German weekly newspaper, printed the headline "The mullahs sabotage a major event in Berlin at the very last

---

[142] Grigor, *Building Iran*, 21.
[143] See the Coversheet *Monopol*, Magazin für Kunst und Leben, 'Der Schatz der Kaiserin und die Berliner Museen,' December, 2016.
[144] Parzinger, 'On the Unifying Power of Art,' 12.

moment."[145] The perception that Iran's refusal to send parts of the TMoCA's collection evolved from Iran's troubled relationship with modernity or its rejection of cultural exchange neglects the Iranian discussions of the exhibition project. First, the idea of cultural exchange, which was strongly promoted by the German side, was not part of the domestic debate in Iran, which centered around the protests mobilized by Tehran's artistic community against the exhibition in Berlin and Rome for political reasons and as a critique of the government's dealing with Iran's cultural heritage.[146] Many artists, gallery owners, and art practitioners protested against the exhibition due to a lack of information, clandestine exhibition preparations, and secrecy about selecting the artworks which were supposed to travel to Europe. The protestors were concerned that works belonging to the museum might be jeopardized or not returned to Iran.[147]

The protest's discourse was rooted not only in the physical manifestation of the TMoCA's modernist collection but also in the symbolic value of the museum's treasury and political agency in postrevolutionary Iran. On the one hand, the protests against the collection's export were informed by national sentiments regarding the museum's collection and the wish to protect national heritage. On the other hand, the collection became the bone of contention in the struggles for democracy between the artistic community and the government.

The art scene demanded that the museum's work be transparent and comply with the laws and regulations of the Islamic Republic. The protest against *The Tehran Modern* exhibition expresses a democratic culture that is part of an oppositional movement in Iran. As Ali Mirsepassi explains, "The popular protest arises from the perception of Iranians across the spectrum that their democratic rights are being routinely violated by the existing governing regime."[148] This public protest stood in the tradition of peaceful mass protest in Iran's history,

---

[145] Werner Bloch, 'Warten auf Farah,' *DIE ZEIT*, no. 49 (2016).
[146] Mohammed Salemy and Stefan Heidenreich, 'Vultures over TMOCA? What's behind the Cancellation of the Berlin Exhibition from the Collection of Tehran Museum of Contemporary Art,' *E–flux*, 2016, https://conversations.e-flux.com/t/vultures-over-tmoca-what-s-behind-the-cancellation-of-the-berlin-exhibition-from-the-collection-of-tehran-museum-of-contemporary-art/5438, accessed 23 February 2018.
[147] Ibid.
[148] Ali Mirsepassi, *Democracy in Iran: Islam, Culture, and Political Change* (New York: New York University Press, 2010), xiv.

from the Tobacco Revolt (1891–1892) to the Constitutional Revolution in 1906, Mohammad Mosaddeq's National Front for the nationalization of Iran's oil, and the Green Movement in 2009.[149] These movements for reform wanted "to create a more open, transparent, and democratic political system through existing institutions."[150] These demands are also mirrored in the discussion about more transparency in the curatorial and administrative decisions concerning the TMoCA. On a broader scale, these discussions show the complexity of Iranian cultural politics and also reveal the reductionist views of the German exhibition partners, who think of Iran as one monolithic state.

Second, one should not forget that, as a state-funded institution of the Islamic Republic of Iran, the TMoCA does not function as a secular institution like those in a Euro-American setting. As an important political agent, the museum functions according to the logic of the Islamic Republic. It does not promote a "strict dichotomy between the secular and religious realms – between the sacred and the profane."[151] In the Islamic Republic, museums follow a strict agenda and "seek to celebrate and strengthen modern Islamic subjectivities."[152]

The History of Tehran Museum of Contemporary Art in Iran

The TMoCA's institutional history underscores the complex underpinnings of national and international points of contention. The museum's legacy, history, and role in the Iranian cultural discourse were not part of the patronizing debate of the Berlin exhibition. Outside Iran, the museum is famous for its exceptional collection of Western modernist artworks, assembled under Queen Farah's auspices. In the Islamic Republic, the collection plays only a minor role in the institution's exhibition activities. A close analysis of the TMoCA's history reveals the museum's ideological function for the political framework in Iran both before and after the Iranian Revolution.

The history and development of the museum have been shaped by six different periods, which are closely connected to the respective

---

[149] Ibid., x. [150] Ibid., xiii.
[151] Christiane Gruber, 'The Martyrs' Museum in Tehran: Visualizing Memory in Post-Revolutionary Iran,' *Visual Anthropology*, vol. 25, nos. 1–2 (2012), 68–97, 69.
[152] Ibid., 70.

governments: the foundational years under the Pahlavi monarchy (1977–1979), postrevolutionary Iran and the years of the Iran–Iraq war under Ayatollah Khomeini (1980–1988), the postwar years of political and cultural reconstruction (1990–1998), President Khatami's reform movement (1998–2005), Mahmud Ahmadinejad's regressive presidency (2005–2013) followed by the Green Movement in 2009, and the last phase under President Rouhani, which saw the signing of the nuclear deal (2013–2018).[153]

The *Muzeh-ye honarha-ye mo'aser Tehran* (Tehran Museum of Contemporary Art) is situated in Laleh Park, part of Tehran's vibrant city center. The museum was inaugurated in October 1977. Established during the Pahlavi monarchy (1925–1978), the collection and exhibition of modernist art were staged as signs of Mohammad Reza Shah's successful modernization and secularization projects. As a prestige object for the Pahlavi government, the museum was supposed to prove that Iran had caught up, done away with its "backwardness," and was ready to take its place in the Western world order. It is important to emphasize that the museum operated only briefly under Pahlavi rule before the revolutionaries took over when the Shah fled the country with his family in January 1979. This means that while the museum's legacy dates back to the Pahlavi monarchy, its specific political and artistic direction was shaped under the Islamic Republic of Iran.

As a "previous Pahlavi incarnation"[154] for the revolutionaries, the institution symbolizes the modernization attempts of the Pahlavi state and embodied the monarchy's decadence. One of the most important goals of the Iranian Revolution was to erase the visible traces of the Pahlavi past and to replace them with Shi'ite culture.[155] This applies to the case of the museum, which the revolutionaries appropriated as an

---

[153] See Alisa Eiman, 'Shaping and Portraying Identity at the Tehran Museum of Contemporary Art (1977–2005),' in Staci Gem Scheiwiller (ed.), *Performing the Iranian State: Visual Culture and Representations of Iranian Identity* (London: Anthem Press, 2013), 83–99; Helia Darabi, 'Tehran Museum of Contemporary Art as a Microcosm of the State's Cultural Agenda,' in Hamid Keshmirshekan (ed.), *Contemporary Art from the Middle East: Regional Interactions with Global Art Discourses* (London: I. B. Tauris, 2015), 221–245.
[154] Eiman, 'Shaping and Portraying Identity,' 92.
[155] Talinn Grigor, *Contemporary Iranian Art: From the Street to the Studio* (London: Reaktion Books, 2014), 37.

institution for the dissemination of the new ideology of the Iranian Republic through artistic propaganda. After the revolution, in the newly established Islamic Republic, the collection of Western modernist artworks played a subordinate role in Iranian cultural politics since modernist arts were "considered as Western-orientated, and thus politically and religiously suspicious,"[156] as the art historian Hamid Severi states. Nevertheless, the museum functioned as an essential space in Iranian society, serving as a seismograph reflecting social, political, and artistic circumstances.

To this day, the museum is one of the major contemporary institutions representing the official cultural politics of the Islamic Republic of Iran. Despite its ideological realignment after the revolution, the TMoCA's objective as an institution remained the display of artistic production from Iran. The reason, however, that the museum could retain its artistic focus was that, since the 1980s, the Iranian government had funded other institutions that fulfilled propagandistic needs, such as the martyr museums for "commemorating the deceased heroes of the Revolution (1979) and the martyrs of the Iran–Iraq War (1980–88)."[157] Memorializing and exhibiting the personal belongings of the martyrs, the "contemporary war and history museums in the Islamic world have much light to shed on how official memory, alongside sanctioned religious and national values, is articulated and strategically positioned through the authoritative voice of the museum," as Christiane Gruber explains.[158]

Formative Periods in the Development of Tehran Museum of Contemporary Arts

The promotion of art and culture was an essential part of Pahlavi politics, which was not only a matter of royal patronage but also pursued a political agenda. After the 1953 coup d'état, the Pahlavi government feared a further politicization of society.[159] The government strictly monitored all areas of cultural life. Governmental

---

[156] Hamid Severi, 'Mapping Iranian Contemporary Publications and Knowledge-Production,' in Keshmirshekan, *Contemporary Art from the Middle East*, 69–88, 71.
[157] Gruber, 'The Martyrs' Museum,' 70.   [158] Ibid., 69.
[159] See James C. Hook and Adam Howard (eds.), *Foreign Relations of the United States*, Iran 1951–1954, Volume XIX (Washington: United States Government

institutionalization and appropriation were part of the royal strategy to control artistic and cultural production, and "the evolution of national museums and monuments as public spaces reserved for the display and consumption of high art was buttressed by the institution of monarchy, as the leading patron of that culture."[160]

The museum's foundation was also part of the so-called White Revolution's cultural politics; the Shah's radical modernization program aimed to transform Iran into a Western industrial nation.[161] Art became a symbol of the country's progress on the domestic level and Iran's foreign policy. Iran was a close ally of Western powers in the ideological struggle against Soviet socialism during the Cold War.[162] The appreciation, promotion, and collection of modernist art were necessary political means to establish a connection with Western nations.[163]

Due to a lack of exhibition spaces, artists had demanded the establishment of a contemporary-art museum since the early 1960s. To fill this institutional gap, Kamran Diba, Farah Diba's cousin, was commissioned to design the building for the museum.[164] The oil revenues enabled the museum's construction and the acquisition of the collection. With the assistance of national and international curators, the Queen's office (*daftar-e makhsus-e shahbanu*) purchased the works in the TMoCA's famous collection on the international art market.[165] The collection started with Impressionism and comprises around 4,000 pieces by Western and Iranian modernist artists.[166]

When the Shah and his family left due to the upheavals of the Iranian Revolution in January 1979, the museum had not even been in operation for two years. Due to the immense significance of visual and artistic material for the revolutionary ideology, it is not surprising that the TMoCA was only closed for approximately two weeks during the peak of the revolution before a new team of museum workers resumed work. The successful dissemination of revolutionary ideas and the

---

Publishing Office, 2017). https://static.history.state.gov/frus/frus1951–54Iran/pdf/frus1951–54Iran.pdf, accessed 23 October 2017.
[160] Grigor, 'Building Iran,' 137.
[161] Darabi, 'Tehran Museum of Contemporary Art,' 222.
[162] Roham Alvandi, *Nixon, Kissinger, and the Shah: The United States and Iran in the Cold War* (Oxford: Oxford University Press, 2014), 7–27.
[163] Saunders, *Who Paid the Piper?*, 1–7.
[164] Eiman, 'Shaping and Portraying Identity,' 87.   [165] Ibid., 85.
[166] Ibid., 91.

revolution's success were closely linked to Iranian media. Ayatollah Khomeini spread his revolutionary messages not only through cassette tapes but also used visual materials, such as posters, murals, and stamps, which became a key factor in the political upheaval in Iran.[167]

After months of restructuring the museum, the TMoCA reopened, and "emerged as an ideological arena, visibly juxtaposing Islamic values and principled character to the memory of Pahlavi Westernization and decadence."[168] In 1982, President Seyyed Khamenei, who has been Iran's Supreme Leader since 1989, emphasized in the museum's mission statement the significance of art for political and societal change.[169] During this time, the TMoCA did not exhibit its collection of modernist art since it functioned as a place to promote the new ideology of the revolution and "was intended to support the State and memorialize the revolution and martyrs" and "link struggles against the United States and Israeli imperialism."[170]

The revolution and its aftermath were a turning point for Iranian society as well as for Iran's cultural politics. At the time, the cultural politics of the Iranian state followed two major tendencies. The state's goals were to Islamize all cultural fields to "install a revolutionary spirit into the country's cultural and artistic life"[171] and to replace Pahlavi aesthetics with those of the Islamic Republic.[172] These new tendencies in cultural politics strongly affected the TMoCA. As a "previous Pahlavi incarnation," the museum became a highly symbolical space for the revolutionaries' implementation of their new ideology.[173] The first step was to open the museum to a broader audience since, before the revolution, the museum as an institution had been reserved for an elite audience.[174] The exhibitions concentrated on Iranian arts and artists and presented "ideological and propagandistic" exhibitions, which promoted war photography of the Iran–Iraq war and revolutionary artists. During this time, "the group of revolutionary, left-wing and religious artists, with radical ideas and aspirations,

---

[167] See Chelkowski and Dabashi, *Staging a Revolution*.
[168] Eiman, 'Shaping and Portraying Identity,' 92.
[169] Darabi, 'Tehran Museum of Contemporary Art,' 227–228.
[170] Eiman, 'Shaping and Portraying Identity,' 92.
[171] Hamid Keshmirshekan, 'Reclaiming Cultural Space: The Artist's Performativity versus the State's Expectations in Contemporary Iran,' in Scheiwiller, *Performing the Iranian State*, 145–155, 146.
[172] Grigor, *Contemporary Iranian Art*, 37.
[173] Eiman, 'Shaping and Portraying Identity,' 92. [174] Ibid.

gradually developed an established genre and became assimilated into the system."[175]

The end of the Iran–Iraq war in 1988 and Ayatollah Khomeini's death in 1989 marked a major shift in Iran's foreign and economic policies. The "era of reconstruction" (*sazandegi*), under the presidency of Ali Akbar Rafsanjani (1989–1997), is characterized by economic reforms. Ansari explains: "the wartime era of austerity was declared to be over, and the era of 'reconstruction' was to begin; Iran was open to business."[176] Despite economic liberalization during Rafsanjani's administration, the fields of arts and culture were still subordinate to revolutionary and military ideology. Although the TMoCA increased its exhibition activities during this period and resumed holding painting biennials, the museum also tried to institutionalize revolutionary artists by adding new kinds of artworks and new artists to its collection of Western modernist arts. As a result, paintings of the revolution were shown "in a prestigious museum with spectacular architecture, in which their paintings nevertheless acquired the status of transcendent, high art, taking the place of the museum's internationally reclaimed works."[177] Thus, the collection of modernist Western and Iranian art was still not officially celebrated as part of Iran's national heritage, although pieces of the collection were occasionally exhibited in the museum (without any historical contextualization).[178]

With the reform period of President Seyyed Mohammad Khatami (1997–2005) and the appointment of Alireza Sami-Azar as the new director of the TMoCA in 1998, the museum gained new importance. Ironically, the state-run museum became a space of artistic and social exchange at a time when hardly any institutions offered a space for debate. Under the umbrella of the state, the museum provided students and artists the opportunity to see exhibitions and to gather and converse in the museum's café, go to the library, or see movies in the cinema.[179]

The directorship of Sami-Azar is often regarded as an essential turning point in the TMoCA's exhibition practice, as the museum not only started to work with its collection but also held international

[175] Darabi, 'Tehran Museum of Contemporary Art,' 230.
[176] Ali Ansari, *Iran under Ahmadinejad: The Politics of Confrontation* (London: Routledge, 2017), 11.
[177] Darabi, 'Tehran Museum of Contemporary Art,' 234.   [178] Ibid., 237.
[179] Eiman, 'Shaping and Portraying Identity,' 94.

exhibitions. In the early 2000s, the museum organized the exhibition series *Pioneers of Iranian Modern Art* and held solo exhibitions devoted to prominent Iranian modernist artists, such as Parviz Tanavoli (2003) and Charles Hossein Zenderoudi (2004), both of whom returned to Iran for their respective exhibitions. Collaborating with scholars and art historians, the museum published the exhibition catalogs for these projects in both Persian and English, thus also making modernist Iranian art accessible to non-Persian speakers.[180]

Due to the museum's new politics, Sami-Azar's tenure was often heralded as a "Curatorial Revolution"[181] or even a "Cultural Revolution at the TMOCA."[182] The new orientation of the museum's curatorial program was not only the result of a change in personnel but was also made possible by the liberal politics of the reform period. Khatami's reform program was based on "the message of civil society and Islamic democracy" and aimed to reform Iranian politics within the framework of current law and the Iranian constitution.[183] This younger generation had an especially strong desire for change and democratization since the old ideologies had lost their impact. For, at the time, as the artist and theorist Iman Afsarian explains,

A generation who had lost faith in ideology was gaining power. Both leftist and religious discourse had lost strength; whether theoretically or aesthetically. The reign of rigid and dogmatic ideologies was over – not merely in Iran, but everywhere.[184]

The museum director, Sami-Azar, a Western-trained architect, was himself a former revolutionary and later became a reformist. As Afsarian further argues,

Sami-Azar, and many of his peers were revolutionary, religious and radical adolescents in the early years of the revolution and were supported by studentships from the government to attend postgraduate courses in

---

[180] See Ruyin Pakbaz and Yaghoub Emdadian, *Pioneers of Iranian Modern Art – Charles Hossein-Zenderoudi* (Tehran: Tehran Museum of Contemporary Art, 2001); Ruyin Pakbaz and Yaghoub Emdadian (eds.), *Pioneers of Modern Iranian Art – Parviz Tanavoli* (Tehran: Tehran Museum of Contemporary Art, 2003).

[181] Darabi, 'Tehran Museum of Contemporary Art,' 234.

[182] Eiman, 'Shaping and Portraying Identity,' 92.

[183] Ansari, *Modern Iran*, 319.

[184] Iman Afsarian, 'The Fortunate Adolescents (Part 1).' https://iran.britishcouncil.org/en/underline/visual-arts/fortunate-adolescents, accessed 23 July 2018.

Europe back in the day. More or less repentant of their background, these people gradually pretermitted their initial radicalism and became the only group who were able to introduce reforms within the governing managerial system. If any reforms were meant to occur, the revolutionaries themselves had to turn into reformists; and so they did.[185]

One of the major reforms accomplished during Sami-Azar's directorship was the reevaluation of its modernist collection. He became familiar with Western modernist art and its international art market during his time as an architecture student in the United Kingdom. After his return to Iran and as director of the TMoCA, he saw the enormous capital and cultural value of the museum's collection.[186] In 2005, Sami-Azar and his curatorial team provided the first postrevolutionary overview exhibition *The Modern Art Movement* of the TMoCA's Western collection. During the reform period, modernist art became a parameter for negotiating red lines with the government of the Islamic republic. Showing works by American artists, such as Jackson Pollock, or images of unveiled women were not censored, even though these works do not correspond to the official politics of the Islamic Republic. The depiction of homoerotic contents, as in Francis Bacon's triptych *Two figures lying on a Bed with Attendants*, on the other hand, fell victim to the censorship of *Ershad* (The Ministry of Culture and Islamic Guidance) and had to be removed from the exhibition.[187] Due to the inclusion of prerevolutionary art in the TMoCA's official curatorial program, the sharp line distinguishing officially acclaimed revolutionary artists and modernist artists from one another began to vanish.[188]

The reform period opened up the museum and provided foreign curators, such as Tirdad Zolghadr, a writer whose work has been published in international art magazines and curator of international exhibitions, with the opportunity to work at the museum. In his publication *Traction*, Zolghadr reflects on his experiences in Tehran and harshly criticizes the museum. According to Zolghadr, the museum does not reflect a "definition of the contemporary" regarding how contemporary art museums should function. The museum's

---

[185] Ibid.
[186] As advisor for the auction house Christie's, Sami-Azar helped to develop a presence of Iranian art on the international art market.
[187] Interview by the author, Tehran, August 2013.
[188] Afsarian, 'Fortunate Adolescents.'

refusal to be part of a global art scene should not be misunderstood as a postcolonial attitude, as Zolghadr further argues, because,

> The muzeh has nothing in common with a documenta workshop in Kabul, or Okwui Enwezor pitching 'off-center' curating in Venice, not to mention a Zolghadr criticizing Tehran museums in a Sternberg book. In the eyes of people who use 'postcolonial' in the way I do, the muzeh is a corrupt, frustrating, and self-provincializing stick-in-the-mud.[189]

Zolghadr's description demonstrates that the TMoCA is not a global art space but, instead, closely tied to Iranian domestic politics and that it functions as an ideological arena for the Islamic Republic. With the election of conservative forces in 2005, the reformist period came to an end. The conservative shift in Iranian politics was also mirrored in the program of the TMoCA. The museum began to focus on revolutionary paintings and religious art again. During this period, the museum continued to present parts of its modernist collection, though it concentrated on Iranian artworks. Modernist Iranian art gained importance as the museum began actively incorporating the modern period into its official cultural politics. With exhibitions and projects about Iranian modernist art movements, the museum tried to establish a narrative continuity in the history of Iranian art.[190] The created continuity was based on the visual incorporation of Iranian elements, colors, and designs used in Iranian handicrafts, architecture, and Persian painting to create a formalist art history. The institutionalization of modernism also suggests that the Pahlavi era is no longer seen as a threat to the Islamic Republic but has instead turned into a chapter of Iran's history displayed as a regular part of museums' inventories. Concomitantly, the constructed continuity results in an odd narrative about modernist art, which, according to the former museum director, Abdolmajid Hosseini-Rad, finds its culminating expression in the works of revolutionary artists.

---

[189] Tirdad Zolghadr refers to the Tehran Museum of Contemporary Art as "*muzeh*," the Persian expression derives from French and is, according to Zolghadr, the common way to refer to the Museum of Contemporary Art in the art community. See Tirdad Zolghadr, *Traction* (Berlin: Sternberg Press, 2016), 13.

[190] See, for example, the exhibition, *A Retrospective Exhibition of Works of Saqqakhana Movement* (Tehran Museum of Contemporary Art, 20 August–12 November, 2013).

This inclination assumed more depth and appeal after the Islamic revolution and generated a predilection among artists, not least the younger generation ... A special appeal in the works of a group of revolutionary painters was shaped within this general tendency to present national identity and spirituality in art which had its roots in the convictions that shaped the Revolution and Islamic and Shiite tenets.[191]

As one can see from this quote, state-sponsored Iranian art historiography intertwines artistic creativity and innovation as results of the ideology of the Iranian Revolution.

Protests against the Cultural Politics of the Tehran Museum of Contemporary Art

The museum continued to promote contemporary art, exhibit new artistic media, and hold biennials.[192] Contrary to the Western general perception, the museum continually expanded its collection of Iranian art and bought numerous artworks over the years.[193] Despite the curatorial program's regressive turn, the museum remained an important space of exchange and debate for artists until 2009. During the 2009 election, many artists supported the moderate candidate Mir Hossein Moussavi. But, after the controversial election, many artists participated in the Green Movement to protest against Ahmadinejad's second presidency. Because of the government's violent repression of the Green Movement, "a majority of the artistic community, including all the artists' associations, issued manifestos and signed declarations advocating a boycott of collaboration with government institutions, and declaring the new government illegitimate."[194]

Following the Green Movement's protests, major demonstrations in front of the museum took place in the spring of 2016. After documents were leaked about the transfer of the museum ownership to the private Roudaki Art and Culture Foundation, demonstrators rallied to protest

---

[191] Abdolmajid Hosseini-Rad, 'Iranian Contemporary Art,' in *Iranian Modern Art Movement: The Iranian Collection of the Tehran Museum of Contemporary Art* (Tehran: Tehran Museum of Contemporary Art, 2006), (without page numbers).
[192] Eiman, 'Shaping and Portraying Identity,' 95.
[193] Hosseini-Rad, 'Iranian Contemporary Art.'
[194] Darabi, 'Tehran Museum of Contemporary Art,' 239.

against the museum's privatization.[195] Protestors insisted that the museum and its collection are part of Iran's national heritage and should not be left in the hands of the private Roudaki Foundation. The Tehran art scene feared the private foundation might sell off parts of the collection. The Roudaki Foundation operates as a private institution with the declared goal "of promoting and developing the field of art inside the country and in so doing making it globally known."[196] The foundation's board of trustees includes the minister of Islamic Culture and Guidance and other governmental representatives. This is why artists such as Jinoos Taghizadeh call this kind of initiative "*khossulati*," a portmanteau of "*khossusi* = private and *doulati* = state."[197] Taghizadeh maintains that the neoliberal approach of privatizing public property brings with it the risk that the museum could operate beyond any form of government or parliamentary control.[198]

Only shortly after the spring protests, the TMoCA concluded the contract with the German government to export works of the collection to Berlin and Rome. The Tehran art scene was highly skeptical about sending parts of the collection abroad, and the Association of Iranian Painters (*Anjoman-e honarmandan-e naqash-e Iran*) even published a statement on their website to explain why it was calling for a boycott of the exhibition. In their statement, they criticized the clandestine exhibition preparations and the lack of information from *Ershad*, the Ministry of Culture and Islamic Guidance responsible for the museum's operation. The Iranian Painters Association was not provided with any information about the selection of the artworks from the Tehran collection, which were supposed to travel to Europe. Nor did they have any access to the loan contract or information about guarantees and dates concerning the return of the artworks. Their major criticism was the lack of clarity regarding the artworks'

---

[195] 'Protest held against privatization of Tehran Museum of Contemporary Art,' *Tavoos Art Magazine*, 2016. http://tavoosonline.com/News/NewsDetailEn.aspx?src=23605, accessed 12 August 2017.
[196] See http://bonyadroudaki.com/PContent.aspx?id=46&&lang=en-US
[197] Jinoos Taghizadeh, 'Jinoos Taghizadeh,' in Hannah Jacobi (ed.), *Stimmen aus Teheran. Interviews zur zeitgenössischen Kunst im Iran* (Frankfurt am Main: Edition Faust, 2007), 55–67, 55.
[198] Ibid.

ownership. Many works in the collection were bought by the royal family and still nominally belong to their former owner, if their ownership has not been transferred to the TMoCA in their certificates after the revolution. The art scene in Tehran was concerned that secret deals could have been made and that the artworks would not be returned to Iran due to demands by former owners that the paintings be returned to them.[199] Following all these rumors, the former queen, Farah Diba, stated in an interview with Kayhan London that the collection of the museum in Tehran belongs to the Iranian people and that she would not claim ownership of them.[200]

The Exhibition Berlin–Rome Travelers *in Tehran (2017)*

In March 2017, after the cancellation of the exhibition in Berlin and as a reaction to the harsh criticism from the Iranian art scene, the TMoCA opened the exhibition *Berlin–Rome Travelers* [sic], which presented the sixty artworks that had been selected for the Berlin show. The exhibition was advertised with the painting *Trinidad Fernandez* (1907) by the Fauvist painter Kees van Dongen. The choice to promote the exhibition with van Dongen's portrait of a woman conveys an important message in response to the rumors that the artworks would not be returned to Iran after their export. In 2011, *Trinidad Fernandez* was sent on loan to the Museum Boijmans Van Beuningen in Rotterdam for the exhibition *All Eyes on Kees Van Dongen*.[201] After the exhibition, the artwork returned safe and sound to Iran. This painting was also the first work in the *Berlin–Rome Travelers exhibition*. With the selection of this image, the museum presents itself as operating on an international level and open to the international system of loaning artworks. This also becomes clear in Majid Mollanoroozi's foreword to the exhibition catalog, in which the museum director describes the importance of the collection.

---

[199] Press release *Anjoman-e honarmandan-e naqash-e Iran*, 10 October 2016. www.iranpainters.com/?m_id=793&id=39, accessed 12 August 2017.

[200] Farah Diba, 'Tavaghof-e ersal-e azar-e muze-ye honarhaye moaser be Berlin va Rome va vakansh-e Farah be shayat,' Interview with Kayhan London, 28 November 2016. https://kayhan.london/fa/1395/09/05/این-%8C%80%E2-لندن-کیهان-با-گفتگو-در-فرح-شهبانو, accessed 12 August 2017.

[201] See *All Eyes on Kees Van Dongen*, Exh.-Cat. Museum Bojmans von Beuningen, 2010.

Tehran Museum of Contemporary Art 81

The history of modern art cannot be complete without the study and analysis of the treasures at the Tehran Museum of Contemporary Arts and without such an approach it would be seriously deficient.[202]

Due to the great significance of the collection of Western and Iranian works, Mollanoroozi suggests that "with these attributes TMoCA may have more exposure and be more active in the world."[203] He further states that the collaboration with international curators and institutions and the presentations of the collection's artworks "have elevated the museum's status and credit."[204]

After the heated discussions around this exhibition, the artworks' presentation at the TMoCA was surprisingly austere. Aesthetically, the exhibition's presentation resembled an art fair more than a content-curated museum exhibition. As underlined by the statement on the museum wall,

With its exceptional architecture and collection, the Tehran Museum of Contemporary Art is a multicultural space for the people of the world wishing to experience the Orient and to see the Western concept of the world, in its clearest manifestation, i.e. artistic creation.[205]

These lines shed light on the museum's self-conception, which relies on a strict division between Iran and the West and hardly tries to establish a dialog between Western and Iranian works.

This separation of Iranian and Western works was reiterated in the structure of the exhibition *Berlin–Rome Travelers*. The exhibition tried to chronologically narrate the formalist development of modernist art from the late nineteenth century to the present, sketching the transition from naturalistic modes of expression toward abstraction and later figurative tendencies, as, for instance, practiced in Andy Warhol and Robert Rauschenberg's pop art. With a focus on formal innovations, the exhibition created two parallel histories of modernist art, Western modernism, and Iranian modernism. Although the exhibition points to

---

[202] Majid Mollanoroozi, *Selected Works of Tehran Museum of Contemporary Art: Berlin – Rome Travelers*. Exh.-Cat. (Tehran: Tehran Museum of Contemporary Art, 2017), 5.
[203] Ibid.   [204] Ibid.
[205] This citation was displayed at the museum's entrance during the exhibition Selected Works of Tehran Museum of Contemporary Art. Berlin–Rome Travelers. Exhibition visited on 15 April 2017.

similarities between twentieth-century artistic practices in Iranian and Western art, it dispenses with any cross-cultural interdependences.

Directly after the entrance area, the rotunda's walls, a dominant feature of the TMoCA's architecture, were adorned with posters of portraits and names of the exhibited artists. The posters' design was very similar to Piet Mondrian's geometric paintings and underlined the exhibition's focus on modernisms. Circulating downward through the labyrinthine galleries arranged in a spiral around the building's rotunda, the visitor could see which artworks had been chosen from the museum's collection. Beginning with Kees van Dongen's Expressionist painting, *Trinidad Fernandez*, and continuing to Max Ernst's surrealism, the first gallery showed development in painting toward abstraction, with works by Franz Kline and Willem de Kooning.

This was followed immediately by Jalil Ziapour's painting *Zaynab Khatoun*, which opened the Iranian section. Departing from Ziapour's figurative depiction of a female nude, the presentation sketched the Iranian path to artistic abstraction. The first Iranian abstract work in the museum was one of Monir Farmanfarmaian's mirror works. In her artistic works, Farmanfarmaian uses mirror mosaics found in mosques and sacred sites in Iran. The prominent position of Farmanfarmaian's work at the beginning of the exhibition suggests that, in the Iranian context, abstract art is less an imitation of Western modernist art discourses and more the result of its own unique Persian pictorial tradition.

Alternating between Western and Iranian works, the exhibition displayed works by Mark Rothko, Jackson Pollock, and Michelangelo Pistoletto, followed by Iranian modernist artists, such as Charles Hossein Zenderoudi, Gholam Hossein Nami, and Massoud Arabshahi, among others. Even Francis Bacon's triptych, *Two Figures Lying on a Bed with Attendants* (1968), was shown in the exhibition. Yet, due to the homoerotic depiction of two male nudes, the middle section of this work had to remain in the vaults, even though the picture was reproduced in the catalog with the men's genitals pixelated.[206] Figurative works by the Iranian female artists Parvaneh Etemadi and Leili Matin Daftari complemented Robert Rauschenberg and Andy Warhol's pop-art pieces.

---

[206] Francis Bacon, *Two Figures Lying on a Bed with Attendants*, 1968, Oil on Canvas, 198 × 442.5 cm (3 panels). See also *Berlin – Rome Travelers*. Exh.-Cat. (Tehran, 2017), 40.

The Iranian section of the exhibition also included pieces made after the revolution. The inclusion of later works is important because it shows that the museum's collecting activities were not restricted to the Pahlavi era alone. It also underscores the museum's active, agitating character as an institution in Iranian society. With Jafar Rouhbakhsh, the museum chose a modernist artist who was both very active during the modernist period in Iran and associated with the artistic movement of *Saqqakhaneh*.[207] Another example was the surrealist painter Ali Akbar Sadeghi, who became famous for his animated films for children in the 1970s. His films and paintings are inspired by Persian miniature painting and the epic literary tradition, as can be seen in his work *Piano War* (2011) from the series *Unwritten Collection*. These two artworks augment the existing collection.

With semi-abstract works by Kazem Chalipa and Habibollah Sadeghi, the TMoCA integrated two well-known and officially acclaimed revolutionary painters in the exhibition.[208] Kazem Chalipa, in particular, is one of the most prominent revolutionary painters. His painting *Self-sacrifice (Izar)* became one of the first large martyr murals in Tehran. It would later be widely reproduced and circulated as a postage stamp.[209] The image visually synthesizes the martyrs of Karbala with Iranian soldiers fighting in the Iran–Iraq war.[210] The veiled mother figure is the protagonist of the image. She holds her son's dead body, ready to sacrifice her child for Iran's war. Her lower body has the shape of a red tulip, the symbol of martyrdom, emphasizing the image's message of self-sacrifice for the good of the state.

But what, the question arises, does this inclusion of representatives of officially acclaimed revolutionary art mean? Is it a political strategy to counteract the selection made by the German curators? Or is it instead an attempt to exhibit the officially sanctioned Iranian style of modernism within the museum's broader collection and to make a statement about the museum's collecting activities? Is it a critique of the art-historical canon? How can one reconcile a collection that is so

---

[207] Javar Rouhbakhsh was presented in the exhibition with his work *Composition*, 1994, Oil on Canvas, 100 × 100 cm. Tehran Museum of Contemporary Art.
[208] Habibollah Sadeghi, *Untitled*, 2014, Oil on Canvas and Kazem Chalipa, *The Burnt Garden*, 2008, Oil on canvas, 150 × 150 cm. Both Tehran Museum of Contemporary Art.
[209] Grigor, *Contemporary Iranian Art*, 100.
[210] Kazem Chalipa, *Izar (Self-sacrifice)*, 1981, Oil on Canvas, 300 × 200 cm.

closely tied to the Pahlavi monarchy with artworks promoting the Islamic Republic of Iran?

Afshin Parvaresh's Practice of Institutional Critique

One of the most outspoken critics of the museum and the export of its works to European institutions is Afshin Parvaresh. Parvaresh is an artist, photographer, and internet activist based in New York, where he creates and coordinates his artistic campaigns. Parvaresh presents his artistic activities and the results of his research through social media platforms, on which he has almost 80,000 followers.[211] On June 16, only shortly before the end of the exhibition, *Berlin–Rome Travelers*, Parvaresh called on his social media followers to protest the artworks' export with a post bearing the headline "breaking news" (*khabar furi*) printed in red. In a second paragraph, he explains that "the most valuable works of the Museum of Contemporary Art will be secretly exported from Iran to Berlin under the supervision of Kamran Diba."[212] In the post's closing lines, Parvaresh implores his readers to take action with the following words, "Do not leave the museum alone! We have suffered enough to protect it!"[213] To emphasize the urgency of this "breaking news," Parvaresh created a poster-like message in Persian with red and black lines that evoked the image of a warning sign. In the comment column, he provides more information about the poster. He repeats his accusation that works from the museum will be exported to Europe without the necessary permission of the parliamentary Cultural Commission and the Iranian Guardian Council. He also accuses the German Foreign Office of ignoring his requests for information regarding the export of the artworks. Parvaresh further states that there is little time left to protect "our" national treasures and to prevent their theft by the international art mafia. He calls upon all compatriots to save Iran's national heritage from being looted.

---

[211] Afshin Parvaresh uses Telegram, Instagram, and his Facebook Account for the dissemination of his artistic reports. His posts are published in Persian. All translations by the author, unless otherwise indicated.

[212] Kamran Diba is the architect of the TMoCA building and was also director of the museum until 1979. Since the Iranian Revolution Diba resides outside of Iran.

[213] Afshin Parvaresh, 'Khabar Furi,' 15 June 2017. www.instagram.com/p/BVVyNHqhIqv/?taken-by=afshin_parvaresh, accessed 12 August 2017.

Tehran Museum of Contemporary Art 85

Figure 1.6 Afshin Parvaresh, *Khabar Furi (Breaking News)*, June 15, 2017. Instagram.

Figure 1.7 Afshin Parvaresh, Emrooz *Ekhtetamiyeh, Fardah Sham-e Akheir (Today is the closing day, tomorrow the last supper)*, June 15, 2017. Instagram.

According to Parvaresh, the claim that Iranian political hardliners blocked the export of the works is only propaganda, also disseminated in foreign media by what he calls the art mafia. In reality, however, the artist's engagement in the protest stopped the export of the artworks. Parvaresh's main charges are directed toward the opaque structures behind the artworks' ownership and the museum's lack of a collection catalog. He elaborated on this topic in another post the following day, in which he formulated controversial questions such as, where is the list with the artworks belonging to the collection of the TMoCA? Why is the original list still in Farah and Kamran Diba's possession? Why do the works officially still belong to the royal family, and why hasn't the Islamic Republic of Iran not transferred their ownership during its thirty-eight years of existence? And why is the loan contract with Germany under seal?[214]

Parvaresh is fully committed in his artistic practice to the investigation of the TMoCA's inventory of modernist art. His posts and messages read like a detective story, in which he identifies the deceitful actions of former museum directors and other complicit artists, especially when he accuses museum staff of stealing and forging artworks. Parvaresh claims that the reasons for this misconduct are to be found in the lack of transparency in the museum's work, the lack of an inventory catalog, and the lack of research on the collection. He criticizes not only the Museum of Contemporary Art in Tehran but also the cultural politics of the Iranian Government in general. He demands a democratization of cultural politics and articulates his critique by demanding transparent museum politics and the disclosure of the collection's history and ownership structures. After years of artistic research to investigate the precise number of artworks held in the collection of the TMoCA, in October 2017, Parvaresh informed his followers on social media that the collection had 3,478 artworks, stating that the artworks belong to the Iranian people. Since, according to Parvaresh, the Iranian nation entrusted the museum with the preservation of the collection for following generations, he demands that the museum fulfill its duty to increase security measures, make the museum's politics transparent, and promote research.[215]

[214] Ibid., 16 June 2017. www.instagram.com/p/BVYQrfuBiQq/?taken-by=afshin_parvaresh, accessed 12 August 2017.
[215] Ibid., 29 October 2017. www.instagram.com/p/Ba0Ni7Nh7Ho/?taken-by=afshin_parvaresh, accessed 29 October 2017.

Parvaresh's accusations are very precise and detailed, though it is not entirely clear what his sources are and if his critique is based on true facts. Yet, Parvaresh's artworks should be regarded less as a source of information and more as a practice of institutional critique. As an artistic practice, institutional critique examines and analyses art institutions, such as museums and art galleries, and questions art's social function. For instance, the German artist Hans Haacke is an important representative of the artistic deployment of institutional critique. In his artworks, he often engages with the institution of the museum. Like an investigative journalist, Haacke tries to reveal hidden power relations that define the work of art institutions. Using charts, texts, and photographs, Haacke reveals the complex political and economic relationships between the institutions, the state, and the economy. One outstanding example among his works is *Shapolsky et al. Manhattan Real Estate Holdings, A Real Time Social System, as of May 1, 1971*, in which Haacke uncovers the secret affairs of the real estate group Shapolsky et al. Manhattan Real Estate Holdings, which owned the majority of real estate in New York during the 1970s. Haacke's work consists of 142 photographic images documenting the buildings, combined with typewritten charts and texts revealing their position within the company's network. With this work, Haacke strongly criticized the dichotomy between capitalist profit optimization and the housing shortage faced by the city's residents. This work was supposed to be shown in a major solo exhibition of Haacke's works in New York's Guggenheim Museum in 1971. This site-specific artwork transgresses the museum walls and actively engages with the architectural and urban discourse of the city in which the museum is located. Haacke's critical investigation of property relations in New York led to the cancellation of his exhibition at the Guggenheim museum, presumably due to the links between the Guggenheim's board of trustees and the real estate group.[216] In *Shapolsky et al. Manhattan Real Estate Holdings, A Real Time Social System, as of May 1, 1971*, Haacke demonstrates, with reference to Rosalyn Deutsche, that "the city – constructed in mainstream architectural and urban discourses as a strictly physical, utilitarian, or aesthetic space – and the museum – conceived in idealist art discourse as a

---

[216] Rosalyn Deutsche, 'Property Values: Hans Haacke, Real Estate and the Museum,' in Rosalyn Deutsche (ed.), *Evictions: Art And Spatial Politics* (Cambridge, MA: MIT Press, 1996), 159–192.

purely aesthetic realm, appear as spatial forms marked by a political economy."[217]

As Haacke stated in an interview with the French philosopher Pierre Bourdieu, he tries to escape the logic of the art market with his artistic works. For Haacke, his works function as a means of free expression and are supposed to "represent symbolic power, power that can be put to the service of domination or emancipation, and thus has ideological implications with repercussions in our everyday lives."[218] A parallel can be drawn between this statement and Parvaresh's artistic practice, which also rejects the financial marketing of his art. His artworks are not sellable products; his works circulate mainly on social media and consist of images and texts. Parvaresh produces his artworks for an Iranian audience, his posts are all in Persian and primarily address domestic political issues in Iran. Parvaresh's works are intentionally not addressed to a global art market to avoid the self-orientalizing and self-exoticizing tendencies often demanded by a global art market interested in the identity politics of non-Western artists' work as part of its strategy of "ethnic marketing."[219]

Like Haacke, whose artistic productions have been described by the artist Andrea Fraser as often being a way of "fearlessly speaking truth to power,"[220] Parvaresh also tries to protect art institutions from political and economic instrumentalization. In his use of George Orwell's famous quote, "in a time of universal deceit, telling the truth is a revolutionary act." as his Facebook cover photo, Parvaresh identifies his social media activities with the practice of "telling the truth."[221] His status as an emigrant artist living in New York allows him to address political subjects more openly than other artists living in Iran, who have faced severe repercussions for criticizing the state apparatus. Parvaresh uses this acquired liberty as a voice to protect Iran's national heritage. At the same time, he is conscious that his investigative practice can have devastating consequences.

---

[217] Ibid., 171–172.
[218] Hans Haacke, 'Helmsboro Country,' in Pierre Bourdieu and Haacke (eds.), *Free Exchange* (Cambridge: Polity Press, 1995), 2–23, 2.
[219] See Tirdad Zolghadr, *Ethnic Marketing* (Zurich: JRP/Ringier, 2006).
[220] Andrea Fraser, 'From the Critique of Institutions to an Institution of Critique,' *Artforum*, vol. 44 (2005), 100–106.
[221] See Afshin Parvaresh's Facebook profile. www.facebook.com/parvareshafshin/, accessed 12 October 2017.

As an investigative journalist, it is my job to deal with crimes harming public policy. My research leads sometimes to situations that put my life and the lives of my research sources at risk. I only identify the problems; the prosecution of these deeds is the task of legal services. The same is true for the art museum and the international art mafia.[222]

This statement shows that, contrary to earlier generations of exiled artists and art practitioners who rejected the legitimacy of the Islamic Republic for their present life realities, Parvaresh believes the Islamic Republic of Iran has a responsibility to take legal actions against violations of current law. This significantly differentiates Parvaresh from the Iranian diaspora community in general and other exiled Iranian artists, such as Shirin Neshat, whose artistic oeuvre is deeply rooted in her personal discourse of exile and diaspora and often functions as a symbolic return to an imagined homeland.[223] As one can see from the analysis of *Iran Modern* in this chapter, the diaspora community has actively tried to establish a national art historiography outside of Iran without, however, engaging with art institutions and historiographical processes in Iran. *Iran Modern* promoted the idea of a nostalgic return to a prerevolutionary and secular Iran, and, in this context, the modernist artworks of the 1960s and 1970s functioned as witnesses of the golden age of Iranian secularism. Consequently, the *imagined community* of Iranian curators, critics, historians, and art practitioners living in the diaspora ignores today's Islamic Republic of Iran as the legitimate successor to the Pahlavi monarchy.

Likewise, the planned *The Tehran Modern* exhibition in Berlin was also plagued by its tendencies to ignore the realities of contemporary Iran and craft a nostalgic version of Iran's past. The Berlin project used Tehran's modernist artistic heritage as a currency of soft power to seal the deal during the nuclear negotiations with Iran. To justify the nuclear deal with Iran, Germany tried to establish an idea of cultural exchange, which was based on an allegedly shared heritage of secularism and democracy. However, this chapter's analysis of *The Tehran Modern* project shows that Germany largely neglected its negotiation partner, the Islamic Republic of Iran, particularly the TMoCA. The German

---

[222] Afshin Parvaresh, Instagram Post, 19 June 2017. www.instagram.com/p/BVhdyZuBb2O/?taken-by=afshin_parvaresh, accessed 12 October 2017.
[223] See Katrin Nahidi, '"How it breaks my heart to leave you" – Images of Women in Shirin Neshat's Video Works,' Exh.-Cat. *Shirin Neshat*, Kunsthalle Tübingen (Tübingen: Stiftung Kunsthalle Tübingen, 2017), 135–147.

side crafted an imaginary Persian past similar to the diaspora community's, which glorified the Pahlavi monarchy as enlightened and oriented toward the West. In this equation, modernist art turns into evidence for the value Pahlavi-era Iran placed on freedom of expression. This imagined historical narrative starkly contrasts Germany's history and the decisive contribution made by Iranian resistance against the Shah's autocracy to the politicization of the German student movement in the late 1960s.

The analysis of *Iran Modern* and *The Tehran Modern* presented in this chapter has shown how the discourses of the diaspora and Germany's use of soft power instrumentalized Iran's modernist artistic heritage to different political ends. What they have in common, however, is how they craft their own discourses and histories of Iranian modernism while ignoring the TMoCA's legitimacy as an official institution of the Islamic Republic of Iran.

2 Cultural Politics in Pahlavi Iran
The TMoCA's Architecture and the Evolution of Gharbzadegi in Arts and Politics

Museums and exhibitions play a crucial role in the depoliticization of modernist art production in Iran. In these contexts, modernist Iranian art often functions as evidence of purely formalist experiments with the aesthetics of Western modernity. Queen Farah Diba's efforts to promote art and culture in the 1960s and 1970s reinforce this impression and foster the reception of modernist art from Iran as primarily a result of royal patronage and as a sign of the Pahlavis' successful secularization programs. A closer look at the sociopolitical debates at the time reveals how cultural politics in the Pahlavi era responded to the growing critique of modernization and its implementation in Iran.

Structurally, this chapter has three parts; it discusses the evolution of the term *gharbzadegi* (westoxification), cultural politics as means of soft power in Pahlavi Iran, and previously untranslated art criticisms of Jalal al-e Ahmad.

Gharbzadegi denotes the most substantial political discourse critical of Pahlavi's implementation of Western modernity and dismantles Iran's history of colonial modernity. As an expression of anticolonial critique and decolonial theory, the term reached new heights after the publication of Jalal al-e Ahmad's eponymous essay, *Gharbzadegi*, in 1962.

The critique of Iran's westoxification was also reflected in Pahlavi cultural politics, as one can see in the way Farah Diba's cultural efforts mirror her attempt to modernize the country on Iranian terms. Not only did her politics of conservation and preservation represent a "feminized version of modernity," but her more liberal politics were also invested in fostering democratic institutional structures.[1] As a case study, the architecture of Tehran Museum of Contemporary Art (TMoCA) illuminates how Pahlavi cultural politics in the field of architecture shifted from an international modernist style to

---

[1] Grigor, *Building Iran*, 184.

architectural designs that embraced local building traditions. The analysis of the museum's architecture will highlight the instrumentalization of art and architecture in Pahlavi Iran, as means of soft power meant to communicate the country's successful modernization. The institutionalization of modernist art and architecture in the Pahlavi era was immensely successful and staged Iranian art production as a sign of modernization in service of the monarchy.

When considering this depoliticized perception of modernist Iranian art, however, it is important to note that al-e Ahmad's antimodernist and anticolonial discourse on *gharbzadegi* was not limited to politics and history but encompassed all fields of cultural productions and, especially, modernist art production. Al-e Ahmad expressed his thoughts and ideas about modernism in various writings about Iranian artists and exhibitions, implementing his concept of an alternative modernity, which is opposed to westernization, and attempts to construct a significantly different version of Western modernity.

Westoxification: The Discourse of *Gharbzadegi*

While the museum's cultural politics and architecture were, on the one hand, means to communicate Iran's successful modernization, they were, on the other hand, also intended as domestic political responses to the ongoing discussions about Iran's westernization. In the 1960s and 1970s, many intellectuals took a critical stance on the Shah's top-down modernization program and demanded an alternative concept of modernity, not exclusively based on Western paradigms of rationality, secularity, and technical progress. Resistance grew under the banner of *gharbzadegi*, a term encompassing a number of critiques of Western colonialism and imperialism. The term *gharbzadegi* (westoxification) became the most influential political slogan for a critique of the Pahlavi monarchy and its modernization programs, as well as the colonial politics and imperial interference of the Allied forces. To this day, *gharbzadegi* has not lost any of its importance in the Islamic Republic and continues to represent a significant political slogan for critiques of Western influence in Iran.

The rise of political Islam in Iran is often understood as a rejection of Western modernity that favored tradition and religion over the *ratio* and modernity of the West. In various writings, Ali Mirsepassi demonstrates that westoxification arose among Iranian intellectuals out of their interest in German and French antimodernist and counter-Enlightenment theory. The concept of *gharbzadegi*, in other words, is not an Iranian concept opposed to Western modernity but rather itself a product of European thought, which was turned into a transnational idea that would ultimately shape Iranian discourse in meaningful ways.[2] Iran's quest for an alternative modernity was also highly welcomed by Western intellectuals, who engaged in a critique of modernity and Enlightenment discourse. For example, Iran's political turn to religion proved to be very influential for Michel Foucault's idea of political spirituality. Before and during the Islamic Revolution, Foucault traveled to Iran several times and met Ayatollah Khomeini during his exile in Paris. He enthusiastically described Khomeini and Shi'ism as harbingers of spiritual politics in his articles and interviews.[3]

Al-e Ahmad, as a fervent critic of colonialism and modernization theory, intensifies the *gharbzadegi* debate and outlines "the Iranian encounter with colonial modernity."[4] He questions the linear history of the progress of Western modernization, which as an assumed tabula rasa moment, radically breaks with any premodern traditions. In recent years, *gharbzadegi* has been reframed as an essential concept for decolonial theory. As "a counter-hegemonic critique of the entwined global processes of racialization and colonial exploitation," it analyzes how colonial modernity's racist structures shaped "the lived experiences of colonial and semi-colonial subjects" in Pahlavi Iran.[5]

Ahmad Fardid's Concept of Westoxification

Until his death in 1994, the Iranian philosopher Ahmad Fardid claimed intellectual ownership of the idea of *gharbzadegi* for himself. Fardid articulated major features of *gharbzadegi* in postwar Germany, where fascism had destroyed the promises of modernity. After graduating with a degree in philosophy and education from Tehran Teachers'

---

[2] Ali Mirsepassi, *Political Islam, Iran, and the Enlightenment: Philosophies of Hope and Despair* (Cambridge: Cambridge University Press, 2010), 274.
[3] For further investigation on this topic, see Janet Afary and Kevin B. Anderson, *Foucault and the Iranian Revolution: Gender and the Seductions of Islamism* (Chicago: University of Chicago Press, 2005).
[4] Hamid Dabashi, *The Last Muslim Intellectual: The Life and Legacy of Jalal Al-e Ahmad* (Edinburgh: Edinburgh University Press, 2021), 9.
[5] Eskandar Sadeghi-Boroujerdi, 'Gharbzadegi, Colonial Capitalism and the Racial State in Iran,' *Postcolonial Studies*, vol. 24, no. 2 (2021), 173–194, 174.

College in 1935, Fardid translated numerous works by Western philosophers, such as Henri Bergson and Henri Corbin, into Persian and also published essential articles about Kant and Heidegger. Fardid was awarded a state-sponsored scholarship and left Iran for Paris, where he pursued his philosophical studies at the Sorbonne from 1946 to 1951. In 1951, Fardid moved to Heidelberg, Germany, to deepen his knowledge of German philosophy, where he would remain until 1955.

During this time, Fardid studied Martin Heidegger's philosophy, which would exert a decisive influence on his development of the concept of westoxification. Fardid was a passionate and fervent adherent of Heidegger's thought, whose ideas he translated into the Iranian context, in which he was later known as the "Iranian Heidegger" and regarded as the leading authority on Heidegger's philosophy.[6] As a radical critic of the Enlightenment and secularism, Heidegger's counter-Enlightenment discourse provided Fardid with the right tools to express his critique of modernity. As Mehrzad Boroujerdi explains, "Persuaded by Heidegger's views on the spirit of historical eras, the philosophy of being, and the imprisoning nature of modern technology, Fardid speaks of *gharbzadegi* as the interlude between the self and the being."[7]

After his return from Germany, Fardid "crafted the Islamist discourses of authenticity as a form of romantic nativism"[8] and coined the term *gharbzadegi*, which served him as a mode of articulating his opposition to the secularism, colonialism, and Orientalism that he experienced in Iran. To formulate his idea of *gharbzadegi*, Fardid "borrowed from a counter-modern discursive narrative already existing in the West as well as the Islamic and Persian mystical tradition."[9] According to Fardid, most Iranians were not just influenced by the West, they had been contaminated by Western influence and had lost the connection to their authentic being. The resurrection of Islamic spirituality was, for Fardid, the only way to differentiate Iran from the West and for Iran to return to an "authentic" self.[10]

---

[6] Ibid., 112.
[7] Mehrzad Boroujerdi, *Iranian Intellectuals and the West: The Tormented Triumph of Nativism* (New York: Syracuse University Press, 1996), 65.
[8] Ibid., 68.   [9] Ibid.
[10] Ali Mirsepassi, *Transnationalism in Iranian Political Thought: The Life and Times of Ahmad Fardid* (Cambridge: Cambridge University Press, 2017), 141.

Fardid's conception and introduction of *gharbzadegi* significantly changed the political discourse in Iran. Since the Constitutional Revolution (1906–1911), political opposition and resistance toward the prevailing system were rooted in a secular position that aspired to democratize Iran. Fardid, however, located resistance against injustice within the discourse of Islamic authenticity.[11] With his discourse on Islamic authenticity, Fardid especially attacked liberalism and democracy as alien to Islamic societies. For Fardid, democracy was a Greek invention and, thus, westoxified.

There is no way to find democracy in the Qur'an. The day before yesterday's truth, and the day after tomorrow's truth, is the one that materializes in the Islamic government. Democracy belongs to Greece, and idolatry is embodied in Greek.[12]

Fardid did not consult Islamic sources, such as the Qur'an or Hadith, when making such statements about authenticity but rather legitimized his strong proclamations by referring to Martin Heidegger's philosophical discourse on the history of being: "The fate of our epoch [*havalat-e tarikhi*] is total forgetfulness of Being – or the true God."[13]

For Fardid, democracy and liberalism were not the only signs of westoxification, which also included Western intellectual production about the "Orient," as he stated in a 1972 article. Unlike Edward Said's later critique of Orientalism, Fardid does not emphasize power relations, hegemony, and colonialism.[14] The reason why the "West's" knowledge is never able to meet the "authentic East's" lies, according to Fardid, in the fact that modern Western sciences are based on rationality and not spirituality:

Today when East and West are discussed, often two distinct geographical entities are imagined. However, the geographical East is so much under the Western civilization and influenced by its thoughts that it is no longer expedient to have recollection of what Eastern authenticity is. However, it is easy to distinguish between the appearance of East and West. But what is important is that the essence of the East, for the time being, is hidden.[15]

---

[11] Ibid., 5.   [12] Ibid., 241.   [13] Ibid.
[14] See Edward Said, *Orientalism: Western Conceptions of the Orient* (New York: Penguin Books, 1978).
[15] Mirsepassi, *Transnationalism in Iranian Political Thought*, 156.

In this statement, Fardid points out that the so-called East exists only in the Western imagination. Western imperialism led to the loss of the East's authentic character. Yet, he is convinced that the East's authenticity has not been permanently lost and might be rediscovered by dismissing Western modernity and Enlightenment.

Mirsepassi argues that Fardid's critique of Orientalism should be understood in the larger context of postcolonialism. Similar to Said, Fardid contests the idea that the "Orient" is but a Western construct based on colonialism and imperialism. Mirsepassi maintains that Fardid's ideological adherence to Heidegger's anti-Enlightenment thought and critique of Western modernity corresponds to Said's work, which was strongly influenced by Michel Foucault's philosophy. Given how influential Heidegger was for Foucault's theoretical works, Mirsepassi concludes that "Fardid's view is an earlier version of Said's idea of Orientalism."[16]

As Ali Shariati writes, Fardid enthusiastically welcomed the Iranian Revolution because he saw in it the fulfillment of his philosophical ideas:

Fardid claimed that he was the theoretician of the revolution. According to him, it was possible that even the leaders and the actors of the revolution did not have a clear idea about its meaning. Fardid had the illusion that he was the ideologue of the revolution. He is quoted as saying that, while Imam Khomeini had talked about Westoxification, he fortunately had not said what its essence was, and Fardid was the one who could explain this essence.[17]

This quote demonstrates how Fardid defined himself as the leading authority on Heidegger, from whom he drew his concept of *gharbzadegi*. Fardid combined his idea, rooted in the European philosophical discourse, with his own (invented) spiritual politics. The complexity of Fardid's concept made it incomprehensible to the masses, and his teachings remained reserved for a small group of committed followers. Most of his followers were former students from Tehran University, where he became a professor in 1960. As a philosopher, Fardid never published a single book and very little otherwise, preferring to communicate his thoughts orally. Thus, to use Fardid's own words, not

---

[16] Ibid., 164.
[17] Ali Shariati, cited in Mirsepassi, *Transnationalism in Iranian Political Thought*, 338–339.

only is "the essence of the East ... hidden," Fardid's thoughts themselves remain hidden "for the time being."

Jalal al-e Ahmad's Westoxification *(Gharbzadegi)*

Yet, not Fardid but the writer Jalal al-e Ahmad popularized the concept of *gharbzadegi* in Iran during the 1960s. Al-e Ahmad articulated his idea of westoxification in the aftermath of the 1953 coup d'état against Mohammad Mosaddeq's government and his attempted nationalization of Iranian oil revenues. The coup d'état, carried out by members of the royalist army and financed by British and US secret services, led to the reinstatement of Mohammad Reza Shah as the autocratic ruler of Iran. With their devastating consequences for power politics and the end of Mosaddeq's democratically elected government, these imperialist interferences constitute a major source of trauma for the Iranian intelligentsia. These political events gave rise to the establishment of anticolonial political discourse in Iran.[18]

In 1961, together with Fardid, al-e Ahmad participated in the meetings of the *Council of the Goals of Education in Iran*, at which a number of intellectuals discussed the reformation of education in the country. It was during these meetings that Fardid introduced his concept of westoxification. After these meetings, the writer, ethnographer, and social critic al-e Ahmad wrote his influential essay, *Gharbzadegi*. In his preface to *Gharbzadegi*, al-e Ahmad explains that he "borrowed the term *gharbzadegi* from conversations I had with my other mentor Ahmad Fardid."[19] Al-e Ahmad turned the idea of westoxification into a book and transformed Fardid's interpretation of the Heideggerian concept into a more accessible political vision of postcolonial thought. Al-e Ahmad's concept of *gharbzadegi* is a critique of colonialism and Orientalism rooted in an anticapitalist critique of Western modernity and Iran's blind imitation of it, which leads to a call for an alternative modernity based on Iran's Islamic heritage and articulated in a comprehensible, yet polemical language. For the critics of the Pahlavi nation-state, *gharbzadegi* "denoted a national pathology, a state of cultural schizophrenia that divorced the true Iranian self from its

[18] Ansari, *Modern Iran*, 162.
[19] Jalal Al-e Ahmad, *Plagued by the West [Gharbzadegi]*, translated by Paul Sprachman (Delmar, NY: Center for Iranian Studies Columbia University, 1981), 2.

wellspring of ideational purity." Thus, *gharbzadegi* became a utopian "promise of hope in a hopeless world" that could "deliver the radical new order that is imagined with a good dose of intoxicating, positivistic certainty."[20]

This one-hundred-page essay would become one of the most important books in Iranian history. As Ehsan Yarshater states, "No other essay in modern Persian history has had the same vogue or has achieved comparable success. Its title has become a catchphrase, used to epitomize in four syllables the basic ill of modern Persian society."[21] Describing *gharbzadegi's* tremendous impact, Dabashi makes clear that "in constituting the very vocabulary of Iranian social criticism in the two decades preceding the Revolution, and in formulating the most essential 'anti-Western' disposition of the Islamic revolutionary discourse, no other text comes even close to *Westoxification*."[22] Reza Baraheni, author and colleague of al-e Ahmad, even goes a step further and compares *gharbzadegi's* significance to that of Karl Marx and Friedrich Engels' *Communist Manifesto*:

Al-e Ahmad's *Gharbzadegi* ... has the same significance in determining the duty of colonized nations vis-à-vis colonialist nations that the Manifesto of Marx and Engels had in defining the responsibility of the proletariat vis-à-vis capitalism and the bourgeoisie, and that Franz Fanon's *The Wretched of the Earth* had in defining the role of African nations vis-à-vis foreign colonialists. Al-e Ahmad's *Gharbzadegi* is the first Eastern essay to make clear the situation of the East vis-à-vis the West – the colonialist West – and it may be the first Iranian essay to have social value on a world level.[23]

Al-e Ahmad was born in 1923 to a religious family in northern Iran. Like his father and grandfather, al-e Ahmad was supposed to pursue a career as a cleric, and, accordingly, al-e Ahmad's father sent him to Najaf, Iraq, to study Islamic theology. After only a few months, however, al-e Ahmad left Najaf and decided to continue his studies at secular institutions in Iran. He graduated from Tehran Teachers' College in 1946. In the late 1940s, he became a member of the Marxist

---

[20] Arshin Adib-Moghaddam, *What Is Iran? Domestic Politics and International Relations in Five Musical Pieces* (Cambridge: Cambridge University Press, 2021), 34.
[21] Ehsan Yarshater, 'Foreword,' in al-e Ahmad, *Plagued by the West*, VIV.
[22] Hamid Dabashi, *Theology of Discontent: The Ideological Foundation of the Islamic Revolution in Iran* (New York: New York University Press, 2006), 74.
[23] Boroujerdi, *Iranian Intellectuals*, 67.

Tudeh Party, which was founded in 1941 as a protest against the Allied Forces' occupation of Iran and the forced abdication of Reza Shah.[24] Al-e Ahmad's membership in the communist party not only was a political decision but also marked his break from religion. Although al-e Ahmad had a high-ranking position in the Tudeh Party, he left the Tudeh in 1948 over conflicts within the party. Though he remained politically active after his break with the Tudeh Party, al-e Ahmad refrained from joining any major political organizations. During the reign of Mohammad Mosaddeq, al-e Ahmad advocated Mosaddeq's liberal politics and supported the campaign to nationalize Iran's oil.[25] After the 1953 coup, al-e Ahmad withdrew from his political affiliations. He focused more on writing fiction and ethnographic reports, for "the whole idea of organized political action and, perhaps more important, the very secular and imported ideological foundations of these movements seem to have lost their interest or relevance for al-e Ahmad."[26]

Illness as Political Metaphor in Gharbzadegi

The publication of his essay *Gharbzadegi* in 1962 marked al-e Ahmad's return to the political stage in Iran. Al-e Ahmad transformed Fardid's concept of *gharbzadegi* into the umbrella term for anticolonial resistance in Iran. From his subaltern position, al-e Ahmad voices a powerful Marxist critique of colonialism, global capitalism, modernization, and economic inequality. As a former member of the communist Tudeh Party, Marxism provided al-e Ahmad with the right vocabulary and the theoretical framework necessary to criticize Western economic and cultural domination, as well as the opportunity to examine ways of resisting hegemonic powers. Al-e Ahmad's essay criticizes colonial power politics and sharply attacks the Pahlavi monarchy and its suppression of Iranian citizens' democratic rights. The politicization of the concept of *gharbzadegi* turned his essay into a

---

[24] For a more detailed investigation of Tudeh Party, see, for example, Cronin, *Reformers and Revolutionaries in Modern Iran*.
[25] For al-e Ahmad's detailed biography, see J. W. Clinton, 'ĀL-E AḤMAD, JALĀL,' *Encyclopædia Iranica*. www.iranicaonline.org/articles/al-e-ahmad-jalal-1302-48-s, accessed 5 May 2019; also see Dabashi, *The Last Muslim Intellectual*.
[26] Dabashi, *Theology*, 51.

political manifesto and initiated the revolutionary mobilization of the masses. Al-e Ahmad's polemical and provocative essay starts with a powerful message that diagnoses Iran as being infected by the West and declares its intention to find a cure for the illness:

> I speak of being afflicted with "westitis" the way I would speak of being afflicted with cholera. (...) Have you ever seen how wheat rots? From within. The husk remains whole, but it is only an empty shell like the discarded chrysalis of a butterfly hanging from a tree. In any case, we are dealing with a sickness, a disease imported from abroad, and developed in an environment receptive to it. Let us discover the characteristics of this illness and its cause or causes and, if possible, find a cure.[27]

In al-e Ahmad's work, the allegory of the disease becomes a primary structural principle for his critique of westernization. After diagnosing Iran with "westitis," al-e Ahmad traces westoxification back to its roots. He observes the beginnings of the West's infectious influence even in premodern times, such as in Iran's mythology and ancient history. From a postcolonial standpoint, al-e Ahmad constructs a historiographical narrative that explains Iran's economic and industrial inferiority and its dependency on Western countries as the results of continuous imperialist and colonial interferences dating back to the time of the Crusades. His account of history does not seek to establish an accurate historiography of Iran but rather "to find out how the worm actually got into the tree."[28] Severe signs of decay had already appeared, according to al-e Ahmad, in Safavid and Qajar times, when the former rulers of Iran could not resist imperialism and the Qajar king, Mozaffer din Shah, sold the oil concession to William Knox d'Arcy. He writes, "as a direct result of our recent quiescent history, the fate of our politics, economy, and culture went directly into the hands of the companies and western nations which backed them."[29]

For al-e Ahmad, westoxification represents a severe problem that permeates all sectors of society, including the clergy, intellectuals, villagers, the newly established middle class, and, in particular, the ruling elite and the monarchy, and which has, thus, led to Iran losing its identity:

> The basic point of this book is that we have not been able to preserve our "cultural-historical" personality in the face of the machine and its

[27] Al-e Ahmad, *Plagued by the West*, 3.   [28] Ibid.   [29] Ibid., 32.

unavoidable onslaught. Rather we have been crushed by events. The point is that we have not been able to maintain a well-thought-out and considered position vis-à-vis this monster of the modern ages. The fact is that until we have actually grasped the essence, basis, and philosophy of western civilization and no longer superficially mimic the West in our consumption of western products, we shall be just like the ass who wore a lion skin.[30]

Al-e Ahmad's theory of westoxification centers around two major subjects: a critique of the colonial "other" and a simultaneous reflection on the Iranian "self" and the inherent inferiority complex that leads Iran to imitate the West. In al-e Ahmad's thought, the West and, in particular, the machine as a symbol of modernity pose a severe threat to Iranian identity. To sustain a structural difference between Eastern and Western countries in his book, al-e Ahmad employs an essentialist dichotomy between "West" and "East." For al-e Ahmad, "'West' and 'East' have neither political nor geographical meaning. Instead, they are two economic concepts. 'West' means the well-fed countries, and 'East' means the hungry countries."[31] Western countries are, according to al-e Ahmad, characterized not only by "high wages, low mortality rate, low birth rates, well organized social services, sufficient food (at least 3000 calories per day)" but by "trappings of democracy and a liberal inheritance from the French revolution"[32] as well. Eastern countries, on the contrary, suffer from economic and social poverty due to an "inheritance" that goes "back to the very beginnings of colonialism."[33]

By pointing out the economic inequality between East and West, al-e Ahmad utters a critique of modernization theory. Modernization theory refers to a set of theories that emerged from various social science disciplines. In the 1950s and 1960s, it gained prominence in understanding economic and social developments in so-called Third World countries. Modernization theory casts social transformation and development as a linear path of evolution from assumed traditional, rural societies to industrial, modern, and urban nation-states. This theory "supposed that the world was converging from tradition into a single modernity."[34] In particular, theorizing the route to

---

[30] Ibid., 7.   [31] Ibid., 4.   [32] Ibid.   [33] Ibid.
[34] Roland Popp, 'An Application of Modernization Theory during the Cold War? The Case of Pahlavi Iran,' *The International History Review*, vol. 30, no. 1 (2008), 76–98, 79.

Western modernity influenced policy-making and scholarship toward Pahlavi Iran. During the Cold War, this ideology promised to preserve Iran's independence from the Soviet Union and guarantee access to Iran's oil revenues, thus informing US foreign policy, development aid, and scholarship. The anthropologist Michael MJ Fischer states: "Iran has been a major test case for modernization theory" and "the case where transformation from the third world into the first world was expected to be most feasible."[35]

In his essay, al-e Ahmad clarifies that Iran's identification with Europe is misleading and calls for postcolonial solidarity between "developing nations."[36] Sadeghi-Boroujerdi argues that Al-e Ahmads's critique is not directed against modernization per se but instead criticizes the racist undertone of this theory, which "locked countries in the Global South into a deeply hierarchical and stratified economic system." This way, the theory fails in itself because it prevents modern transformations.

Al-e Ahmad's Adaptation of Marxism and Shiism

Al-e Ahmad's adaptation of Marxist thought becomes visible in his critique of capitalism and his use of dependency theory to describe the inequality between colonizing and colonized countries when he "rehearses his own specific iteration of dependency theory,"[37]

> Just as Marx pointed out about his age, we today have two worlds in a state of conflict. But these two worlds have attained dimensions much wider than those of his time, and the conflict has taken on more complexity than the conflict between worker and boss. Ours is a world of confrontation between rich and poor, extending over the entire globe.[38]

In their *Communist Manifesto*, Karl Marx and Friedrich Engels ascribed a decisive role to colonialism and imperialism in developing global capitalism. In his essay, al-e Ahmad also refers to the relationship between imperialism and capitalism and states, as explained by Margaret Kohn and Keally McBride, that Iranians contribute to the economic inequality between Eastern and Western countries by

---

[35] Michael M. J. Fischer, *Iran: From Religious Dispute to Revolution* (Madison: University of Wisconsin Press, 1989), 8.
[36] Sadeghi-Boroujerdi, 'Gharbzadegi, Colonial Capitalism,' 175. [37] Ibid.
[38] Al-e Ahmad, *Plagued by the West*, 6.

consuming Western goods. They write, "In consuming commodities, the Iranian bourgeoisie fails to recognize the underlying social relations of production that such consumption is reinforcing. In other words, westoxification is a form of commodity fetishism."[39]

Capitalism represents a significant thread in al-e Ahmad's thought. Not only did the export of capitalism to non-Western parts of the world create a system of economic inequality and dependency, but the liaison between imperialism and colonialism also put a halt to the socialist revolution in Europe, for reasons that Marx elaborated on in his writings.[40] Al-e Ahmad adopts Marx's argument and states that capitalism has led political ideologies to lose significance.

Our age is no longer one in which people in the "West" can be made to fear "Communism" and people in the "East" made to fear the bourgeoisie and liberalism. Nowadays even kings can appear revolutionary on the surface and use suspicious leftist language, and Khrushchev can buy wheat from America. Today all of the "isms" and ideologies have become paths leading to the exalted throne of "mechanism" and mechanization.[41]

Throughout his book, the machine as an embodiment of capitalism plays a crucial role in al-e Ahmad's argument about the economic dependency of Eastern countries. Al-e Ahmad does not demand an abolition or rejection of machines and the modernization brought about by industrial manufacturing. Instead, the appropriation and acquisition of the means of production represent for him the only way to dissolve Eastern countries' economic dependency on Western nations and cure them of the accompanying westoxification.[42]

Despite the Marxist tradition of his critique, for al-e Ahmad, religion represents the only successful remedy for westernization. This is because, according to al-e Ahmad, Iran's Shi'ite religion was the crucial factor that prevented Iran from ever being fully colonized. Or, as he put it, "[I]t was our lot then to be the only ones, both in the guise and the reality of an Islamic totality, to stand in the way of the advance of European civilization (read: colonialism; Christianity)."[43]

---

[39] Margaret Kohn and Keally McBride, *Political Theories of Decolonization: Postcolonialism and the Problem of the Foundation* (New York: Oxford University Press, 2011), 42.
[40] Robert J. C. Young, *Postcolonialism: An Historical Introduction* (Oxford: Blackwell, 2001), 105.
[41] Al-e Ahmad, *Plagued by the West*, 5.   [42] Ibid., 7.   [43] Ibid., 9.

Throughout his book, however, al-e Ahmad maintains a critical stance toward the clergy, criticizing them as westoxified as well as for hiding in their ivory tower. He writes,

> From the time of the Constitutional Revolution, our clergy who were the last line of defense against the foreign onslaught, had retreated so deeply into their shells in the face of the preliminary wave of mechanization and had shut out the outside world to such an extent and had woven cocoons around themselves so well, that only the Day of Judgement could rouse them.[44]

Despite the clerics' passivity in political matters, for al-e Ahmad, the Shi'ite religion and Iran's clergy seemed to harbor the potential to preserve Iran's cultural identity because "Shi'ism had acquired a special position within the core of the Iranian social psyche."[45] Al-e Ahmad argues that clerics are the least westoxified group in Iranian society and, thus, calls for cooperation between secular intellectuals and the ulema regarding orchestrating their resistance against Western domination and mechanization. According to al-e Ahmad, politicizing the clerical class is a simple task due to the character of the clerics.

> they tend to be men of learning by the very nature of their profession; they tend to be radically minded, coming mainly from lower class backgrounds; they tend to be trusted by the masses as guardians of the faith; and, finally they can be agents for social or political uprising as a result of their ability to speak the language of the masses.[46]

Al-e Ahmad's argumentation draws on the historical role played by the clergy in earlier political events, such as the Tobacco Revolt in 1890–1891 and the Constitutional Revolution of 1906, as well as the years of the oil industry's nationalization, when the ulema's call for political action efficiently mobilized the masses.[47]

Despite his ideological admiration of the clergy, al-e Ahmad's book should not be interpreted as a nationalistic or nativist work. Sadeghi-Boroujerdi convincingly argues that interpreting *gharbzadegi* under the established paradigms of "nativism" and search for cultural authenticity is an outcome of colonial modernity itself, silencing its critical voices.[48] Instead, the interplay of a Marxist critique of global capitalism and al-e Ahmad's critique of Islam aims to establish a critical and

---

[44] Ibid., 32.   [45] Boroujerdi, *Iranian Intellectuals*, 72.
[46] Al-e Ahmad, *Plagued by the West*, 72.   [47] Ibid.
[48] Sadeghi-Boroujerdi, 'Gharbzadegi, Colonial Capitalism,' 175.

universal perspective on mechanization and globalization, which seeks "to reinvent global modernity in Iranian-Islamic terms."[49] This emerges with particular clarity in his work's last chapter, "The Hour of Resurrection Drew Near," in which Al-e Ahmad draws parallels between his concept of *gharbzadegi* and Albert Camus's book *La Peste*, published in 1947, when he writes, "I realized that 'the plague' for Camus was 'mechanization,' the killer of beauty, poetry, humanity, and heaven."[50]

Yet, the feeling that mechanization represents a threat to humanity is hardly unique to French existentialism and also appears in the works of many other Western artists and writers. For al-e Ahmad, the central theme of Eugène Ionesco's play, *Rhinocéros*, as well as Ingmar Bergman's film, *The Seventh Seal*, is the fact that "[t]he era of belief is at an end and the age of experimentation is at hand and experimentation leads to the atomic bomb." Al-e Ahmad understands "these fictional destinies to be omens, foreboding the Hour of Judgement, warning that the machine demon, if not harnessed and put back in the bottle, will place a hydrogen bomb at the end of the road for mankind."[51]

The analysis presented by al-e Ahmad in *Gharbzadegi* is an outstanding response to Western domination and colonialism, articulating an alternative conception of Iranian modernity while refraining from returning to a pre-modern age. Instead, thinkers such as al-e Ahmad and Fardid tried to renegotiate and reinvent an Iranian identity based on the cultural heritage of Islam. In other words, as Shirin S. Deylami points out,

> They have developed a vision of religious and national identity that is both conscious of and adaptive to global changes, that is both a receiver of cultural globalization and its catalyst, and that demands an input into a system that has silenced Iranian, Islamic and, more broadly Third World voices.[52]

It is in this sense that al-e Ahmad closes his book with a verse from the Qur'an referring to the miraculous splitting of the moon attributed to

---

[49] Shirin S. Deylami, 'In the Face of the Machine: Westoxification, Cultural Globalization, and the Making of an Alternative Global Modernity,' *Polity*, vol. 43, no. 2 (2011), 242–263, 247.
[50] Al-e Ahmad, *Plagued by the West*, 110.   [51] Ibid.
[52] Deylami, 'In the Face of the Machine,' 246.

prophet Muhammad: "The hour of resurrection drew near and the moon was rent in twain."[53] It was this miracle that convinced the polytheists in Mecca of Mohammad's legitimacy as a prophet and demonstrated the veracity of his proclamations. To emphasize that he is speaking truth to power and that his allegations of Iran's westoxification are accurate, al-e Ahmad calls upon the authority of the Qur'an.[54]

Publication and Distribution Processes

Due to strong censorship, al-e Ahmad's *Gharbzadegi* remained unpublished, and circulated only as unofficial copies among friends and colleagues who distributed the writing in communist circles inside and outside Iran. In the spring of 1962, al-e Ahmad tried to publish the first chapter of his book in the magazine *ketab-e mah*, yet, once again, it fell victim to state censorship. Later that year, al-e Ahmad published his text independently, but further editions of his essay were again banned from being published.[55] In his foreword to the English edition of *Gharbzadegi*, al-e Ahmad ironically describes the clandestine distribution processes, which, while a natural reaction to state censorship, also contributed to the book's immense success.[56]

After Ayatollah Khomeini embraced Al-e Ahmad's battle cry of westoxification and integrated this term into his sermons, Al-e Ahmad's book became "the essential reading for Iranian revolutionaries of all stripes."[57] Though his book has often been categorized as part of an Iranian discourse on political Islam, the preceding analysis demonstrates that it is a postcolonial critique of colonial modernity. It should be noted here that al-e Ahmad died in 1969. This means that, for al-e Ahmad, the idea of *gharbzadegi* remained an intellectual experiment and he did not witness Khomeini's appropriations of his rhetoric in service of the revolution's ideology. Furthermore, al-e Ahmad was not an Islamic thinker per se but educated as a secular intellectual whose turn to religion stemmed from its potential as a means of political resistance against the ruling system.

[53] Al-e Ahmad, *Plagued by the West*, 111.
[54] Franz Lenze, *Der Nativist Ǧalāl-e Āl-e Aḥmad und die Verwestlichung Irans im 20. Jahrhundert* (Berlin: Klaus Schwarz Verlag, 2008), 174.
[55] Al-e Ahmad, *Plagued by the West*, 1–2.   [56] Ibid., 2
[57] Deylami, 'In the Face of the Machine,' 248.

Al-e Ahmad's book owes its success, in part, to its sensational title, which conveys not only a conceptual meaning but also the uncanny emotion that Western dominance had left behind. The translation of *gharbzadegi* is an ambiguous and often discussed matter.[58] *Gharbzadegi*, as plague, was theoretically borrowed from Fardid and metaphorically from "Camus, Ionesco and Bergman and the colonization of the life-world it enacts."[59] The expression has various meanings and refers to *gharb*, which, in Persian, means "West" in the sense of the cardinal direction. But, the word *gharb* is also etymologically similar to the Persian word, *gharib*, which denotes a stranger or an unknown person. This etymological similarity resonates in the term *gharbzadegi* and thus "associates the West with both strangeness and the unknown," as Shirin S. Deylami explains.[60] The suffix, *zadegi*, is the past participle of *zadan* ("to strike") and denotes the idea of being "'stricken' as in 'plague-stricken,'" as the translator, Paul Sprachman, remarks.[61] As a result, the Persian neologism *gharbzadegi* unfolds a suggestive impact. Elaborating on this, Deylami interprets gharbzadegi as a "western strangeness" with an "intoxicating character,"

The strangeness of the Other becomes the strangeness of members of the body politic. It hypnotizes subjects believing that what the West has to offer is what they should desire; that they must mimic the West in order to progress.[62]

Queen Farah Diba and Her Support of Arts and Culture

The monarchy's lack of democratic structures is al-e Ahmad's significant criticism. In his essay, he states that there exists in Iran only "a pretense of having a western democracy," which he describes as "a show of democracy," in which fundamental rights such as "freedom of

---

[58] See the following translations Jalal Al-e Ahmad, *Occidentosis: A Plague from the West (Gharbzadegi)*, translated by R. Campbell (Berkeley: Mizan Press, 1983); Al-e Ahmad, *Plagued by the West (Gharbzadegi)*, translated by Paul Sprachman (Delmar, NY: Caravan Books, 1981); Al-e Ahmad, *Weststruckness (Gharbzadegi)*, translated by John Green and Ahmad Alizadeh (Costa Mesa: Mazda Publisher, 1997). This study employs the translation of *gharbzadegi* as westoxification because of its predominance in Iranian studies literature.
[59] Sadeghi-Boroujerdi, 'Gharbzadegi, Colonial Capitalism,' 186.
[60] Deylami, 'In the Face of the Machine,' 246.
[61] Al-e Ahmad, *Plagued by the West*, XI.
[62] Deylami, 'In the Face of the Machine,' 246.

speech, freedom of belief, freedom to use the media (which in our country is a government monopoly), freedom of publishing opinions opposed to the authority of prevailing" are not guaranteed.[63] For al-e Ahmad, "pretending to be a western democracy is in itself another symptom of westitis."[64] The primary opponent of implementing democracy in Iran was, according to al-e Ahmad, the Shah's secret police, SAVAK, which "defeats the country's intellectuals" "with terror, threats, co-optation, imprisonment, and exile." Thus, for al-e Ahmad, the Shah's pseudo-democracy epitomized just another means of power politics for a ruling class who needs "national elections in order to justify their own positions."[65]

Against this sociopolitical background, Queen Farah "emerged as the liberal ruler who would bring moderate reforms."[66] With her coronation in October 1967, she became Iran's first *Shahbanou* (empress) since pre-Islamic times. In the case of his sudden death, Mohammad Reza Shah decreed that Queen Farah should become his successor until his son was old enough to ascend the throne. The empress assumed leadership of the royal court's cultural politics and the Ministry of Culture and Arts. With her engagement in cultural affairs, "the queen was offering Iran, and the world, an alternative model of being modern," as Talinn Grigor explains. Although Farah Diba carved out an important political position for herself with her engagement in cultural affairs, "she remained, like most of the upper class and upper middle class of the 1970s Iran, a product of the depoliticized Pahlavi society."[67] In this way, the empress "offered to Iran and the (Western) world the image of the ideal Iranian woman as modern" while, at the same time, accepting and supporting the Shah's modernization program with her cultural politics.[68]

Before her marriage, Farah Diba had studied architecture at the École Spéciale d'Architecture in Paris. She was convinced that "good architecture could not only avert a revolution from below" but also "acculturate the nation."[69] Thus, architecture became a crucial element in the queen's cultural agenda. Queen Farah also tried to preserve Iran's architectural heritage. However, this did not always harmonize with the Shah's modernization projects at times when the "King and his architecture were the ultimate symbols of modernity" on which the

---

[63] Al-e Ahmad, *Plagued by the West*, 83.   [64] Ibid., 84.   [65] Ibid., 85.
[66] Grigor, *Building Iran*, 176.   [67] Ibid., 185.   [68] Ibid.   [69] Ibid., 183.

new Pahlavi country was being built.[70] These politics often deliberately destroyed monuments and cultural sites in favor of new buildings promoting the Pahlavi ideology. With her commitment to the protection of monuments and older architectures, Queen Farah's cultural politics represented a "feminized version of modernity," which "was not destructive but constructive through all-embracing policies of preservation."[71]

The foundation and establishment of museums was an important strategy for Farah Diba's politics of cultural preservation. Examples include the Negarastan Museum (founded in 1975), a former Qajar palace presenting objects, paintings, and jewelry from Qajar times; as well as the Carpet Museum, built in 1976 near the TMoCA, which, to this day, displays Persian carpets from the sixteenth century to the present. For the collections of the newly established museums, the queen not only identified objects that had been located in Iran but, in collaboration with her office (*daftar-e makhsus-e shahbanu*), also repurchased artworks from abroad that belonged to Iran's national patrimony, as she stated in an interview:

We created a number of museums to house our beautiful objects and treasures ... It was unbelievable to me that we didn't have one museum for our carpets. Over many years we located the valuable carpets in Iran – sometimes in palaces and government offices. After identifying what was in our country, we purchased some special collections and brought them back to Iran for The Carpet Museum in Tehran.[72]

Though the preservation of Iran's cultural heritage was one focus of the queen's politics, she simultaneously promoted and fostered the development of contemporary arts in Iran, as evident in the example of the TMoCA. The foundation of the TMoCA was a major project of Pahlavi cultural politics. Financed by the revenues from Iran's oil business, the museum was intended to provide an exhibition space for contemporary artists and to be the home of a significant collection of modern art by Iranian and Western artists. Generously endowed with Iran's oil money, the Queen's office (*daftar-e makhsus-e shahbanu*) was able to compile the TMoCA's famous collection, which consists of

[70] Ibid., 184.   [71] Ibid.
[72] Farah Diba, 'For the Love of Her People: An Interview with Farah Diba about the Pahlavi Programs for the Arts in Iran,' in Scheiwiller, *Performing the Iranian State*, 75–82, 80.

more than 4,000 artworks and includes important Western art movements through purchases made on international art markets.[73]

Collecting modern art offered an opportunity for artistic exchange and the aesthetic education of Iranian artists. It was also an effective means of laying a material claim to partial ownership of Western modernity. In other words, the material possession of modern European art as a signifier of Western modernity was one of many means to achieve modernization and to turn Iran into a modern Westernized state. Farah Diba's confidence in the quotation above illustrates Iran's claim to be an equal partner of Western states. Farah Diba even argues that Iran should collect and acquire Western art as a reverse practice of Western countries' collecting of Persian arts, stating, "Eventually, we decided to establish a museum of Western art for our people to see contemporary developments outside of Iran. After all, the Metropolitan Museum of Art exhibits Near Eastern art."[74]

The TMoCA was conceived as a place for the specialized production of knowledge about Western modernity and, in particular, artistic production. The example of this museum in Tehran illustrates the idea that material possession of objects is a necessary precondition for the appropriation of knowledge. This concept dates back to the French Revolution and the period of the Enlightenment in Europe, during which, for instance, the material possession of antique objects became mandatory for studying antiquity. The close relationship between material ownership and the intellectual acquisition of knowledge informs the conceptual heritage of many art and history museums to this day.[75] Practices of collecting objects and creating anthropological images became even more important in colonial and imperialist discourses since they helped divide and classify non-Western civilizations and create the West's cultural "Other." Collecting art and objects from other cultures became a key factor in colonial discourse's knowledge production and was a "crucial process of Western identity formation."[76]

In Pahlavi Iran, collecting Western modernist arts was less intended to produce knowledge about the West as Iran's significant "Other."

---

[73] Ibid., 85.   [74] Diba, 'For the Love of Her People,' 80
[75] Bénédicte Savoy, *Die Provenienz der Kultur: Von der Trauer des Verlusts zum universalen Menschheitserbe* (Berlin: Matthes & Seitz Berlin, 2018), 20–21.
[76] James Clifford, *The Predicament of Culture: Twentieth-Century Ethnography, Literature, and Art* (Cambridge, MA: Harvard University Press, 1998), 220.

On the contrary, the appropriation and adaptation of Western modernity were essential means of modernizing Iran and spreading the idea of Iran "being modern" through the country's cultural institutions. In this regard, the establishment of museums became a vital instrument in Iranian cultural politics. As Tony Bennett explains, "the birth of the museum is coincident with, and supplies a primary institutional condition for, the emergence of a new set of knowledges."[77] Thus, the foundation of the TMoCA represented a demonstration of royal power and, as an essential means of mediating a specific version of Pahlavi modernity, also highlighting the relations between culture and government. In this respect, Bennett notes that the museum often displays "the development of modern forms of government" and functions as an "educator for the people,"[78]

The purpose, here, is not to know the populace but to allow the people, addressed as subjects of knowledge rather than as objects of administration, to know; not to render the populace visible to power but to render power visible to the people and, at the same time, to represent to them that power as their own.[79]

Taking on the role of an educator transforms "the entire function of the state." In light of Bennett's statement, the foundation of museums in Iran can be interpreted as evidence of Farah Diba's liberal cultural politics and her attempt to promote Iran's democratization since, as Bennett further explains, "The museum emerged as an important instrument for the self-display of bourgeois-democratic societies."[80] This transformation is possible because,

The migration of the display of power from, on the one hand, the public scene of punishment and, on the other, from the enclosed sphere of court festivals to the public museum played a crucial role in this transformation precisely to the degree that it fashioned a space in which these two differentiated functions – the display of power to the populace and its display within the ruling classes – coalesced.[81]

This demonstrates that, as a pseudo-democratic institution, the museum could easily be employed as an expression of Iran's alleged democratization. In the broader sociopolitical discourse of the Pahlavi

---

[77] Tony Bennett, *The Birth of the Museum: History, Theory, Politics* (London: Routledge, 2005), 96.
[78] Ibid., 98.   [79] Ibid.   [80] Ibid.   [81] Ibid.

era, the establishment of museums was a clear sign of liberalization for the Shah's opposition, who fervently criticized the violations of the constitutional monarchy and fundamental democratic rights.

The appropriation and acquisition of modernist art by the Pahlavi government helped identify the monarchy itself with modernism and portrayed it as possessing the relevant knowledge to understand modern Western art. During this time, viewing art and visiting museum exhibitions allowed Iran's middle and upper classes to perform their modernity. In particular, members of the royal families dressed in the latest Western fashion trends and were often depicted in the media visiting museums and exhibitions.[82] As a patron of modernist arts, Queen Farah Diba not only was an observer of modernist art production but also inaugurated many modernist art exhibitions. Her presence and involvement in the arts also affected art criticism and the public discourse on modernist arts. Due to Mohammad Reza Shah's censorship of the media, both private and state-run newspapers and magazines and state-run television channels had to announce and promote the exhibitions and portray the royal family in a positive light.[83] Against this backdrop, the collection of the TMOCA not only embodies financial capital but can also be understood in terms of symbolic capital. As the sociologist, Pierre Bourdieu explains,

Of all the conversion techniques designed to create and accumulate symbolic capital, the purchase of works of art, objectified evidence of 'personal taste,' is the one which is closest to the most irreproachable and inimitable form of accumulation, that is, the internalization of distinctive signs and symbols of power in the form of natural 'distinction', personal 'authority' or 'culture.'[84]

For Queen Farah, the establishment of the museum and the collecting of art functioned as a way to accumulate symbolic capital and to communicate, through the museum, the process of nation-building, and the overcoming of an "inferiority complex." As she explained in an interview,

---

[82] Grigor, *Building Iran*, 139.
[83] Gisela Fock, *Die iranische Moderne in der Bildenden Kunst: Der Bildhauer und Maler Parviz Tanavoli* (Vienna: Verlag der Österreichischen Akademie der Wissenschaften, 2011), 231.
[84] Bourdieu, *Distinction*, 282.

I had such high hopes for the preservation of my country's heritage and Iran's emergence as a contemporary force ... Like other developing countries, we had an inferiority complex about the advanced world, and everything outside Iran was admired and considered more beautiful. But in the last years of the monarchy, we had passed through this period of emulation, and our identity was secure.[85]

This statement by Farah Diba demonstrates that she was aware of the ongoing political discussions, which demanded modernization on Iranian terms. Yet, the further course of Iran's history and the revolutionary ideology has disproved the idea that Iran's "identity was secure."

As our analysis of al-e Ahmad's essay, *Gharbzadegi*, has shown, these questions of identity became the theoretical foundation for revolutionary discourse. Despite his critique of the West's hegemony and his diagnosis of the country's intoxication with the West, al-e Ahmad, and other revolutionary ideologues, like Shariati, did not discard the project of modernization per se. Instead, they called for modernization on the cultural and ideological basis of authentic Islamic culture and demanded a return to a true Iranian identity grounded in Shi'ite belief. The idea of a "return to the self" (*bazgasht beh khish*) became a central notion and contributed to the mobilization of the masses.[86]

These discussions of a possible Iranian identity in the 1960s and 1970s, at once modern and still distinctly "Iranian," were also reflected in Pahlavi cultural politics and, particularly, in the architectural field. The architecture of the Pahlavi monarchy's prestige project, the TMoCA, is a prominent example of the attempt to reconcile modernist architecture with local Iranian building traditions. In this attempt, the museum's architectural design becomes a visual metaphor highlighting Pahlavi cultural politics. As one can see, Pahlavi cultural politics were a means of modernizing and secularizing the country and were also deeply invested in exercising political power.

The Architecture of Tehran Museum of Contemporary Art

Since its inauguration in 1977, *Muzeh-ye honarha-ye mo'aser Tehran* (Tehran Museum of Contemporary Art) has been the home of modernist and contemporary arts in Iran. Over the last forty years, the

[85] Diba, 'For the Love of Her People,' 76.   [86] Dabashi, 'Theology,' 144.

museum has presented widely divergent concepts and ideas of art. Founded by the Pahlavi monarchy, the museum's collection and exhibition practices functioned as a symbol of the successful modernization and secularization efforts under Mohammad Reza Shah. The building's regional brutalist architectural language also served as a visual message to the critics of the Pahlavi state, who accused the monarchy of being too westernized. By the same token, the museum's architectural appearance and its visual proximity to ancient clay-built towns in Iran also correspond to the ideology of the Iranian Revolution. The revolution's key message was its demand for a return to a genuine and authentic self, as prominently articulated by the theoreticians al-e Ahmad and Shariati, who criticized the Western hegemony from an anticolonial standpoint. After the revolution, the museum became a symbol embodying Pahlavi decadence while at the same time functioning as an important platform for the implementation of the new revolutionary ideology.

To this day, the museum has remained architecturally unchanged. The architectural design of the TMoCA is characterized by a synthesis of traditional Iranian elements and industrial architecture. On the one hand, the architectural language of regional brutalism was a sign of Iran's appreciation of modernism under Pahlavi rule. On the other hand, the references to Iranian desert architecture were in line with the Shah's ideological embracing of pre-Islamic achievements as a means of reconstructing a tradition of secularism in Iran's history.

The TMoCA's Architectural Design

The TMoCA is located in Laleh Park, close to Tehran's vibrant city center. The juxtaposition of different cubic elements makes the museum appear as a type-case fortress. The outer shape of the massive walls, which are characterized by a prominent division between stone façade and exposed concrete, as well as the lack of windows or any architectural openings providing a view into the interior of the building, reinforce the fortress-like impression. The yellowish and brown colors remind the spectator of Iranian clay-built towns in desert areas, such as Yazd and Kashan, whose ancient city centers inspired the museum's architect, Kamran Diba. As Diba himself explains, with the museum's design, he tried to establish a synthesis between traditional Iranian elements and modernist industrial architecture.

Architecture of Tehran Museum of Contemporary Art

Figure 2.1 Exterior view of the TMoCA (*Muze-ye honarha-ye moaser-e Tehran*). Architects: Kamran Diba and Nader Ardalan.

The unique skylines, characterised by ancient, dramatically shaped, mud-covered, desert wind towers, or *Badgirs*, on one hand, and modern industrial architecture with its roof-sourced lighting (sky lighting) on the other gave rise to light-catchers that would form the striking roof-scape of the Tehran Museum.[87]

The combination of the modules' quadratic roofs and their varying heights creates a dynamic and wavy landscape of metal roofs. Four elevated light catchers, taller than the rest of the building, immediately follow the entrance area. The tower's square formation creates a cross in which the half cupolas face one another, while the tinted window sides are placed outward and thus function as light catchers for the museum's interior space. These four towers lend the museum building its characteristic outer appearance.

The interior design refrains from incorporating local architectural elements and is characterized by the dominance of exposed concrete,

---

[87] Kamran Diba, 'The Origins of TMoCA: A Personal Account,' in Brill et al., *The Tehran Modern*, 24–37, 25–26.

from which the brutalist style draws its name. The anthracite concrete makes the museum's interior very dark, as very little light shines through the tinted skylights of the light catchers. The museum's central architectural element is a monumental rotunda between the light catchers that extends down to the basement of the building. The eight columns in the rotunda indicate the position of the wind towers' front corner pillars.

The prominent architecture of the museum determines the direction in which visitors must walk. Starting from the first of seven altogether galleries, which can be accessed from the rotunda, the museum visitor moves through the museum in a downward spiral. The individual galleries are not visible because of their helical arrangement around the rotunda. Corridors, some of which also turn into exhibition spaces themselves, connect the individual rectangular galleries. As a result, the architectural structure of the museum becomes a canal-like network leading the museum visitor along a downward spiral through the labyrinthine building. The visit to the museum ends at the bottom of the rotunda on the basement floor, where a ramp along the rotunda leads visitors back up to the exit. Located at the bottom of the museum's rotunda, the permanently installed artwork *Matter and Mind* by Noriyuki Haraguchi, first exhibited in 1977 at *documenta 6* and later purchased for the TMOCA, is evidence that the museum was literally built on Iran's oil business. The artwork consists of a rectangular metal tank filled with used engine oil. Thus, the site-specific installation and the use of oil transform the artwork into a symbolic foundation of the institution.

The newly built museum's architecture successfully communicated Iran's modernization and its "world-class status," bringing the museum international recognition, as the architect and critic John Morris Dixon wrote in the magazine *Progressive Architecture* in 1978.

For a bustling city that already has the requisite high-rise offices and apartments, freeways, bosky suburbs, and plans for rapid transit, this museum could be seen as one more essential of world-class status. Not that Tehran would be culturally impoverished without Western institutions. Though a relatively new city – looking very much like Houston transferred to the high desert setting of Albuquerque – it already has rich collections of antiquities.[88]

---

[88] John Morris Dixon, 'Tehran Museum of Contemporary Art: A Cultural Hybrid,' *Progressive Architecture*, no. 5 (1978), 68–71, 68.

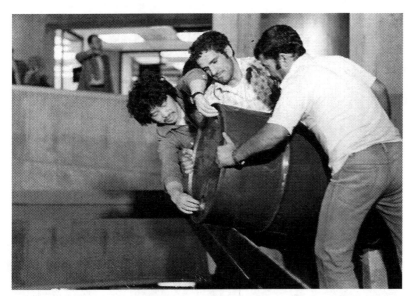

Figure 2.2 Noriyuki Haraguchi installing *Matter and Mind* (1971) at the TMoCA, 1977.

Dixon's description of the Iranian capital demonstrates that Tehran resembled major American cities visually and that, for Dixon, the adaptation of an international architectural language helped establish a relationship between "them" and "us," that is, Iran and the United States. For a brief moment in history, the Pahlavi monarchy's primary aspiration to transform Iran into a secular Western nation-state seemed successful.

Architecture and National Identity in Pahlavi Times

The TMoCA is only one example of architecture's important role in the twentieth century in Iran when architectural innovation played a crucial role in legitimizing the kingship of both Reza Pahlavi Shah (1925–1941) and his son Mohammad Reza Shah (1941–1979). During this time, architecture became an important means of conveying Iranian identity politics. Architectural programs visually implemented the specific concepts of race and nationality propagated by the Pahlavi government.

The history of the Pahlavi kingship starts with Reza Khan, a commanding officer of the Persian Cossack Brigade. Due to his clever

Figure 2.3 Interior view of the TMoCA with Haraguchi's oil pool.

political and military maneuvers, the parliament declared Reza Khan Shah in 1925.[89] Since he had no hereditary claims to the Persian royal throne, Reza Shah created an imaginary continuity with the antique Persian Empire to legitimize his succession.[90] In 1935, Reza Shah ordered the renaming of Persia as Iran. It is often said that the designation Iran originates from *Iranshahr* ("Empire of the Aryans"), which was used in Sassanid Persia during the third century for power-political

---

[89] Ansari, *Modern Iran*, 25–26.
[90] Talinn Grigor, 'Kingship Hybridized, Kingship Homogenized: Revivalism under the Qajar and the Pahlavi Dynasties,' in Sussan Babaie and Talinn Grigor (eds.), *Persian Kingship and Architecture: Strategies of Power in Iran from the Achaemenids to the Pahlavis* (London: Tauris, 2015), 219–254, 234.

reasons.[91] Reza Zia-Ebrahimi argued that the Persian word *ariya*, found in pre-Islamic sources, should not be confused with the ethnonym "Aryan," since "the antique incidences of ariya can in no way be used to support the claims of Aryan."[92] According to Ebrahimi, the "Aryan" discourse does not date back to Iran's antiquity but was imposed on Iran by European Orientalists in the nineteenth century and later disseminated in Iran through German National-Socialist propaganda. Iran's adaptation of "Aryanness" thus, denotes not a glorious antique past but is "rooted in a dethroned and inglorious European ideology."[93]

For Reza Shah, however, the turn to Iran's pre-Islamic past was an important strategy to weaken the powerful position of the *ulema*, the clerics, and lead Iran into a secular and modern age. The new name, Iran, was an ideological means of helping to establish the nation-state and to construct an "imagined community" based on a shared common identity.[94] While the Eurocentric name "Persia" did not comprise all groups in the heterogeneous multi-ethnic state, Iran was seen as "culturally inclusive."[95]

In particular, European archaeology and archaeologists leading excavations in Iran supported the ideas of a collective Iranian national identity dating back to ancient times. For instance, Ernst Hertzfeld, who was responsible for the excavations in Persepolis, explained in 1925 that the "true" Iranian heritage was to be found in pre-Islamic times, "Since the Aryan tribes, or more precisely because of them, this country is called 'Iranshahr,' that is about nine centuries before Christ, and the true ancient heritage of Iran dates from that period."[96] Archaeology, Orientalism, and cultural heritage became essential

---

[91] Sussan Babaie and Talinn Grigor, 'Introduction,' in Babaie and Grigor, *Persian Kingship*, XVII–XXIII, XVIII.
[92] Reza Zia-Ebrahimi, 'Self-Orientalization and Dislocation: The Uses and Abuses of the "Aryan" Discourse in Iran,' *Iranian Studies*, vol. 4, no. 4 (2011), 445–472, 460
[93] Ibid.
[94] Benedict R. Anderson, *Imagined Communities: Reflections on the Origin and Spread of Nationalism* (London: Verso, 1991).
[95] Ansari, *Modern Iran*, 103.
[96] Ernst Herzfeld, cited in Talinn Grigor, 'Recultivating "Good Taste": The Early Pahlavi Modernists and Their Society for National Heritage,' *Iranian Studies*, vol. 37, no. 1 (2004), 17–45, 27.

agents of modernization during Pahlavi rule. As Talinn Grigor explains,

> Modern Iran's relationship to its patronage provided ideological justification for Iran's place in the network of modern nations and for the political struggles aimed at radical secular reforms, territorial integrity, and national unity. In short, Iran's cultural heritage was modern Iran's political raison d'être.[97]

Under Reza Shah, architecture reflected, on the one hand, his radical modernization programs and, on the other hand, the attempts to construct a pre-Islamic national identity. State-sponsored programs invited foreign architects, such as the German archaeologist and architect Ernst Herzfeld, the French archaeologist André Godard, the US art historian and dealer Arthur Upham Pope, and the French architect Maxime Siroux, to materialize concepts of a secular identity in Iran's architecture. In 1928, André Godard became director of the archaeological museum *Iran Bastan Museum* (*Muzeh-ye Iran-e bastaan*). Godard and Siroux designed the modernist museum building, whose distinctive façade was inspired by past Persian architectural traditions. The monumental entrance gate is an allusion to *Taq-e Kasra*, also known as the Archway of Ctesiphon, the last remaining element of a former Sassanian palace complex in the city of Ktesiphon in present-day Iraq. Godard and Siroux did not aim to imitate the antique model, but rather, by borrowing various motives from different periods, to improve on ancient architecture with their modernist designs.[98]

But, not only foreign architects were engaged in the discourse of Iran's architectural secularization. In 1922, only shortly after the dissolution of the Qajar monarchy, a group of statesmen and intellectuals founded the Society for National Heritage (*Anjoman-e Asar-e Meli*) to both protect and reinvent Iran's heritage. According to the society, Iran's "true" heritage was to be found in the times of the Achaemenid Empire (ca. 550–330 BC). This idea was again closely tied to archaeological excavations performed at the beginning of the twentieth century, which unearthed ancient relics of palaces, such as Persepolis, which had been one of the capitals of the ancient Achaemenid Persian Empire. To reinvent Iran's heritage, the society collaborated with the architects mentioned above and created mausoleums and

---

[97] Grigor, *Building Iran*, 9.   [98] Ibid.

monuments to establish their version of a secular Iranian history. This agenda led to demolishing monuments and tombs associated with any Islamic religious context and replacing them with modern and allegedly secular mausoleums.[99] A good example is the Tomb of Hafez in Shiraz, planned by Siroux in 1935–1938 and, today, a popular tourist attraction in Iran. The reconstruction was intended not only to create a monument to one of Iran's most famous poets but also to separate Hafez's poetry, which is deeply embedded in Sufism, from any religious connotations and to celebrate Hafez as a secular Iranian hero.[100]

Many architects opposed the architectural recourse to tradition and did not endorse this eclectic architectural style. In particular, Iranian architects who had studied abroad and returned to Iran to participate in the construction of the new nation-state advocated a radical break with past Iranian building traditions. The architect Vartan Hovanessian (1896–1982), who studied at the École Speciale d'Architecture in Paris, was an outspoken supporter of Reza Shah's modernization program.[101] For Hovanessian, Reza Shah's decree banning the Islamic veiling of women, which was forcefully and violently implemented in 1936, corresponded to the architectural innovations that opposed the introverted architectures often found in Islamic countries:

Similar to the women who were imprisoned at home and used to live as prisoners, buildings and gardens and other edifices of the capital were enclosed and veiled within high walls; and like the women's face free from any smile or happiness, the appearance of the buildings inside the dark and sometimes towering muddy walls seemed very sad and grumpy.[102]

To incorporate openness and transparency in his architectural designs, Hovanessian employed a modernist language of forms based on glass, concrete, and steel. Architects such as Hovanessian built for a new society, a Western elite comprised of the newly established middle class who wanted to spend their free time in cinemas, restaurants, and hotels. One of Hovanessian's major buildings is Hotel Darband in Northern Tehran. Commissioned by Reza Shah, Hovanessian designed a hotel complex, which was especially popular with the wealthy

---

[99] Ibid. [100] Ibid., 95–99.
[101] Reza M. Shirazi, *Contemporary Architecture and Urbanism in Iran: Tradition, Modernity, and the Production of "Space-in-Between"* (Cham: Springer, 2018), 14.
[102] Vartan Hovanessian, cited in Shirazi, *Contemporary Architecture*, 15.

Figure 2.4 The monument *Shahyad Aryamehr*. Architect: Hossein Amanat. Tehran, 1971. After the Iranian Revolution renamed to *Freedom Tower* (burj-e azadi).

Western elite, who spent their leisure time in the hotel's restaurants and casino.[103]

Mohammad Reza Shah, who succeeded his father, Reza Shah, in 1941, also saw himself as the legitimate heir to the throne of ancient Persia. Like his father, Mohammad Reza Shah resolutely pushed forward Iran's modernization, technological progress, and industrialization. The ideal Iranian nation-state was a synthesis of antique dynasties and Western progress. To display this allegedly successful synthesis, in 1971, the Pahlavi government organized the celebration of the Persian Empire's 2,500th anniversary at the excavation site of Persepolis.[104] The ancient city was transformed into a tent village meant to give international state visitors a vivid impression of the antique opulence and greatness of the Persian Empire. To simultaneously celebrate Iran's successful modernization, the second part of the celebration was held in Tehran, where the monument *Shayad Aryamehr* was inaugurated as a representation of 2,500 years of

---

[103] Shirazi, *Contemporary Architecture*, 16.   [104] Ansari, *Modern Iran*, 218.

tamadon-e bozorg, the Great Civilization of Iran.[105] The monument plays with pre-Islamic architectural references and marks the western entrance to the city.

The monument complex, which, in addition to the prominent tower, also accommodates a museum, was designed by the architect Hossein Amanat. The integrated museum was supposed to illustrate Mohammad Reza Shah's ambitious reform program, the so-called White Revolution.[106] After the 1979 revolution, the monument *Shahyad Aryamehr* was renamed the Freedom Tower (*burj-e azadi*). Throughout Iran's history in the twentieth century, the tower gained significance as "the architectural manifesto of the king's monarchy," as Grigor explains,

It became the symbol of the modern nation, marching forward, captured in the dynamic form of the landmark and connected to the past with the general configuration of the plan and the elevation along with the decorative details and prototypes. As in the nation, in Shahyad the new and the old were omnipresent: a gate to the Great Civilization (*darvazeh-ye tamaddon-e bozorg*).[107]

The Invention of the TMoCA's Architecture

Like the Freedom Tower, the design of the TMoCA also bridges new and old architectural elements. Thus, the museum building articulates a specific concept of modernity, in which tradition and modernity stand not in a dialectical relationship but rather bifurcate one another and create a local modernist expression. To establish an intensive dialogue with the newest trends in Western architecture, several conferences were organized in Iran. In 1970, the architects Louis Kahn, Paul Rudolf, and Buckminster Fuller were invited to present their work and designs at the conference *The Interaction between Tradition and Technology* held in Isfahan. In particular, Louis Kahn's remarks about the relationship between tradition, history, and design became decisive for Iranian architects such as Nader Ardalan.[108]

---

[105] *Shayad Aryamehr* (Persian) translates into English as the Shah's monument or Light of the Aryans.
[106] Grigor, 'Kingship Hybridized,' 245. [107] Ibid.
[108] Shirazi, *Contemporary Architecture*, 56–57.

Figure 2.5 Interior view of the TMoCA with view of the rotunda.

The museum's interior design demonstrates that the architects deliberately imitated major Western museum buildings like, for example, Frank Lloyd Wright's Guggenheim Museum in New York.[109] Both museums provide a sculptural impression and present the prominent rotunda as their architectural protagonist. The museum's character reminds one of a factory, the preferred exhibition space for contemporary arts since the 1960s. The architectural integration of a cinematheque, auditorium, and library emphasizes the museum's participative and contemporary orientation. This has led the architect Kamran Diba to try and establish structural similarities with the Museum of Modern

---

[109] Diba, 'The Origins of TMoCA,' 25.

Art in New York, such as the Tehran Museum of Contemporary Art, abbreviation as TMoCA.[110]

The regional brutalist style of the museum demonstrates that the architects were familiar with contemporary architectural discourses on an international level. Both Kamran Diba and Nader Ardalan, the architects in charge of the TMoCA's construction, hold degrees from US universities. Diba studied architecture and sociology at Howard University in Washington. After his return to Iran, he founded DAZ Consulting Architects and Engineers, an architectural office that also planned other important projects, such as the *Niavaran Cultural Centre* in Tehran (1970–1978) and the housing project *Shustar New Town*. Diba not only was one of the leading architects behind the TMoCA's design but also became the museum's artistic and managing director from 1976 to 1978. As a cousin of the queen, Kamran Diba had privileged access to the royal family and received many important architectural commissions.

Ardalan studied architecture at Harvard University. With Diba, he was responsible for designing the TMoCA. Shortly before the Iranian Revolution, Ardalan migrated to the United States. He engaged deeply with vernacular architecture and elaborated his ideas in numerous articles. After graduating, Diba and Ardalan returned to Iran, where their designs became formative for Mohammad Reza's project to build a new nation-state.[111] Together with Amanat, these architects belonged to a new generation in Iran. Their orientation toward traditionalism distinguishes them from earlier modernist architects, such as Hovanessian, whose architectural practices were committed to the International Style. In 1973, the magazine *Art and Architecture* called on Iranian architects to design regional buildings because "the King of

---

[110] Ibid., 24.
[111] Kamran Diba studied architecture and sociology at Howard University in Washington. After his return to Iran, he founded DAZ Consulting Architects and Engineers. Diba was not only the architect for the TMOCA, but he realized other significant architectural projects in Iran, for example Niavaran Cultural Center, Teheran (1970–1978), Shustar New Town (Residential Area), Shustar, Iran. From 1976–1987 he was director of the TMoCA. Nader Ardalan studied architecture at Harvard University. After his return to Iran, he contributed to the architectural design for the TMoCA. He planned also the Center for Management Studies in Teheran (1972). Ardalan left Iran before the revolution and moved to USA. He wrote numerous articles about vernacular architectures and is responsible for international architectural projects.

Kings himself often said that there should be Iranian solutions to Iranian problems."[112] Students and professors in architecture departments tried to implement this principle and searched for Iran's "original" and authentic architecture in rural areas and villages. This regionalism was supposed to replace the strict formalist principles of past modernist architecture.

Nevertheless, this practice was also very eclectic. The new architects preferred a specific Persian past that could be classified with labels such as "folklore," "vernacular," and "tradition" and used as a point of reference for an imagined secular past. Religious cities such as Qom and Mashhad were not part of their new architectural language.[113]

With its visual references to ancient desert cities, the museum was in line with the secularist guise of Mohammad Reza Shah's efforts to modernize and nationalize Iran. The nation-building project often requires an active engagement with "invented traditions" to create a continuity with the past and thereby legitimize the newly established nation-state.[114] The integration of a regional stylistic language shows how the architects considered local conditions when thinking about how to create a new kind of architecture in a modernist language: "Brutalism, as an equally global and regional movement, is the architecture of nation building."[115] In its combination of brutalism and regionalism, the museum building can be understood as an early example of critical regionalism. Critical regionalism, as explained by the architectural theorist Kenneth Frampton in a 1980 article, is an "architecture of resistance" that criticizes universalist approaches to modernity; "The fundamental strategy of Critical Regionalism is to

---

[112] 'Iran Yesterday, Today, Tomorrow,' *Art and Architecture*, nos. 18–19 (June–November 1973), 140.

[113] Talinn Grigor, 'Shifting Gaze: Irano-Persian Architecture from the Great Game to a Nation State,' in Rujivachkurul Vimalin (ed.), *Architecturalized Asia: Mapping a Continent through History* (Honolulu: University of Hawai'i Press, 2013), 217–230, 229.

[114] Eric Hobsbawm, 'Introduction: Inventing Traditions,' in Habsbawm, *The Invention of Tradition*, 1–14, 13.

[115] Oliver Elser, 'Just What Is It That Makes Brutalism Today So Appealing? A New Definition from an International Perspective,' in Oliver Elser, Philip Kurz, and Peter Cachola Schmal (eds.), *SOS Brutalism: A Global Survey*, Exh.-Cat. German Architecture Museum, Frankfurt am Main (Zurich: Park Books, 2017), 15–19, 16.

mediate the impact of universal civilization with elements derived indirectly from peculiarities of a particular place."[116]

Though the museum's architecture is directed against universal conceptions of modernity, the building is not an act of resistance toward the ruling system. Financed and commissioned by the monarchy, the instrumentalization of a regional architecture was intended to weaken accusations by revolutionary ideologues, such as al-Ahmad and Shariati, who criticized the Pahlavis' westernization of Iran.[117] In *Gharbzadegi*, al-e Ahmad harshly criticizes the Shah's architectural program of urbanization when he states,

It is on account of him that we have such unauthentic and unindigenous architecture and such sham urbanization. It is on account of him that the avenues and intersections of our cities have been turned into sideshows under the ugly glare of the neon and florescent lights.[118]

The modern architecture promoted by the two Pahlavi kings was, according to al-e Ahmad, one of many signs of Iran's westernization and loss of its national identity,

We have spurned Iranian architecture with its symmetry, central reflecting pools and fountains, gardens, cool subterranean rooms, *howzkhana*, sash windows and carved wooden window sets. We have closed the doors of the traditional athletic clubs (*zurkhanas*) and forgotten how to play polo.[119]

On the one hand, with its synthesis of modernist and traditional elements, the architecture of the TMoCA responded to the accusations mentioned above. On the other hand, its architecture could easily be adapted to serve on a political level the Pahlavi state's logic. The external design and the structure of the museum building refer to Yazd, widely known in Iran as the city of wind catchers (*shahr-e badgirha*).[120] *Badgirs*, or wind towers, are architectural elements built primarily to cool the interiors of houses. But Yazd is not only known for its architecture. It also stands at the center of Zoroastrianism, the

---

[116] Kenneth Frampton, 'Towards a Critical Regionalism: Six Points of Architecture of Resistance,' in Hal Foster (ed.), *The Anti-aesthetic: Essays on Postmodern Culture* (London: Pluto Press, 1983), 16–30, 21.
[117] Grigor, *Building Iran*, 183.   [118] Al-e Ahmad, *Plagued by the West*, 71.
[119] Ibid., 102–103.
[120] S. Roaf, 'BĀDGĪR,' *Encyclopædia Iranica*, Online edition, 2011. www.iranicaonline.org/articles/badgir-traditional-structure-for-passive-air-conditioning, accessed 4 February 2017.

pre-Islamic religion practiced by the ancient rulers of Persia, such as Cyrus the Great, who was Mohammad Reza Shah's great role model. The recourse to Zoroastrianism was not religiously motivated but helped to reduce Islam's cultural meaning and construct a tradition of secularism in Iran.[121] The museum's iconography is characterized by the interweaving of constructed and imagined national traditions with the architecture of Western museums. This visual strategy helped present the museum as a sign of the Shah's successful modernization efforts.

By integrating regional elements, the TMoCA's architecture meets Frampton's demands for integrating topographical characteristics. In particular, this is achieved through the visual integration of *qanat* (aqueduct system) and *badgir* (wind tower) in the museum's architecture. Initially, these architectural structures often functioned as technical aids to cope with climate conditions and to create an inhabitable environment. In the TMoCA's architecture, however, these elements function merely as visual and decorative references. Neither the wind towers nor the aqueduct system has any functional purpose. The term *qanat* refers to Iran's millennia-old subterranean canal systems used for irrigation and the transport of drinking water, which operate using hydraulic systems and gravity.[122] A closer look at the museum shows that *qanat* was the conceptual framework for the museum's floor plan. Similar to the way water rises from a source and springs through a tunnel system, visitors flow in circulating movements through the building's labyrinthine corridors. At the same time, the metaphor of flowing is an important topos of modernist architecture in the designs of Le Corbusier and Bruno Taut.

The architects, Diba and Ardalan, implemented additional elements of Iranian architecture in their museum design. For example, the museum's interior is only accessible through the main entrance and cannot be seen at all from the outside. This kind of introverted architecture, which created a secluded courtyard through its helical floor plan, was considered a characteristic feature of Islamic architecture.

---

[121] Janet Kestenberg Amighi, 'ZOROASTRIANS IN IRAN iv. Between the Constitutional and the Islamic Revolutions,' *Encyclopædia Iranica*, Online edition, 2016. www.iranicaonline.org/articles/zoroastrians-in-iran-parent, accessed 4 February 2017.

[122] Reza Daneshmir and Catherine Spiridonoff, 'Subterranean Landscape: The Far-Reaching Influence of the Underground Qanat Network in Ancient and Present-Day Iran,' *Architectural Design*, 82, No. 3 (2012), 62–69, 65.

For Ardalan, integrating Islamic aesthetic principles was an essential strategy for developing vernacular architecture. In 1973, Ardalan published his book *The Sense of Unity: The Sufi Tradition in Persian Architecture* in collaboration with Laleh Bakhtiar. As they write, the return to Islamic architectural traditions provided them with the possibility of realizing a social utopia, "In the art and architecture of a traditional society, the principles of the traditional inspire man's creative energies and integrate the whole of a society into a totality."[123] The idea of a return to an authentic self, which Ardalan and Bakhtiar advocated in architecture, resonates with the prerevolutionary discourse in Iran. In particular, the revolutionary spokespersons al-e Ahmad and Shariati called for a "return to the self" (*bazgasht be khish*) based on an "authentic" Islamic culture. This "return to the self" became a vital message of the revolution, which contributed to the success of the Iranian Revolution.[124]

The TMOCA's architecture is, consequently, an echo of the architectural and sociopolitical discourses of its time. While one might classify the museum building's vernacular architecture as an early example of critical regionalism, the question poses itself, is the museum an example of an "architecture of resistance?"[125] And, if so, against what, or whom, is the resistance directed? The incorporation of local and vernacular elements helps to counteract universal conceptions of Western modernity, but the architects often achieved this "through the lens of cultural essentialism" and, in doing so, "they helped promote the notion that the Orient could only valorize itself through Western tropes. These modern traditionalists condemned Westernization while embracing the Western episteme."[126]

Inaugurated as a prestige object by the Pahlavi government, the museum was supposed to prove that Iran had caught up, overcome its "backwardness," and was prepared to take its place in the Western world order. As discussed in Chapter 1, the museum was only briefly closed during the revolutionary upheavals before it became an important space to disseminate the Islamic Republic's new ideology. Although the revolution was a major turning point in Iran's modern history,

---

[123] Nader Ardalan and Laleh Bakhtiar, *The Sense of Unity: The Sufi Tradition in Persian Architecture* (Chicago: The University of Chicago Press, 1973), 3.
[124] Dabashi, *Theology*, 1996, 144.
[125] Frampton, 'Towards a Critical Regionalism.'
[126] Grigor, *Building Iran*, 165.

Figure 2.6 Andy Warhol and Iran's Empress Farah Diba, in front of a screen print portrait by Warhol during a reception at the Waldorf Astoria Hotel.

which profoundly influenced the museum's exhibition politics, the museum remained – at least architecturally – in its original state. With its location in central Tehran and its architecture's use of national traditions, the TMoCA helped promote the ideology of the new Islamic Republic. The museum's architecture, which promised a return to an Iranian identity, also accorded with the national architecture later supported by the Islamic Republic.[127] The architectural references to the city of Yazd were agreeable to the new government. Yazd was known not only as the city of Zoroastrianism but also for its "Islamic

---

[127] Farshad Farahi, 'World of Similitude: The Metamorphosis of Iranian Architecture,' *Architectural Design*, vol. 82, no. 3 (2012), 52–61, 59.

religious conservatism."[128] During the month of mourning, *Muharram*, Yazd serves as one of the most important settings for *Ashura* (Shi'ite Passion Plays), where millions of mourners commemorate Imam Hussein's martyrdom with numerous rituals and performances. Although the newly established state's system adopted the concrete works of architecture from Pahlavi times as necessary infrastructure without any problem, they denounced the architects as political enemies. In particular, due to their "Western" designs, those architects who had built the urban landscape of Pahlavi Iran, among them Diba and Ardalan, were accused of cooperating with the royal regime and forced into exile.[129]

Iranian Modernist Art and Jalal al-e Ahmad's Concept of *Gharbzadegi*

Jalal al-e Ahmad's Art Criticism

A closer look at Pahlavi cultural politics shows that this means of soft power played a crucial role in the legitimation of the monarchy. The instrumentalization of art and architecture has not only led to a depoliticized reception but also often situates these artistic expressions in the service of the monarchy and thus erases any political agency of the artists and their artistic works. In contrast to the perception of Iranian modernist art as merely the expression of a successful Western modernization, al-e Ahmad's art criticism helps to paint a different picture of modernist art production in Iran. His discussion of *gharbzadegi* and call for the creation of alternative versions of Western modernity, which, according to al-e Ahmad, was based on concepts of progress and rationality, were also reflected in the cultural realm. In various essays about Iranian modernism, al-e Ahmad analyzed Iranian contemporary artists' artistic practice and exhibitions. His essays clearly demonstrate that he did not disregard the achievements of the modern age, such as modernist artistic expression, but instead demanded an Iranian version of modernization. In his writings, al-e Ahmad communicates a postcolonial concept of modernist art, advocating an Iranian modernism based on hybridity and mimicry as sources of artistic

---

[128] Mirsepassi, *Transnationalism in Iranian Political Thought*, 8.
[129] Grigor, *Contemporary Iranian Art*, 126–127.

innovation. To create new means of expression, al-e Ahmad calls for a hybrid merging of European artistic discourses with Iranian topics. Or in other words, as Homi Bhabha states, "the importance of hybridity is not to be able to trace two original moments from which the third emerges, rather hybridity is the 'third space' which enables other positions to emerge."[130] This kind of hybridity is, for al-e Ahmad, the creative source of a modernist art that is not simply decorative but rather politically committed to serving in the fight against colonization and westernization. For al-e Ahmad, modernist art is a means to express the political desire for a better society whose goal is "to eliminate poverty and to provide spiritual and material welfare for all people."[131] In his essay, *Gharbzadegi*, and articles for cultural magazines, al-e Ahmad formulates essential points for achieving an artistic modernity based on "Iranianness." Iranian artists should not seek recognition and validation for their artworks from Western authorities or institutions but produce their works for an Iranian audience, not for the Western gaze.

Al-e Ahmad's art criticism provides a valuable source for a better understanding of Iranian modernism on several levels. First, these documents offer a rare look into the development of modernist art and the accompanying intellectual discourses of the Iranian art scene. They also present different strategies with which artists negotiated modernist expression and the adaptation of Western modernity in Iran. At the same time, these writings also contributed to the establishment of the new literary genre of art criticism. Stylistically, these experimental writings are very similar to his fictional literary works, such as his short stories and novels. Al-e Ahmad illustrates his relationships to the artists and their works with personal anecdotes in which biographical and personal descriptions play a significant role.

Surprisingly, Iranian art history has largely neglected al-e Ahmad's writings about Iranian modernism, even though he was one of the most prominent intellectuals of his time. The reason for al-e Ahmad's exclusion lies in the dominance of a methodologically formalist aesthetic approach in Iranian art historiography, which concentrates on visual innovation when dealing with modernist art productions. The art

---

[130] Jonathan Rutherford, 'The Third Space: Interview with Homi Bhabha,' in Rutherford (ed.), *Identity, Community, Culture, Difference* (London: Lawrence and Wishart, 1990), 207–221.

[131] Al-e Ahmad, *Plagued by the West*, 60.

historian Combiz Moussavi-Aghdam, for instance, explains the past neglect of al-e Ahmad's art criticism in Iranian art historiography as follows,

> The wide gap between the literary intellectuals and artists was never bridged ... there was no compatibility between the visual artists (mainly painters) and literary circles at the time. While most of the painters in the 1960s and 1970s were dealing with the aesthetic aspects of modern art with no intellectual potential and interest to consider socio-political criticism in their work, their literary peers underestimated the visual qualities of artworks.[132]

Moussavi supports his argument with a statement by Ruyin Pakbaz, a witness of modernist art and art historian, who is considered a leading authority in Iranian art history. Pakbaz refers to al-e Ahmad's art criticism as "nonsense texts" because "they failed to acknowledge the visual arts as a field with its own intrinsic values."[133] However, this dominant thread in Iranian art history leads to a depoliticized and decontextualized reception of Iranian modernism with a focus on formal-aesthetic criteria in the analysis of modernist works, which treats the artwork as if it existed in a vacuum separated from the time and place of its production. On the contrary, we see that, from the beginnings of modernism in Iran, there has always been a close connection between visual and literary production.

Al-e Ahmad's writings about modernism in Iran follow artistic developments from the first exhibitions of modernist art, covering the crucial development of this art in the 1950s and 1960s when modernist expression was still a relatively new phenomenon. In an article from 1950, al-e Ahmad introduced the Apadana Gallery, one of the first exhibitions spaces for artistic exchange in Tehran, which was founded in 1949 and run by the artists Mahmoud Javadipour, Hossein Kazemi, and Hooshang Ajoodani.[134] Al-e Ahmad highly appreciated the artists' initiative to provide a platform for Iranian artists to discuss and disseminate modernist paradigms. The collective exhibition presented

---

[132] Combiz Moussavi-Aghdam, 'Art History, "National Art" and Iranian Intellectuals in the 1960s,' *British Journal of Middle Eastern Studies*, vol. 41, no. 1 (2014), 132–150, 144.
[133] Ibid., 144.
[134] Moeini Seyed Hossein Iradj, Mehran Arefian, Bahador Kashani, and Golnar Abbasi (eds.), *Urban Culture in Tehran: Urban Processes in Unofficial Cultural Spaces* (Cham: Springer, 2018), 130.

works by Houshang Pezeshkian, Ahmad Esfandiari, Mehdi Vishkaie, and Jalil Ziapour. In merging Cubist and Impressionist formal languages with the Iranian tile tradition, the paintings by Pezeshkian (1917–1972) represent positive examples of local Iranian modernism, according to al-e Ahmad. By doing so, Pezeshkian succeeds in recreating the colors and atmosphere of Iran. Thus, Pezeshkian's art does not remain merely decorative but has a solid political significance because it depicts the labor conditions of Iranian farmers and illustrates their hopelessness, something highly welcomed by the Marxist author. Although al-e Ahmad criticizes one of Ziapour's paintings as pornographic, he acknowledges Ziapour's attempt to include Iranian topics in his paintings while using Cubism as his preferred means of expression, for instance, in the picture *Sepah Selar Mosque* (1949). Despite al-e Ahmad's critique of some of the works exhibited, he demands more public attention and support for this new generation of artists and the commitment of their artistic practice not only to the depiction of "truth" but also to addressing socially relevant topics. Each of the artists exhibited searches for his own means of artistic expression, creating "hope and ideals" and actively engaging in the sociopolitical discourses of their time. Al-e Ahmad concludes that combining Iranian traditions with modernist European discourses is the right strategy and proves that "our artists are on the right track."[135]

Colonialism and Orientalism as Agents of Modernization in Iran

In the 1960s, al-e Ahmad and his circle understood artistic production as a powerful means of establishing difference based on notions of national and cultural Iranian identity. Contrary to art historiography's apolitical perception of modernist art in Iran, al-e Ahmad articulates a political understanding of modernism far beyond formalism. He illustrates the dimensions of cultural imperialism as an agent of colonialism and Orientalism when he sharply criticizes orientalist production of knowledge as a means of exercising Western power and questions the discipline's scientific nature:

But an orientalist in a general sense? What does that mean? Does it mean that he knows all the secrets of the East? Are we living in the age of Aristotle? This

---

[135] Al-e Ahmad, 'Painting Exhibition in "Apadana",' in Zamaninya, *Adab wa hunar-i imruz-i Īrān*, 1286–1293, 1293.

is why I call orientalism a parasitic growth on the roots of imperialism. What is really amusing is that these orientalists have organizations affiliated with UNESCO, biennial and quadrennial congresses, gatherings and such nonsense.[136]

These cultural institutions are, according to al-e Ahmad, further means of cultural imperialism to maintain Western hegemonic powers:

The issue is not only that Europe exports its mercenaries with the machines, but more importantly that it ensures the health and safety of its cities, museums, and theatres at the price of depriving colonial and backward states of their freedom.[137]

In particular, for al-e Ahmad, modern European artistic innovation was closely tied to colonialism.

Gauguin brought distilled sunlight and color in his canvases to Europe and so revolutionized the somber and grey painting of Flamand that the antics of Picasso and Dali seem old hat today.[138]

European artistic innovation often took place at the expense of the colonized countries and through the incorporation of their cultural heritage as an enabling force for European artistic innovation, as al-e Ahmad further explains,

The West slowly realized that (...) the East also contained many nonmaterial goods, commodities which universities and laboratories could use. (...) And now in addition to all of these material goods, the spiritual exports of the East and Asia and Africa and South America form the intellectual baggage of an educated western man, e.g., those sculptors who search for motifs in the primitive sculpture of Africa.[139]

In this regard, al-e Ahmad strongly criticizes Iran's reaction to European artistic innovation, which is often based on Eastern cultural heritage. Instead of turning to Iran's visual traditions as a source of inspiration, al-e Ahmad argues that Iranian artists neglect their national heritage as long as it is not valorized and mirrored by the Western episteme. Still, al-e Ahmad does not advocate a return to past artistic traditions. He acknowledges that Iran is in a transformative stage in its history and that the advancement of art forms is an effective tool for the completion of Iran's transformation:

[136] Al-e Ahmad, *Plagued by the West*, 73.   [137] Ibid., 98–99.   [138] Ibid., 101.
[139] Ibid., 102–103.

But as for returning to our old cocoons, no caterpillar has ever done such a thing. We after all, are a changing nation, and if we are plagued by anxiety about our values and ways of thinking, it is precisely because we are shedding our old skin. So the road back to the past or to stagnation is closed.[140]

Critique of Biennials in Iran

As lecturers at the College of Decorative Arts, al-e Ahmad and his wife, the author and art historian Simin Daneshvar, stood in active dialog with the visual arts scene. The magazine *ketab-e mah* (Book of the Month), edited by al-e Ahmad, regularly invited painters to roundtable discussions to investigate the modernist art's state and impact.[141] The discussions between modernist artists and literary critics demonstrate that the artists dealt not only with the question of how to integrate formal-aesthetic aspects of European modernism into their artworks. These documents also provide valuable insights into processes of negotiating modernity, colonialism, and imperialism in the fields of artistic production. During the first meeting in May 1962, the participants discussed the following main questions:

Is painting a belated art? What are the sources for the inspiration of Iranian artists? What are the adequate means of expression? What is the spectator searching for? How far should art fulfil the spectator's expectations or is it necessary to ignore the spectator? Is the foreigner's critique and judgement of taste crucial?[142]

Daneshvar's last question is a critical allusion to the exhibition practices of the Tehran Biennial, which invited a European selection committee to award Iranian artists with prizes and to evaluate their artworks. The Tehran Biennial was the first major state-sponsored initiative to promote modernist art in Iran. From 1958 to 1966, the Ministry of Fine Arts organized five biennial exhibitions. In 1958, the artist Marcos Grigorian organized the first Tehran Biennial based on the model of the Venice Biennial. In his foreword to the catalog, Grigorian states that the exhibition's main aim was to reconnect to

[140] Ibid., 56.
[141] Simin Daneshvar, 'Painters' Roundtable Report,' in Zamaninya, *Adab wa hunar-i imruz-i Īrān*, 1297–1325.
[142] Ibid., 1300.

the great achievements of Persian arts and recover Iran's status as an empire through modernist art. Since modernist art was a relatively new phenomenon in Iran, the exhibition was also intended to acquaint the audience with modernist expression and establish a connection between the artists and the people. A committee of Iranian and Western experts was invited to select the best artistic works for Iran's national representation at Venice Biennial. Iran's participation at Venice Biennial was, for Grigorian, an important step for the further advancement of modernist art and Iran's artistic connection to Western modern art.[143] For the Shah's government, the Tehran Biennial and Iran's participation in Venice Biennial were important means of communicating the country's world-class status and a vital strategy to signal Iran's modernity internationally. Cultural critics such as al-e Ahmad and Daneshvar understood and exposed the instrumentalization of modernism as royal propaganda intended to illustrate Iran's successful modernization programs. For al-e Ahmad, the government's promotion of modernism and the artistic practice of imitating Western means of expression were, above all, results of cultural imperialism, as he explained in his essay, *Gharbzadegi*:

> However, a quick glance at the walls of the art galleries which have been recently become fashionable and quick stroll down the city's lanes and avenues allow one to see the results of these artists. With a few exceptions, most of their work results in the use of paint, canvas, glass, and iron, which means the use of western manufactured products again. One rarely finds among Iranian architects and artists a person who does not imitate the West or in whose work that quality exists which provides originality and artistic innovation or whose work adds something to the sum of artistic endeavour in the world. Things have gone so far in this respect that we even import judges and critics from Europe and America to judge the work of our own artists.[144]

Criticism of Orientalism and Exoticism in the Visual Arts

For al-e Ahmad and Daneshvar, the employment of Western means of expression represents colonial domination and leads Iranian artists to produce their artworks for a Western market and implement exoticism

---

[143] Marcos Grigorian, 'Foreword,' in *Catalogue First Tehran Biennial* (Tehran: Ministry of Art and Culture Tehran, 1958), 2–8.
[144] Al-e Ahmad, *Plagued by the West*, 90.

in these works. To communicate with the Western observer, artists create mere orientalizing and exoticizing decorations for the Western gaze. Thus, their works lose their topicality for Iranian discourses and become insignificant on a local level. In particular, for al-e Ahmad, the deployment of Persian and Arabic script to achieve abstract expression represents a significant case of exoticism. Without reading knowledge of Persian, the painted words become, for the observer, "a kind of talisman, exoticism, or expression of primitivism. It becomes a reminiscence to Africa, India, colonialism, sun, and power."[145] Yet, al-e Ahmad observes that these self-exoticizing tendencies are present not only in the artworks of Iranian artists but in the works of Turkish and Pakistani artists as well, whose countries also participated in the Fifth Tehran Biennial in 1966. While al-e Ahmad understands the employment of Arabic writing in the works of the Turkish and Pakistani artists as forgivable experiments of form, he condemns the thoughtless use of Persian words and text by Iranian artists as an expression of their westoxification, primarily when they use the "word" as mere "wall decoration" and deprive the word of its meaning in order "to create mere visual pleasure."[146]

The usage of the "word," as for example in a talisman for luck, is a kind of mystification to create fear and reverence in a general public who cannot read the "word" and understand its meaning.[147]

Al-e Ahmad's Texts about Bahman Mohassess

Despite arguing for Iran's need for transformation, al-e Ahmad warns of the blind adaptation of Western modernity. In his text *About Mohassess* from 1966, al-e Ahmad depicts Western modernity as a double-edged sword.

"Hamlet" is one side of the coin, "Vasco de Gama" is the other side. These are the two sides of the coin of the West. Coincidently, they were contemporaries. The first honorable intellectual in practice. The second, the perfidy, the decision to spread Christianity all over the world. The first, an honor to Western culture, the second, the executioner of colonialism.[148]

[145] Al-e Ahmad, 'The Fifth Triple Yolk Egg,' in Zamaninya, *Adab wa hunar-i imruz-i Īrān*, 1377–1385, 1380.
[146] Ibid., 1382. [147] Ibid., 1384.
[148] Al-e Ahmad, 'About Mohassess,' in Zamaninya, *Adab wa hunar-i imruz-i Īrān*, 1357–1340, 1359.

For al-e Ahmad, the juxtaposed figures of Shakespeare's Hamlet and the fifteenth-century Portuguese explorer Vasco de Gama, who discovered the sea route to India and contributed to the development of global imperialism and Western expansion, represent the two faces of Western modernity. He elaborates on this idea when he explains that existentialism and colonialism mutually determine and influence each other:

> In these days Hamlet is embodied by his majesty Jean Paul Sartre, who hates himself, according to the magazine *Encounter*, because of being European; Vasco de Gama is embodied in the great general Westmoreland in Vietnam. The second is a sharp, heavy sword in the hands of the European and American arms industry.[149]

For al-e Ahmad, the Vietnam war represented one of the worst excesses of Western modernity. Yet, for him, even French existentialism, which had become a crucial philosophical inspiration for articulating his thoughts and views, turned into a sign of a Western colonial attitude. As the translator of numerous works by French existentialist authors, such as Jean-Paul Sartre and Albert Camus, he acquired a profound knowledge of existentialist literature.[150] But, in the same article about Mohassess, he also strongly criticizes European intellectuals such as Sartre. Al-e Ahmad refers to Sartre as "the moral ace up the untrustworthy Western sleeve. His majesty named himself the 'troubled consciousness' of the West so that African and Asian intellectuals regard him as the executioner of Asian impoverishment."[151] He further states that Asian and African intellectuals had no hesitations about sharing their material and spiritual knowledge with Western intellectuals since they hoped to participate and contribute to the critical anticolonial discourse of their time. For non-Western thinkers, intellectual and financial profit became a strong incentive. But, as al-e Ahmad further explains, even self-appointed spokespersons such as Sartre benefited from Third World knowledge and presented these appropriated ideas as their own intellectual productions.[152] For this reason, as al-e Ahmad saw it, existentialism was only a further agent of Western expansionism.

---

[149] Ibid., 1360.
[150] Examples of Al-e Ahmad's translations into Persian include (selection): Fyodor Dostoevski *The Gambler* (1948); Albert Camus *The Stranger* (1949); Jean Paul Sartre *Dirty Hands* (1952); Eugène Ionesco *Rhinoceros* (1966).
[151] Al-e Ahmad, 'About Mohassess,' in Zamaninya, *Adab wa hunar-i imruz-i Īrān*, 1359–1360.
[152] Ibid., 1360.

In Mohassess' paintings and the mutilated bodies of their lonesome creatures, however, al-e Ahmad saw the realization of an artistic version of his critique of modernity. The amputation of the figures' arms and legs alludes, according to the author, to the mutilation of humanity in the twentieth century. Although the approach of his visual representation was good, Mohassess was not radical enough for al-e Ahmad because his paintings could still be used as wall decorations. And he warns the painter that once "the Western flood" is over, "the skeletons of your works will be like the sludge remaining after the flood."[153] For him, the only way to preserve paintings from decoration and insignificance was to create artistic works based on the concept of hybridity:

> He [Mohassess] asked, what should we do then? I said, what else could you do than the painters of Timurid and Safavid era? They knew the artistic styles from China, India, and Moghul and mixed them together and put something from our self, and created thus, the schools of Heart, Shiraz, or Tabriz, etc.[154]

"To Mohassess and for the Wall"

Al-e Ahmad's writings about modernist art convey his Marxist and political understanding of art. This can be observed in his text "To Mohassess and for the Wall," one of his most significant writings about modernist art. The text is not only a piece of art criticism but also gives one an insight into al-e Ahmad's literary practice as the author of numerous short stories and novels. Conceptually, the text builds on the Persian proverb *beh dar miguyam ta divar beshnavad*, which literally means *I tell it to the door so the wall will listen*. This proverb is best translated with a certain "innuendo," a "remark that suggests something but does not refer to it directly, or this type of remark in general."[155] In "To Mohassess and for the Wall," al-e Ahmad addresses the work and life of the painter Mohassess as a positive and leading example of modernist expression while at the same time sharply attacking other painters whose expression remains mere decorative. A close examination of this text shows that al-e Ahmad articulates his specific understanding and definition of

---

[153] Ibid.   [154] Ibid.
[155] https://dictionary.cambridge.org/de/worterbuch/englisch/innuendo

modernist arts in Iran. Choosing a personal approach, al-e Ahmad begins by introducing his friend, the painter Mohassess, to his readers:

I have known Bahman Mohassess since the years 1951–52. Beside this familiarity, I like him as well. Because he is warm. And literate and more importantly, he is a 'phenomenon'. A man from Rasht became Italian! And I doubt that anyone else has ever seen anywhere else such a 'phenomenon'! Generally speaking, Mohassess story is for me, the story of today's painting. It is a strange world, where fools recently invented a new secret language, communicating internationally with each other and sending messages. But their message is not a message, and if you don't understand its stutter, nothing remains. And more interestingly, he himself is the story of our painting today. Removing a sapling and replanting it somewhere else in another climate and pruning the twigs and leaves it had and growing new leaves.[156]

Al-e Ahmad establishes a crucial point with his first meaningful sentence, "I have known Bahman Mohassess since the years 1951–52." His contemporary Iranian readers would have immediately recognized these dates as the years of historical turmoil leading to the shah's temporary dismissal and, simultaneously, the prelude that would eventually lead to the coup against Prime Minister Mohammad Mosaddeq. In 1951, Mosaddeq successfully mobilized the masses, calling for the people of Iran to take to the streets. After the oil strike in April of the same year, the Iranian parliament had to approve his nationalization bill and appointed Mosaddeq prime minister. When Mosaddeq, now Prime Minister, started to implement his program to nationalize Iran's oil, the British government opposed Mosaddeq's attempts and blockaded the export of Iranian oil in support of the Anglo-Iranian Oil company. In this situation, Mosaddeq tried not only to put an end to the colonial interferences of imperial forces but also to strengthen the constitutional system in Iran and to weaken the shah's power. As prime minister, Mosaddeq requested control over the military to secure and, if need be, defend his plans for the nationalization of Iran's oil.[157] But, when the shah refused to transfer royal command of his armed forces to Mosaddeq, Mosaddeq sought support from the masses and called for public demonstrations and protests via radio broadcast.

---

[156] Al-e Ahmad, 'For Mohassess and the Wall,' in Zamaninya, *Adab wa hunar-i imruz-i Īrān*, 1343–1344.
[157] Abrahamian, *A History of Modern Iran*, 116.

The consequences of this were, as Ervand Abrahamian explains, "The public promptly poured into the streets and, after three days of general strikes and bloodshed, forced the shah to back down. The crisis became known as the 30th of Tir (July 21st)."[158]

According to al-e Ahmad, it was precisely during this turmoil that Mohassess joined in his political activism. While al-e Ahmad was working on his newspaper, Mohassess painted political posters for the demonstrations depicting high-ranking politicians and diplomats. With high hopes for the nationalization of Iran's oil and the resulting democratization of Iran, artists and intellectuals joined the mass protests on the streets. The further course of history, the coup against Mosaddeq, and the reinstatement of Mohammad Reza Pahlavi as Shah of Persia caused trauma, disappointment, and the political retreat of many activists. As al-e Ahmad explains with disappointment, "In those days, we hurried to make history. But even though his [Mohassess] posters had no political benefit, at least they were drawing exercises."[159]

Contrary to Iranian art history's general perception of modernist art as a period of apolitical formal experiments, al-e Ahmad's text demonstrates a close relationship between artists and political activism in Iran. The socialist *Niru-ye Sevom* ("Third Force") party, founded by al-e Ahmad and Khalil Maleki in 1948 after their split from *Tudeh* party, constituted the left wing of Mosaddeq's National Front coalition. In the same years, 1951–1952, Third Force hosted an exhibition presenting an overview of Mohassess's artistic works.

Al-e Ahmad's and Mohassess's collaboration was characterized by their use of one another's work. Even after Mohassess left for Italy, he produced illustrations for al-e Ahmad's books and Nima's poems. During this time, al-e Ahmad and Simin Daneshvar, also traveled to Italy, where Mohassess introduced them to Rome's painting and architecture. They also met other Iranian artists living in Italy, such as Behjat Sadr, Mansoureh Hosseini, Mohsen Vaziri-Moghaddam, and Mortezza Hannaneh. Despite al-e Ahmad's appreciation of other modernist Iranian artists' works, Mohassess's artistic practice was an

---

[158] Ibid., 117.
[159] Al-e Ahmad, 'For Mohassess and the Wall,' in Zamaninya, *Adab wa hunar-i imruz-i Īrān*, 1344.

outstanding example because "he is continuously searching. He searches for an escape route from contemporary art's stutter."[160]

Nevertheless, modernist expression often took on the form of "stuttering" since, for al-e Ahmad, artistic production only articulates itself in an incomprehensible language that the general public cannot understand. To give his voice more authority, al-e Ahmad backs his argument with the statement attributed to Jean-Paul Sartre, "the painter is a fool when he does not put any signs (e.g., words) on his canvases unless he creates something."[161] Based on Sartre's statement, al-e Ahmad concludes,

> And could this not also be the reason, why the majority of our contemporary artists are idols? Quiet like rocks – and no matter how you address them, they hide themselves in silence? This means our words are on our canvases. In any case, in this particular situation Mohassess is a gift of god, who employs the means of painting to eliminate the evil spirit and he does not hide himself behind his canvas. And one can easily sit beside him and speak a few words about these subjects.[162]

The question of art's purpose is the central question in his texts about modernist painting. For al-e Ahmad, decorative painting is neither insignificant nor meaningless. Decoration also poses a political threat since modernist art, which experiments only with formalist elements, can also easily be instrumentalized for political power, as he explains,

> My main point about contemporary 'modern' painters is that our current state of affairs and our governmental institutions ... use your foolish language and your deceptive colors with nothing behind them to fool the people. This is history's judgement about Mohassess, although he does not fall in this trap, I tell it to the door, so that the wall will listen.[163]

Once again, al-e Ahmad uses the Persian proverb, which is also the title of his text addressed to Iranian artists. Art without a message remains for him mere decoration or, as he put it, "It is only a door in the wall, and you color it. But the wall's structure is weak."[164] For al-e Ahmad,

> The foundation is not stable, and no matter how much you embellish the evil spirit [*ifrit*] on the arch of the veranda, it will still be in ruins and in such a crumbling state, that for its destruction you won't even need this fragile pen to act as an axe to destroy it.[165]

[160] Ibid., 1350. [161] Ibid., 1350–1351. [162] Ibid., 1351. [163] Ibid.
[164] Ibid., 1352. [165] Ibid.

Furthermore, he states not even the art critic has the power to change the disastrous state of painting at the moment. This leads him to reflect on his role as an art critic, which he interprets as just another sign of his own westoxification. Modernist art critique was a relatively new phenomenon in Iran without a local literary tradition to build on. Al-e Ahmad recognized that the Western tradition of art criticism legitimated his authority as a critic. He describes this transfer of cultural knowledge and tradition from West to East as leading to a condition of homelessness and rootlessness when he explains the migratory experience of Iranian artists as "the sapling's story, which is one of being moved, losing its roots, becoming decoration, and needing a greenhouse and other disasters."[166] Yet, this applies not only to Iranian artists living in the West but also concerns Iranian artists living in Iran, when, for example, foreign judges are invited to evaluate artworks and select the winners for Tehran Biennials. For al-e Ahmad, the attempt to seek the West's validation and recognition is an expression of a significant inferiority complex resulting from colonial interdependence and Iran's westoxification. Thus, the international participation of Iranian artists in international exhibitions is not a distinction bestowed on their artistic achievements but rather part of the state's deeply propagandistic cultural politics.

And now you assume that you can master the spider web of Western techniques. Because they represented you at Venice Biennial under the rubric of the foreigners? And when you are being with the foreigners, what is your contribution to the Western world? And what if it is already agreed that you remain a consumer of the West?[167]

Even though al-e Ahmad does not provide his readers and the artists addressed with a simple solution and practical advice, he asks the artists to at least communicate their artworks' messages to prevent them from being misunderstood and politically instrumentalized:

I don't ask you to move your brush under the rules of our tradition, local achievements and so on, nor to work as beginners work in some established and old methods and traditional arts. But I am asking you to come and take my hand and take me up on the ladder of your canvas, and accomplish something in this market.[168]

---

[166] Ibid.   [167] Ibid., 1354.   [168] Ibid., 1354–1355.

Al-e Ahmad shows he understands Iranian artists who seek to achieve artistic recognition in an international art market. Yet, he asks artists to refrain from orientalizing and exoticizing tendencies in their artworks because this, for him, represents just another sign of the artists' westoxification and their inferiority complex regarding Western arts. Instead, al-e Ahmad calls for artists to liberate themselves from the market and customers' needs and use artistic production as a tool to communicate and address local topics. In his articles, al-e Ahmad incorporates his Marxist thoughts and formulates an antiformalist approach toward modernist arts. So long as they do not use their potential to convey a message to the audience, new techniques and the employment of Western means of expression remain empty shells devoid of any context for him.

Somebody who has something to say or to show does not require any help and, by trying to satisfy your "snobbism," you do not scare off the viewer and you can't fool anybody with your westernization. And my last point is, if you have roots in this land, don't blossom in fall, that means bad luck. And if you have become the decoration of these circles and are not one of us, then forget about what I have written.[169]

Although al-e Ahmad criticizes painting's decorative function, he still sees its crucial potential as a significant instrument of free speech and political potential. His criticisms are not so much directed against the artistic practice of modernist Iranian artists as they function in his anticolonial discourse of *gharbzadegi* as a call for political participation. His texts encourage artists to use creative means of expression to develop their voices and to strive for democratization and adherence to democratic standards. Seen especially against the background of cultural politics in the Pahlavi era and the depoliticization of all fields of cultural production, al-e Ahmad's texts help us question the perception of modernist art as a primarily formalist experience that evolved within a sociohistorical vacuum.

---

[169] Ibid.

3 "Saqqakhaneh *Revisited*"
The Art-Historiographical Construction of a Local Modernism

When reading about Iranian modernist artistic production, one regularly encounters the name *Saqqakhaneh*. Generally speaking, *Saqqakhaneh* describes the creative practice of a group of Iranian artists, who were active in the creation of a local artistic modernism during the 1960s. In order to achieve such innovation in the Iranian context, they merged elements from Persian visual heritage with Western means of modernist expression. Their artistic turn to Shi'ite and Persian iconography is considered to this day as the peak of Iran's modernist art history. *Saqqakhaneh* is, thus, often regarded as a successful illustration of how Western modernity can be adopted, while simultaneously preserving and promoting Iranian identity politics.

In Iranian art historiography, *Saqqakhaneh* represents the first movement of modernist art that was not disparaged as a belated imitation of Western artistic styles. It has therefore often been described as superior to earlier artistic experiments with modernist arts in Iran. This well-established way of reading and reciting *Saqqakhaneh* as local translations of a global modernist movement has gained even more prominence in recent years, thanks to recently emerged art-historiographical endeavors, which have renewed the interest in these modernist artists, their artworks, and the various written records associated with *Saqqakhaneh*.

Yet, this renewed interest also raises a fundamental question: What exactly is *Saqqakhaneh*? Far from being a self-styled movement, the artists associated with *Saqqakhaneh* collaborated with each other only occasionally, had no common aesthetic principles, and never wrote an artistic manifesto. While some texts speak of *Saqqakhaneh* as a school of modernism, others define it as an artistic group or even as an independent art movement. As this chapter will demonstrate, *Saqqakhaneh* was less an artistic group than an art-historiographical construction fueled by art critics and individual artists.

Recognizing this distinction opens the door to understanding the complex political shifts, in which these works should be situated, both in their original context and in the process of memorializing prerevolutionary Iran. On the one hand, *Saqqakhaneh* has been remembered as an apparent celebration of the Pahlavi state's liberal support of the arts. On the other hand, it also emerged as part of a discourse in resistance to the very westernization that led to the widespread dissatisfaction with the regime expressed in the revolution. The art critic Karim Emami and the artist Parviz Tanavoli were key figures who described the idea of *Saqqakhaneh* as an expression of an Iranian modernism. Yet, Emami's writings show that the works identified through this description were deeply rooted in an anticolonial discourse that was connected to the debates about westoxification (*gharbzadegi*) in Iran. Emami's classification of *Saqqakhaneh* as a cultural practice of resistance was, thus, an attempt to establish a counter-narrative within the field of cultural politics in Pahlavi Iran.

The idea of *Saqqakhaneh* as a specifically Iranian version of modernism was, however, also highly welcomed by the Pahlavi state, which underwent a cultural shift toward Islamic spirituality in the 1970s. During this time, the ambiguity of the artworks' meaning allowed the style to be used both as a form of resistance against the state and as an ideological tool by that very state. When the Tehran Museum opened its doors on Queen Farah Diba's birthday in October 1977, for example, the exhibition *Saqqakhaneh* was one of four curated shows inaugurating the new museum for modern and contemporary art. In fact, in this context, *Saqqakhaneh* offers an illustrative example of how the Pahlavi state institutionalized the common aesthetic practice of a loosely connected group of artists and transformed it from a cultural practice of resistance into material for state propaganda used to communicate Iran's successful modernization to the world. The instrumentalization of *Saqqakhaneh* and art-historical discourses have largely hidden the oppositional nature of the artists' work in their proper context. This, in turn, has prompted a depoliticized narrative of the artists' work, in which their artistic productions were often understood as signs of a negotiation of cultural identity. Ignoring *Saqqakhaneh*'s political implications continues to constitute a major paradigm in Iranian art historiography to this day.

In accordance with this dominant narrative, transcultural processes of institutionalization have staged *Saqqakhaneh* as the decisive manifestation of a local Iranian modernism. This mechanism's success is clearly visible in *Saqqakhaneh*'s dominance, to this day, as an ideological model in Iranian art historiography. *Saqqakhaneh* and its nostalgic longing for an authentic Iranian past have become such a dominant concept that they absorb, even in retrospect, almost any kind of artistic practice incorporating local elements. To deconstruct the category of *Saqqakhaneh* and to make its historiographical construction as an "imagined community" visible, this chapter traces the historiographical emergence of *Saqqakhaneh* in detail, while shedding light on its political instrumentalization.

Shi'ite Material Culture in Modernist Iranian Art

Hossein Zenderoudi's Incorporation of Islamic Iconography

In 1960, the artist Hossein Zenderoudi presented his work, *Who is this Hossein the World is so crazy about?* (1958/59), at an exhibition at Reza Abbasi Hall.[1] In this work of art, Zenderoudi depicts the tragic death of Imam Hussein in the battle of Karbala, so central to Iranian hagiographic iconography. Zenderoudi's linocut is a significant example of how artistic expression at the time sought its inspiration from Shi'ite religious traditions. This connecting of modernist visual expression and religious iconography is said to be the beginning of *Saqqakhaneh*. Zenderoudi's example demonstrates that *Saqqakhaneh*'s modernist expression was not a secular enterprise to explore Western means of expression from a formalist point of view. The exploration of Shi'ite iconography in a modernist language was, rather, an important tool to situate artistic expression in the ongoing political debates about Iran's westoxification. With his artwork, Zenderoudi suggests that a possible modern Iranian identity is to be found in the alliance of Iranian and Islamic identity. Thus, Zenderoudi questions the country's allegedly successful secularization and shows that his search for an Iranian artistic modernity was based on an immersion in Iran's religious traditions. This new artistic language

---

[1] Hossein Zenderoudi, 'Who is this Hossein the world is crazy about?,' Linocut print on textile, 228.52 cm × 148.5 cm, 1958/59, British Museum London. Unfortunately, due to copyright, the picture cannot be reprinted in this book, but it can be found on the British Museum's website www.britishmuseum.org/collection/object/W_2011-6034-1

enabled the artist to explore Shi'ite iconography from a fresh perspective and to bring Shi'ite traditions back to the present.

In particular, in Persian visual arts, the battle of Karbala and the cult of martyrs not only are important elements in Shi'ite belief but also form the narrative content of its iconographic tradition. Shi'ite iconography strongly shaped Persian visual arts and has a strong presence in Iran, in both public and private spheres. Despite Reza Shah's 1932 prohibition of *ta'ziyeh* (passion plays), a religious performative ritual commemorating Imam Hussein's martyrdom, this tradition of Shi'ite mourning was still an actively practiced part of rural life in Iran.[2] *Ta'ziyeh* became an integral part of the Shiraz Arts Festival. The annual festival, held from 1967 to 1977, brought together Iranian and international artists in Iran to give a stage to works from different fields of performing arts. Due to its transcultural character and importance for Iran's modern history, the festival represents a "cultural model for a post-colonial necessity," as Vali Mahlouji explains.[3]

Zenderoudi's work, *Who is this Hossein the World is so crazy about?* also reflects the topicality of this specific hagiographic iconography. Using a powerful black-and-white aesthetic, similar in style to a comic strip, Zenderoudi depicts ten episodes of Hussein's political and religious fight against Yazid, the Caliph of Damascus, whom Imam Hussein, the grandson of the prophet Muhammad, refused to recognize as the rightful successor of the prophet. With his family and a group of loyal followers, Hussein left Medina to support his adherents in Kufa, who were fighting against the Caliphate. In Karbala, Yazid's troops cut Hussein and his followers off from any water supply. Yazid's forces expected Imam Hussein's capitulation and his ensuing return to Medina. But, on the tenth day of the occupation (*Ashura*), fighting broke out. Yet, Hussein and his followers were powerless against the military superiority of Yazid's troops. The prophet's grandson and his armed retinue were violently murdered in the battle of Karbala and the women and children were taken hostage and brought to Damascus. For Shi'ites, the battle of Karbala is the cornerstone in the struggle for the line of succession to the prophet Muhammad and the cause of the division of the Muslim community into *Sunni* and

---

[2] Rebecca Ansary Pettys, 'The Ta'ziyeh: Ritual Enactment of Persian Renewal,' *Theatre Journal*, vol. 33, no. 3 (1981), 341–354, 347.
[3] Vali Mahlouji, 'Perspectives on the Shiraz Arts Festival: A Radical Third World Rewriting,' in Daftari and Diba, *Iran Modern*, 87–91.

Shia. As a result, Karbala functions as an important trope for Shi'ite identity formation and has left "an indelible mark on Muslim consciousness."[4] As Syed Akbar Hyder explains,

> History is actively reconstituted through the affective power of prose and poetry, oral as well as written forms, and through a galaxy of images, as the event of Karbala has been emplotted over a millennium in a multitude of traditions.[5]

In his artistic rendition, Zenderoudi particularly emphasizes the most dramatic scenes in the course of the battle. For example, the rectangular scene in the second row from above shows how Hussein cries over the death of his son Ali Akbar in the midst of the battlefield. The next scene illustrates Hussein's decapitation in front of Yazid's army. The soldiers are carrying the severed heads of Hussein's followers on top of lances. In the last scene, Zenderoudi depicts Imam Hussein's defeat. Yazid sits, together with the battle's only survivors, surrounded by Hussein's female relatives, with Hussein's head on a tray in front of him as a spoil of war.

With his illustration of Karbala, Zenderoudi clearly refers to the artistic tradition of *pardeh* (curtains). These portable linens are important means for oral visual storytelling in Iran, which became very famous in the nineteenth and early twentieth centuries. The historical events of the battle of Karbala are the main subject of *pardehs*. Executed on linen, these portable screens serve to illustrate Hussein's suffering to the audience during storytellers' recitations of these events.[6] These narrative paintings play a major role in the annual reenactments (*ta'ziyeh*) commemorating the martyrdom of Hussein and his followers. The *pardeh*'s portability meant that the religious "performance could take place anywhere in the city or village – from coffeehouses, which have always been a locus of these kinds of popular arts, to the broken wall of deserted house in a village."[7] As a space for social gatherings, the coffeehouse became an important locus for

---

[4] Syed Akbar Hyder, 'Iqbal and Karbala: Re-reading the Episteme of Martyrdom for a Poetics of Appropriation,' *Cultural Dynamics*, vol. 13, no. 3 (2001), 339–362, 340.

[5] Ibid.

[6] Hamid Dabashi, 'Ta'ziyeh as Theatre of Protest,' *TDR*, vol. 49, no. 4, *Special Issue on Ta'ziyeh* (2005), 91–99.

[7] Amir Lashkari and Mojde Kalantari, 'Pardeh Khani: A Dramatic Form of Storytelling in Iran,' *Asian Theatre Journal*, vol. 32, no. 1 (2015), 245–258, 253.

religious storytelling. Coffeehouses also often "served as the ateliers of the painters," with the owners commissioning the painters to realize religious narrative works for their interiors.[8] Thus, the genre of *pardeh* became highly influential in the development of coffeehouse paintings, making them another important means for the depiction of Imam Hussein's martyrdom.

The outer frame surrounding the episodes represents a significant compositional and textual means of identifying the theme of Zenderoudi's images. In the inscriptions framing the composition, one repeatedly encounters the sentence, which also serves as the painting's title, *In Ḥoseyn kist ke delhā hama divāna-ye ust?* (*Who is this Hossein the World is so crazy about?*). The very title itself illustrates that, in his work, Zenderoudi is exploring the narrative pattern that has evolved around the prominent religious figure of Imam Hussein. Due to Zenderoudi's significant use of inscriptions, Alice Bombardier associates his work with the wall hangings (*parcham*) used during the mourning month of *Muharram* to decorate assembly halls.[9] As an essential part of Shi'ite material culture, *parchams* not only display figurative images derived from the iconography of Karbala but also incorporate *ashura* elegies to commemorate the martyrdom of Imam Hussein. The Safavid court poet Muhtasham Kashani (d. 1587) is a prominent representative of the literary genre of elegiac poetry in Persian literature. His twelve-stanza elegy to honor Imam Hussein's martyrdom achieved an immense popularity and became a major work referred to in various mourning rituals.[10] More specifically, Bombardier compares Zenderoudi's work with a particular *parcham* from 1959, which was displayed at a ritual assembly hall and employed Kashani's poem as "calligraphic inscriptions" in a similar way.[11]

Textually, one can observe that Zenderoudi's question, *Who is this Hossein the World is so crazy about?*, is closely modeled after the

---

[8] Peter Chelkowski, 'Narrative Painting and Painting Recitation in Qajar Iran,' *Muqarnas*, Vol. 6 (1989), 98–111, 108–109.

[9] Alice Bombardier, 'A Contemporary Illustrated Qur'an. Zenderoudi's Illustration of Grosjean's Translation (1972),' in Alessandro Cancian (ed.), *Approaches to the Qur'an in Contemporary Iran* (Oxford: Oxford University Press, 2019), 325–352.

[10] For further investigation on the topic of *parcham*, see Ingvild Flaskerud, *Visualizing Belief and Piety in Iranian Shiism* (London: Continuum, 2010).

[11] Bombardier, 'A Contemporary Illustrated Qur'an,' 332.

famous lines in Kashani's lamentation poetry, which continues to be part of mourning rituals in Iran:

Baz in che shuresh ast keh dar khalq alam ast.
Baz in che nowheh che 'aza va che matam ast.

[Again, what is this revolt that is among the people of the world?
Again, what is this lament, this condolence and this mourning?][12]

Parchams do not always necessarily display Kashani's poem in its entirety, but may also use only a few lines. Thus, the depiction of the "incomplete version of the poem suggests that it is expected to be known in the interpretive community" and requires no further explanation for the participants of mourning ceremonies.[13] It can be inferred that contemporary viewers of Zenderoudi's artwork had the cultural knowledge to connect the linocut's lines to Kashani's famous lamentation.

The second sentence, inscribed only once at the bottom of the frame in Zenderoudi's print, translates to "*Who is this flame [candle], for which all souls are moths?*"[14] The image of the moth and its "fateful attraction to flame" dates back to Umayyad religious poetry and symbolizes "an imaginative motif for satire, panegyric and love poetry."[15] The moth and the flame metaphor is a widespread motif in Sufi literature and denotes the concept of *fana*, the annihilation of the self, that leads to the seeker's eventual unification with God.

As human beings, we have the ability to reach the state of extinction and annihilation and yet have the consciousness that we are nothing in ourselves and that all being belongs to God. We can reach a state of unitive consciousness prior to bifurcation into object and subject.[16]

The experience of *fana* is like that of the moths, whose desire for unification with the flame is so strong that they consciously accept this unification despite it meaning the extinction of their own life. Sufis

---

[12] Cited in, Flaskerud, *Visualizing Belief*, 94.   [13] Ibid.
[14] Ladan Akbarnia, 'Curator' s Comment,' Collection Online, The British Museum. www.britishmuseum.org/research/collection_online/collection_object_details.aspx?objectid=3421951&partid=1, accessed 21 October 2019.
[15] Muḥammad Mansour Abaḥsain, 'The Supra-Symbolic Moth in Arabic Religious Poetry from the Late Ottoman Period,' *Journal of Arabic Literature*, vol. 24, no. 1 (1993), 21–27, 24.
[16] Seyyed Hossein Nasr, *The Garden of Truth: The Vision and Promise of Sufism, Islam's Mystical Tradition* (New York: Harper Collins, 2007), 135.

often used this metaphor to explain the concept of *fana*. As Annemarie Schimmel states, "when the divine light fully appears in the mystic's consciousness, all things disappear instead of remaining visible" and this "is the experience of fana – a blackout of everything."[17]

The Sufi allegory of the moth and the flame is very prominent in Persian poetry and can, for instance, be found in the works of Omar Khayyam, Attar, Rumi, and Jami. In the *Conference of the Birds*, the twelfth-century poet Attar employs the metaphor of the moth and the flame as an "allegorical portrayal of the longing of the human soul for union with the Divine."[18] In this story, an assembly of birds sets out to seek the mystical bird Simorgh. Under the leadership of a hoopoe, the birds' journey leads them through seven valleys representing the Sufi seeker's spiritual path. In order to depict the seventh valley of self-resignation and annihilation (*faqr* and *fana*), Attar includes the metaphor of the moth and its irrepressible desire to seek unification with the flame. Attar's *Conference of the Birds* was highly influential on modernist art production in Iran and will be further investigated in the next chapter.

In his linocut, Zenderoudi brings together two inscriptions, one referring to the metaphor of the moth and the flame, the other referring to the martyrdom of Imam Hussein. The symbol of the moth also recalls the martyrdom of Hossein and his companions, memorialized as the ultimate signs of annihilation and unification with God. In this context, Syed Akbar Hyder writes,

Sufis, through anagogical readings, have frequently remembered Ali's son Husayn and his companions as paragons of virtue and lovers of God who annihilated themselves in the divine (*fana fi'llah*) in order to attain subsistence in God (*baqa bi'llah*) by receiving God's promised sustenance for the martyrs.[19]

Zenderoudi employs these inscriptions as a textual framework for the dramatic battle scenes of Karbala and clearly refers to Kashani's lines. Zenderoudi uses his inscriptions *Who is this flame [candle], for which*

---

[17] Annemarie Schimmel, *Mystical Dimensions of Islam* (Chapel Hill: University of North Carolina Press, 1975), 144.

[18] A. V. Williams Jackson, 'The Allegory of the Moths and the Flame. Translated from the Manṭiq aṭ-Tair of Farīdad-Dīn 'Attār,' *Journal of the American Oriental Society*, vol. 36 (1916), 345–347, 345.

[19] Hyder, 'Iqbal,' 339.

all souls are moths? and *Who is this Hossein the World is so crazy about?* to explore Imam Hussein's hagiographic tradition. In addition, contemporary art critics recognized Zenderoudi's question not only as a reference to Imam Hussein but also as a reference to the artist himself. This is also amplified by Zenderoudi's artistic signature in the bottom-left part of the print. Zenderoudi signed his painting with *kar-e al-haqir-e Hossein Zenderoudi*, which translates as "a work by the humble Hossein Zenderoudi."[20]

The example of Zenderoudi shows how artists investigated local religious iconographies in the language of modernist expression. The art historian Fereshteh Daftari states that it was the artist Marcos Grigorian who introduced Zenderoudi to the printmaking technique of linocut during his studies at the Boys' Art College *Honarestan-e Honarha-ye Ziba* (1958–1960). Grigorian was deeply engaged not only in printmaking but also in the preservation of coffeehouse painting, which was not considered part of Iran's official cultural heritage at that time and thus not part of Pahlavi preservation policies. To promote a modernist expression rooted in Iran's own visual traditions, Grigorian encouraged his students to seek artistic inspiration in Iranian folk culture, such as coffeehouse painting. He researched this topic and exhibited the works of the contemporary coffeehouse painters Qolar Aghassi and Mohammad Modabber in his Galerie Esthétique.[21] In Daftari's view, Grigorian was highly influential in Zenderoudi's artistic career because the latter "found compelling inspiration in the local primitivism of the coffee-house paintings."[22] Daftari considers Zenderoudi's linocut a modernized and updated version of the established painterly genre because "the humour and the irreverence endow Zenderoudi's work with a modernity absent in coffee-house painting."[23] Due to his visual adaptation of this kind of folk aesthetics, "Zenderoudi embodies 'the authentic local' with whom a movement away from Western idioms and back into the depths of Shi'ite iconography began."[24]

Looking at Zenderoudi's artwork, however, it also becomes clear that he broke with the pictorial traditions of *pardeh* as an artistic

---

[20] Fereshteh Daftari, 'Another Modernism: An Iranian Perspective,' in Lynn Gumpert (ed.), *Modernisms: Iranian, Turkish, and Indian Highlights from NYU's Abby Weed Grey Collection* (New York/Munich: Grey Art Gallery, New York University, 2019), 43–63, 50.
[21] Ibid. [22] Ibid. [23] Ibid., 30. [24] Ibid.

genre. As a painterly genre, *pardehs* and coffeehouse painting share distinctive features that support the storyteller's oral recitation. The storyteller plays a crucial role in providing his viewers orientation regarding the painting. The story unfolds horizontally, such that the storyteller can walk back and forth in front of the painting during the performance and the depicted episodes of the narration are visually intertwined and cannot be separated from another. The painter often arranges scenes and characters into a sequence without visual divisions or blank spaces between its parts. To distinguish the opposing fronts, however, artistic designs are used to establish pictorial distinctions, such as portraying Yazid and his troops as monstrous and ugly in order to make clear their role as oppressors. In order to preserve conventions of decorum and distinguish them as "good," Hussein and his followers, the holy persons, however, are portrayed in a visually appealing manner. Despite their suffering amid the battle, their faces usually bear no signs of the pain they are enduring. This distinction is also reflected in the colors' symbolism, as "green was indicative of sacredness, yellow suggestive of distress, and red implied oppression."[25] Due to the symbolic employment of colors, *pardehs* and coffeehouse paintings are often very colorful in appearance.

In contrast to this tradition, Zenderoudi depicts his scenes in black and white. Zenderoudi's narration unfolds vertically, not horizontally, and follows a clear narrative structure from top to bottom. Zenderoudi cut each episode in linoleum sheet and printed the compilation of the partitioned scenes on a large linen cloth.[26] Thus, as a printmaking technique, linocut supports the specific compositional organization and the partitioning of the single episodes.

As an artistic medium, the use of linocut also supports Zenderoudi's Expressionist figurative execution of Hussein's martyrdom. Zenderoudi carves sharp sketch-like drawings into linoleum in order to depict his version of Karbala in rough scratches without refined details. Zenderoudi's expressive execution of the portrayed figures and his selection of linocut as an artistic medium recall Expressionist aesthetics, which can also be found, for instance, in the prints of German Expressionism. Aesthetically, Zenderoudi's visual turn to

---

[25] Lashkari and Kalantari, 'Pardeh Khani,' 247–248.
[26] Ruyin Pakbaz, 'The Originality of Repetition,' in Pakbaz and Emdadian, *Charles Hossein Zenderoudi*, 28–29, 28.

Expressionism also represents a significant strategic turn meant to present him and his artwork as "modern." Thanks to its international dissemination in the twentieth century, Expressionism was considered a major avant-garde movement and had become a signifier of Western modernity. Having emerged as a rejection of Impressionism's success and its depiction of nature, Expressionist tendencies embraced a subjective focus on feeling and emotion. Before World War I, the Expressionist discourse had a multidimensional character and encompassed various artistic theories and national politics. Thus, the label "Expressionism" was used as an umbrella term to designate any kind of modernist art that radically broke with past visual traditions.

With his 1914 book, *Der Expressionismus*, art critic Paul Fechter helped propagate the idea that Expressionism was a distinctively German artistic phenomenon and Germany's contribution to Western modernism. In particular, the artists' respective groups, *Die Brücke*, founded in 1905 in Dresden, and *Der Blaue Reiter*, founded in 1910 in Munich, were presented as Germany's avant-garde movements. The immense success of these groups can also be attributed to the media of printmaking and graphic arts as important means for artistic exchange across Europe. In the aftermath of World War I, Expressionist and leftist artists devoted their artistic practice to posters, leaflets, and pamphlets and, following the October Revolution in Russia in 1917 and the November Revolution 1918 in Germany, Expressionism became the artistic language of revolutionary art. Expressionist printings helped both realize Marxist ambitions to produce art for the masses and to disseminate Expressionist artists' political program. After the November Revolution, various groups of artists in Germany promoted politically engaged art.[27] In the *Novembergruppe*'s 1919 pamphlet, the artist Max Pechstein, a member of the politically active faction of the group, appealed to artists to use their art to help establish a new society based on a socialist government.[28] Especially after the traumatic war experiences

---

[27] Isabel Wünsche, 'Expressionist Networks, Cultural Debates, and Artistic Practices: A Conceptual Introduction,' in Wünsche, *The Routledge Companion to Expressionism in a Transnational Context* (New York: Routledge Taylor & Francis Group, 2019), 1–30.

[28] Franziska Lampe, 'Zum Holzschnitt als visuelle Strategie um 1918/19,' in Nils Grosch (ed.), *Novembergruppe 1918. Studien zu einer interdisziplinären Kunst für die Weimarer Republik* (Münster: Waxmann, 2018), 43–60, 45.

during and after World War I, Expressionist aesthetics became an effective language to articulate destruction and human loss, as, for example, in Käthe Kollwitz's antiwar prints, which circulated widely and were highly influential on leftist art. With its specific visual characteristics, such as distortions and stark contrasts between light and dark, Expressionism provided the right stylistic elements to paint "images of apocalypse, universal suffering, and redemption."[29]

These kinds of aesthetics are also observable in Zendeorudi's artwork. In light of Expressionism's political agency, it becomes evident that Zendeorudi's turn to Expressionist forms was far more than a mere signifier of modernity. Expressionism provided a political legacy and an effective yet figurative language to reject the decorum of the established Shi'ite iconography in Iran. Instead, it represented a visual means of intensifying Imam Hussein's suffering as an experience of pain, misery, and devastation. In his linocut, Zenderoudi articulates the suffering and murder of Hussein in contemporary language and thus points to the timeless und universal validity of Hussein's martyrdom in Shi'ite belief, which also informed the political and intellectual discourse in Iran from the 1960s on.

Zenderoudi narrates the events evolving around the battle of Karbala in a clearly structured composition from top to bottom. This meant that contemporary viewers equipped with the necessary and widespread cultural knowledge about Imam Hussein's suffering could easily follow Zenderoudi's presentation in a gallery space. Not only did the image's comprehensibility make the oral recitation of the traditional storyteller redundant in a certain sense, the linocut itself tells the story. Thus, the gallery space displaying *Who is this Hossein the World is so crazy about?* turns into a ritual space to memorialize the martyrdom of Imam Hussein, at a time when Shi'ite mourning rituals were not part of the Shah's ideology of modernization. Zenderoudi's artwork shows how modernist art provided fertile ground to delve into Shi'ite iconography and explore Iran's discourse of martyrdom on visual terms. This also clearly refers to the ongoing debates about *gharbzadegi* in Iran, which saw Iran's Shi'ite religion as the only possible cure for the country's westoxification.

[29] Wünsche, 'Expressionist Networks,' 18.

Parviz Tanavoli and His Rendition of Saqqakhaneh's *Emergence*

The sculptor, painter, and collector Parviz Tanavoli came across Zenderoudi's artwork in 1960 at the exhibition at Reza Abbasi Hall and became acquainted with it as his teacher at the newly founded College of Decorative Arts in Tehran. After Tanavoli had returned to Iran from his study of sculpture with Marino Marini in Milan, the young sculptor obtained a teaching position at the newly established College of Decorative Arts. During this time, he also opened Atelier Kaboud, a studio, and workshop. In this studio, he not only produced his own artworks but also held exhibitions for artist friends, such as Zenderoudi, for instance, who showed his work there in 1961.[30] In this way, his atelier became an alternative space for informal artistic exchange in Tehran.

Tanavoli played an important role in establishing the idea of *Saqqakhaneh* as an artistic group in Iranian art historiography. Alongside Zenderoudi, Tanavoli is often considered a founding member of the so-called *Saqqakhaneh School*. In his own rendition of *Saqqakhaneh's* genesis, Tanavoli significantly connects this phenomenon of Iran's contemporary arts to religious objects as a creative source, which can be found around *Saqqakhanehs* and other religious sites, such as shrines and *emamzadehs*. Recalling his visit with his friend Zenderoudi to the shrine of Abdol-Azim, Tanavoli states,

> One day on a visit to the Shrine of Shah 'Abd al-'Azim, I bought my usual stock of pilgrimage prayers, religious posters and other souvenirs. We returned to the studio and I got to work, while Zenderoudi painted by himself in a corner. A couple of hours later he had completed a sketch on cheap packing paper of one of these religious posters. This sketch, which may still be extant, resembled one of the religious posters and showed a hand embellished with writing.[31]

The Role of Shi'ite Shrines

The art historians Keshmirshekan and Daftari have pointed out that the incorporation of Persian traditional visual elements into artworks

---

[30] See Pakbaz and Emdadian (eds.), *Charles Hossein Zenderoudi*, 34.
[31] Ibid., 69.

by artists associated with *Saqqakhaneh* can, in particular, be seen as a visual manifestation of the search for a specific Iranian identity, a major element in the discourse on westoxification.[32] This meant that art criticism and art production associated with the category of *Saqqakhaneh* were situated in the ongoing political debates about Iran's westoxification (*gharbzadegi*). In her article, Alice Bombardier shows that al-e Ahmad's short story, *Ziyarat* (*The Pilgrimage, 1945*), in particular, played a crucial role in *Saqqakhaneh* artists' turn to Shi'ite iconography.[33] In his autobiographical account, al-e Ahmad narrates his pilgrimage to Imam Hussein's shrine in Karbala, Iraq. In this short story, Al-e Ahmad paints a vivid picture of his experience as a pilgrim and recounts in great detail the religious rites and prayers of the "ordinary" and "simple" people at the shrine.[34] As a "writing photographer," al-e Ahmad vividly depicts the religious objects of the shrine, such as textiles, inscriptions, padlocks, and grillwork, in order to grasp the pilgrims' emotional worlds.[35]

Similar to al-e Ahmad, Tanavoli also deliberately situates *Saqqakhaneh*'s emergence in relation to a visit to the shrine of Abdol-Azim. This not only explains the artistic inspiration but also alludes to the meaning of Islamic pilgrimage and the associated tradition of political activism in Iran. The Holy Shrine of Hazrat Abdol-Azim is a prominent site for Shi'ite pilgrimage in the city of Ray, near Tehran. Ray, which dates back to the Achaemenid Empire, was a central site for Islam's replacement of Zoroastrianism as the official state religion and remains a significant place for Shi'ite Islam to this day. With the advent of Islam, the citizens of Ray "accepted the Sunni sect of Islam, but during the first half of the eighth century AD the majority converted to *Imami* Shia, which later assumed the title of 'national religion' of Iran."[36]

---

[32] Hamid Keshmirshekan, 'Neo-Traditionalism and Modern Iranian Painting: The "Saqqa-khaneh" School in the 1960s,' *Iranian Studies*, vol. 38, no. 4 (2005), 607–630; Daftari, 'Another Modernism'; Daftari, 'Redefining Modernism'; Daftari, 'Persia Reframed.'

[33] Bombardier, 'A Contemporary Illustrated Qur'an,' 327.

[34] Ibid. and Bozorg Alavi, *Geschichte und Entwicklung der modernen persischen Literatur* (Berlin: Akademie Verlag, 1964), 221.

[35] Alavi, *Geschichte*, 221.

[36] Fakhri Haghani, 'The City of Ray and the Holy Shrine of Shah/Hazrat Abdol Azim: History of the Sacred and Secular in Iran through the Dialectic of Space,'

The shrine was built on the burial site of Abdol-Azim. Abdol-Azim was the son of Imam Hassan, the grandson of the prophet Muhammad, and "the third Imam in the Islamic sect of the Shi'a."[37] Abdol-Azim, the "faithful follower," had extensive knowledge of the Qur'an but was forced to live a "nomadic life, moving from one city to another, in order to escape the orders of the despotic caliphs."[38] A famous account of his death says that Abdol-Azim was murdered because he converted to Shi'ite Islam.[39] Thus, the faith of Abdol-Azim functions in Iran's discourse of Shi'ite martyrs and can easily be connected to the religious subtext of *Saqqakhanehs* as religious sites.

The shrine of Abdol-Azim, however, not only refers to Iran's religious history but also has a significant meaning for Iran's political history. The history of Shi'ite shrines, for instance, was closely connected to the practice of *bast*, which allowed taking sanctuary in shrines in order to escape governmental prosecution, since state forces were not permitted to enter these spaces. Or, as Peyman Eshaghi explains,

Taking sanctuary in Shi'ite shrines in Iran was a key practice in Iran's premodern legal system. It was understood through the framework of the authority of Shi'ite clergies and the sacredness of Shi'ite shrines for Iranians.[40]

The practice of *bast* was often accompanied by sit-ins at the shrine, which challenged the state's power and strengthened the clergy's authority in Iranian politics. It is often said that the Constitutional Revolution of 1905 started inside a holy shrine, when a sit-in of members of the clergy, *bazaaris*, bankers, and merchants forced the Qajar Shah Muzaffar al-Din to accept and introduce constitutional monarchy in Iran.[41] In the course of modern Iranian history, the Shrine of Abdol-Azim became an important institution of religious shelter for Iranian protestors and took on an important role in public memory. As Fakhri Haghani points out,

---

in Soheila Shahshahani (ed.), *Cities of Pilgrimage* (Berlin: Lit, 2009), 159–176, 163.
[37] Ibid.   [38] Ibid.   [39] Ibid.
[40] Peyman Eshaghi, 'Quietness beyond Political Power: Politics of Taking Sanctuary (Bast Neshini) in the Shi'ite Shrines of Iran,' *Iranian Studies*, vol. 49, no. 3 (2016), 493–514, 494.
[41] Ibid., 505.

For over a century, Iranian dissidents have utilised the religious space of Hezrat Abdol 'Azim as a crucial setting for tahasson (taking a refuge, lasting days, months, or years), exercising a civil resistance method against the injustice of despotic rulers. Tahasson, more effective and successful than the political parties in Iran, led to a rapid formation of a unified objective for mobilisation of the masses.[42]

Only during the reign of Reza Shah, and as a result of modernization and judicial reforms, did the new Pahlavi king abolish the century-old practice of taking political sanctuary in shrines. Thus, Tanavoli's conceptual emphasis on the Holy Shrine of Abdol-Azim as the site of the *Saqqakhaneh* movement's origin can be interpreted as an attempt to situate his conceptual understanding of *Saqqakhaneh* in the discourse of political resistance and the fight for political participation in Iran.

Purchasing and collecting common religious objects from their journey to the shrine enabled Tanavoli and Zenderoudi to develop a new artistic language of Iranian modernism. As the example of Zenderoudi's early works demonstrated, a shift in media transformed the religious objects of Shi'ite material culture into signs of refined aesthetic taste. At the same time, however, these religious objects also help establish an important link to the subject of pilgrimage. As Soheila Shahshahani points out,

To take relics from this experience, be it in the form of address, pictures or objects, help to remember the experience and to transmit it to others. Gifts and relics of religiosity bring others to the site.[43]

Creating modernist expression by drawing on religious objects as a source should be understood less as an expression of religiosity and rather as a symbol of cultural belonging, for, "this interest in material things seems opposed to spirituality," and "it is through these objects that one is reminded of the experience of pilgrimage."[44] The visual deployment of and references to items related to popular belief functions in the works of Tanavoli and Zenderoudi as signs of a specific Iranian and Shi'ite context, since "having gone to a pilgrimage is related to a chain of other identities and worldviews which going to a tourist site does not involve" and since in "a place of pilgrimage

---

[42] Haghani, 'The City of Ray,' 167.
[43] Shahshahani, 'Introduction and Cities of Pilgrimage in Iran,' 11–32, 14.
[44] Ibid., 17.

presence of others is confirmation of one's faith and being on the right path."[45] As the source of their artistic inspiration, the pilgrimage objects purchased refer to the broader issue of identity politics in Iran during the 1960s. This is possible because these "objects are the aid for reminiscence, for making one's house a sacred place and for making the experience last. In this way, the objects help to empower the person who wants to keep the feeling of transcendence."[46] During Reza Shah's rule and up until Mohammad Reza Shah's White Revolution, both kings tried to produce a politics of Iranian identity by excluding religiosity. As the discussion in Chapter 2 demonstrated, the Pahlavi kings instrumentalized the fields of archaeology, architecture, and literature to create alternative identity discourses based on Iran's imagined secular heritage, which persist until today in some parts of Iran's diaspora community. The transformation of religious objects into signs of modernist art functioned on a similar level. Modernist art based on religious items opens up an alternative discourse about a possible Iranian identity that places Islamic religiosity at the very core of this process. The artistic works relying on religious objects, thus, also represent an attempt to refute the accusations that Iranian modernism is a mere expression of Western imitation and to establish an Iranian version of modernist art.

Politics of the Period

From the 1953 Coup d'état to the "Quiet Revolution"

Scholarship on twentieth-century Iranian history often depicts the Shah as a resolute modernizer, whose secularization efforts triggered clerical opposition and organized resistance eventually leading to the Islamic Revolution. After the rise of the westoxification discourse, however, the Pahlavi state's relationship with Islam was framed through a complex negotiation of aestheticism and the reconceptualization of Shi'ite traditions through Western scholarship, as for instance that of the French philosopher Henry Corbin. The Pahlavi's instrumentalization of Islamic spirituality illustrates an important discursive shift in the royal politics that tried to create new visions of possible Iranian identity conceptions beyond Western rationality and secularism.

[45] Ibid.   [46] Ibid., 16.

A closer look at the ideological foundations of this new Pahlavi nationalism, however, demonstrates that "the quest for a modern Iranian identity embedded in a reconstructed Shi'ism owed more to European counter-Enlightenment discourses than any specific element in an indigenous Iranian tradition."[47] Thus, the new Pahlavi nationalism was "a bizarre mix of the growing gharbzadegi ideology and Corbin's eternal Iran."[48] Both ideologies, *gharbzadegi* and Corbin's spiritual findings, emerged as results of a close reading and translation of European anti-Enlightenment thought into the Iranian context, which eventually led to the politicization of Islam and the downfall of the monarchy.

Especially after the CIA-sponsored coup d'état in 1953 and the resulting reinstatement of Mohammad Reza Shah, the Shah's legitimacy as ruler of Iran was questioned. During this time, oppositional voices that perceived the monarchy as an outdated and contradictory model of power in the age of modernization demanded political participation and democratic rights.[49] The institutionalization of *Saqqakhaneh* as the decisive reflection of a state-promoted modernism and its political instrumentalization to display Iran's modernity in the arts, however, were closely tied to the Shah's modernization program, the White Revolution, as developed between 1958 and 1963. The White Revolution not only was a program of modernizing reforms to transform Iran into an industrialized Western country but rather also served the construction of a suitable ideology. As Ali Ansari explains,

The 'White Revolution' can be interpreted as an attempt by the Shah and his supporters to provide a legitimating myth for the Pahlavi monarchy by reconciling the contradictions implicit in these various ideologies in the person of the monarch.[50]

Particularly, after the publication of al-e Ahmad's essay, *Gharbzadegi*, oppositional forces used the trope of westoxification to criticize the autocratic rule of Mohammad Reza Shah and Western cultural domination. Most interestingly, a cultural and intellectual shift occurred

---

[47] Ali Mirsepassi, *Iran's Quiet Revolution: The Downfall of the Pahlavi State* (Cambridge: Cambridge University Press, 2019), 160.
[48] Ibid., 167.   [49] Ibid.
[50] Ali M. Ansari, 'The Myth of the White Revolution: Mohammad Reza Shah, "Modernization" and the Consolidation of Power,' *Middle Eastern Studies*, vol. 37, no. 3 (2001), 1–24, 2.

during this time, and the Pahlavi state itself started to embrace and appropriate the *gharbzadegi* discourse and its critique of Western modernity. The scholar Mirsepassi has used the phrase "Iran's Quiet Revolution" to describe the cultural transformation that occurred, when the Pahlavi elites contributed to the distribution of *gharbzadegi's* inherent antimodern ideology.[51] Although both the Pahlavi state and the opposition used the antimodern critique for different political ends, for both sides, *gharbzadegi* represented an important device in the nation-building process and means to stage an allegedly binary opposition between the secular West and the spiritual East. Or, as Mirsepassi explains, "it provided a powerful sense of national solidarity, invoking Iranian and Islamic past traditions and identity as an alternative to Western values."[52]

For the Shah, the appropriation of an anti-Western critique was a political strategy to justify his royal dictatorship, defame Iranian leftists as Westernized, and eventually declare democracy as alien to Iranian culture. This strategy "appropriated the anti-Western, and deeply anti-secular, Westoxification discourse that had been voiced by religious and leftist regime opponents" with the goal of weakening the public movement that demanded liberalization and democratic rights.[53] According to Mirsepassi, the instrumentalization of *gharbzadegi* had ideological motives:

By defining both the radical Iranian left and liberals as Western-inspired, and alien to Iranian and Islamic tradition, the Pahlavi endeavored to establish itself as the authentic governing force of Iran, against the historical tide of political and cultural imperialism.[54]

Concomitantly, the Pahlavi state appropriated the Iranian-Islamic concepts of identity, which had evolved from the opposition's debates about westoxification, as evidence that the Iranian people did not have "the required education and intellectual maturity" for democratic principles and thus were not ready for democracy.[55]

This historical background explains why the monarchy could easily adopt the political implications of the *gharbzadegi* discourse and ultimately *Saqqakhaneh* for its own political purposes. The oppositional discourse of *gharbzadegi* was not only articulated by leftists

---

[51] Mirsepassi, *Iran's Quiet Revolution*.   [52] Ibid., 3.   [53] Ibid., 27.
[54] Ibid., 3.   [55] Ansari, 'The Myth of the White Revolution,' 18.

intellectuals, such as Fardid and al-e Ahmad but also institutionalized by the Pahlavi monarchy through important and close associates of the Pahlavi court, such as the philosophers Seyed Hossein Nasr and Daryush Shaygan. Moreover, the sociologist Ehsan Naraghi and, most prominently, the French orientalist Henry Corbin (1903–1978) promoted Islamic spiritual heritage as a major part of Iranian nationalism.[56]

Henry Corbin's studies on Persian and Islamic philosophy and his promotion of "Spiritual Islam" as a specific Iranian expression of Islam, in particular, provided the Pahlavi state with fertile grounds on which to embrace Shi'ite religion as an essential part of Iranian identity. Corbin maintained a close relationship to the Pahlavi court and was also involved in the conceptual planning of celebrations for the Persian monarchy's 2,500th anniversary in 1971. In turn, the monarchy sponsored Corbin's research on Iran's ancient and spiritual heritage under the institutional roof of the Imperial Iranian Academy, founded by Queen Farah Diba in 1974 and directed by Corbin's former student, Seyed Hossein Nasr.[57]

Trained as a philosopher, Corbin encountered Persian mysticism, when Louis Massignon, director of the Islamic Studies department at the Sorbonne in Paris, introduced him to the teachings of Shahab al-Din Yahya ibn Habash Suhrawardi (d. 578/1191). For Corbin, becoming acquainted with the Persian philosopher Suhrawardi was a life-changing event. As he recalls, "By my encounter with Suhrawardi, my spiritual destiny in my passage through this world was sealed. This Platonism of his expressed itself in terms belonging to the Zoraoastrian angelology of Ancient Persia and in so doing illuminated the path I had been searching for."

In an interview with *Bonyad Monthly*, a magazine published by the Shah's sister, Ashraf Pahlavi, Corbin explains his ideas about Iran's spiritual heritage, which seem, to him, to represent a cure for the rationality of Western modernity.

You live in a space filled with spiritual and mystic traditions. You live in a world in which Avicenna, Molla Sadra, and Sohrewardi have existed. In fact, you live in a world that has all the necessary essentials for the spiritual

---

[56] Mirsepassi, *Iran's Quiet Revolution*, 27.
[57] Steven M. Wasserstrom, *Religion after Religion. Gershom Scholem, Mircea Eliade and Henry Corbin at Eranos* (Princeton: Princeton University Press, 1997), 151.

transformation of the human condition. In the poor and miserable West, there is no spirituality, which is humanity's most important need.[58]

Corbin's critique of Western modernity was based not only on medieval Persian philosophers but also on his studies of the German philosopher Martin Heidegger. The latter played a decisive role in Corbin's interpretation of Islamic and Sufi traditions as part of a possible alternative modernity. Corbin became most well-known as a translator of Heidegger's work into French. For Corbin, Heidegger's writings constituted an important methodology for approaching Islamic philosophy und mysticism. Contrary to the orientalist tradition, Corbin did not try to paint a picture of the "oriental other" but rather operated on the "premise that," as Nile Green explains, "there is neither truly east nor west in the geographical sense, that there is no dichotomy of 'Western philosophy' and 'Islamic philosophy', but only philosophy, only phenomena, can come as a welcome relief, and indeed escape."[59]

With his turn to Iran's spiritual tradition, Corbin also contributed to the creation of a timeless and universal ideal of ancient Persia, which strongly ignored the sociopolitical conditions of contemporary Iran. In his 1946 publication, *Les motifs Zoroastrien dans la philosophie de Sohrawardi*, Corbin maps out a meta-historical narrative "from the ancient Persian prophet Zoroaster through the gnostic prophet Mani, spanning the medieval philosophers Suhrawardi and Mulla Sadra, and eventuating in the Peacock Throne of Reza Shah Pahlavi."[60] This trajectory of an alleged continuity from pre-Islamic times to the present enabled Corbin's "distinctively Persianizing approach to Islam."

The idea of a Persian Islam was also highly welcomed by Mohammad Reza Shah, who, on the one hand, "showed himself as a Western, modern king to the international community," but, on the other hand, "invoked the rituals of Islamic kingship, with their ancient roots, in his performance of kingship at the local and provincial levels."[61] Contrary

---

[58] Henry Corbin, 'An Interview with Henry Corbin: The Inner East,' *Bonyad Monthly*, no. 1 (1977), 6. Cited from Mirsepassi, *Iran's Quiet Revolution*, 40.

[59] Nile Green, 'Between Heidegger and the Hidden Imam: Reflections on Henry Corbin's Approaches to Mystical Islam,' *Method & Theory in the Study of Religion*, vol. 17, no. 3 (2005), 219–226, 220.

[60] Wasserstrom, *Religion after Religion*, 134.

[61] Ali Karjoo-Ravary, 'Shi'i Rituals in Pahlavi Iran: Audio Recordings from the Ajam Archive,' https://ajammc.com/2017/11/10/archive-iranian-islam-1979-shii-rituals-mohammad-reza-shah/, accessed 14 January 2020.

to general perception, Mohammad Reza Shah, who is often seen as a ruler who aimed for radical modernization and secularization, also performed religious services and went on pilgrimages to holy Islamic sites, such as his *hajj* to Mecca and other sites of importance for Islam in Iran.[62] The royal attention to Iran's Shi'ite religion enabled the Shah to propagate a new, state-sponsored version of modernity, which embraced Iranian-Islamic traditions. This unfolded primarily against the backdrop of the growing *gharbzadegi* discourse and its inherent critique of Western modernity. In his 1973 book, *Toward the Great Civilization*, Mohammad Reza Shah emphasized his divine right to rule Iran, recalling his divine visions and telling of how Imam Reza himself saved his life during an illness in his childhood. This illustrates how the Shah staged himself as God's chosen leader and how he used the adaptation of "an anti-Western and nativist vision of Iran" as a decisive political tool in the 1960s to "offer a legitimizing ideology for an increasingly autocratic monarchical rule and rapidly modernizing society."[63] In reaction to the *gharbzadegi* discourse, the Pahlavi state tried to reconcile its modernization programs with a "new Pahlavi nationalism" propagating "Iranian identity politics inspired by an intellectual combination of Henry Corbin's Orientalist worldview and the gharbzadegi ideology (two overlapping visions) popularized during this period."[64]

In the late 1970s, during the years leading up to the Islamic Revolution, the Shah had fully embraced Islam as part of Iranian cultural identity and propagated Islamic religion as a means to repel imperialist and colonialist interference. Following this view, he states:

> Our fundamental aim in building Iran's society of today and tomorrow is to promulgate and fortify as much as possible the true meaning of Islam in our society, so that the society of the era of the "Great Civilization" will be one truly blessed with faith, purity, virtue, and maximum spirituality.[65]

The Naming of *Saqqakhaneh*

The term *Saqqakhaneh* as a designation for modernist art in this period emerged in two phases. In newspaper articles published between 1963 and 1968, the art critic Emami recognized similarities in the

[62] Ibid.   [63] Mirsepassi, *Iran's Quiet Revolution*, 153.   [64] Ibid., 154.
[65] Mohammad Reza Pahlavi, *Toward the Great Civilization: A Dream Revisited* (London: Satrap Publishing, 1994), 161.

artistic practice of a loose group of artists whose works he had encountered in Tehran's art galleries and at Tehran Biennials and whom he called the *Saqqakhaneh* School. In his texts, Emami conceptualized *Saqqakhaneh* in the broader discussion of westoxification, one of the most substantial leftist and intellectual political debates of the 1960s, and its demands for an alternative modernity.

The state's propagation of *Saqqakhaneh* as a movement deflected attention away from the anti-Western underlying many of the works. The fact, that many artists referenced traditional culture independent of one another suggests how dispersed this critique was. Turning this artistic critique into a movement and institutionalizing it as a state-sponsored reflection of modernism minimized the critical impact of their artistic production. *Saqqakhaneh*'s memorialization as an apolitical movement and the erasure of its ideology of resistance become visible in the 1977 catalog published on the occasion of the *Saqqakhaneh* exhibition at the TMoCA, which continues to characterize the reception of *Saqqakhaneh* until today. This small book represents the only primary source of *Saqqakhaneh*. The catalog features works by the artists Hossein Zenderoudi, Parviz Tanavoli, Faramarz Pilaram, Massoud Arabshahi, Sadeq Tabrizi, Mansour Ghandriz, Nasser Ovissi, and Jazeh Tabatabaie.

Emami's Rendition of Saqqakhaneh's *Artistic Evolution*

Through the nomenclature *Saqqakhaneh*, Emami created an unprecedented connection between modernist art, associated with Europe, and an element of Iranian culture that intimately connected everyday life to Shi'ite faith. Modernist Iranian expression that patently had no relationship with religion could not avoid its imprint; such art questioned the very possibility of the modern secular state's mandate to separate religion and society.

To designate this modernist art movement, Emami used the word for sacred public fountains. *Saqqakhanehs* provide water for Shi'ite believers and people passing through public spaces. These architectural spaces are mainly found in older parts of Iranian cities and in bazaars. Their decoration may range from a simple brass hand and drinking bowl to calligraphic texts, candles, and objects such as padlocks or pieces of cloth, knotted around the grillwork, indicative of private devotion and prayers. Installed in a niche and connected to a cistern,

The Naming of Saqqakhaneh

Saqqakhanehs function as memorials for Imam Hussein and his followers, who were denied access to water in the heat of Karbala.

In the 1960s and 1970s, many artists frequently included recognizable elements of the visual culture of *Saqqakhanehs*. Emami identified features characteristic of *Saqqakhaneh* in Zenderoudi's artworks, in particular, and his incorporation of Shi'ite visual traditions. According to Emami, Zenderoudi recreated, in particular with his linocut *Who is this Hossein the World is so crazy about?*, which was analyzed earlier in this chapter, the atmosphere of *Muharram* mourning rituals to commemorate Hussein's martyrdom, which is also the main function of *Saqqakhanehs*.

I also remember, years later, looking at another early work of Zenderoudi at the home of another friend. This was a huge lino-cut that traced the events of Kerbala in numbered sequence, not unlike a Coffeehouse painting. By looking at these Zenderoudi canvases, the viewer was reminded of Shi'ite shrines and assemblies. The atmosphere was one of Moharram mourning, of candles reflected in shiny brass bowls, of chants of "Ya Hossein" and "Blessed be the prophet." The atmosphere was a religious one, but not as lofty and grand as that of the Shah Mosque in Isfahan, nor as spacious and impersonal as that of the Sepahsalar Mosque in Tehran, but intimate and close at hand as that of the neighborhood Saqqakhaneh round the corner.[66]

For Emami, Zenderoudi's painting not only refers to traditional arts but rather takes Persian visual heritage as an inspirational point of departure to create a modern visual code for a religious story. Zenderoudi's paintings unfold, according to Emami, an emotional impact that transports the viewers from a gallery space straight into their "neighborhood Saqqakhaneh round the corner."[67] This shows that, for Emami, modernist art was not an expression of the state's secularity but rather both a way to revoke and preserve Shi'ite traditions, which had been excluded from official cultural politics.

In June 1963, after seeing works by Tanavoli, Zenderoudi, Mansour Ghandriz, Faramarz Pilaram, Nasser Oveissi, and Behzad Golpaygani at an exhibition at Gilgamesh Gallery in Tehran, Emami composed a written record of his idea of *Saqqakhaneh* up to that point. He explains,

I first noticed the converging paths of these artists in Third Tehran Biennal (1962) and gave them a name, and I said that as a group they were the most

[66] Emami, 'Saqqakhaneh School Revisited.' [67] Ibid.

dynamic and presented the most promise among all those who were trying to pull off something Iranian.[68]

On the basis of visual similarities in the artworks and the artists' attempt to incorporate traditional Iranian elements into their artistic practice, Emami summarized their works under the rubric of *Saqqakhaneh* because they were "embracing the strongest and newest trends in Modern Iranian Painting."[69]

Due to their revival of Persian visual traditions in their artworks, *Saqqakhaneh* artists were more innovative in achieving a local modernism than any earlier modernist artists, as Emami states,

> So far most attempts at creating something new out of the old by Iran's contemporary artists have failed, because these attempts have been aimed at maintaining the stylized forms of Persepolis, or at dislocating the equally stylised forms of Persian miniatures for the sake of the new, an act which was foredoomed because it was undertaken with a total disregard for the characteristics of the rigid frozen forms it set out to wreck. But now the lowly materials, which Zenderoudi and his friends have put their hands on, show a much larger degree of flexibility and adaptability.[70]

In Emami's appreciation of *Saqqakhaneh*, one can see that he also promoted a socialist understanding of modernist art. The *Saqqakhaneh* artists' selection of cheap materials, instead of an emphasis on high art, functioned as a source of artistic innovation. For Emami, the integration of popular materials, such as talismans, prints, and metal works, which were often perceived as cheap ephemera and not as high art, made *Saqqakhaneh* superior to other so-called neo-traditionalist artistic movements.[71] Indeed, the conditions of artistic productions were a major concern in Emami's texts and articles. Between 1962 and 1968, he mentioned them several times in his journalistic texts about cultural life in Tehran for the English daily newspaper *Kayhan International*. He strongly promoted the development of an active art market with an adequate infrastructure of art

---

[68] Karim Emami, 'Making Reciprocity Stick: Artists are Becoming Critics,' in Houra Yavari (ed.), *Karim Emami on Modern Iranian Culture, Literature & Art* (New York: New York: Persian Heritage Foundation, 2014), 226–227.
[69] Karim Emami, 'A New Iranian School,' in Yavari, *Karim Emami*, 160–162, 161.
[70] Ibid., 161.   [71] Ibid., 160–162.

institutions, collectors, and buyers.[72] In his articles, Emami constantly reflects on the role and responsibility of a critic in a newly emerging artistic scene experimenting with modernist forms of expression. With his writings, Emami tried to make modernist art more accessible to a broader public and to narrow the gap between the audience and artists. Most people attending events such as the first exhibitions of modernist visual arts and film screenings belonged to a privileged audience composed of artists, intellectuals, and foreigners living in Tehran. For the newly established middle class and the growing number of university students, participation in the newly founded cultural life became a very important way of indicating their affiliation with an educated urban elite.

The College of Decorative Arts, where many artists associated with *Saqqakhaneh* taught or studied, also became a space for political discussions. In a personal interview, the artist Parviz Tanavoli recalled how al-e Ahmad used his teaching position at the school to discuss politics and the consequences of westoxification with students.[73] Thanks to their shared time teaching at the College, Emami was personally acquainted with al-e Ahmad's thought. Emami translated many of al-e Ahmad's works into English and made them available to non-Persian readers.[74] For Emami, al-e Ahmad was one of the most important contemporary writers in Iran, and his interpretation of *gharbzadegi* was the crucial contribution that opened the discourse on westernization to a broader audience.

His last published work is the much discussed Gharbzadegi, which criticized westernization in Iran. Possessing a sharp analytical mind, Al-e Ahmad in his writings bombards the reader with pungent ideas that are wholly stimulating and thought-provoking, if not always acceptable or practical. And to sugarcoat the pill, there is his delightful racy prose which sheds many of the more

---

[72] Karim Emami, 'Artists Must Be Able to Sell, April 21, 1964,' in Yavari, *Karim Emami*, 173–175, 174.
[73] Personal interview with Parviz Tanavoli by the author, 12 August 2015, Tehran.
[74] Emami translated, for example, Jalal al-e Ahmad, 'Crisis in Education: The School Principal,' in Michael Hillmann (ed.), *Iranian Society: An Anthology of Writings by Jalal Al-e Ahmad* (Lexington, KY: Mazda Publication, 1988), 80–88. Emami translated numerous works by Iranian writers into English language, including, for instance, works by authors such as Forrukh Farrokhzad, Nima Yushij, Ebrahim Golestan, and Golam Hossein Saedi. At the same time, Emami also translated English literature into Persian, including Scott Fitzgerald's *The Great Gatsby*, which he translated as *Gatsby-e Bozorg* in 1965.

usual writing conventions and finds strength instead in a generous dose of living colloquialisms.[75]

Emami's Concept of Saqqakhaneh *in the Context of Anticolonial Resistance*

The epistemic violence of westernization had only increased since the 1953 military coup, backed by the United States and Great Britain, and the reinstitution of Mohammad Reza Shah, all of which led to a politicization of society. Al-e Ahmad's essay, *Gharbzadegi*, is a significant example of how intellectual circles inside and outside Iran condemned the imperial interferences of foreign powers as acts of colonialism, leading to the rise of the anticolonial resistance in Iran. Emami's critical approach to the modernist expression of *Saqqakhaneh* and classification of it in the context of an Iranian, rather than a European modernity is tremendously important for the political discourse in Iran during the 1960s. This strategy helped establish a counter-narrative to the dominant perception of modernist arts as a symbol of successful modernization and secularization in Iran. Similar to al-e Ahmad and other members of the opposition, Emami demands an Iranian modernism not based on the imitation of Western paradigms of modern art and uses terms of hybridity as a creative source to achieve artistic innovation. In his texts, al-e Ahmad focuses on the imperial and colonial aspects of modernity and hegemonic power relationships between the East and the West, while highlighting the effects of Western modernity on Iran and its population. Emami, in turn, uses Al-e Ahmad's postcolonial critique of modernity to establish the concept of *Saqqakhaneh* as a subversive counter-narrative in the fields of visual arts. Emami's recognition of the power of popular forms to undermine the imposition of modernism suggests that he saw artistic modernism as a form of epistemic violence. As Gayatri Spivak argues, a central role of the postcolonial scholar is to distinguish between the truth and fiction of imperialist historiography. According to Spivak, historiography is not primarily an act of juxtaposing objective facts because the history of modernity is often conceived of from a Western or colonialist perspective based on the "epistemic violence" of "an

[75] Karim Emami, 'The School Principal, October 19th, 1964,' in Yavari, *Karim Emami*, 74–79, 74.

The Naming of Saqqakhaneh 173

alien ideology established as the only truth, and a set of human sciences busy establishing the 'native' as self-consolidating Other ('epistemic violence')."[76]

Against this background, Emami's classification and categorization of *Saqqakhaneh* exemplify a significant attempt to create an alternative representation against imperial conceptions of modernity and modernism in Iran. In this context, Emami's conceptual creation of *Saqqakhaneh* can also be understood as an endeavor to "produce an alternative historical narrative of the 'worlding' of what is today called 'the Third World.'"[77] Two significant strategies Emami employs in his writings are the "other" and the staging of Iran's artistic difference to the dominant Western modernist styles of expression. In his texts, Emami repeatedly accentuates the particularity of Iran's modernist expression by emphasizing the topic of rediscovery and the revival of folkloristic elements of Shi'ite culture as a source of artistic innovation. The topic of rediscovery is, according to Spivak, an important strategy of differentiation that allows one to "think of the Third World as distant cultures, exploited but with rich intact heritages waiting to be recovered, interpreted, and curricularized in English translation."[78] It is also an important tool that supports Iran's participation in the "emergence of the 'Third World' as a convenient signifier."[79] Although Iran was never formally colonized, Iran's nineteenth- and twentieth-century political leaders gave economic power to foreign companies and governments in exchange for military or financial support. Western political influence and imperialist ambitions decisively shaped Iran's modern history. The Iranian political discourse in the 1960s and 1970s condemned Western interference in Iran and merged global anticolonialism with a politicized radical Islam, which led to the downfall of the monarchy.[80] For many Iranian intellectuals, such as Fardid, al-e Ahmad, Shariati, and Bahman Nirumand, Iran was suffering deeply from Western imperialism and colonialism. In his publications, the exiled Iranian intellectual Bahman Nirumand

---

[76] Gayatri Chakravorty Spivak, 'Three Women's Texts and a Critique of Imperialism,' *Critical Inquiry*, vol. 12, no. 1, *Race, Writing, and Difference*, Autumn (1985), 243–261, 254.
[77] Gayatri Chakravorty Spivak, 'The Rani of Sirmur: An Essay in Reading the Archives,' *History and Theory*, vol. 24, no. 3 (1985), 247–272, 247.
[78] Ibid.   [79] Ibid.
[80] Kohn and McBride, *Political Theories of Decolonization*, 35–36.

disseminated the idea that Iran was politically dependent on foreign powers due to its "colonization." This would have a decisive influence on the politicization of the German student movement.[81] For Frantz Fanon, the case of Iran illustrates a new twentieth-century version of colonialism, which is "more elegant, less bloodthirsty" and for which "the important thing is not whether such-and-such a region in Africa is under French or Belgian sovereignty, but rather that the economic zones are respected."[82] Fanon sees the 1953 coup as a colonial crime, which overthrew a national liberation movement for decolonization because Mosaddeq's attempt to nationalize Iran's oil threatened Western capitalist interests and the flow of global capital.[83]

In this context, Emami's historiographical invention of *Saqqakhaneh* and its references to Persian arts can be interpreted as an attempt to situate Iran in the broader context of a "Third World" country participating in the global anticolonial movement. This stands in stark contrast to Pahlavi Iran, which, as a close ally of Western powers during the Cold War, sought an equal partnership with Western nations.

Emami conceptualized *Saqqakhaneh* at a time when popular Shi'ite rituals such as *ta'ziyeh* and religious institutions such as *Saqqakhanehs* had declined in their significance for official cultural politics in the 1960s due to the Shah's modernization and secularization programs. Nevertheless, metaphors and images borrowed from Shi'ite theology played a major role in the intellectual discourse of the 1960s, when Iranian leftist intellectuals merged elements from Marxism and Shi'ite Islam to establish a political opposition toward Pahlavi rule.[84] This phenomenon connected leftists with members of the clergy, as Janet Afary and Kevin Anderson explain,

The new discourse also expressed solidarity with several more traditional figures, especially Ayatollah Khomeini, who opposed the government of Muhammad Reza Shah and his agenda of reform.[85]

In reaction to Khomeini's critique, Mohammad Reza Shah held a referendum in 1963 to demonstrate that his ambitious reform program, the White Revolution, enjoyed widespread public approval. The so-called White Revolution included several points intended to

---

[81] See Slobodian, *Foreign Front*. [82] Fanon, *The Wretched of the Earth*, 66.
[83] Ibid. [84] Afary and Anderson, *Foucault and the Iranian Revolution*, 57.
[85] Ibid.

modernize the country, among them land reform, women's suffrage, and the formation of literary corps.[86] But, these reforms also meant a loss of power for the clergy, which turned the clergy and their ideological leader Ayatollah Khomeini into fervent critics of the Shah and his political programs. In this context, Said Arjomand writes,

> In March 1963, holding a copy of the Koran in one hand and a copy of the Constitution in the other, Khomeini publicly accused the Shah of violating his oath to defend Islam and the Constitution.[87]

After Khomeini's verbal outbursts, Mohammad Reza Shah attacked Khomeini's headquarters in Qom and arrested several students. In June 1963, during *Ashura* (the days of commemoration of Imam Hussein), Khomeini condemned the Shah's politics in his sermons. In his speech delivered in Qom, Ayatollah Khomeini drew parallels between the tyrant Yazid and the Shah. For Khomeini, the Umayyad Caliphate not only claimed religious leadership but also attempted to uproot the prophet's family and, thus, the religion of Islam as a whole. Khomeini and other members of the opposition effectively staged Mohammad Reza Shah as contemporary personification of Yazid and, therefore, as a threat to Islam, the Qur'an, and the clergy. Consequently, Khomeini and his followers presented their political opposition toward the ruling system of the Pahlavi monarchy as a reenactment of the battle of Karbala and claimed for themselves the role of Imam Hussein and his fellow martyrs. During the Revolution, the topic of Karbala and the discourse of Shi'ite martyrdom became the central paradigm for the revolutionaries.[88] Khomeini's 1963 speech would later become a central document for later revolutionary discourse, since, in it, Khomeini established a close connection between Shi'ite mythology and leftist critiques of Western imperialism. After Khomeini's speech, the Shah detained him and sent Khomeini into exile in Najaf.[89]

It was only two days after Khomeini's speech that Emami established a crucial link between modernist artistic expression and Shi'ite mythology in his article. Emami deliberately situated his art-historiographical invention of *Saqqakhaneh* within the intellectual

---

[86] Said Amir Arjomand, *The Turban for the Crown: The Islamic Revolution in Iran* (New York: Oxford University Press, 1988), 85.
[87] Ibid., 85–86.
[88] Afary and Anderson, *Foucault and the Iranian Revolution*, 57–58.
[89] Ibid., 58.

discourse of the 1960s in Iran. Many of the artworks referencing religion preceded this crisis, however, and Emami's own designation of *Saqqakhaneh* was applied only in retrospect. Emami coined the term *Saqqakhaneh* at a time when the discourse of *gharbzadegi* was in full swing and clerics and liberal intellectuals contributed equally to the resistance movement against the Shah's politics and, as they saw it, blind adoption of Western modernity in Iran. In the broader discourse of *gharbzadegi*, Emami tried to establish a concept of modernist art, which could be easily distinguished from Western modernism because of its deep roots in Shi'ite Islam. Thus, the conceptual creation of *Saqqakhaneh* helped Emami communicate artistic modernism as a specific Iranian achievement, which was not alien to Iranian traditions but rather emerged from Iran's own cultural past. Like al-e Ahmad and other Iranian intellectuals, Emami demanded an artistic expression, which was politically committed and which refused to be reduced to mere decoration. He explains,

There are many genres that a modern artist may turn to, but what is really important for him is to remain honest and sincere to himself, to do what he is doing with conviction and to avoid blind imitation of others, be they European, American or Iranian.[90]

In Emami's view, the abstract art displayed at the Fourth Tehran Biennial in 1964 was especially at risk of pursuing mainly decorative purposes.

At the exhibition, one can see tens of characterless 'hodge-podge' abstracts whose forms or colors are neither evocative nor suggestive in any sense, and whose compositions are certainly no shining examples of inner constructions. I think it would be safe to say in their case that the paintings are aesthetically meaningless to the artist as to the viewer.[91]

Saqqakhaneh's Existence as a Group

Saqqakhaneh: *A "School" of Modernism*

The artists associated with *Saqqakhaneh* had no artistic manifesto stating the group's artistic or ideological goals. The term

[90] Karim Emami, 'Saqqa-khaneh Dominant, April 14, 1964,' Yavari, *Karim Emami*, 170–172, 170.
[91] Ibid.

Saqqakhaneh unites a wide range of artists and artworks and encompasses highly diverse forms of artistic expressions. What they all have in common is their incorporation of local elements from Iran's visual heritage into their artistic expression. This common aesthetic strategy of seeking artistic inspiration in Iran's past became particularly visible in curated exhibitions, such as the Tehran Biennial, gallery shows, or presentations in spaces run by artists. More than their artistic collaboration, it was the art criticism that evolved from reviews of these curated exhibitions, in particular, which contributed to *Saqqakhaneh*'s consolidation. Emami and Tanavoli's various writings, in particular, demonstrate that they did not use a consistent term to define *Saqqakhaneh* in their texts. In some texts, they speak of *Saqqakhaneh* as a school, a style, or even a movement. To further investigate *Saqqakhaneh's* existence as a group, in this section, I will discuss the tension between Emami's notion of *Saqqakhaneh* as a school of Iranian modernism and its stylistic manifestation of a local modernist expression.

In his texts, Emami speaks of *Saqqakhaneh* as school of modernism and attributes to this aesthetics a political impetus. The naming and classification of artistic "schools" is a central art-historiographical practice established in the eighteenth century which, when applied to *Saqqakhaneh*, makes the term appear to be a major art-historical paradigm. The designation "school" is usually connected to a person or a geographical region and speaking of schools often indicates certain stylistic and visual characteristics, which were adopted by students and successors of "great master artists." Not only artists, however, but topographies too can produce schools with distinctive regional and national features in the respective artworks.[92] Especially in Iranian art history, the categorization of Persian painting into various schools represents an important formalist tool of classification, which is reflected, for example, in the Shiraz School, the Herat School, the Tabriz School, or the Isfahan School. The Isfahan school of painting and calligraphy, for instance, is a term used to refer to Safavid painting from the first half of the seventeenth century. In an Iranian context, Western scholarship has contributed decisively to the classification and

---

[92] See Ulrich Pfisterer, 'Schule,' in Ulrich Pfisterer, *Metzler Lexikon Kunstwissenschaft: Ideen, Methoden, Begriffe* (Stuttgart: Metzler, 2019), 402–406.

categorization of Persian arts.[93] The term "Isfahan School" was applied in the 1950s to describe Safavid paintings under the patronage of Shah Abbas I, which, on a stylistic level, referred to the Safavid court painter Reza Abbasi, who experimented with Western pictorial concepts, such as perspective, shading, and modeling.[94]

In his conceptualization of *Saqqakhaneh*, however, Emami does not use the school's characteristic features to define a style but instead connects it to the socialist legacy of art movements. According to Emami, the artists had "several things in common: their friendship, the Tehran School of Decorative Arts, where they have been or still are students, and their tapping of the most popular, and hither-to, not-so-respected domains of Persian art to obtain their raw material."[95] The College of Decorative Arts (*Honarkada-e honar-hāy-e taz'ini*) was founded in 1961 and provided instruction in "various fields of study such as decorative painting, graphic design, sculpture, and interior architecture with a major emphasis on applied arts."[96] The program encouraged the students "to seek local sources of inspiration, symbols and idioms, and to familiarize themselves with Iran's decorative heritage."[97] For Emami, the College's establishment was a "landmark in the history of modern art in Iran" because, with its focus on applied arts and iconographies from Persian popular culture, it represented a "breeding ground" for Iranian modernism.[98]

Due to the school's focus on traditional craft techniques and "aim of training experts in the applied arts,"[99] the College is often called "Iranian Bauhaus." For the artist and graduate of the College of

---

[93] See Arthur Upham Pope and Phyllis Ackerman, *A Survey of Persian Art from Prehistoric Times to the Present* (London: Oxford University Press, 1938).

[94] Massumeh Farhad, 'Isfahan xi. SCHOOL OF PAINTING AND CALLIGRAPHY,' *Encyclopædia Iranica*, Online edition (2007), www.iranicaonline.org/articles/art-in-iran-xi-post-qajar, accessed 23 October 2019.

[95] Ibid.

[96] Abbas Mashhadizadeh, 'Abbas Mashhadizadeh Talks History of Iranian Academic Art,' *Honaronline* (2007), www.honaronline.ir/Section-visual-4/96791-abbas-mashhadizadeh-talks-history-of-iranian-academic-art, accessed 23 October 2019.

[97] Keshmirshekan, 'Saqqa-kana.'

[98] Emami, 'ART IN IRAN xi. POST-QAJAR,' *Encyclopædia Iranica*, Online edition (2009), www.iranicaonline.org/articles/art-in-iran-xi-post-qajar, accessed 23 October 2019.

[99] Ibid.

Decorative Arts, Abbas Mashhadizadeh, for instance, the only differences were only its location in Tehran and Hushang Kazemi's directorship instead of Walter Gropius'.[100] Art historian Combiz Moussavi Agghadam has pointed out that during the 1960s and 1970s, the concepts of Bauhaus became an important model for Iranian artists to enhance art's social function in the Iranian context.[101] This is reflected in Emami's text, when he compares the practice of *Saqqakhaneh* artists with that of Iranian craftsmen.

Saqqā-ḵāna canvases or sculpture pieces bore direct links with Iran's cultural heritage; these artists could be in fact considered descendants of Iran's famous craftsmen of earlier centuries – illuminators, goldsmiths, engravers, and calligraphers – who beautified a thousand and one utilitarian objects with intricate floral scrolls or calligraphic lines.[102]

The implicit connection of the Tehran School with the German modernist Bauhaus movement (1919–1933) locates the artistic practice of the Iranian artists ideologically within the genealogy of Socialism's influence on art. Bauhaus's return to craftsmanship was highly influenced by William Morris and the British Arts and Crafts Movement. As a confessing socialist, William Morris "politicized the discourse of functionalist aesthetics" and transformed the question of nineteenth-century artistic production in terms of a recovery of medieval craft traditions.[103] To articulate his socialist understanding of art and architecture, Morris employed Karl Marx's dialectical materialism. As Lauren S. Weingarden explains, "Morris identified a system of craft values to facilitate the process of disalienation and, in turn, a peaceful revolution from capitalism to socialism."[104] Walter Gropius appropriated Morris's socialist utopian thoughts on art and their impact on the democratization of society for the conception of Bauhaus. Like Morris, Gropius tried to overcome the separation of traditional craftsmanship and "high art" by demanding the equality of artists and craftsmen. Gropius regarded Bauhaus as a "new guild of craftsmen" and

---

[100] Abbas Mashhadizadeh, 'Honar dar zendegi va zendegi dar honar: Darbare-ye Lilit Teryan,' http://old.sharghdaily.ir/pdf/90-09-03/vijeh/22.pdf, accessed 21 October 2019.
[101] Moussavi-Aghdam, 'Art History,' 147.   [102] Emami, 'ART IN IRAN.'
[103] Lauren S. Weingarden, 'Aesthetics Politicized: William Morris to the Bauhaus,' *Journal of Architectural Education*, vol. 38, no. 3 (1985), 8–13.
[104] Ibid., 9.

established traditional workshops.[105] The goal of this newly established community of artists and architects was described by Gropius with the following words: "A new cathedral of the future will one day rise toward heaven from the hands of a million workers like the crystal symbol of a new faith."[106]

Aesthetically, Bauhaus design and the artworks of artists associated with *Saqqakhaneh* seem to have only little in common. The socialist overtone, however, persists in Tehran's College of Decorative Arts program and in *Saqqakhaneh's* historiographical accounts. Similar to Morris and Bauhaus, the artistic practice promoted at the College was also rooted in traditions of craftsmanship and attempted, to a greater degree than Morris and Bauhaus had, to connect modernist art with local cultural practices. Denoting *Saqqakhaneh* as a "school" of Iranian modernism thus functions on two levels. On the one hand, it is a tool to categorize Iranian art history and produce a modern history of schools and different styles. On the other hand, the categorization of *Saqqakhaneh* as a school and its connection to Bauhaus was also an important strategy employed to politicize modernist art production in Iran.

Saqqakhaneh *as a "Style"*

Zenderoudi and Tanavoli did not use the term *Saqqakhaneh* to describe their artistic practice in their early artworks. In his art-historiographical rendition of *Saqqakhaneh's* emergence, however, Tanavoli acknowledges art critic Emami's attempt at a classification and his contribution to the development of a modernist artistic discourse in Iran. About Emami, Tanavoli writes,

He was the first critic to use the term to describe a particular artistic style, applying it to a group whose work shared certain distinct features. One of these common characteristics was the use of folk art or commonly held beliefs which found expression in inscriptions, talismans and depictions of famous love stories.[107]

---

[105] Edmund Goldzamt, 'Das Erbe von William Morris und das Bauhaus [1],' *Hochschule für Architektur und Bauwesen*, vol. 23, no. 5–6 (1976), 485–488.
[106] Walter Gropius, cited in Weingarden, 'Aesthetics Politicized,' 11.
[107] Parviz Tanavoli, 'Atelier Kaboud,' in David Galloway (ed.), *Parviz Tanavoli: Sculptor, Writer, and Collector* (Tehran: Iranian Art Publishing, 2000), 53–113, 84.

It is very significant that Tanavoli calls *Saqqakhaneh* "a particular artistic style." Referring to this aesthetics as a style places it in an art-historical context and its practice of stylistic categorization and classification of periods and people. Style often implies stark categorization of works based on formalist principles, which contributes to a decontextualization of the artworks and pays little attention to their meaning and the larger question of an artwork's function. As a categorical tool to analyze artistic production, style has been subject to substantial criticism in the field of art history. The reason for this was primarily the National-Socialists' misuse of the term in racist and nationalist art discourses as a way to identify a nation's collective will.[108]

For Georg Wilhelm Friedrich Hegel, style reflects a period's *Zeitgeist*. Consequently, all fields of cultural expression harmoniously mirror, according to Hegel, the spirit of their respective historical period. This means that artistic productions communicate their inherent *Zeitgeist* through their shared shapes and forms. Thus, the period's spirit creates a unified and coherent expression, which "disallows the accidental and bends everything to a unified law."[109] Hegel's conception of style resonates very well with Tanavoli's thought and his classification of *Saqqakhaneh* artistic productions as a particular style denoting "a distinct group whose members had, in a brief span of time, come to comprise the first movement in contemporary Iranian art."[110] For Tanavoli, the group's historical achievement represented the first truly Iranian artistic innovation because, "unlike the larger body of painters who took the West as their model, these artists traced their roots to Iran's cultural soil."[111] By adapting Hegel's concept of style, it is possible to situate their artistic production and rediscovery of Iran's visual heritage as reflections of the sociopolitical discourses of their time. In Tanavoli's case, this means that the rhetorical use of style is not only a superficial category to denote formalist qualities of an artistic practice. Characterizing *Saqqakhaneh* not only as a style but also as a movement enhances Tanavoli's attempt to establish

---

[108] For a deeper discussions of style as an art-historiographical classification, see, James Elkins, 'Style,' Grove Art Online, Oxford Art Online, 2003. https://doi.org/10.1093/gao/9781884446054.article.T082129, accessed 23 October 2019; Hubert Locher, 'Stil,' in Pfisterer, *Metzler Lexikon Kunstwissenschaft*, 414–419.

[109] Elkins, 'Style.'   [110] Ibid.   [111] Ibid.

Saqqakhaneh as an art-historiographical concept, as James Elkins explains,

> Hence, at the most profound level, style may be understood as a moment in the ongoing dialogue between the constructing of history and the constructing of the self, a moment that is sustained by not pressing the illogic of the argument of style on towards its crippling conclusions.[112]

Tanavoli's rendition of *Saqqakhaneh* demonstrates that he accepted Emami's classification. The concept of *Saqqakhaneh* was thus a significant trope for the establishment of a canon in modern Iranian art history. In this context, *Saqqakhaneh* helped to connect art criticism and production with the discourse of identity formation in the age of Iran's modernization.

Artistic Reactions to Saqqakhaneh's *Dominance*

In the course of state-sponsored exhibitions such as the Tehran Biennials and Iran's participation in major international shows such as the Venice Biennial, as well as due to developments within art criticism, *Saqqakhaneh* became the dominant concept in Iranian modernist art in the 1960s and 1970s. Many artists associated with *Saqqakhaneh*, however, disagreed with this kind of classification and the decontextualization of their artistic productions. In reaction to this decontextualized approach to modernist arts, a group of Iranian artists founded *Talar-e Iran* as an alternative and independent artistic platform in Tehran. *Talar-e Iran*, which was renamed *Talar-e Qandriz* after the death of painter Mansour Ghandriz, lasted from 1964 to 1977.[113] In their numerous publications, discussions, and exhibitions, *Talar-e Qandriz* tried to establish a socially committed version of modernist expression, which refrained from decorative tendencies, exoticism, and the longing for a nostalgic and orientalist past. Contrary to *Saqqakhaneh*, *Talar-e Qandriz* was a self-organized artistic platform, which was based on artistic collaboration and explicitly stated creative goals.[114] A look at the participating artists, however, reveals that *Talar-e Qandriz* can hardly be seen as an artistic opposition to *Saqqakhaneh*, since Faramarz Pilaram, Mansour Qandriz,

---

[112] Ibid.   [113] See *Talar-e Qandriz* (Tehran: Herfeh Honarmand, 2016).
[114] See, Moussavi-Aghdam, 'Art History'; *Talar-e Qandriz*.

Massoud Arabshahi, and Sadegh Tabrizi were active in *Talar-e Qandriz* and also exhibited under the rubric of *Saqqakhaneh*. It also demonstrates that the categorization of artists into groups in Iran was more of a historiographical process than an artistic one.

In their writings and artworks, the artists Tanavoli and Arabshahi reflected critically upon and discussed the negative consequences of merely formal and aesthetic incorporations of traditional elements in their artworks. Their artistic critique of creating exoticist, Orientalist artworks for the international market resonated well with al-e Ahmad and Emami's further accusations that Iranian modernism was a mere empty decoration for the Western gaze. During his career, the artist Arabshahi tried to distance himself from the label of a *Saqqakhaneh* artist. Arabshahi does not refer to religious visual material in his works. As the *Saqqakhaneh* exhibition catalog explains, Arabshahi "is the only artist in the group who has not drawn on religious art, and his kinship with the others is a matter of the spirit."[115] In his works, Arabshahi uses monochromatic ornaments with tactile surfaces to achieve an abstract expression, often described as evoking associations with Iran's ancient heritage. For this reason, Firooz Shirvanloo sharply attacks Iranian art criticism and their attempt to classify Arabshahi as a *Saqqakhaneh* artist, since he does not reference Islamic elements in his works.

Arabshahi has mistakenly been named among the followers of the Saqqakhaneh School, if it can be construed as a school at all. Such negligence, which is practically an indication of indifference and lack of true comprehension of art, is one of the reasons for today's dishevelled cultural state. Maybe from now on it might be proper to awaken the easy-going authors to this matter with a hint and if a hint isn't effective then with a blow.[116]

For Shirvanloo, Arabshahi's deployment of ancient, non-Islamic visual elements represents the distinctive feature of his works that sets him apart from *Saqqakhaneh* artist. Nevertheless, Arabshahi belongs to the generation of modernist artists that benefitted from the state's promotion of modernist art. Arabshahi was commissioned to decorate the

---

[115] Emami, 'Saqqakhaneh School Revisited.'
[116] Firooz Shirvanloo, 'Creative Return to Iran's Ancient Art' (Tehran, 1977), cited in Pakbaz and Emdadian (eds.), *Massoud Arabshahi: Pioneers of Iranian Modern Art* (Tehran: TMoCA, 2001), 8–9, 9.

walls of new modernist administrative buildings several times. In 1969, for instance, Arabshahi was commissioned to adorn the walls of the auditorium of the building *Sazeman-e Shir-o Khorshid Sorkh* (the Lion and Red Sun Organizations, then counterpart of the Red Cross). For this building, Arabshahi created a large terra-cotta relief (30 × 16 × 12 meters) experimenting with abstract forms, which can be related to patterns from Iran's pre-Islamic past, such as Achaemenian rock carvings and inscriptions on Sasanian tombs. This artistic strategy accorded well with Pahlavi cultural politics, which used Iran's ancient past as proof of the country's secular tradition.[117]

In his own account, Arabshahi reflected critically upon the superficial incorporation of traditional elements in modernist art production to achieve a local expression of modernism, writing in 1972,

In those days, we expected too much from our heritage and worst of all we infused calligraphy in our works. When calligraphy enters a work it is followed by repetition and after a while if the calligraphy is expunged nothing will be left. It is dangerous to overindulge in traditions, but at the same time we shouldn't disregard them. That is what the young artists, whom [*sic*!] had witnessed our bitter experience, did. They began from nothing and that is the reason behind the bewildered state of our painting.[118]

Parviz Tanavoli's Heech

Generally speaking, Parviz Tanavoli accepted and continues to use the term *Saqqakhaneh* as it was applied to him by Emami. At the same time, however, Tanavoli questions Emami's concept of *Saqqakhaneh*, when he doubts his authority as a critic and states that he was not an active member of Tehran's art scene. Or, in Tanavoli's words,

Inconsistent accounts of the birth of the Saqqakhaneh School have made it imperative for me to set the record straight here. When the Saqqakhaneh School was taking shape, Karim Emami, who named it, was not even aware of its existence. Although he was then (1960–61) a professor of English at the College of Decorative Arts, he had still not developed an interest in art. Nor do I recall ever meeting him at the exhibitions of the time, most certainly not at those held in the Atelier Kaboud, where the Saqqakhaneh School came into existence.[119]

[117] Ibid.   [118] Massoud Arabshahi, *Massoud Arabshahi*, 20.
[119] Tanavoli, 'Atelier Kaboud,' 84.

Despite his criticisms, Tanavoli continues to use Emami's concept. In doing so, he preserves Emami's version of *Saqqakhaneh*, which stresses its crucial ties with the Iranian Shi'ite martyr discourse. In fact, the material culture evolving around *Saqqakhaneh* as a religious site became a source of great inspiration for his artistic practice. As Tanavoli explains, "Saqqakhaneh items nonetheless hold a tremendous spiritual power. Their popular associations with talismans and magic set them apart from other artefacts."[120] Tanavoli sees the collaborative work on religious objects as an important quality of "these items, cruder than the work of professional artists such as calligraphers and painters" and "produced collaboratively by average people on the street."[121]

The incorporation of Iranian subjects represents an important artistic strategy in Tanavoli's works. This was not only a creative means but also an artistic language and tool Tanavoli used to express his critique of the empty use of tradition merely as a source of visual pleasure for the Western gaze. For him, the use of traditional objects was an essential element in the establishment of a modernist expression based on Persian idioms. To achieve this, Tanavoli often refers to Sufi tropes, which frequently reoccur in his artistic works. His series, *Heech*, which depicts the word *heech* (meaning *nothing*) in Persian script, would become the creative trademark of Tanavoli's artistic career. With his artistic rendition of the word *heech*, Tanavoli reflects the idea of *fana*, one of the key concepts of Sufi belief, as we have already seen. As Nina Chichoki points out, "Tanavoli's nothingness was a spiritual one, and its origin was the theme of annihilation, cherished in Persian Sufi Poetry."[122]

The highest goal of Sufism's adherents is the attainment of unification with God. *Fana*, the destruction of the self and the annihilation of their own existence, is an important stage in order to achieve unification with the divine. Jalal al-din Rumi illustrated this in his Matnavi, in which the famous thirteenth-century Sufi poet continuously emphasizes the central meaning of *fana*. As Jawid Mojaddedi explains,

Rumi often describes Man's relationship with God by using the scholastic language of Islamic theology and philosophy. God is described as Absolute

---

[120] Ibid., 93.   [121] Ibid.
[122] Nina Chichoki, 'Sculpted Poetry,' in Pakbaz and Emdadian, *Parviz Tanavoli*, 9–15, 13.

Being, while humans are non-beings who merely imagine that they have their own independent existence. They are urged to recognize their non-existence and to strive to become effaced in God, in order to truly exist through Him.[123]

The poet Rumi was an important artistic inspiration for Tanavoli, whose rendition of *heech* functions in the same Sufi context.[124] It is in this sense that Tanavoli is said to have announced that "'nothing' is an aspect of God. God is in all things and therefore in everything. The 'nothing' is not God, but is a place where God could be in his purest state."[125]

Tanavoli reflected Rumi's concept of *fana* in his artistic version of *heech* by transforming calligraphy into sculpture. The sculptures show the Persian word *heech*, with a special emphasis on the first letter, ha, roughly equivalent to "h," known in Persian as the "two-eyed h." Because of its shape, traditional Islamic calligraphy often used the letter "heh" to depict a crying face.[126] The semi-circular shape of the last letter "che" in combination with the face-like form of the first letter lends Tanavoli's sculptures the physical appearance of human beings or animals. This strategy lends the sculptures from the series a great flexibility. By varying the scripture and the distance between the letters, *heech* can adopt different shapes and positions as, for example, in *Heech and Table* (1973) and *Heech and Chair*. In this work, for instance, *heech* takes on the shape of a cat sitting on a chair, while in other works *heech* appears as a valuable piece of jewelry. Nonetheless, it is important to note that *heech* remains legible and recognizable in all of Tanavoli's artistic renditions. This constitutes a major difference from other Iranian modernist artists, who used calligraphy in their artistic works mostly as a means to achieve an abstract form of expression.

In this context, Tanavoli's *heech* turns into a mirror-like reflection of the empty adaptation of calligraphy in modernist Iranian arts and shows that these arts literally depict nothing. Tanavoli's critique of the merely formal employment of calligraphy resonates well with al-e Ahmad and Emami's further observations and accusations that Iranian

---

[123] Jawid Mojaddedi, 'Introduction,' in Rumi Jalal al-Din and Jawid Mojaddedi (eds.), *The Masnavi. Jalal al-din Rumi* (Oxford: Oxford University Press, 2004), XI–XXVI, XXV.
[124] Chichoki, 'Sculpted Poetry,' 13.   [125] Ibid.   [126] Ibid., 12.

Saqqakhaneh's *Existence as a Group*

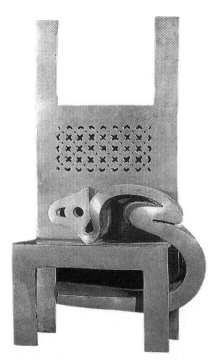

Figure 3.1 Parviz Tanavoli, *Heech and Chair II*, 1973. Bronze, 79 × 45 × 26 cm. Collection of Manijeh Tanavoli

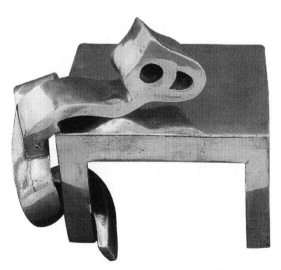

Figure 3.2 Parviz Tanavoli, *Heech and Table I*, 1973. Bronze, 20 × 24 × 15 cm

artists were consciously exoticizing and orientalizing Iran for the Western gaze. According to Tanavoli, *heech* grew out of his discontentment with the common practice of employing calligraphy solely as an aesthetic means, without paying attention to its historical and religious meaning.

As I will explain, everything conspired to lead me to this figure. Without a doubt, the artistic environment of the time, the school whose methods and pedagogy I could not believe in, the thinkers and artists who were trumpeting some new artistic phenomenon from the West every day, and the aristocrats who proudly bought their second-hand merchandise, provoked in me a reaction of protest. *Heech* was the voice of this protest. However, as I will explain, this protest had wider scope and included myself in its purview, for it was dedicated against the *Saqqakhaneh* painters.[127]

Thus, Tanavoli's series, *heech*, becomes an artistic reaction to the excessive use of calligraphy in modernist Iranian art. In many artistic works, the calligraphic script employed is only a loose, illegible assemblage of Persian letters devoid of meaning. Without any inherent meaning, calligraphy becomes merely a formalist means of expression to examine abstract paradigms of Western modernism. In this way, calligraphy turns out to be an artistic endeavor without any political or social commitment and hence a kind of modernism that has degenerated into mere decoration. As Tanavoli states,

From the mid-1960s onwards, the Saqqakhaneh movement was on the rise, with increasing numbers of painters joining it ranks- or, if you like, jumping on its bandwagon. Most of them used calligraphy as the basis of their work and often simply covered their paintings with script. Although this development seemingly meant that the Saqqakhaneh School was growing, it filled me with disgust rather than pleasure.[128]

Tanavoli's critical statement against *Saqqakhaneh* illustrates his personal discontent with his artistic colleagues' removal of traditional Iranian elements from their religious and cultural contexts and exclusive focus on formalist experiments. Although Tanavoli's critique is directed toward the visual adaptation of Western modernity, it can also be situated in the broader debate about Iran's westernization. The

---

[127] Tanavoli, 'Atelier Kaboud,' 96–97.   [128] Ibid., 97.

preceding analysis of al-e Ahmad and Emami's art criticism showed that the discourse of westoxification was also reflected in modernist art. In these contexts, modernist art served as a case study to discuss how to reconcile tropes of Western modernity with Iranian discourses.

Tanavoli's critical account of the so-called school of modernism also shows that *Saqqakhaneh* was a very imprecise and nebulous term in Iran. Due to this lack of a clear definition or any kind of artistic cooperation, the idea of *Saqqakhaneh* became a very elastic concept that could be used to characterize all kinds of artistic positions depicting any elements of the Persian visual tradition. Although Iran's modernist art history has witnessed the emergence of different artistic groups and association of artistic collaboration, such as the *Fighting Rooster Association* (which will be discussed in Chapter 4) or *Talar-e Qandriz*, only *Saqqakhaneh* entered the canon as a specific expression of Iranian modernism. *Saqqakhaneh*'s dominance in the art-historiographical canon is therefore also a result of the successful processes of its institutionalization and promotion by the Pahlavi monarchy in its staging of *Saqqakhaneh* as an example of a specifically Iranian modernism.

The State's Recognition of *Saqqakhaneh* as an Expression of a State-Sponsored Modernism

The state's promotion of *Saqqakhaneh* as the official style of Iranian modernism culminated in the eponymous exhibition on the occasion of the TMoCA's opening in 1977. The Pahlavi state's cultural and discursive shift to Islamic spirituality in the late 1960s and 1970s, a political reaction to the ongoing debates about the regime's westoxification, enabled the instrumentalization of *Saqqakhaneh* as a state-sponsored school of modernism. The appropriation of oppositional discourses, such as the critique of the country's westernization, became an important political strategy to silence voices critical of the monarchy in Pahlavi Iran. Artistic productions related to *Saqqakhaneh* resonated well with the conceptions of national identity propagated by the Pahlavi state, which framed the topic of religion as a matter of the difference between Iran and Western states. As the scholars Ali Mirsepassi and Hamed Yousefi have pointed out, "Saqqakhaneh artists operated with a similar network of relations" and also shared "the image of Iranian identity that was aestheticized in their works," with which the "artists offered modernist renditions of traditional, devotional motifs."[129]

A strong example of this approach is the catalog of the *Saqqakhaneh* exhibition, which was published by the TMoCA in 1977. This catalog's visual design gives a vivid impression of how the monarchy started to fully embrace Islamic spirituality in order to craft new Iranian-Islamic identity discourses for the Iranian people. At the same time, however, the Persian-English bilingual design of the catalog helps situate the exhibition not only in a local but also in a global context of art as a universal sign of modernity. While the exhibition was supposed to provide an overview of modernist art production in Iran, the catalog paints a different picture. The visual design and the images reproduced in the catalog create the impression that the museum had actually organized a presentation about the material culture of Shi'ite Islam, rather than modernist arts. This impression is immediately suggested by the cover, which displays an image of a green wooden lattice with cloth strips and small metal elements attached to it. Behind the latticework, one can read, in Arabic, "*Saqqakhaneh*." It is very significant that the title is written not with Persian but rather Arabic letters, whose diacritical marks call forth associations with the Arabic language, in which the holy book of the Qur'an is written. The photographs in the rest of the catalog reinforce the topic of religious devotion, not only by depicting black-and-white close-ups of architectural elements, such as a metal grillwork and water taps with drinking bowls attached to them but also by portraying women praying in their *chadors*. Objects connected to popular Shi'ite belief's material culture also played a major role within the exhibition and were featured in the catalog. The visual representation of the devotional objects actually takes up more space than the documentation of the modernist artworks displayed. Entire pages display objects, such as *panj-tan*, in the form of a brass hand symbolizing the five holy persons of Shi'ite Islam, namely, Mohammad, Ali, Fatima, Hussein, and Hassan. Other pages show the wide range of different talismans, such as talismanic spoons with inscriptions, talismanic seals for witchcraft, sun and lion talismans used on both arms to give one strength, brass objects for fortune telling, and many more such items. The street photographs in the

---

[129] Ali Mirsepassi and Hamed Yousefi, 'Abby Weed Grey's Journey to the East: Iranian Modernity during the Cold War,' in Gumpert, *Modernisms*, 65–77, 69.

Figure 3.3 *Saqqakhaneh* Exhibition Catalog, 1977. Tehran Museum of Contemporary Art

catalog illustrate this strong focus on material culture in Shi'ite religious practice. These objects represented an integral part of the exhibition and helped to situate modernist artistic practice not only in a local but also in a specifically Shi'ite religious context. One picture, for instance, depicts a father dressed in Western clothes, who has stopped at a *Saqqakhaneh* to give his thirsty daughters water from the public water fountain, while a boy passes by with ice cream in his hand. This image promotes the impression that religious practice and daily life in modern Pahlavi city coexist with one another in a well-balanced harmony. Or, in other words, modernity and the practice of religion are no longer in conflict but rather both function as important markers for the definition of modern Iranian identity. This is also mirrored in the exhibition's name, *Saqqakhaneh*, which represents, on the one hand, religious practices revolving around the battle of Karbala as the defining paradigm of Shi'ite belief, and, on the other hand, a modernist Iranian artistic practice. In this process, the exhibition and its catalog can be interpreted as a visual answer to the pressing charges against the Pahlavi monarchy in the 1960s and 1970s, when intellectuals like al-e Ahmad and Shariati accused the Shah and his government of being too westernized and secular.

In addition to the catalog's images, the texts also emphasize the exhibition's connections to the Iranian context. The former museum director, Kamran Diba, for instance, who also designed the museum building's architecture, explains in his curatorial statement that the "Saqqakhaneh exhibition is an attempt to register vernacular aspects of contemporary art in Iran."[130] In his opinion, this was an exceptional moment in the history of Iran's modernist art because it was "the first time the western-oriented Iranian artist has looked inward in search of his cultural identity." For him, the reason for this kind of introspection was that the "discovery of concepts and visual symbols of primitive religious rituals, in the form of prayers and spells devoid of traditional formalism excited the artist."[131] In the broader discourse of *gharbzadegi*, Diba's appreciation of Queen Farah's efforts to promote modernist arts is not only the act of a loyal citizen but also an attempt to prove that the monarchy was not too westernized.[132]

Sadegh Tabrizi and Nasser Oveissi did not consider themselves part of the group of *Saqqakhaneh* artists and, as the art critic Emami states, "they have never admitted, to the best of my knowledge, to being members of this school."[133] Nevertheless, Emami associates their practice with *Saqqakhaneh* because "they had more or less independently worked their way towards the utilization of traditional material."[134] While Emami has no doubts about including male artists

---

[130] Diba, 'Preface,' in *Saqqakhaneh* (Tehran: Tehran Museum of Contemporary Art, 1977).
[131] Ibid. [132] Ibid. [133] Ibid. [134] Ibid.

working in different artistic styles, he excludes any female artists because of their varying artistic expression.

There are also some other painters, such as Ms. Mansoureh Hoseini and Ms. Iran Darrudi, who have used calligraphic elements in their works in one period or another but they have turned to other styles, and so do not qualify as bona fide Saqqakhaneh artists.[135]

This suggests that Emami's categorization of *Saqqakhaneh* is rather selective and was not based on common characteristics of form or content. Emami's vision of *Saqqakhaneh* clearly lacks a clear stylistic definition and was conceived of as an entirely male association of artists. As argued above, Emami's attempt at classification should be understood in the context of an anticolonial discourse, in which he tried to establish a counter-narrative to the dominant discourse of modernization in Iran. This also becomes clear in his introductory text to the exhibition catalog, when he tries to distance himself from *Saqqakhaneh*. In 1977, Emami considered his exhibition text "Saqqakhaneh School Revisited" a "nostalgic piece about a past page of Iran's art history" and thus as a historical matter, which had died out by the late 1970s. Nevertheless, Emami saw *Saqqakhaneh*'s significance in the artists' creation of "an Iranian school of modern art," which "had been a dream of the Iranian modernists who had earlier returned to Iran from study periods in Europe."[136] Earlier generations of artists, such as Jalil Ziapour and Houshang Pezeshknia, according to Emami, had not been successful in establishing a national style of modernism because they were "clinging – with little success – to Cubist or Expressionist techniques."[137] For Emami, the merit of *Saqqakhaneh* artists was that they "came along and showed us how much could be done just by drawing on the familiar materials available close at hand."[138]

Saqqakhaneh's Discursive Afterlife

The exhibition at the TMoCA and its accompanying catalog, in fact, shaped the reception of *Saqqakhaneh* as an artistic expression of Pahlavi's successful modernization programs in all fields of Iran's society. In his foreword to the exhibition catalog, Kamran Diba claims

[135] Ibid.   [136] Ibid.   [137] Ibid.   [138] Ibid.

the *Saqqakhaneh* artists for the regime by declaring that their work had been made possible by a framework of royal patronage. As he states, "without the Tehran Biennials and the consistent encouragement of Her Imperial Majesty, such movements in Iranian art would not be possible."[139] Thus, he reframes an oppositional movement as an achievement of Iran's modernization. As discussed in Chapter 2, Queen Farah Diba's royal patronage and her cultural politics were deeply rooted in the state's modernization and secularization programs. Beyond that, her support of modernist art led to the infrastructure that provided the right conditions for oppositional art to emerge. This means, in other words, that the Pahlavi state had provided the very framework, which enabled artistic critique and resistance. The case of *Saqqakhaneh* demonstrates that modernist art served as a platform for critical reflection on pressing questions, which evolved due to the transformative modernization programs of the Pahlavi state.

The apparently contradictory phenomena of *Saqqakhaneh*'s simultaneous political opposition to the state and its institutionalization by that very state can be captured theoretically with Gilles Deleuze and Felix Guattari's concept of a *minor literature*.[140] A *minor literature* is an analytical method of grasping the cultural and artistic productions "which a minority constructs within a major language."[141] Deleuze and Guattari developed their concept in light of Franz Kafka's literary practice in Prague. According to the authors, *a minor literature* has three main features,

The three characteristics of a minor literature are the deterritorialization of language, the connection of the individual to a political immediacy, and the collective assemblage of enunciation. We might as well say that minor no longer designates specific literatures but the revolutionary conditions for every literature within the heart of what is called great (or established) literature.[142]

Emami's and Tanavoli's common conception of *Saqqakhaneh*, which, in its conceptual and aesthetic renditions relied on Islamic faith and Shi'ite martyr discourse, was deeply rooted in the sociopolitical discourse of Iran's westoxification. This strategy represented a significant

---

[139] Ibid.
[140] Gilles Deleuze and Félix Guattari, *Kafka: Toward a Minor Literature* (Minneapolis: University of Minnesota, 1986).
[141] Ibid., 16.   [142] Ibid., 18.

attempt to establish a counter-discourse to the Shah's modernization programs. The modernization programs of the Pahlavi dynasty had the goal of secularizing the country, reducing the clergy's political influence, and downplaying Islam's religious legacy. Culture became the main venue to illustrate Iran's successful secularization. The Shah regime deployed tropes of Iran's antiquity to establish imagined traditions of secularism, which became visible in the architectural programs as well as in the festivities held for the 2,500th anniversary of the Persian Empire in 1971.

Rapid modernization, westernization, and secularization, however, have spurred intellectual debates about preserving an Iranian identity while, at the same time, modernizing the country. Iran's immense transformation from an agricultural country to a modern nation-state in the course of the twentieth century led, in part, to feelings of estrangement and the fear of losing their cultural identity. Estrangement, a lack belonging, and rootlessness are not only phenomena of Pahlavi Iran but rather one of the many conditions of life in modernity. As Deleuze and Guattari write,

> How many people today live in a language that is not their own? Or no longer, or not yet, even know their own and know poorly the major language that they are forced to serve? This is the problem of the immigrants, and especially of their children, the problem of minorities, the problem for all of us: how to tear a minor language away from its own language, allowing it to challenge the language and making it follow a sober revolutionary path? How to become a nomad and an immigrant and a gypsy in relation to one's own language?[143]

To compensate for this state of deterritorialization, the artistic turn to religious traditions and well-known iconographies was an effective strategy to deal with Western modernist expression, which constituted a language that many modernist artists in Iran experienced only through translations. Or, in other words, their language was not that of modernist expression, since Western modernism was equally appropriated by both the state and the artistic opposition. The incorporation of motives and techniques from Iranian artistic traditions was an important strategy to appropriate modernist expression. Persian visual traditions, however, did not provide a vocabulary capable of depicting

[143] Ibid., 19.

the intellectual debates and the conditions of life and artistic production in the modern age. This becomes evident in Emami's foundational texts, which created the concept of *Saqqakhaneh*, as well as in the artistic works of Zenderoudi and Tanavoli. These artistic productions inspired Emami to invent a term that described artworks with the potential to express a critical resistance against the dominant system, while also enabling artistic innovation. As Deleuze und Guattari write,

> To make use of the polylingualism of one's own language, to make a minor or intensive use of it, to oppose the oppressed quality of this language to its oppressive quality, to find points of nonculture or underdevelopment, linguistic Third World zones by which a language can escape, an animal enters into things, an assemblage comes into play.[144]

Transcultural Processes of Institutionalization

The idea of *Saqqakhaneh* as the mature expression of a specific version of Iranian modernity in the fields of arts was met with a warm welcome, both inside and outside Iran. In particular, due to transcultural processes of institutionalization in the Cold War era, *Saqqakhaneh* was staged as a representative reflection of an Iranian version of global modernism. This transcultural institutionalization was so successful that to this day, *Saqqakhaneh* is seen globally as the decisive expression of an Iranian modernism, even though the synopsis of Emami's text and the analytical comparison of *Saqqakhaneh* artworks above demonstrated that the associated artists worked in varying styles, employed different iconographical traditions and followed diverse artistic goals. Thus, it can be inferred that *Saqqakhaneh* was not so much a creative collective with common artistic goals as it was a historiographical construction, which reflected the quest for a decolonized Iranian modern identity beyond Western tropes of modernity, such as secularity, technical progress, and rationality.

Ironically, *Saqqakhaneh*'s prominence is a result of Cold War cultural politics indebted to the art patron Abby Weed Grey's (1902–1983) personal engagement. The latter played a major role in the transcultural and transnational institutionalization of *Saqqakhaneh* and its global dispersion. Her collection of Iranian modernist arts represents "the largest public holding of Iranian modern art outside of Iran." In 1974,

---

[144] Ibid., 27.

Abby Weed Grey donated her collection to New York University, leading to the establishment of the Grey Art Gallery and Study Center.[145] This research institution facilitates the display, preservation, and study of modernist Iranian arts, a research area with very few scholarly archives. Thus, on the one hand, Grey's art collection provides an important infrastructure for global research and scholarship on modernist Iranian arts and "helped give Saqqakhaneh an international currency that subsequently fed back into a local context."[146] On the other hand, however, the collection perpetuates the myth of *Saqqakhaneh* in the broader discourse of Cold War politics and the art movement's ideological instrumentalization for the purpose of legitimating the Pahlavi monarchy.

Abby Weed Grey encountered Iranian modernist expression for the first time on her trip to Iran in 1960, when she visited the Second Tehran Biennial. Her collection of modernist arts from Iran unites diverse forms of expression and gathers a wide group of artists, such as Ahmad Esfandiari, who belongs to the first generation of Iranian artists who introduced European modernist means of expression into the Iranian context. One can also find more abstract positions, such as those of Ruyin Pakbaz, Behjat Sadr, and the poet and painter Sohrab Sepehri. With Tanavoli, Zenderoudi, Ghandriz, Pilaram, Tabatabaie, Tabrizi, and Ovissi, however, the collection follows a clear focus on artists associated with *Saqqakhaneh* and thus contributes to the continued reproduction of the *Saqqakhaneh* myth. One reason for this was Grey's close friendship with the artist Parviz Tanavoli, whom she met in 1961 in Tehran and who later became her personal protégée. Grey not only acquired almost eighty works by Tanavoli for her collection but also supported his artistic career by establishing contact with the Minneapolis School of Art, where Tanavoli deepened his knowledge of bronze casting during an artistic residency. With her personal promotion of Tanavoli's artistic development, Abby Weed Grey also exerted an important influence on the art scene in Tehran. After Tanavoli's return to Tehran in 1964, the Ben and Abby Weed Grey Foundation sponsored a bronze foundry at the Academy of Fine Arts in Tehran and provided Tanavoli with a position as a professor of sculpture. His new

---

[145] Lynn Gumpert, 'Reflections on the Abby Grey Collection,' Balaghi and Gumpert, *Picturing Iran*, 17–19, 17.

[146] Mirsepassi and Yousefi, 'Abby Weed Grey's Journey,' 70.

bronze sculptures led to Tanavoli's artistic breakthrough and his commissioning by the royal couple Mohammad Reza Shah and Farah Diba to realize official representational sculptures of the royal family.[147]

With her art foundation, Abby Weed Grey played an important role in the promotion of new arts not only in Iran but also in the West. Her numerous journeys took Abby Weed Grey to countries such as Iran, Turkey, Japan, and Thailand, where she compiled an astonishing collection of modernist arts from non-Western countries. With her foundation, Abby Weed Grey organized several touring exhibitions in the United States that presented her collected artworks. At the 1972 Minnesota State Fair, she organized the exhibition "One World Through Art," which displayed 1001 artworks from the Middle East. New York University became home to Grey's modernist art collection in 1974.[148] Abby Grey and her foundation's goal of supporting non-Western modernist artists had the programmatic title "Communication through Art." It clearly corresponded to the idea of modernist art as a universal language, one of the outcomes of Cold War politics, which staged modernist art as a cultural weapon against the socialist East and its allegedly representational styles of art. Given that Iran was a close political ally of the United States during the Cold War, it is not surprising that "Saqqakhaneh was the Iranian version of Cold War modernism."[149] The combination of tradition and modernity under the umbrella concept of *Saqqakhaneh* became a very powerful expression of Iranian modernism. This took place mainly, thanks to the close connection between royal patronage and the advancement of the idea that *Saqqakhaneh* was the expression of an Iranian school of modernism, which was reiterated by Abby Grey and her foundation and eventually contributed to *Saqqakhaneh*'s global recognition. This promotion of *Saqqakhaneh* is reflected in scholarly research in Iranian art history, which commonly stages the term *Saqqakhaneh* as the central concept in modern Iranian art history.

Saqqakhaneh *in Art Historiography*

In the 1960s and 1970s, the Ministry of Art and Culture published scholarly overviews in Persian, English, and French of the evolution of

---

[147] Fock, *Tanavoli*, 118–120.
[148] Gumpert, 'Reflections on the Abby Grey Collection,' 18.
[149] Mirsepassi and Yousefi, 'Abby Weed Grey's Journey,' 66.

modernist arts in Iran. As one can see in the publications by the authors Tadjvidi and Pakbaz, for example, the history of Iranian modernism presented was modeled predominantly after the categories of Western art history. Similar to Emami, these authors argue that after years of imitation and immature experiments with Western modernist styles, such as Impressionism, Cubism, and Fauvism, *Saqqakhaneh* was a promising artistic answer to the question of how to incorporate local Iranian elements. For Tadjvidi, earlier modern Iranian art styles had failed to meet the artists' and public's aesthetic needs. Only the artists associated with *Saqqakhaneh* merged modernist expression with "leur propre vie intérieure et de leur propre heritage culturel."[150]

The artist and art critic Pakbaz also stresses that the Third Tehran Biennial in 1962 demonstrated how previous trends of introducing "an Iranian aura to painting, now became transformed into a virtually unanimous tendency."[151] Pakbaz saw this trend realized in the artworks of many artists who were included neither in Emami's list of *Saqqakhaneh* artists nor among artists later canonized as part of *Saqqakhaneh*, such as the calligraphic works of Mohammad Ehsai, Bahram Alivandi, Mehri Bakhsha, and Reza Mafi. The inconsistency of the members associated with the so-called national school of modernism is also observable in Tadjvidi's list of artists, who also considers Pakbaz a *Saqqakhaneh* artist, although he later became very critical of the so-called *Saqqakhaneh* style. In 1979, Ehsan Yarshater stated that artists associated with *Saqqakhaneh* do not comprise a defined group of artists and that they "vary considerably in their modus operandi; but they share a consistent reference to themes and symbols of traditional Persian life and art."[152] For Yarshater, *Saqqakhaneh*'s employment of traditional, religious, and literary subjects occurred only on a formal level and "in a non-partisan, apolitical, and asocial guise." As he goes on to explain,

The themes more often utilized are reminiscent not of ancient or medieval Persia and not of her past glories, but of a mode of life within the reach of one's memory: a life that the artist's parents or grandparents lived, a life still undisturbed by the pervasive presence of the Western world and free from claims of modernization, a life reflecting the languid pace of centuries past, a

---

[150] Tadjvidi, *L'art moderne en Iran*, 43.
[151] Pakbaz, *Contemporary Iranian Painting*, 30.
[152] Yarshater, 'Contemporary Persian Painting,' 363–377, 365.

life familiar and yet removed, a life suddenly and inexorably relegated to history within a single generation, a life within reach and yet irretrievable.[153]

The emphasis on *Saqqakhaneh's* "romantic nostalgia" and the decorative character of their artistic productions helped establish *Saqqakhaneh* as a depoliticized and secularized version of Iranian modernism whose goal was to participate in a global modernity shaped by Cold War ideologies.

Nevertheless, it is important to note that the historiographical accounts of *Saqqakhaneh* before the revolution were very limited and mostly concentrated on art criticism and short overviews, which participated in linear narratives about the evolution of modernist arts in Iran. A short overview of the relevant literature shows that *Saqqakhaneh* only became part of a canonized art historiography in the course of the globalization of the art world's discourse and art history's global turn starting in the early 2000s. During and after the revolution of 1978/79, many artists left Iran and took up residency in Western countries. During this time, there were very few attempts to display and study Iranian modernist arts. This gradually changed in the late 1980s and 1990s, when *Saqqakhaneh* became an official part of Iranian historiography, as one can see, for example, in Emami's entry on Post-Qajar Painting in the *Encyclopaedia Iranica*, where he describes *Saqqakhaneh* as a "soul searching" movement whose members tried to differentiate their artistic expression from other modernist artists while exploring questions such as "what was 'Iranian' in their work? What was the relationship between the paintings and sculptured pieces that they were turning out and their country's cultural heritage?"[154]

In 1989, Kamran Diba, the former director of the TMoCA, facilitated *Saqqakhaneh*'s inclusion into the canon of global modernism by naming it "spiritual pop art." As he explained,

There is a parallel between Saqqa-Khaneh and Pop Art, if we simplify Pop Art as an art movement which looks at the symbols and tools of a mass consumer society as a relevant and influencing cultural force, Saqqa-Khaneh artists looked at the inner beliefs and popular symbols that were part of the religion and culture of Iran, and perhaps, consumed in the same way as

---

[153] Ibid. [154] Karim, 'ART IN IRAN xi. POST-QAJAR.'

industrial products in the West (but for different reasons and under dissimilar circumstances).[155]

In *Encyclopedia of Art – Painting, Sculpture, and Graphic Arts*, which was published in Persian in 1999, the art historian Pakbaz explained that *Saqqakhaneh* was neither a specific school nor a unified group of members but rather more of an artistic style in search of new means of expression based on Iran's visual heritage.[156]

Generally speaking, *Saqqakhaneh*'s reception often concentrates on its incorporation of past visual traditions as a source of artistic inspiration. Thus, various scholars see artworks by *Saqqakhaneh*-related artists as the result of an artistic quest for an Iranian identity that could reconcile the tropes of modernity with Iranian elements. In his book, *Jostejoo-ye hoviyat dar naqqashi-ye mo'aser-e Iran*, the revolutionary painter Mortezza Goudarzi interprets Iranian art history as a series of artistic attempts to create national or religious identity in the arts. For Goudarzi, *Saqqakhaneh*, with its turn to religion and Shi'ite iconography, represents an artistic reaction to the ongoing antiwesternization debates articulated by writers and intellectuals such as al-e Ahmad and Shariati, who, according to Goudarzi, were highly influential on the art critic Emami and artists associated with *Saqqakhaneh*.[157]

The question of Iranian identity politics as a result of the discourse about how to negotiate modernity also forms the focus of art historian Hamid Keshmirshekan's scholarly contributions concerning *Saqqakhaneh*'s artistic production. According to Keshmirshekan, *Saqqakhaneh* is an expression of neo-traditionalism that tried to bridge the allegedly dialectical relationship between tradition and modernity. Its artistic style is not necessarily limited to a certain group of artists, since it "later was extended to all the artists, both painters and sculptors, who drew directly on the traditional art forms of Iran as raw material for their work."[158] For Keshmirshekan, artists associated with *Saqqakhaneh* used Iranian visual heritage for mostly formalist reasons in order to "create an identifiable traditional and sometimes religious atmosphere rather than specific subject matter" in order to

---

[155] Kamran Diba, 'Iran,' in Wijdan Ali (ed.), *Contemporary Art from the Islamic World* (London: Scorpion Publication, 1989), 150–158, 153.
[156] Pakbaz, *Encyclopedia of Art*, 893.
[157] Mortezza Goudarzi, *Chostoochooy-e hoviat dar naghashi-e moaser-e Iran [The Search for Identity in Iran's Modern Painting]* (Tehran, 2002).
[158] Keshmirshekan, 'Neo-Traditionalism,' 614.

"Iranicize their works."[159] The artists' exploration of possible concepts of Iranian identity through their works of art took place, according to Keshmirshekan, in full harmony with modernization and westernization because the artists referred "to their own roots without turning away from the West."[160]

Iranian modernism also gained international recognition, when the Grey Art Gallery hosted the exhibition "Between Word and Image: Modern Iranian Visual Culture" at New York University's Fine Arts Museum in 2002. In particular, the accompanying publication, *Picturing Iran: Art Society and Revolution*, addressed "questions of modernity in Iran through the lens of visual culture."[161] Due to Abby Weed Grey's activities as a collector and her friendship with Tanavoli, *Saqqakhaneh*-related artworks were a major part of the exhibition. For the curators, Lynn Gumpert and Shiva Balaghi, the example of *Saqqakhaneh* helped to demonstrate that non-Western modernist arts are not at all "a simple act of imitation and mimicry."[162] By employing vernacular elements of Persian culture and transferring them into a new context of meaning, these "artists imagined ways to exist as Iranians within a modern consumer society" and suggest "that modernity in the Iranian context was a complex field of negotiation and accommodation."[163]

The art world's internationalization and globalization reinforced the concept of *Saqqakhaneh*, especially when the TMoCA was revived under the directorship of Alireza Sami-Azar (1999–2005) and held exhibitions and published catalogs about artists associated with *Saqqakhaneh*, such as Parviz Tanavoli, Charles Hossein Zenderoudi, and Massoud Arabshahi.

The above-mentioned scholarly positions and exhibition initiatives have set the stage for the further reception of *Saqqakhaneh* as a central element in Iranian modernist art historiography and led to its scholarly canonization both inside and outside Iran. Not only do exhibition projects reiterate and perpetuate *Saqqakhaneh* as a constituent factor of Iranian art history, numerous articles and scholarly contributions also discuss the concept of *Saqqakhaneh*. In Iran, a new peak of publications about *Saqqakhaneh* was reached after the TMoCA

---

[159] Ibid., 628. [160] Ibid.
[161] Gumpert, 'Introduction,' in Balaghi and Gumpert, *Picturing Iran*, 11–16, 11.
[162] Ibid. [163] Balaghi, 'Iranian Visual Arts,' 25.

Saqqakhaneh's *Discursive Afterlife*   203

Figure 3.4 *Saqqakhaneh* Exhibition Catalog, 2013. Tehran Museum of Contemporary Art

organized a major exhibition about *Saqqakhaneh* in 2013, initiated by the artist and critic Mehdi Hosseini and strongly modeled after the first *Saqqakhaneh* exhibition at this institution in 1978. It is interesting to note how easily the Islamic Republic of Iran could host a *Saqqakhaneh* exhibition in a prominent state institution, despite Farah Diba's former promotion and instrumentalization of this style as a modernist national artistic language.

This ideological appropriation was possible because *Saqqakhaneh*-related artworks employ timeless religious and traditional subjects in their visual language and also because, as was shown earlier, art historians such as Mortezza Goudarzi likened *Saqqakhaneh* to the anti-Western sentiments of the 1960s and 1970s. Thus, these artworks can easily operate in the broader discourse of Iranian identity politics, while also fitting with the Islamic Republic's official ideology. Ehsan Aghaee, the director of the museum at the time, has clarified how this artistic development took place in his writings.

The Iranian society, which in those days lacked the necessary infrastructures for change, was suddenly faced with a phenomenon called modern art, which was unknown in the subconscious minds of the Iranians as a whole. The changes brought about in the technique and content by modern painting, lacked the necessary intellectual and spiritual backing among our nation's artists. After many years and from the early sixties, the Iranian genius came forth once again and the Iranian modern art was born.... This art was in line with the religious and national beliefs, which today can be recalled as modern Iranian art.[164]

In the Iranian context, in particular, *Saqqakhaneh* turned into a general term denoting any modernist arts that made reference to local content or Persian visual traditions. This term has since become so powerful that, to this day, many artists and art historians debate *Saqqakhaneh*'s emergence and impact on following generations of artists. Art magazines in Iran, such as *Tandis* and *Herfeh Honarmand*, continuously review the *Saqqakhaneh* movement and discuss the ways in which modernism in general and Iranian modernism in particular took shape.[165] After the 2013 exhibition at the TMoCA, *Saqqakhaneh* experienced a strong revival in publications and interviews.[166] In a round table talk, for instance, the artists and writers Behrang Samadzadegan, Behnam Kamrani, and Siamak Delzendeh not only discussed *Saqqakhaneh*'s heritage but also questioned its legacy and art-historiographical dominance, in light of the lack of a major scholarly work on its evolution and emergence. From a postcolonial standpoint, these artists and scholars demanded a critical reflection on the myth of *Saqqakhaneh* and a deeper investigation of the subject beyond the limits of mere formalism.[167] This reflects a new approach toward *Saqqakhaneh* artistic production, which has often been staged as a mere reflection of Pahlavi modernism. The Islamic Revolution in 1978/79 and the sudden end of modernism and modernity as promoted by the Pahlavi monarchy also had a dramatic effect on *Saqqakhaneh*'s reception. Generally speaking, the revolution was often depicted as a failure of Pahlavi modernization programs and a sign of the Iranian people's political immaturity and the victory of

---

[164] Ehsan Aghaee, *A Retrospective Exhibition of Works of Saqqakhana Movement*, Exh.-Cat. (Tehran: Museum of Contemporary Art Tehran, 2013), 5.

[165] In 2019, the newly established magazine *Poshtebaam* published a special issue on *Saqqakhaneh*, providing a collection of articles as well as bibliographies on the topic. See, *Poshtebaam, Art Magazine*, Issue 1, 2019.

[166] For example, see Javad Mojabi's book containing collected interviews with Iran's modernist artists, *Saramdan-e Honar-e Noh [The Pioneers of New Art]* (Tehran: Behnegar, 2015).

[167] For a further examination, see roundtable discussion about Saqqakhaneh's heritage with Behran Samadzadegan, Behnam Kamrani and Siamak Delzendeh, 9 April 2014, Etemad Newspaper. www.magiran.com/article/2926864, accessed 23 October 2019.

Islamic traditions over Western modernity. Consequently, the merging of Western means of expression with Islamic and Persian visual elements in *Saqqakhaneh*'s artistic production no longer represented a reconciliation of tradition and modernity but was rather seen as Iranian art's failed attempt to become truly modern. The artist Parvaneh Etemadi, for example, claims that the incorporation of past traditions contradicts contemporaneity per se.

If there were such a thing as Saqqakhaneh School, what it was doing was copying compositions on magic, superstition and ... having enchanting visual effects, appearing very native and original in the eyes of foreigners. If we work in a contemporary way, what have we to do with superstitious or traditionalist traditions?! Unless we are producing works which tourists would love.[168]

More recent positions critically reflect upon the notions of modernity and observe the turn to tradition as a specific feature of modernization in "Third World" countries. For the art historian Combiz Moussavi-Aghdam, *Saqqakhaneh* represents a state-sponsored modernism operating in the global art discourse of Cold War politics. Moussavi, however, sees it as an attempt to "overcome the sense of inferiority caused by the aforementioned Orientalist attitude of Westerners toward 'Third World' art and culture."[169] Nevertheless, according to Moussavi, *Saqqakhaneh* could not satisfy society's needs of a specifically Iranian modernism and remained reserved exclusively for an elite circle. He argues,

For the cultural officials and artists alike, the idea of national art, which presented an 'authentic', 'homogeneous' and 'monolithic' self as indicative of national autonomy, was concealed in the treasury of pre-Islamic and Islamic tradition and had to be explored by connoisseurs and linked to the politics of a modern nation-state.[170]

For the painter and writer Iman Afsarian, the artistic return to the self represents a romanticist reaction to the political trauma caused by the 1953 coup d'état against Mohammad Mosaddeq, the hindrance of Iran's oil nationalization, and the suppression of the communist

---

[168] Parvaneh Etemadi, 'In Order to Create, One Must First Destroy': An Interview with Parvaneh Etemadi,' *Payvand*, 2017. www.payvand.com/news/17/apr/1123.html, accessed 23 October 2019.

[169] Moussavi-Aghdam, 'Art History,' 146.   [170] Ibid.

Tudeh party. Seeking artistic inspiration in Iran's indistinct past functioned, according to Afsarian, as a strategy of repression and means of forgetting to cope with the destruction of the Mosaddeq years' hopes for democratization. In his opinion, *Saqqakhaneh* was highly welcomed by the Pahlavi state as the official form of modernism not only due to its apolitical outlook, but also because, by choosing only those elements from their Persian and Islamic heritage which functioned visually in the discourse of Western modernism, the artists created artworks that aimed to please Western modes of perception.[171]

This selection of art-historiographical positions demonstrates that *Saqqakhaneh* is a complex concept of categorization in Iranian art history, which has nearly attained the status of a dogma of Iranian modernism. The foregoing synopsis of the respective designations, however, has demonstrated that, as an art-historiographical category, *Saqqakhaneh* is nebulous and lacks a clear definition, while our analysis of the few original written sources shows that the use of *Saqqakhaneh* as a term and category is not only inconsistent but also insufficient as a description for such diverse artistic expression by such diverse artists.

Looking at *Saqqakhaneh*'s history as an idea, Emami's attempt to create a counter-narrative to the instrumentalization and institutionalization of all cultural production in the Pahlavi era, it seems almost ironic that *Saqqakhaneh* has become a symbol of the monarchy's modernism. This institutionalization was possible because of the Pahlavi regime's discursive shift and embracing of Iran's spiritual heritage in the 1970s. Thus, artists such as Tanavoli, who depicted themes from Persian Sufi traditions in their artworks, became the perfect protagonists in the enactment of a state-sponsored modernism. This strategy became so powerful that the myth of *Saqqakhaneh* has led to works by artists that incorporate Iranian or Islamic iconography easily being categorized as *Saqqakhaneh* works, without a deeper investigation of the image's content, its history, or visual techniques. As an art-historical category with various connotations, such as, for example, its being a reflection of Pahlavi modernism, the term *Saqqakhaneh* not only prevents a deeper look at the various works of art and the diversity of artistic expression but is also a hindrance to seeing artistic production as a historical source that can help us gain a

---

[171] Afsarian, *Talar-e Qandriz*, 12–21.

better understanding of the sociopolitical discourses surrounding that work. The art-historiographical processes and their establishment of *Saqqakhaneh* as a global category for Iranian modernism demonstrate art history's decisive contribution to the depoliticization of *Saqqakhaneh*'s artistic production. It is, for this reason, necessary to look at the works and artistic production from this period without the reductive historiographical framework of *Saqqakhaneh*, which continues to prevent deeper investigation of the topic.

4 | *Jalil Ziapour and the* Fighting Rooster Association *(Ḵorūs-e Jangī)*

Cubist Aesthetics in Iran

In 1948, together with his artistic colleagues, the writer Gholam Hossein Gharib (1923–2003), playwright Hassan Shirvani, and composer Morteza Hannaneh (1922–1989), the Iranian painter Jalil Ziapour (1920–1999) founded the *Fighting Rooster Association* (*Anjoman-e Ḵorūs-e Jangī*) to promote the newly emerging modernist arts in Iran. Jalil Ziapour and the *Fighting Rooster Association* were the leading representatives of Cubism in Iran, which arose as a movement in the 1940s and offered Iranian artists such as Ziapour a suitable vocabulary to elaborate an artistic subjectivity based on Iranian heritage.[1] At the same time, it also helped to promote the *Fighting Rooster Association*'s own aim of fostering the democratic hope for an Iranian nation. This chapter focuses on the group's works and texts in light of Orphic Cubist theory and highlights the beginnings of modernist art in Iran, the global entanglements of modernism, and the search for an Iranian art beyond orientalist painting traditions and exotic depictions of being the "other."[2]

Jalil Ziapour's artistic practice illustrates how experiences of migration and transcultural processes of translation shaped the development of modernist arts in Iran. Ziapour became familiar with European modernist art during his studies at the École-des-Beaux-Arts and with

---

[1] I would like to thank the two anonymous peer reviewers for their fruitful comments; part of Chapter 4 is based on a revised version of the essay Katrin Nahidi, 'Cubism in Iran: Jalil Ziapour and the Fighting Rooster Association,' *Stedelijk Studies Journal*, vol. 9 (2019), doi:10.54533/StedStud.vol009.art08.

[2] For further examination of the theoretical terms of "orientalism" and "exoticism" in relation to Iranian art, see Hamid Keshmirshekan, 'The Question of Identity vis-à-vis Exoticism in Contemporary Iranian Art,' *Iranian Studies*, vol. 43, no. 4 (2010) 489–512. Also see Keshmirshekan, 'Globalization and the Question of Identity: Discourses on Contemporary Iranian Art during the Past Two Decades,' in Keshmirshekan, *Amidst Shadow and Light*, 64–81.

Cubism, in particular, at André Lhote's private art school. As one of the representatives of Orphic Cubism, Lhote provided his students with an insight into the Cubist language of forms.[3] Orphic Cubism was strongly shaped by the writings of the philosopher Henri Bergson. The antirationalist and antipositivist underpinnings of Bergson's thought helped to establish Cubist artistic language and theories of visual perception. Bergsonian theory also provided the basis for their political efforts to articulate an alternative, leftist nationalism before World War I. The strong connection between political commitment and artistic expression had a crucial impact on the *Fighting Rooster Association*'s activities, and a closer examination of their writings will demonstrate that their aesthetic principles were also informed by Bergson's thought as translated in the Iranian context through tropes of Sufism. The recourse to Bergson's philosophical ideas enabled the Iranian artists to proclaim an alternative cultural identity rooted in Iran's spiritual heritage to counteract modern rationality as it was adopted in Iran.

A close reading of the first issue of the eponymous journal demonstrates that the *Fighting Rooster Association* was deeply engaged in articulating new aesthetics with the ideal of educating the masses. The group's central thought was based on a socialist understanding of art that was intended to promote a leftist nationalism. Their ideologically leftist alignment, however, is also the reason why the group has never been fully institutionalized in Iran's modernist art canon, which, as we have seen, was largely established against the background of anticommunist Cold War ideology. To this day, Iran's modernist canon functions to illustrate the Pahlavi state's alleged secular modernization.

Jalil Ziapour's Zaynab Khatoun

Jalil Ziapour's painting *Zaynab Khatoun* (1953, repainted in 1962) is a prominent example of his translation of Cubist aesthetic principles into a local context and helped to spread Cubism as a modernist language of expression in Iran (Figure 4.1). *Zaynab Khatoun* was

---

[3] For further investigation of André Lhote's Art Academy, see Zeynab Kuban and Simone Wille (eds.), *André Lhote and His International Students* (Innsbruck: Innsbruck University Press, 2020).

Figure 4.1 Jalil Ziapour, *Zaynab Khatoun*, 1953, repainted in 1962. Oil on canvas, 127 × 117 cm. Tehran Museum of Contemporary Art

displayed at the first Tehran Biennial in 1958, where it won Ziapour the gold medal.[4]

Zaynab Khatoun shows a woman combing her hair in a public bath, a so-called *hamam*. The figure crouches in an unnatural, twisted pose in front of a yellow, green, and bluish tile panel. While the strong grid structure of the tile pattern creates a geometrical linear composition, the yellow part of the background illuminates her naked and cubic,

---

[4] *The First Exhibition of Tehran Biennial*, Exh.-Cat. (Tehran: General Administration of Fine Arts, 1958).

sculptural body. Her bronze-colored body and her dark hair, which waves around her silhouette like a sheet, take center stage. The figure stretches both her arms in a triangle above her head, while holding a turquoise comb in her hands. Against the illuminated yellow tile background, the viewer's focus falls on the turquoise comb and contrasts with the female's red, henna-colored hands and feet. The color palette of the woman's body consists mainly of shades of brown and black. The depiction of the female model from various viewpoints makes her posture appear unnatural and twisted. Even though the woman's sculptural body and the way she balances on a frame indicated in the painting suggest a certain three-dimensionality, the painting remains flat and devoid of any depth. The flatness of the pictorial space and the emphasis on the tiled structure create a geometrical impression. The tiles' strong lines are the dominant feature of the image and simultaneously disassemble and reassemble the painting. The tiles (which are used in the Iranian tradition for both ornamentation in mosques and the depiction of high-ranking personalities in palaces) are not only a geometric pattern but can themselves also turn into an independent element, which breaks up the space of the painting.

A closer look at the painting reveals a text banner surrounding the female figure with the lines of a children's poem by the poet Parvin Dowlatabadi (1924–2008). This use of writing is an important feature of *Zaynab Khatoun*, as the interplay between text and image reveals the picture's complex textual and visual program. For Persian-literate viewers, the poem indicates that the painting illustrates a bathing scene in a *hamam*.

> Chamchomak the autumn leaf,
> Zaynab Khatoun is my mother,
> Her hair is as long as a bow,
> It is longer than a bow,
> It is blacker like sabagh,
> She wants to stay thirty days in the hamam,
> She wants a turquoise comb.[5]

With his reference to the *hamam*, Ziapour's painting offers an alternative depiction of oriental bathing scenes that stands in stark contrast to

---

[5] Translation by the author from the painting. See also Mehdi Hosseini, 'Obituary on Jalil Ziapour,' www.ziapour.com/memorial/هرگز-نمیرد-آنکه-دلش-زنده-شد-به-عشق-2/, accessed 26 April 2019.

those of orientalists such as Jean Léon Gérôme (1824–1904) and Dominique Ingres (1780–1867). In this way, Ziapour deconstructs the orientalist erotic imaginary of public baths as created, for instance, by Ingres in his 1862 painting *The Turkish Bath* (1862).[6] Ingres' painting creates a spatially realistic impression. The depicted scene presents countless naked white women sitting and reclining on cushions on the floor. The relaxed intimacy in this exclusively female space constructs a homoerotic atmosphere as we perceive the intertwined bodies in their erotic postures. Ziapour's painting differs not only in its lack of eroticism but also in its concentration on one single female figure performing various bath-related actions. Ziapour's figure is shown from the front and seems to seek eye contact with the viewer, allowing her nudity to appear more provocative. While, in Ingres' painting, the naked figure depicted with its back toward the viewer functions as a possible means of identification for what Roger Benjamin has described as "the dominating masculine voyeurism suggested by the construction of a picture as a peephole view onto a zone forbidden to male access."[7]

Instead, Ziapour offers an unconventional concept of a bathing scene that is rooted in a local pictorial tradition. This is very significant because an earlier generation of Iranian art, namely, Qajar photography in the nineteenth century, undoubtedly borrowed from orientalist image conventions. As Ali Behdad states, "Having internalized the discourse and practices of Orientalism, Nasir al-Din Shah depicts himself and his wives in the same stereotypical way as European artists represented Middle Eastern women and the oriental despot."[8]

In the Persian painting tradition, the depiction of a nude woman bathing often also refers to the iconography of Khosrow and Shirin. The legendary love story between the Sassanian King Khosrow and the Armenian princess Shirin dates back to the poetry of Nizami Ganjavi (1141–1209), who became very popular for the stories in his famous poem collection *Khamseh*. One of the tale's climaxes is Khosrow's

---

[6] Jean-Auguste-Dominique Ingres, *The Turkish Bath* (*Le Bain turc*), 1862, Oil on canvas, 108 × 110 cm, Musée de Louvre, Paris.

[7] Roger Benjamin, *The Oriental Mirage, Orientalism: Delacroix to Klee* (Sydney: Art Gallery of New South Wales, 1997), 15.

[8] Ali Behdad, 'The Powerful Art of Qajar Photography: Orientalism and (Self)-Orientalizing in Nineteenth-Century Iran,' *Iranian Studies*, vol. 34, no. 1/4, 'Qajar Art and Society' (2001), 141–151, 148.

discovery of Shirin bathing in a pool. This very popular scene has been depicted in miniatures, tiles, and many other visual forms throughout the history of Iran's visual art production.[9] The iconography of Shirin taking a bath often concentrates on the crucial moment of recognition between Khosrow and Shirin, in which both believe they have glimpsed their respective beloved. One prominent example of this moment's depiction is the Safavid miniature from Nizami's Khamsa (1539–1543) at the British Library in London.[10] The miniature painting's diagonal composition divides the scene into two parts and depicts Shirin and Khosrow in two separate settings. Shirin occupies the lower-left corner of the image and is depicted sitting half-nude in a pool with black water, her braids covering her breasts. The meeting of their gaze functions as the unifying element that connects the separated parts of the image. In his painting, Ziapour reduces the scene to a depiction of Shirin bathing. Ziapour's female nude is seeking eye contact with the beholder, who, by making eye contact, slips into Khosrow's role. This is a significant artistic strategy meant to emphasize the figure's gaze and the moment of recognition as the painting's central element.

Textually, the work's title, *Zaynab Khatoun*, and the employment of the poem open an ambiguous space of interpretation. The combination of poem and image not only connects religious and national discourses with one another but also forms a new moment of transgression. This allows for different interpretations because the religious implications of the Shi'ite figure of Zaynab are connected to the familial imagery of modern nations, personified in this case by the mother. This enables Ziapour to express his idea of a possible Iranian national identity rooted in local traditions. By naming his painting *Zaynab Khatoun*, Ziapour evokes different religious and cultural associations in the mind of the viewer.

Zaynab is the daughter of Fatima and Imam Ali, the sister of martyr Hussein, the granddaughter of the prophet, and an important figure in the Iranian Shi'ite context. She is often represented in hagiographic literature because of her significant role during the tragic events of the battle of Karbala, where she was part of her brother's resistance

---

[9] Peter J. Chelkowski (ed.), *Mirror of the Invisible World: Tales from the Khamseh of Nizami*. Exh.-Cat. (New York: Metropolitan Museum of Art, 1975).

[10] *Khusraw spies Shirin bathing*. Miniature: Nizami, *Khamsa*. Tabriz, 1539–1543. 36 × 25 cm. Manuscript on paper. London, The British Library, Oriental and India Office Collections.

against the tyrant Yazid and witnessed the killing of seventy-two men in the battle of Karbala. After the brutal murder of Hussein and his followers, Zaynab became a prominent exponent of the Shi'ite message.[11]

As a legitimate representative of the party of Hussein, Zaynab represents the opposition to Yazid. The speeches she delivered in Kufa and Damascus at Yazid's court are seen as a continuation of Hussein's battle. For Shariati, Zaynab incorporates a feminized version of resistance, as he later stated.

Whereas Zainab, the sister of Imam Hosein, who takes a heavier mandate, the mandate of Hosein in her Ali-like hands, continues the movement of Karbala, which opposed murders, lying, terror and hysterics. She continues the movement at a time when all the heroes of the revolution are dead and the breath of the forerunners of Islam has ceased in the midst of our people, when commanders of the Islam of Mohammad and the Shi'ism of Ali are gone. But she has been turned into 'a sister who mourns.'[12]

Ziapour's reference to Shi'ite history is not an endless delving into the past but rather the testimony of a living tradition. Zaynab's character was kept alive because her mourning for the martyring of her brother and nephews is a major feature in *ta'ziyeh*, the Iranian passion plays, a yearly reenactment of the battle of Karbala during the month of Muharram. As mentioned, in 1932, during the rule of Reza Shah, *ta'ziyeh* was prohibited because, for Iran's government, it epitomized backwardness as seen from the perspective of modernization. Nonetheless, the century-old practice of reenacting the battle of Karbala could not be restricted entirely and survived in rural areas and villages. The imposition of these religious limitations popularized the symbols of the *ta'ziyeh* and "became the artillery of the religious revolution which toppled the Pahlavi regime."[13]

Ziapour's painting could also be a visual implementation of the Qur'anic figure of Zaynab bint Jahsh, one of prophet Muhammad's

---

[11] Peter J. Chelkowski, 'Iconography of the Women of Karbala: Tiles, Murals, Stamps, and Posters,' in Kamran Scot Aghaie (ed.), *The Women of Karbala: Ritual Performance and Symbolic Discourses in Modern Shi'i Islam* (Austin: University of Texas Press, 2005), 119–138, 120.

[12] Ali Shariati, *Fatima Is Fatima*, translated by Laleh Bakhtiar (Tehran: Shariati Foundation, 1981), 42–43.

[13] Rebecca Ansary Pettys, 'The Ta'zieh: Ritual Enactment of Persian Renewal,' *Theatre Journal*, vol. 33, no. 3 (1981), 341–354, 347.

wives. After the prophet had arranged a marriage between Zaynab and his adopted son, Zaid ibn Harithah, he accidentally saw Zaynab taking a bath and immediately fell in love with her.[14] Still, the prophet married his cousin Zaynab to his adopted son Zaid ibn Harithah. One day, the prophet paid a visit to Zaid's house, but his son was not home and he found only Zaynab. "At the house entrance was a curtain made of pelts, and when the wind lifted this curtain, it revealed the sight of Zaynab 'uncovered' in her chamber."[15] Various traditions embellish the story in various ways. Tabari, for instance, states that Zaynab was not dressed properly, whereas Ibn Babawayh mentions that the encounter took place while Zaynab was taking a bath.[16] The latter version, in particular, corresponds closely with Ziapour's depiction.

When Zaid found out about the meeting, he suggested to the prophet that, if the prophet admired her beauty, he would get separated from Zaynab. Even though the prophet refused, Zaid divorced his wife shortly thereafter and, after observing the waiting period, Muhammad married Zaynab. To avoid being criticized by society for marrying his son's wife, Mohammad had to dissolve Zaid's legal status as his adopted son, as described in Surah 33:37–40.

When you [Prophet] said to the man who had been favoured by God and by you, 'Keep your wife and be mindful of God,' you hid in your heart what God would later reveal: you were afraid of people, but it is more fitting that you fear God. When Zayd no longer wanted her, We gave her to you in marriage so that there might be no fault in believers marrying the wives of their adopted sons after they no longer wanted them. God's command must be carried out.[17]

In the context of the painting, the topic of religion is not, however, an expression of belief but rather functions for Ziapour as a manifestation of cultural belonging, as evidenced by the second line of the children's poem in the painting's poem: "Zaynab Khatoun is my mother." The allegory of the mother alludes to the process of modernization in Iran, mainly in the Constitutionalist era (1906–1910), when new terms such

---

[14] Barbara Freyer Stowasser, *Women in the Qur'an, Traditions, and Interpretation* (New York: Oxford University Press, 1996), 123–124.
[15] Ibid., 88.
[16] Ibid.; see Ibn Babawayh Surah Isra 17:40; *The History of Al-Tabari: The Victory of Islam*, translated by Michael Fishbein (Albany, 1997), vol. VIII, 2–3.
[17] Abdel Haleem Muhammad, *The Qur'an* (New York: Oxford University Press, 2004), 269.

as "nation," "politics," "citizenship," and "homeland" had to be created to name modern political entities. In general, Iranian nationalism was achieved through a reshaping of central concepts. The idea of the modern nation was often articulated through the use of familial metaphors, especially in the Iranian context, where the idea of homeland as "mother" had a special significance for the construction of a national identity.[18]

As Afsaneh Najmabadi has shown, there is a deeply rooted tradition in modern Persian literature of metaphorically portraying the homeland as a mother, which can be traced back to motifs from Sufi literature. The modernist idea of *vatan* has its roots in Sufi thought. *Vatan* is an allegorical term to denote a spatial configuration of the other world, a spiritual abode beyond the material world, where unification with God is possible. In this discourse, the grave can also function as *vatan* because it is the symbol of "the return to the earth, to one's original substance, the beginning of the return to God."[19] The Sufi concept of *vatan* is very similar to the idea of the homeland as mother, as Najmabadi further states because "the return to earth was also a return to the womb whence one had been born."[20] The fetus in the womb is protected from possible contamination by outside world. Najmabadi therefore concludes that "the Sufi desire to reach the grave and to unite with the divine expressed a desire to return to the mother's womb."[21]

The idea of *hubb al-watan min-iman* ("love of homeland is love of the faith") was attributed to the prophet Muhammad and was interpreted in Sufi teachings as a way to attempt to achieve unification with the divine through love.[22] In the twentieth century, its meaning shifted and the Sufi allegory of divine love turned into love for Iran, as, for instance, when a Constitutionalist newspaper used this expression to foster patriotic feelings in their audience. The nationalist alteration of the Sufi concept "was affectively produced through the re-articulation of classical Persian mystical erotic love literature."[23]

With its emphasis on the term *vatan*, this poetic shift produced a new literary genre of patriotic poetry. With the invocation of a fictional "we" and "us," this poetry helped to create the image of Iran's people

---

[18] Afsaneh Najmabadi, 'The Erotic Vatan [Homeland] as Beloved and Mother: To Love, to Possess, and to Protect,' *Comparative Studies in Society and History*, vol. 39, no. 3 (1997), 442–467, 442.
[19] Ibid., 447. [20] Ibid. [21] Ibid. [22] Ibid. [23] Ibid., 451.

as one homogenous nation. The trope of Iran as a mother was also a means of articulating citizens' obligation to respect and love their mother. However, the gendered articulation of the mother as geo-body is also related to the discourse of protection and defense. It also demands a certain degree of nationalism for the protection of the selfless mother. Najmabadi has argued that these familial metaphors played an important role in the process of identity formation and helped to create a specific sentiment of Iranianness based on similarities beyond religious and ethnic differences.

In this context, the sentence "Zaynab Khatoun is my mother" takes on a particularly strong meaning in connection with the metaphor of the mother as homeland, that is, Iran. Jalil Ziapour's image consequently develops the message to suggest replacing the line "Zaynab Khatoun is my mother" with "Zaynab Khatoun is my homeland." With the different textual and visual connotations of the figure of Zaynab, Ziapour expresses his commitment to Iran's cultural-religious heritage.

What is fascinating about this painting is not only Ziapour's personal artistic expression but also how it constitutes the position of the viewer. The nude woman appears to make direct eye contact with the beholder. This compositional strategy goes hand in hand with the different textual implications of the female figure. Common to all the textual references selected by Ziapour is the intimate moment of recognition of the beloved. Even though Khosrow and Shirin had never actually met, during their short encounter, they felt that they were meant for one another. The prophet Muhammad also immediately recognizes Zaynab as his future wife in the moment when the curtain is lifted. In this context, Ziapour's painting loosely plays with various possible associations of the female figure, rendering the precise identity of the female figure less important. This associative process simultaneously takes place on a visual and a textual level. Ziapour concentrates on the depiction of the female nude but represents her without any recognizable iconographic attributes. As a result, her gaze gains in importance and directly involves the observer. The direct eye contact invites the viewer to identify itself with the lover and again stresses the moment of recognition underlying all narrations of Zaynab and Shirin's story. The synthesis of the central moment of recognition and the nationalistic implications of the trope of the mother transform Ziapour's painting into a kind of mirror.

With *Zaynab Khatoun*, Ziapour makes clear stylistic breaks with earlier Iranian painting traditions and demonstrates that he was familiar with modernist European arts. In this work, he employs aspects of the Cubist language of forms, such as the flatness of pictorial space, multiple perspectives, and the abandonment of naturalism. The sculptural portrayal of the female figure evokes associations with Alexander Archipenko's bronze statues; the assemblage of different artistic means, such as tiles, sculpture, and miniature, resonate with the characteristics of the Cubist collages; and the representation of Zaynab recalls Pablo Picasso's depictions of bathers.

Ziapour belongs to the first generation of modernist artists who deliberately abandoned the realistic-naturalistic styles of earlier generations of Iranian painters who had adopted Western painting techniques and aesthetic principles. Due to his artistic innovations and experiments with modernist European expression, Ziapour became known in Iran as a "pioneer" and was even called the "father of modernism."[24] The term "pioneer" is a translation of the Persian word *pishgaman*, meaning "foot soldiers," and is used to refer to the first generation of modernist artists in Iran. This notion of a militant avant-garde refers to their path-breaking achievement in an inhospitable environment still unfriendly to modernist art.[25] The term "pioneer" reinforces the idea of Ziapour, along with other artists, as importers of modernist art, but concomitantly prevents a more in-depth analysis of his artistic work. As a pioneer, he prepared the ground for modernist art at a time when this new form of artistic production was still regarded very critically and had hardly any institutional framework.

Ziapour's decisive role and his agency in the development of modernist expression in Iran have been widely discussed, especially in recent years, in English, French,[26] and Persian

---

[24] Javad Mojabi, *Pioneers of Contemporary Persian Painting, First Generation* (Tehran: Iranian Art Publishing, 1996), 3–21. See also Alice Bombardier, *Les pionniers de la Nouvelle peinture en Iran: OEuvres méconnues, activités novatrices et scandales au tournant des années 1940* (Bern: Peter Lang, 2017).

[25] Mojabi, *Pioneers*.

[26] For further study of the subject, see a selection of important contributions, Bombardier, *Les pionniers de la Nouvelle peinture en Iran*. See also Aida Foroutan, 'Why the Fighting Cock? The Significance of the Imagery of the Khorus Jangi and Its Manifesto "The Slaughterer of the Nightingale",' *Iran Namag*, vol. 1, no. 1 (Spring 2016), XXVIII–XLIX; Parastoo Jafari, *New Word,*

publications.[27] Keshmirshekan, who has studied modern and contemporary Iranian art extensively and contributed tremendously to the study of Iranian modernism in a global context, considers Ziapour's art "as the practical application of the artist's proposal for developing a modern visual language on the basis of Iran's national heritage."[28] Most historiographical renditions follow a formalist approach and see Ziapour's style as one of the first attempts to adopt modernity in the visual arts and to connect Western means of expression with Iranian content.

Nevertheless, Ziapour's works of art are often understood as belated imitations of European modernist art, resulting from an artistic immaturity concerning Western art as well as the belated introduction of Cubism in Iran. In this regard, the art historian Ruyin Pakbaz states that the adaptation of Western art occurred primarily on a stylistic and technical level, without a deeper understanding of Western modernity. In particular, for Pakbaz, Ziapour's artistic practice of merging Cubist expression with Iranian elements, such as mosques and bazaars, represents an irreconcilable conflict with a presumedly universal modernity.[29]

Ziyâ-Poor's "Cubism" was not representative of what the term commonly denotes, for his art lacked some essential elements of cubism. This was basically because Iranian mosques and bazaars, for example, just could not give way to industrial shapes and edifices, nor could traditional Iranian geometrical shapes, mostly curvilinear anyway, simply could (*sic!*) not be replaced by the mechanistic geometrical forms favoured by cubism.[30]

For the art historian Daftari, Ziapour's adaptation of Cubist formal language was an immature attempt to nationalize Iranian art. She argues that during Ziapour's migratory experience in the postwar years in Paris, Cubism and Fauvism were undergoing a renaissance as part of an effort to reconnect with France's prewar and pre-German-occupation cultural past. Thus, according to Daftari, Cubism provided Ziapour with a suitable vocabulary to establish an Iranian modernist art in the service of nationalization.[31] The art critic Bavand Behpoor

Other Value. Artistic Modernism and Private Patronage: Associations and Galleries in Pre-Islamic Revolution Iran (Munich: OPH Press, 2020).

[27] See Farshid Parsikia et al. (eds.), *Horus-e changi, Pazuheshi darbare-ye anjoman-e honari* [*The Fighting Rooster, Research about the Artistic Association*] (Tehran: Poshtebaamag.ir, 2019).

[28] Keshmirshekan, *Contemporary Iranian Art*, 60.

[29] Pakbaz, *Contemporary Iranian Painting*, 14.   [30] Ibid.

[31] Daftari, 'Another Modernism,' 47.

affirms that the adaptation of a Cubist style was a way to connect to the artistic legacy of Picasso, who served as role model for many Middle Eastern artists, and thus a mere signifier of avant-gardism.[32] Mortezza Goudarzi goes one step further and harshly criticizes Ziapour's attempt to link Cubist and Iranian elements as a massive failure and accuses the painter of harming the reputation of French Cubism in Iran.[33] Occasionally, Iranian art historiography also interprets Cubism in Iran as a belated copy of Picasso's artistic practice. This phenomenon not only applies to the Iranian context but is also a wider phenomenon in the study of non-Western art history, which the art historian Partha Mitter has described as the "Picasso manqué syndrome."[34] The Picasso manqué syndrome stems from Western art history's epistemology of creating a history of artistic influence, which also includes the study of artistic production outside the West. Producing a history of Western influence also carries power-political implications and thus contributes to the establishment of a colonial art history. This history tends to present Western artists and their practice of cultural appropriation as superior, whereas the practice of "borrowing by artists from the peripheries becomes a badge of inferiority."[35]

Jalil Ziapour and French Cubism

Both for a better understanding of the practice of Cubism in Iran and to alter the perception of it as belated imitation, however, it is important to note that French Cubism was a pluralistic enterprise with highly diverse forms of expression and creative artistic innovation practiced by various artists. After Ziapour graduated in 1945/46 from the newly founded Faculty of Fine Arts at the University of Tehran, the Ministry of Culture honored his achievements with a state-sponsored fellowship to continue his art education in the French capital.[36] During his stay in

---

[32] Bavand Behpoor, 'Introduction to "The Nightingale's Butcher Manifesto" and "Volume and Environment II",' *ARTMargins*, vol. 3, no. 2 (2014), 118–128, 123.

[33] Goudarzi, Mortezza, *Chostoochooy-e hoviat dar naghashi-e moaser-e Iran* [*The Search for Identity in Iran's Modern Painting*] (Tehran, 2002), 13.

[34] Partha Mitter, *The Triumph of Modernism, India's Artists and the Avant-Garde 1922–1947* (London: Reaktion, 2007), 7.

[35] Ibid.   [36] Mojabi, *Pioneers*, 12.

Paris (1946–1948), Ziapour studied at *l'Académie André Lhote*, a private art school, where the French painter and theoretician André Lhote (1885–1962) trained more than 1,200 students from all over the world. Thus, Cubism became a global enterprise that traveled to Iran and different parts of the world, underwent various local changes, and produced a diversity of modernist expressions. At the beginning of his career, Lhote worked in a Fauvist style, but in 1912 he joined the Section d'Or, an association of Cubist artists also known as the Puteaux Group or Orphic Cubists, which included prominent members such as Jacques Villon, Juan Gris, Robert Delaunay, Marcel Duchamp, Fernand Léger, Jean Metzinger, and Albert Gleizes. Due to their writings and exhibitions in major venues in Paris, such as the *Salon des Indépendants* and the *Salon d'Automne*, the Puteaux Group became the public representative of the Cubist movement. The popular master narrative of modernist art heralds Cubism, in particular, for its sharp break with past pictorial traditions and artistic innovation. This becomes even clearer when one considers the prevailing stylistic distinction in art history, rooted in a focus on Pablo Picasso and George Braque, between analytical and synthetic Cubism. It was the art dealer Daniel-Henry Kahnweiler who first introduced this conceptual differentiation in his text *Der Weg zum Kubismus* (*The Rise of Cubism*), published in 1920. In his book, Kahnweiler promoted the idea that, in particular, the works of Picasso and Braque relied on a "celebration of radical subjectivity and the temporal qualities of consciousness" shaped by the philosophy of Immanuel Kant.[37]

After World War I, this approach became the dominant reading of Cubist works and erased the political engagement and aspirations of French Cubism. In his studies about Cubist aesthetics, however, the art historian Mark Antliff has demonstrated that this artistic movement was less an expression of radical subjectivity and more an artistic reaction to "this atmosphere of rapid change and impending war, shaped partly by a number of artists committed to an idealistic conception of society opposed to war."[38] With their artistic production and theoretical writings, the Puteaux Cubists, in particular, contributed to the discourse about French cultural identity. The debate was

---

[37] Mark Antliff and Patricia Dee Leighten, *Cubism and Culture* (New York: Thames & Hudson, 2001), 204.

[38] Ibid., 8.

strongly shaped by the *Action Française*, a royalist and far-right political movement founded by Charles Maurras in 1899 in reaction to the Dreyfus Affair. This movement strongly opposed republican politics and demanded the reestablishment of the monarchy. The members of the association advocated a return to a golden age of rationality that they saw realized during the reign of Louis XVI.[39] In opposition to the *Action Française*, many leftist parties, including the Puteaux Group, tried to establish an alternative, leftist nationalism. In their political writings, they adopted the French philosopher Henri Bergson's concept of intuition and correlated it to the spiritual aspirations inherent in their ideological writings in opposition to the Cartesian rationality of the *Action Française*. Bergson's antirationalist ideas and his concept of intuition were welcomed among artists and critics of the Parisian avant-garde who considered themselves Bergsonians. Orphic Cubism, especially, developed under the influence of Bergson's philosophy and became the manifesto against the depiction of a recognizable world in response to a general disappointment with nineteenth-century thought, as epitomized by positivism, determinism, and materialism.[40]

Bergson's antirationalist concepts of *durée* (duration) and intuition had an especially great influence on the artistic development of Cubist aesthetics, as Jean Metzinger and Albert Gleizes pointed out in their text *Du Cubisme* (1912), the first major theoretical writing on the subject. The concept of simultaneity, for instance, which is essential for Cubist aesthetics, was developed in connection with Bergson's concept of *durée*. Bergson's *durée* is based on the idea that humans do not experience time in measurable units. Applying this concept to artistic language helped to introduce the element of time on the pictorial space by simultaneously depicting objects from various spatial perspectives and temporal contexts. In their text, Gleizes and Metzinger explained that "moving around an object to seize from it several successive appearances" permits the artist to "reconstitute it in time."[41] According to the authors, this can only be achieved intuitively and the artist "should rely on intuition, an empathetic form of consciousness, to discern the inner nature of reality through the flow of time, which he called 'duration.'"[42] Bergson's concept of intuition

---

[39] Ibid., 112.   [40] Ibid.
[41] Mark Antliff, 'Bergson and Cubism: A Reassessment,' *Art Journal*, vol. 47, no. 4, *Revising Cubism* (Winter 1988), 341–349, 342.
[42] Antliff and Leighten, *Cubism and Culture*, 72.

helped Metzinger and Gleizes promote the abandonment of classical perspective. This intuitionist approach represented an important means to liberate the pictorial space from the Euclidean and Kantian, mathematical conception of perspective. Both Bergson and the Cubists proclaimed that "space is intuited, rather than conceptualized rationally."[43]

The adaptation of Cubist aesthetic language for the Iranian context was not only behind aesthetic innovations but also opened up artistic production as a discursive space for questions of cultural identity based on an alternative, antiroyalist, constitutional, and leftist form of nationalism. The philosophical reference points of Bergsonian thought were productive in the construction of a leftist national artistic expression that could function as an act of resistance toward the royalist forces, as will be discussed later in this chapter.

The analysis of *Zaynab Khatoun* in this chapter has demonstrated how Ziapour employed various references to existing visual traditions to achieve artistic innovation. This strategy refers to Bergson's theory of "successive or accumulated images," as elaborated in *An Introduction to Metaphysics*.[44] For Bergson, the image has to function as an instrument for the apprehension of the inner self.

No image will replace the intuition of the duration, but many different images, taken from quite different orders of things, will be able, through the convergence of their action, to direct consciousness to the precise point where there is a certain intuition to seize on. By choosing images as dissimilar as possible, any one of them will be prevented from usurping the place of the intuition it is instructed to call forth ... By seeing that in spite of their differences in aspect they all demand of the mind the same kind of attention and, as it were, the same degree of tension, one will gradually accustom consciousness to a particular and definitely determined disposition, precisely the one it will have to adapt to ... to produce the desired effort and by itself, arrive at the intuition.[45]

Ziapour's pictorial allusions to different religious, cultural, and literary traditions are not very concrete. Rather, they suggest vague or intuitive associations in the beholder. Only the conjunction of individual images allows for the interplay with the textual elements of the painting as a

---

[43] Ibid., 85.   [44] Antliff, 'Bergson and Cubism,' 344.
[45] Henri Bergson, *An Introduction to Metaphysics* (Indianapolis: Hackett Publishing Company, 1999), 27–28.

whole. This allows Ziapour to verbalize his understanding of Iranian modern art and to construct his idea of the nation through the trope of the mother as a metaphor for Iran. It shows how the translation of Bergson's philosophical concepts into his own artworks provided Ziapour with fertile ground to create a specifically Iranian modernist expression.

Ziapour's Theoretical Translation of Cubism into the Iranian Context

As one of the members of the Puteaux Group, André Lhote introduced Jalil Ziapour to Bergsonian Cubism's body of thought. Lhote and his intellectual circle strongly advocated the active role of the artist and the importance of painting in shaping societal processes through theory, as he pointed out in his 1919 treatise *On the Necessity of Theories*.[46] Lhote's artistic self-conception as theoretician, teacher, and painter became a decisive model for Ziapour. Ziapour's extensive writings and self-understanding as an active educator were integral parts of his definition of the new social functions of art in Iranian society.[47] This, in turn, provided Ziapour with a vocabulary to explore the possibilities of creating a specifically Iranian expression of modernism. In fact, to achieve an Iranian version of modernism, Ziapour merged Cubist aesthetics, such as multiperspectivity, the dissolution and flattening of space, and the introduction of time as pictorial means, with local Iranian motives such as mosques or tribal figures from rural areas. Ziapour not only searched for "true" Iranian art in his own artistic works, he also elaborated on these issues in his theoretical writings. Shortly after his return from Paris, Ziapour proclaimed what steps were necessary to accomplish painting's true purpose in his artistic manifesto *Refute of the Theories of Past and Contemporary*

---

[46] Daniel Robbins, *André Lhote, 1885–1962, Cubism*, Exh. Cat. (New York: Leonard Hutton Galleries, 1976), 5.

[47] During his career, Jalil Ziapour became a proponent of modernist art and advocated his views about modernism through his teachings, lectures, and publications. Ziapour published more than twenty books on a wide range of historical and sociological topics, such as the history of ancient art in Iran, the history of costumes, and ethnographical studies about rural people in Iran. His books include *Antique Costumes in Iran – from Antiquity to Sasanians* (1343/1965), *The Woman. From her Origins to Today* (1344/1965), and *Painting and Sculpture in Iran* (1343/1965).

Ideologies from Primitive to Surrealism, which circulated widely in various newspapers and magazines.[48]

This piece is an important theoretical text about modernist art in Iran and has, thus far, not received the full scholarly attention it deserves.[49] In this text, written at an early stage in his professional career, Ziapour formulates his guidelines for accomplishing the true goals of painting, which lie in antirepresentational styles, the satisfaction of spiritual needs, the self-expression of the artist, and the fulfillment of society's needs. For Ziapour, painting epitomizes a political means of expression and has the important social function of educating the masses, for which reason he strongly criticizes the concept of *l'art pour l'art*, as he stated in the following terms:

> We must remember that the painter cannot remain totally indifferent to social themes, because for him and all the people who live in a community it is impossible to run away from the beliefs and the reactions of the others because of the mutual impact everything has .... We need to know that nothing is created without the need of the environment; and no request can be further than one of its time, because each request has a cause; and naturally the cause of each request comes from the needs of society and, therefore, my request is not beyond the need of our present time.[50]

As his manifesto progresses, Ziapour introduces the idea of a parasite to argue that painting has not yet developed its true purpose and full potential due to its infestation with a parasitic infection. For Ziapour, the parasite represents, on the one hand, naturalist-realistic styles that strive to depict reality and, on the other hand, visual abstract language without any connections to natural forms observable in real life. The parasite, as a figure of thought, helps Ziapour not only to define his concepts of a new art but also to argue for a kind of formalistic revolution in all fields of Iranian art, including music, theater, and painting, and to express his support for a clear break between modernism and earlier artistic styles. He writes,

---

[48] Jalil Ziapour, *Refute of the Theories of Past and Contemporary Ideologies from Primitive to Surrealism* (Tehran, 1948), www.ziapour.com/wp-content/uploads/2008/12/jalil_ziapour_theory.pdf, accessed 4 April 2019.

[49] Ziapour's text, *Refute of the Theories of Past and Contemporary Ideologies from Primitive to Surrealism*, has not yet been fully translated into English; for a translation into French, see Bombardier, *Les pionniers de la Nouvelle peinture en Iran*.

[50] Ziapour, *Refute of the Theories*.

Not even Classicism, Romanticism, Fauvism (except for a bit Impressionism and Cubism), no other movements have done painting justice, nor have they taken into consideration its vast domain and, by infesting painting with parasites, they have hindered painting.[51]

Generally speaking, Ziapour very much appreciates European modernism for its artistic innovation and as a means of reflecting societal needs. At the same time, however, he observes a seemingly global problem of modernist arts, when he explains that "the struggle of all the movements has also been to free themselves from the grip of these parasites, but hence without any success."[52] The remedy for painting's parasitic infection cannot be found on a formalist level, as he goes on to state, since abstract and nonrepresentational forms are not suitable solutions either. In addition, they "have also caused a split from the real intention and have perverted the mind (...) from the true characteristic of painting," for which reason "they are therefore considered the real parasites of painting and they must be destroyed."[53] For Ziapour, Cubism, in contrast, represents the artistic movement with the least shortcomings. And this, even though he criticizes Cubist expression's formal inadequacy as a representation of "true" painting, because, as he elaborates, it was unable to liberate itself completely from the tendency of pictorial images and natural forms.

And cubism, even though in many aspects the most complete movement, has some shortcoming in an artistic sense which I shall explain: a- it can only express limited themes and lacks the ability to express precisely and in depth sensual themes, something very much needed now, b- and since it must change the forms of the objects for an expression and has therefore intrigued the mind to recognize the deformed objects, it has taken the attention from the main intention of painting, which is understanding the beauty of expression.[54]

Ultimately, however, Ziapour acknowledges that Cubist painters came fairly close to his high artistic ideals in that they "turned to unnatural forms to create the kind of themes adequate for their spiritual needs, so we can say they did take steps to free painting from the grip of natural forms."[55] In particular, for Ziapour, Cubism's incorporation of spirituality represented an effective way to overcome the parasite of naturalistic representation.

[51] Ibid.   [52] Ibid.   [53] Ibid.   [54] Ibid.   [55] Ibid.

A second positive aspect of Cubism was, for Ziapour, its turn to "primitivism," which represents for him "the most impressive period in the history of painting."[56] As Ziapour saw it, the Cubists' appropriation of allegedly simplistic and authentic artistic expression from the colonies was an act meant to both oppose the so-called civilized West and transform Western art. In the age of Iranian industrialization and urbanization, Ziapour developed a longing for true Iranian art, which he found in the art of nomads and rural people.

Ziapour's idea of the parasite functions in his texts as a literary figure, which can be connected to his Marxist considerations and socialist understanding of art. He borrowed this literary trope from one of the most famous manifestos in modern history: Marx and Engel's *Communist Manifesto* (1848).

A spectre is haunting Europe – the spectre of Communism. All the powers of old Europe have entered into a holy alliance to exorcize this spectre: Pope and Czar, Metternich and Guizot, French radicals and German police-spies.[57]

In his text, however, Ziapour reverses the idea of the specter into that of a parasite haunting artistic movements. This reference to the *Communist Manifesto* gives Ziapour's writing a political significance at a time when communist discourses had reached new heights in Iran.

Although, in the course of his text, Ziapour harshly criticizes former generations of Iranian artists for their naturalist modes of expression, he also admits that artistic styles and their techniques reflect societal needs during a specific time, stating,

The more the social concepts change, the more visual subjects also change. There were times in life when it was necessary to paint religious themes and to show humans' ascension and parade in outer space and to show them flying in the material and spiritual world, to express their spiritualism, and there have been times when artists painted, instead of flying and religious scenes, objects. So we can see even the most avant-garde painters having one thing in common and that is visual representation of themes in order to express their personal spiritualism. And later we can see that, because natural forms did not adequately represent artist's perceptions, painters

---

[56] Ibid.
[57] Karl Marx and Friedrich Engels, *The Communist Manifesto* (New York: International Publishers, 1948), 8.

started, due to necessity, to adjust the forms, to increase or reduce them to express their ideas more precisely.[58]

In summary, one can say that Ziapour's employment of the parasite metaphor helps him argue for the necessity of introducing an Iranian audience to new artistic discourses, an audience that had not yet developed the familiarity with Western art and viewing habits necessary for understanding modernist expression. For Ziapour, new modes of artistic expression had to be created in reaction to the fundamental changes and rapid transformation that modernization had brought to Iran. In this context, Ziapour transforms his concept of the parasite into a trope to bring into view the shortcomings and failures of earlier artistic styles and thus emphasizes the societal necessity of searching for new means of expression. To overcome these failures, Ziapour includes a list of artistic advice to liberate new Iranian painting at the end of his article:

a. Painting must focus on color, design, form, and composition.
b. The more the subject is distorted the more valuable and complete the painting is.
c. Painting's theme should not have a beginning, information, and conclusion, like a text, because each line, color, form, and composition, is itself a beginning, a novelty, and a conclusion, and is in itself a theme and, thus, any kind of form, picture, or theme close to nature violates painting.
d. The more natural or similar unnatural forms give way to colors and design and other technical elements to the same degree that painting advances toward perfection, by which I mean it reaches a level at which it can better accomplish its beauty.
e. If a painting is depicting natural or similar unnatural forms, then the artist must destroy them so that no similarity between them and nature can be seen and artistic elements can be seen without any parasite.
f. In a nonpictorial painting (a painting that does not have any natural or similar unnatural forms), the artist knows what he should be doing, and it is clear to him that to create aesthetic work, he should pay direct attention to artistic elements (which means creating a more precise and more pleasant harmony and a more expressive

---

[58] Ziapour, *Refute of the Theories*.

drawing). At this stage, the artists and the observers (who, by understanding normal themes and pictures that reminded them of their memories and hopes, have had of an aesthetic experience) know where they stand. From this point on, they will pay attention to artistic elements and not to pictorial themes. Here is the first stage where artists and people realize the meaning of a professional aesthetic.

g. So far painting has not reached its artistic and aesthetic potential and has been mixed with other fine arts and, especially, literature, which describes true events. With my theory, a movement that I call complete comes into existence, which separates the borders of painting from the other arts. From here on, in this completeness, a professional and technical painting separates itself from other arts and comes into an existence with a much broader meaning.

h. Aesthetics in painting is different from the aesthetic of the others arts. One has to study it separately.

i. We need to know that nothing is created without the need of the environment, and no request can be more than one of its time, because each request has a cause, and naturally the cause of each request lies in the needs of society and, therefore, my request is not beyond the need of our present time.[59]

Although Ziapour's list of artistic advice remains rather vague, it is an important document that testifies to how the first generation of modernist artists in Iran conceived of modernism's adaptation in an Iranian context. Ziapour's manifesto thus provides an important insight into the artistic debates about how to create a local modernism that breaks with pictorial traditions of the past, while responding to the social realities of its time.

The *Fighting Rooster Association*

"Cubism or Communism?"

After his return from Paris, Jalil Ziapour cofounded the artistic association *Fighting Rooster* with artistic colleagues of his in 1948. Ziapour's studio became a meeting place, where the group of artists

[59] Ibid.

discussed theoretical issues in contemporary culture on a weekly basis.[60] As a closer analysis of the Fighting Rooster's political and artistic agenda highlights, the association evolved in a crucial period of Iran's modern history, when modernism had close ties to Soviet socialism. And as *Korūs-e Jangī*'s magazines demonstrate, the participating artists appropriated artistic concepts from social modernism and translated them through Sufi tropes into an Iranian context. The group was deeply engaged in articulating new aesthetics, with the idealistic goal of educating the masses. To achieve this, they created images in their various works of poetry, articles, short stories, and visual art that, as we will see, were used by various artists both independently and in close connection with one other.

The years in which the *Fighting Rooster Association* was active span a crucial era in Iran's modern history. The period between 1941, after Reza Shah's abdication, and the 1953 coup, which was sponsored by US and British intelligence services and led to the overthrow of the democratically elected Prime Minister Mohammad Mosaddeq, was a promising era for democracy in Iran. During World War II, the Allies forced the ruling king of Iran, Reza Shah Pahlavi (1921–1941), to abdicate because of his political and economic ties to National-Socialist Germany, after which Crown Prince Mohammad Reza Shah took up the crown and succeeded him as heir to the Pahlavi throne. Up until 1953, Mohammad Reza Shah fully cooperated with the Allies, presented himself as the constitutional monarch respecting the basic rule of law, and started various health campaigns. During this time, political prisoners were released and nationalist as well as socialist groups reorganized. Intellectuals began to reconnect with the central discourse of the Constitutional era, the demand for equality between the monarchy and the people, and to express their hopes for processes of liberalization and democratization. The establishment of the communist Tudeh Party ("Party of the Masses") was part of the historical context in 1941. Many intellectuals became members of the Tudeh Party, including members of the *Fighting Rooster*, such as the poets Nima Yushij and Manouchehr Sheybani. In 1949, however, after a failed attempt to assassinate Mohammad Reza Shah, the parliament voted for the immediate abolishment of the communist party. Despite the ban, the members did not cease their political activities but instead

---

[60] Mojabi, *Pioneers*, 18–43.

joined the National Front, a coalition comprised of different parties and alliances of leftists, liberal, and bourgeois forces, founded in 1949 under the leadership of Mohammad Mosaddeq, who had been responsible for the nationalization of Iran's oil industry. The nationalization of the oil industry was not only financially motivated but also meant to epitomize national independence and the end of imperialist and colonialist interference. During this period, nationalism was seen as possible path to liberation from foreign occupation and became, especially in the arts, a central tool for social mobilization.[61]

It was in this historical context that the *Fighting Rooster Association* published five issues of their eponymous magazine between 1948 and 1950, which was censored and suspended only shortly after its publication because government officials equated Cubism with communism and accused the association of socialist propaganda. To circumvent censorship and continue to spread the aesthetic principles of their new art, the association published their magazine under two new names, *Kavir (Desert)* and *Panj-e ye Khorus (The Rooster's Foot)*. The new magazines were also quickly suspended, both because Ziapour was "suspected of being a communist sympathizer or Communist Party member" and in particular because, as Aida Foroutan has stated, "the association between Cubism and Communism was known in Iran."[62] As Alice Bombardier discerns from his article in the fourth edition of the group's magazine, Ziapour's concept of painting was based on a socialist understanding of art. Bombardier observes that Ziapour appropriated communist ideological language not only to demand an overcoming of earlier representational conventions but also to promote Cubism as an artistic language suitable for the mobilization of the masses.[63] In other words, Ziapour promoted Cubism as a manifestation of modernism and, moreover, as a cultural and political ideology.[64]

---

[61] Abrahamian, *A History of Modern Iran*, 97–122.
[62] Foroutan, 'Why the Fighting Cock?' XLI.
[63] Bombardier, *Les pionniers de la Nouvelle peinture en Iran*, 163.
[64] After the poet and painter Hushang Irani joined the *Fighting Rooster Association* in 1950, the group developed more radical views on avant-gardism as expressed in the *Nightingale's Butcher Manifesto*, published in every issue from 1951. The manifesto demanded a destructive approach to past cultural traditions and a totally new artistic start. This radicalization and the shifting emphasis on literature were the reasons why it no longer met Jalil Ziapour's artistic ideals, which took their artistic inspiration from Iran's past cultural

Especially in the initial phases, modernizing tendencies in the arts were often based on a socialist concept of modernity in Iran. The idea of a socialist modernity was quite dominant in the 1940s and 1950s in Iran, or, as Fereshteh Daftari states, "The Soviet influence was not without ramifications for cultural life in Tehran."[65] In fact, with its organization *VOKS (The Soviet All-Union Society for Cultural Ties)*, the Soviet Union pursued an aggressive campaign to spread socialist modernity in Iran. *VOKS* was founded in 1925 to support Soviet cultural diplomacy's fostering of cultural cooperation between the Soviet Union and foreign countries. In 1942, *VOKS* founded the Iranian Society for Cultural Relations with the USSR in cooperation with Iranian leftists. *VOKS* also worked together with Iranian government officials and hosted numerous cultural events. After the Shah became a close ally of Western powers during the Cold War and, especially after the 1953 coup, began following an antileftist, anticommunist policy, the institution was dissolved in 1955.[66]

While seeming to operate independently, the institution was deeply invested in socialism's ideological dissemination in Iran. James Pickett states that the "intensity of Soviet cultural diplomacy in Iran had little precedent elsewhere in the Third World and was an important component of the USSR's larger bid for geopolitical influence."[67] At the same time, the Society was one of the few institutions that functioned as a cultural space in the 1940s and 1950s in Iran. At the time, works of modernist art received hardly any recognition from the state and were not yet part of official Pahlavi cultural politics. *VOKS*'s space was very well equipped and hosted lectures and exhibitions, such as the writers' congress in 1946, for example, which also featured works by members of the *Fighting Rooster Association*. More than seventy authors and Iranian officials attended the event. The Prime Minister and the Minister of Culture stressed the importance of cultural modernization as a national task. The poet and member of the *Fighting*

traditions, and why he later suspended his membership. See Behpoor, 'Introduction to "The Nightingale's Butcher's Manifesto" and "Volume and Environment II".'

[65] Daftari, *Persia Reframed*, 12.
[66] James Pickett, 'Soviet Civilization through a Persian Lens. Iranian Intellectuals, Cultural Diplomacy and Socialist Modernity 1941–55,' *Iranian Studies*, vol. 48, no. 5 (2015), 805–826.
[67] Ibid., 806.

Rooster Association, Nima Yushij, became well known for a famous speech he delivered at the conference.[68] The Iranian artistic and literary scene did not perceive VOKS and its cultural programs as imperialist interference but rather welcomed the new possibilities as a multiplying platform. James Pickett states that, in this context, "Iranian intellectuals selectively appropriated the resources deployed in this effort and re-articulated the Soviet message in a manner fitting Iran's own national project."[69] The appropriation of a socialist modernity and its translation in the Iranian context was an especially important artistic strategy for the *Fighting Rooster Association* and the articulation of their utopian aspirations to awaken society.

The Incorporation of Sufism as a Means of Political Resistance

In the context of the creation of an Iranian modernist expression, the incorporation of local and vernacular elements became an important tool to counteract universalist conceptions of Western modernity present in Iran. In the discourse on modernization, for many Iranian intellectuals, the inclusion of *erfan*, the spiritual teaching of Shi'ite Islam, became a "potential discursive device for constructing a modern and authentic Iran."[70]

The incorporation of Sufism in literary and cultural productions, however, was highly controversial at the time. At the center of the debate was the question of Iran's transformation into a modern nation-state. Iran's intellectuals discussed the question of the country's modernization in the broader field of literature. This is not surprising, given that Persian literature played a crucial role in the construction of a secular Iranian national identity.[71] The erasure of Islam was an important mission on the path to modernization, especially during the reign of Reza Shah Pahlavi. New monuments and tombstones helped to celebrate the great authors of national literature. A significant example from the 1930s is Hafez's tomb in Shiraz. A monument built in order

---

[68] Ahmad Karimi Hakkak, 'Nima Jushij: A Life,' in Hakkak and Kamran Talattof, *Essays on Nima Yushij: Animating Modernism in Persian Poetry* (Leiden: Brill, 2004), 11–68, 17–18.
[69] Pickett, 'Soviet Civilization,' 806.
[70] Mirsepassi, *Transnationalism in Iranian Political Thought*, 78.
[71] Lloyd Ridgeon, *Sufi Castigator, Ahmad Kasravi and the Iranian Mystical Tradition* (London: Routledge, 2006).

"to appropriate the Sufi significance of the site into Iran's secular historiography" led to the fact that "Hafez's tomb, a real place with a long Muslim history, became just another tourist site, integral to the network of tourist destinations on the map of New Iran (iran-e novin)."[72]

But, governmental officials were not the only ones who tried to downplay the influence of Sufi teachings on Iran's cultural production. The historian Ahmad Kasravi (1890–1946) was one of the major critics of Sufi literature. Kasravi, who published many works in opposition to Sufism and tried to spread the word about the "evil teachings" of religion and mysticism, was very influential. For Kasravi, religion and political Islam were not compatible with modernization and progress. He saw mysticism as a barrier to reforming Iran and to connecting it with Western secularized countries. For Kasravi, modernization was based on reason and science and therefore incompatible with religion. Politically active in Iran's constitutional movement, Kasravi was deeply engaged in Iran's liberal democratization and reform, education of the masses, and a general improvement of social conditions in Iran.[73] In his writings, Kasravi saw Sufism in a context larger than that of secularism alone. For him, the celebration of Sufism was also closely tied to colonialism and Orientalism. He saw the representation of Iran as irrational, spiritual, and inclined to mysticism as a symbolic power-political tool for the justification of imperialism.[74]

In Iran, his sharp criticism was perceived as blasphemy and legal action was taken against him. Kasravi was brutally murdered in 1946 by a member of a Shiite fundamentalist group (*Fedai'an-e Islam*) during a hearing in his court case.[75] Kasravi's nationalist opinion and his criticisms of Sufism strongly affected Iranian intellectuals after him, including al-e Ahmad and Shariati, and contributed to the revival of Islamic influences in society.

In this context, it is important to note, as Mirsepassi explains, that the recourse to Iranian and Islamic tradition in twentieth-century Iran was brought about not only by a revival of local traditions but also through a reflective act of the Western episteme. Though intellectuals

---

[72] Grigor, *Building Iran*, 83. [73] Ridgeon, *Sufi Castigator*, 52.
[74] Kasravi, quoted in Ridgeon, *Sufi Castigator*, 160.
[75] Mohammad Amini, 'Kasravi Ahmad ii. Assassination,' *Encyclopedia Iranica*, 1 May 2012, www.iranicaonline.org/articles/kasravi-ahmad-ii, accessed 15 December 2016.

such as Fardid made decisive contributions to "the revitalization of Iranian *erfan* in the modern context," this happened largely due to his philosophical encounter with Henri Bergson's antirationalist concepts.[76] The connection between *erfan* and Bergson's philosophy and its significance for the process of Iran's national formation were widely discussed, for example, by Taghi Arani (1903–1940), the leading Marxist thinker and ideologue of the communist Tudeh party, who elaborated the relationship between Bergson's teachings and Sufi spiritual theology. In 1933, he published his views on Sufism in *Erfan va osule-e madi* (*Mysticism and the Principles of Materialism*) in the Marxist publication *Donya*, in which he argues that dialectic materialism has the ideological power to dissolve the need for mysticism.

Today, the principles of materialism and logic have connected humans to all sciences, industries, societies and arts, and it has liberated humans from common superstitions whether through nature, biology, physiology or sociology, and it has shown humans the path of happiness.[77]

Despite his critique, Arani understands Sufism as a means of political opposition toward the ruling systems. He argues that Sufism came into existence as a form of resistance to the dictatorial caliphate in Baghdad.[78] Sufism, thus, became an instrumental strategy of resistance and a form of political expression during the early years of Pahlavi rule, when modernity was widely understood as a secularizing process based on the principle of rationality. This makes clear that Sufism only became a major theme in the intellectual discourse of Iran's modernization. More particularly, this new generation of artists and writers employed themes from Iran's Islamic traditions to explore the political dimensions of a local modernism.

The First Issue of the Fighting Rooster Magazine

Jalil Ziapour's Depiction of the Fighting Rooster

In his black-and-white print on the cover of the magazine's first edition, Ziapour gave the association the face of an aggressive rooster angrily looking down its tong-like beak with its forked tongue darting out (Figure 4.2). The image's subtext and its framing are a structural

---

[76] Mirsepassi, *Transnationalism in Iranian Political Thought*, 78.
[77] Taghi Arani, quoted in Ridgeon, *Sufi Castigator*, 27.
[78] Ridgeon, *Sufi Castigator*, 28.

Figure 4.2 Jalil Ziapour, cover of *Fighting Rooster* magazine [Ḵorūs-e Jangī magazine], vol. 1, Tehran, 1948

reference to Iranian miniature painting, which creates a strong interconnection between text and image, as the picture's caption, *horus changi* ("the fighting rooster"), specifies. Strong lines shape the rooster's body; the indicated platform and the walking motion of the rooster suggest a certain three-dimensionality, reinforced by its claw, which extends beyond the frame and brings the bird to life for the viewer; and the strong, curved lines suggest a similarity to calligraphy. In comparison to zoomorphic calligraphy, which writes in the guise of animals, Ziapour reverses this idea. His abstract calligraphic forms function as a deconstruction and division of the pictorial surface.

By using the shape of a bird, Ziapour alludes to the iconographic tradition of writing the word *bismillah*, "in the name of God." Many calligraphers have used such bird-shaped calligraphy as an expression of God's beauty. *Bismillah* is the first word in the Qur'an, and the short form of *b-ismi-llāhi r-raḥmāni r-raḥīmi*, "in the name of God, the most Gracious, the most Merciful." The immense and timeless importance of this expression can be very clearly observed in the contemporary Islamic Republic of Iran, where this confession is obligatory for all

The Fighting Rooster Association

Figure 4.3 *In the name of the merciful*, calligraphy in the form of a hoopoe, Iran, seventeenth/eighteenth century, ink on paper, 42.4 × 35.6 cm. Museum of Islamic Art Berlin

official legal actions, as well as documents. Even though it serves as a political cooptation of Islam, it is obviously an important means of boltering Muslim identity.

In this work, Ziapour mixes traditional iconography with modernist European art, merging the avian calligraphy's religiously loaded symbolism with Picasso's political depictions of the rooster.[79] Picasso's series of roosters, painted during the German occupation, demonstrates his political engagement and represents the possibilities of artistic resistance.[80] Picasso's triumphant rooster as a "messenger of dawn and resurrection" refers to the Gallic rooster, which has a long

---

[79] Foroutan, 'Why the Fighting Cock?' XXXV.
[80] Pablo Picasso (1881–1973), *The Cock of the Liberation* (*Le Coq de la Liberation*), 1944, oil on canvas, Milwaukee Art Museums.

history of being a symbol of French patriotism, and was used as a figurehead by the French Resistance during World War II.[81]

Nima Yushij's About the City of the Morning

It is significant that the first issue of *Fighting Rooster* magazine opens with the poem "About the City of the Morning" by the avant-garde poet Nima Yushij (1895–1959). The poem narrates the journey of a rooster accompanying a caravan through Iran. The rhythm of the movement follows the rooster's crow, "cock-a-doodle-doo," and is an invitation for the audience to join the caravan, to escape night and the darkness, and to strive for a new morning. With his poem, Nima illustrates the *Fighting Rooster*'s goal of educating the audience and changing and revitalizing society, as the statement on the cover also makes clear: "Our declared aim: Increasing the culture of Iranians with the Fighting Rooster association."[82] In this poem, Nima also communicates his political ambitions through a reconfiguration of familiar images of Islamic literature, Sufi metaphors, and motives of traditional Persian literature. The use of images and metaphors from Persian literature made the *Fighting Rooster*'s political messages comprehensible to the Iranian masses, for whom poetry was part of a living tradition and has always been a widely practiced part of Iranian cultural identity, regardless of class or education.

"About the City of the Morning" (1948) demonstrates significant similarities with the well-known Sufi poem *The Conference of the Birds*, by the twelfth-century poet Farid al-din Attar. In his poem, "About the City of the Morning," Nima translates Attar's Sufi metaphors of the self's unification and annihilation into a secular political context as a way to empower the masses. Thus, Nima's poem becomes a political manifesto reflecting a historical moment in which Iran's monarchy seemed outdated and individual political action appeared to be a serious alternative to the centuries of royal dictatorship.

About the City of the Morning
Cockadoodledoo, crows the cock,
Singing from the bottom of his heart,

---

[81] Gertje R. Utlej, *Picasso, The Communist Years* (New Haven: Yale University Press, 2000), 60.
[82] See the cover of *Fighting Rooster Magazine*, no. 1 (Tehran, 1948).

From the depths of the way, like a dry vein.
Blood pulsates through the bodies of the dead,
It surrounds the cool dawn,
Flows in the lake Hamun.

With his song, the paths are filled,
He delivers the message to the free ear,
He shows the caravan
The way to Abadan,
The route through *harab abad*.

He strolls gently,
He sings passionately,
Beating his wings,
Spreading his feathers.

The sound of the bells of the caravan,
Beats to the rhythm of the cock's crow,
On this dark path,
Who is it who has fallen behind?
Who is it, who is tired?

Warmed by his melodious breath,
Cold winter nights,
Reveals dark secrets,
Enlightens the mornings.

It exchanges a kiss with the body of the earth,
The coquetry of the morning, the morning of late travel,
Singing passionately from the bottom of his heart.
Expressing his feelings.

Cock-a-doodle-doo. From a particular place,
Fleeing into the vagueness of the night,
Like the deepest mud,
The everyday noise disappears from dawn,

The cock runs along the rider's way,
Though the horse has fled into the darkness,
The morning dawn tickles the nose,
This is a pleasant plan for a bright morning.

The time in his eyes,
Had brought joy,
Like a bright day,

Enlightening his way,
Riding the horse.
Cock-a-doodle-doo. This makes him happy.
Morning has broken. The cock crows.

Like a prisoner of the night, like a grave,
The bird escaped the confines of the cage,
On a long way through the desert,
Say again, who is it that has fallen behind?
Who is it, who is tired?[83]

The poet Nima Yushij attained great prominence in Persian literature for his stylistic innovations and his radical break with past literary tradition. Celebrated as the founder of the literary genre of *sher-e no* (New Poetry), Nima is often called the "father of modern Persian poetry"[84] and seen as a radical reformer of traditional Persian poetry. As Ahmad Karimi-Hakkak explains, poetry

> was occupied by a set of rules and requirements that governed the system of classical poetry of the Persian language. This poetry, having grown in sophistication over the centuries in philosophical discourse and the discourse of love, seemed to allow little room for the expression of concrete socio-political concerns.[85]

To communicate his political program in the service of Iran's liberalization and democratization, Nima had to free himself from past literary traditions. With poetry, Nima and his followers attacked an imaginary, homogenous, and timeless literary production that had conceived of itself as either mainly subjective or solely an expression of God's beauty. Situating his literary practice of *sher-e no* (New Poetry) in the broader discourse of a radical break with the traditions and strict rules of *sher-e klassik* (classical poetry), Nima explained,

---

[83] Unless otherwise specified, all the translations from Persian texts contained in this dissertation are by the author. Nima Yushij, 'About the City of the Morning,' *Fighting Rooster Magazine* (Tehran, 1948), 1–2.

[84] Hamid Dabashi, 'Nima Yushij and Constitution of a National Subject,' in Davison Andrew and Himadeep Muppidi, *The World Is My Home: A Hamid Dabashi Reader* (London: Transaction, 2010), 147.

[85] Ahmad Karimi Hakkak, *Recasting Persian Poetry: Scenarios of Poetic Modernity in Iran* (Salt Lake City: University of Utah Press, 1996), 30.

My style in poetry is like a poisonous arrow shot to the traditionalists. They consider my poetry unreadable and unpublishable. I have many enemies … I live in Tehran. I write a lot. I publish a little.[86]

Nima Yushij developed his symbolism under the impression of French literature. He attended the Catholic St. Louis College in Teheran, where French poetry formed a major part of the school's curriculum. Kamran Talattof has pointed out that French Symbolism became especially important for the stylistic characteristics of Nima's poetry and writes that "he especially presents form as a distinctive central element in aesthetics."[87]

French Symbolism not only equipped Nima with the tools he needed for formal innovations but also introduced him to Bergsonian thought. The symbolist literary circles in Paris, and particularly the neo-Symbolists, shared with the Cubists their enthusiasm for Henri Bergson's philosophy. Together with the neo-Symbolist poets René Arcos, Henri Martin Barzun, and Jules Romains, the Cubist painter Albert Gleizes founded the Abbaye de Créteil Group (1906–1908). With this association, he pursued utopian aspirations to "escape from corrupt Western civilization to the simplicity of life in the South Seas, as he then believed Gauguin had done."[88] At the same time, however, the group also believed in Jules Romains' idea of *Unanimism*. The concept of *Unanimism* was based on the assumption of collective emotion and group consciousness. His concept of a transcendent consciousness promoted the idea that individuals can immerse themselves in a larger collective. Romains developed this thought with Henri Bergson's concept of intuition in mind.[89]

In contrast to the Symbolists, Nima did not try to escape to other cultural landscapes but found his artistic inspiration in Iran's own cultural past. A closer examination of Nima's poem, *About the City of the Morning*, reveals that his stylistic means are innovative in terms of their less artificial language and rigid formal structures but that his poetic metaphors are deeply rooted in the tradition of Persian poetry. This so-called break is a deliberate transformation of classical tropes

---

[86] Yushij, quoted in Dabashi, 'Nima Yushij,' 147.
[87] Kamran Talattof, 'Ideology and Self-Portrayal in the Poetry of Nima Yushij,' in Hakkak and Talattof, *Essays on Nima Yushij*, 69–98, 90.
[88] Daniel Robbins, *Albert Gleizes, 1881–1953, A Retrospective Exhibition*, Exh. Cat. (New York: Solomon R. Guggenheim Foundation, 1964), 13.
[89] Antliff and Leighton, *Cubism and Culture*, 93.

and metaphors for the purpose of addressing current political and social issues.

This is illustrated by the example of the rooster motif in Nima's work. The metaphor of the rooster is deeply rooted in Persian cultural traditions. In Zoroastrianism, the rooster is regarded as a sacred animal because of its prophetic ability to foresee and warn of coming events. In the Zoroastrian text *Vidēvdād*, the rooster is the companion of the deity *Sraoša* and a guardian that watches over the earth in the time between midnight and dawn. In this context, the bird not only dispels darkness but also calls the faithful to prayer: "Rise up, ye men! Praise ye the best righteousness; abjure ye the demons!"[90] In addition, the rooster's positive characteristics are also heralded in Islamic literature and several relevant hadiths attributed to prophet Muhammad praise the rooster's abilities to tell time, drive away the devil, and see angels:

When you hear the crowing of the rooster, ask God His favour, because it sees an angel, but if you hear the braying of a donkey, seek refuge in God from the devil, because the donkey sees a the devil.[91]

Some other collections report that Mohammad once said, "God has a white rooster with two wings embellished with chrysolite, sapphire and pearls; one of its wings is in the east while the other one is in the west, its head under His Throne while its claws are in the air."[92] Another source reports that God sent a white rooster to Adam to remind him of the times for prayer. Adam's rooster was able to hear the angel reciting *tasbih* and would begin praising God on earth, when it heard the angelic voices. The rooster's most praiseworthy quality is that it wakes people up for prayer. Some hadiths create a connection between the cock's crow and the ritual prayer, for, as the prophet stated, "the crowing of the rooster and the flapping of its wings are its *ruku* and *sujud*."[93] This idea is also reflected in the third verse of Nima Yushij's poem, in which the rooster also performs ritual acts of prayer.

---

[90] Mahmoud Omidsalar, 'Cock,' *Encyclopedia Iranica* (1992), www.iranicaonline.org/articles/cock-the-male-of-the-subfamily-phasianinae-pheasants-usually-having-a-long-often-tectiform-tail-with-fourteen-to-thirty, accessed 3 November 2016.

[91] Roberto Tottoli, 'At Cock-Crow: Some Muslim Traditions About the Rooster,' *Der Islam*, Bd. 76 (1999), 139–144, 140.

[92] Ibid., 142.   [93] Ibid., 141.

He strolls gently,
He sings passionately,
Beating his wings,
Spreading his feathers

The rooster's prayer is its cock-a-doodle-doo, which, "warmed by his melodious breath," "reveals dark secrets, enlightens the mornings" (fourth verse). Nima intentionally plays with these cultural connotations of the rooster in his poem to transform the theological into a sociopolitical context. His rooster not only calls people to prayer but also "reveals dark secrets" and "shows the caravan, the way to Abadan, the route through *harab abad*." This route leads the caravan through *harab abad*, Persian for "devastated land," and refers to the city of Abadan, which had become the country's largest oil refinery. With his play on words, Nima refers to the problematic situation in Abadan. As a metaphor for the artistic association itself or as a cultural symbol of truth speaking, the rooster functions as a way to draw the reader's attention to Abadan. In 1946, only two years before the publication of Nima's poem, oil refinery workers in Abadan had gone on strike to protest the strenuous working conditions, a shortage of food, the increased social control they experienced, and insufficient health services. Organized by the Tudeh party, in July 1946, 65,000 workers stopped working. The strike, however, was soon brutally suppressed, with the government declaring martial law and arresting a huge number of the strikers.[94]

In fact, as Houman Sarshar explains, Nima's strategy of semantically reconfiguring traditional Persian literary allegories is a highly significant novelty, which one also finds in his poetic practice.

Nima keeps the nightingale's basic semantic feature as "bird of song" and changes the two particular semes 'small' and 'bird of flight', ending up with the rooster. In this reconfiguration, both birds still represent the poet in the poem.[95]

Through the shift and extension of the bird's traditional meaning, Nima combines traditional tropes to define the politics of his poetic

---

[94] Ervand Abrahamian, *The Coup 1953, the CIA and the Roots of Modern U.S.-Iranian relations* (New York: New Press, 2013), 20.
[95] Houman Sarshar, 'From Allegory to Symbol: Emblems of Nature in the Poetry of Nima Yushij,' in Karimi-Hakkak and Talattof, *Essays on Nima Yushij*, 99–138, 116.

practice. To express his political aspirations, Nima relies heavily on Sufi concepts of Persian poetry. Significant similarities with the well-known Sufi poem, *The Conference of the Birds* by Farid al-din Attar, can be identified, especially in his poem *The City of the Morning (1948)* and, later, in a more elaborated form, in *The Amen Bird (1951)*.[96] The story of *The Conference of the Birds* centers around a group of birds' pilgrimage to seek a new king.

> The world's bird gathered for their conference
> And said: 'Our constitution makes no sense.
> All nations in the world require a king;
> How is it we alone have no such thing?
> Only a kingdom can be justly run;
> We need a king and must inquire for one.'[97]

In this story, Attar recounts the pilgrimage of thirty birds to seek a new king. Under the leadership of a hoopoe, the birds try to find the mythological bird *Simorgh*. Similar to Nima's poem in its attempt to persuade the listeners to join the caravan, the hoopoe also has to fight with the skepticism of the other birds. The hoopoe is the spokesperson of the group and counters each of his comrades' excuses with an anecdote that confronts them with their underlying fears. During the journey, the hoopoe plays the part of a religious leader advising his followers on their spiritual path. Their arduous expedition to Mount Qaf, *Simorgh's* supposed dwelling place, leads the birds through the seven valleys of quest, love, insight into mystery, serenity, unity, awe and reverence, and unity and nothingness – all essential Sufi concepts. Yet, when they arrive at the destination of their journey, they do not find a new king but rather only their own reflection in a mirror. Through their reflection, the birds understand that they themselves are the long-awaited savior Simorgh, something etymologically attested to by the Persian name *Simorgh*, which can be translated as *Si*, meaning "thirty," and *morgh*, meaning "bird."

Written in 1948, *The City of the Morning* reflects the spirit of the relatively free era after the abdication of Reza Shah Pahlavi and before

---

[96] In my interpretation of Nima's poem, *About the City of the Morning*, I adopt Houman Sarshar comparison of Nima's poem with *The Conference of the Birds*, 125–137.

[97] Farid al-din Attar, *The Conference of the Birds*, translated by Dick Davis (London: Penguin Books, 2005), 57.

the consolidation of power under his successor Mohammad Reza Shah. Contrary to Iranian art history, Iranian literary studies have embedded cultural production under the Pahlavi monarchy in its sociopolitical context. By doing so, literary studies have established a predominately political reading of Nima's poetry, as one can see in the works of various writers who have pointed out how Nima altered familiar literary metaphors from Persian poetry to articulate his political criticism. Paul Losensky, for instance, has shown how Nima employs the motif of the night as a symbol for the Pahlavi monarchy. He explains that Nima's depiction of the night

> is not the night of separation of two sweethearts, and if it is the night of the separation of two lovers, it is talking about some other lovers. If there is any waiting involved, they are waiting for the day to break, and the day is the day of relief, the day of salvation, and not the salvation of a person, but the salvation of the people. This night, which throughout more or less all of Nima's poetry moves with the impetus of a living being, has an aggressive existence.[98]

Employing the night as a symbol of the Pahlavi state, Nima leaves the reader of *The City of the Morning* Nima with a utopian vision:

> Like a prisoner of the night, like a grave,
> The bird escaped the confines of the cage,
> On a long way through the desert,
> Say again, who is it that has fallen behind?
> Who is it, who is tired?

Thus, like Nima as an artist, who also escaped the confines of traditional poetry and could thus enhance the social function of poetry as a politically committed writer striving for political reform, the rooster freed itself and escaped the confines of its cage. This analysis of Nima's and Ziapour's image of the rooster shows that the association's visual productions were closely linked with and responded to each other. Whether in literature or the visual arts, the artists pursued the same goal in their respective creative media and tried to overcome rigid past traditions and establish a new art. This artistic cross-fertilization not only represents an important means of aesthetic expression but also

---

[98] Paul Losensky, "'To Tell Another Tale of Mournful Terror': Three of Nima's Songs of the Night,' in Karimi-Hakkak and Talattof, *Essays on Nima Yushij*, 139–172, 139.

helped to spread the *Fighting Rooster*'s political message and promote their goal of awakening audiences.

Contributions by Sheybani, Gharib, Hannaneh, and Ziapour

Manouchehr Sheybani's Poem

The first issue of the *Fighting Rooster* magazine focuses explicitly on Sufi themes, as can be identified in the contributions by members of the association such as Sheybani, Gharib, and Hannaneh. As an editor, Manouchehr Sheybani, a Marxist activist, was responsible for the poetry section of the *Fighting Rooster* magazine. He became Nima's mentee after the publication of his first collection of poems, entitled *Halqe* (Spark). As a multimedia artist, Sheybani (1924–1991) worked in different genres, including film, theater, opera, painting, and poetry. His painting technique was similar to Ziapour's and also based on traditional Iranian craftsmanship. Working in a traditional textile workshop inspired him to develop his pictorial language based on his professional knowledge of weaving, design, composition, and dyeing.[99]

Significantly, the subject and storyline of Sheybani's poem reference the archetypical topic of wine consumption in traditional Sufi literature, namely, drunkenness and the central search for truth.[100] His poetic protagonists are the *saqi*, or wine bringer, and the *rend*, a Sufi seeker. In Persian, *rend* usually has the rather negative meaning of rogue, debauchee, or libertine. In this context, however, Sheybani refers to the concept of *rend* used in classical Persian literature to describe a Sufi seeker.

In the first verse, Sheybani begins by vividly portraying the surroundings, locating the scene in a wine house in a small gloomy city with winding streets. The night is almost over and the morning stars are rising. The atmosphere in the wine house is quite chaotic, the place is crowded, spilled wine has colored the floor red, and the *saqi* lies drunk under the table. Also very drunk, the *rend* has lost his sense of

---

[99] Mojabi, 'Sheybani: Chani-e Na-aram va chandsaht' (Sheybani: A Restless Spirit and Multidimensional) in Mojabi, *Saramadan-e honar-e no*, 56–63; Saeid Rezvani, 'Sheybani, Manuchehr,' *Encyclopedia Iranica*, www.iranicaonline.org/articles/sheybani-manuchehr, accessed 16 May 2017.

[100] Manuchehr Sheybani, *Poem (Untitled)*, *Fighting Rooster Magazine*, no. 1 (1948), 43–45.

time and space. The *rend* has traveled to every village and city in search of a Sufi master. Finding his master, or essential truth, has been one of his main goals. Suddenly, the silhouette of a Sufi master (*pir-e moqan*) appears in the wine house. The Sufi master, however, challenges the seeker, who has to resist several temptations during his stay in the tavern. In the *rend's* hallucination, the roof of the cupola opens up and gives way to a view of the night sky and its stars. Each sparkling star turns into a beautiful woman with white skin and long black braided hair descending like angelic creatures from the sky. The *rend* tries to escape the women, who are coming closer and closer. Because he ignores their appearances, the female figures turn away and shrink into small bubbles that burst and spill their liquid into the wine.

Stylistically, the repetition of the phrase "the wine pours"[101] connects the strophes and emphasizes the constant drinking and consumption of wine. When the *rend* sees his own face mirrored in the wine, a lightning bolt suddenly strikes the tavern's cupola and angels on horses descend from the heavens. The female figures closely resemble those with white skin and black hair from the *rend*'s first hallucination. The angels fill the room, play the harp, and recite poems. One of the angels with golden wings goes up to the *rend*, who is very intoxicated, and whispers into his ear, "What has happened to you?"

> The wine pours again. Blind people with a sword in their hand.
> Each single one a rider. They fight with each other for an imaginary castle.
> The elderly attack each other, to know where the truth lies.
> The wine pours again. The alchemist is searching for the dream elixir.
> He endeavors. Regardless how often he hammers the copper,
> his copper does not turn into gold. The old master,
> can turn dust into gold with his gaze. His gaze is the elixir.
> And all this makes the old master. The wine pours.
> The tears flow from the rend's eyes. He opens his mouth simultaneously.
> He laughs of joy and says to the saqi: "Oh, you saqi. The water of life!"[102]

At this point, however, the scene in the wine house is interrupted by the sound of trumpets, the city gates open, and the ringing of camel bells announces the return of the caravan from a long journey. The call to prayer, ringing like the crowing of a rooster, indicates the end of the night and the beginning of a new day. People awaken and the wine glasses are emptied. Similar to Nima, Sheybani also describes a

[101] Ibid.   [102] Ibid.

moment of self-recognition and indicates that the search for a master is not expedient for true faith.

The topic of wine, drunkenness, and intoxication is very common in classical Persian poetry and also serves as a major topic depicted in miniature painting. In Sufi belief, wine serves as a binding element between the mystical and the real world and allows humans to alter their perception, as Shahab Ahmed explains,

> Wine is a shared medium that links the existences of the Seen and Unseen worlds: to drink wine is to know and experience something of and like the Unseen even as we cannot see the Unseen ... the lower, real, material, everyday wine of the Seen world is, in other words transporting and transforming the drinkers towards (an altered) consciousness, knowledge and experience of the higher, Real, ideal, eternal Wine of the Unseen world.[103]

In his poem, Sheybani employs the state of drunkenness to depict the ambiguity of experienced reality. Wine's significance lies in the confusion it creates in the reader. As a poetic medium, it serves as a means of oscillating between two worlds,[104] making it difficult for the reader to distinguish between the *rend's* hallucination and the events in the tavern. At the end of the poem, the *rend* recognizes that his personal and spiritual truth lies in wine. Nevertheless, the poem does not evoke a hopeless impression but rather creates a nostalgic atmosphere and refers to a time when people could believe in the miraculous powers of their Sufi master's alchemy.

Not surprisingly, trumpets and the cock's crowing dissolve the scenery and awaken the guests in the tavern. The last lines connect Sheybani's poem to the magazine's overall topic, the *Fighting Rooster Association* and its utopian goal of shaking up society and realizing its vision in Iran's political reality.

The figure of the *rend* can be translated as an "inspired libertine" and is deeply rooted in Persian poetry. Especially in Hafez's poetry, the *rend* functions as a metaphor to identify hypocrisy in Iranian society. Hafez's *rend* often symbolizes a person who is critical toward the clergy and does not obey the rules they have established. As Ehsan Yarshater explains,

---

[103] Shahab Ahmed, *What Is Islam? The Importance of Being Islamic* (Princeton: Princeton University Press, 2016), 422.
[104] Schimmel, *Mystical Dimensions of Islam*, 288.

Hafez's attacks on the pretenders of virtues is not limited to witty or derisive barbs; he employs a stratagem far more effective than merely satirizing them. To humiliate and embarrass self-righteous hypocrites, he takes the dregs and derelicts of society and enthrones them as paragons of virtue, even as *pirs* or saintly Sufi leaders. These are the *rend* "debauchee", the *qalandar* "dissolute hoodlum," the *pir-e meyforush* "wine selling *pir*."[105]

The recourse to and simultaneous transformation of traditional tropes from Sufi poetry were, for Sheybani and Nima, decisive tools for the creation of a socially committed, comprehensible literature for the masses.

Gholam Hossein Gharib's Short Story Nabsh

Unlike Nima and Sheybani, the writer Gholam Hossein Gharib portrays how clinging to traditional and religious roles can lead to the individual's isolation and to even more disastrous consequences beyond that. This illustrates how contemporary writers examined the role of spiritual Islam in the construction of a modern Iranian national identity in their literary works. In a short story entitled *Nabsh*, Gharib presents the life of a Sufi in a negative light. The story highlights the moment of sexual awakening in a Sufi's life. Cut off from the outside world, Sheikh nur al-din lives a lonely, ascetic life in an abandoned *imamzadeh* (a shrine of an Imam's descendants).[106] The title of the short story, *Nabsh*, has several meanings in Persian. While *nabsh can* normally be translated as "corner," through the progression of the plot, the reader gradually comes to understand that, in this particular context, *nabsh* refers to the desecration of dead bodies.

The short story's protagonist, Sheikh nur al-din, is a thirty-five-year-old cleric and janitor of the Imamzadeh Bibi Zakenan. His main duties are lighting candles and reading from the Qur'an at funerals. He lives alone in nearly complete isolation in a small space inside the *imamzadeh*. Located outside of the city, "the imamzadeh was in a sheltered and quiet place and its two half-torn minarets and the dusty cupola were a beacon for the caravan that passed by on its way every now and then."[107]

---

[105] Ehsan Yarshater, 'Hafez i. An Overview,' *Encyclopedia Iranica*, www.iranicaonline.org/articles/hafez-i, accessed 4 November 2016.
[106] Gholam Hossein Gharib, 'Nabsh,' *Fighting Rooster Magazine*, no. 1 (1948), 16–30.
[107] Ibid., 16.

The inhabitant's characterization and the description of the *imamzadeh* reflect the topographical character of the cemetery as an intermediate place between the living and the dead. In this story, the young *sayyed* (cleric), who is feared by most people, has very few visitors at the *imamzadeh*. He is unattractive in appearance, unkempt and skinny, and wears woolen garments and his father's traditional *mullah* clothes (a long robe and a green hat). In addition, people believe that his presence will bring misfortune and blame him for the death of his mother, who died giving birth to him. He lives mainly on donations of *halva* and *horma*, sweets, and dates, which the visitors bring to the graves.

One day during a walk, Sheikh nur al-din discovered a group of people. At first, he remained unimpressed. Later, however, he observed one of the women bathing in a water spring and, for the first time in his life, he saw a naked woman. The woman was sitting on a rock next to the spring, her body visible head to toe, while her long, black, braided hair fell on her white and naked breasts. It is interesting to note how well the literary description of the bather resonates with Ziapour's painting *Zaynab Khatoun*.

However, the cleric's voyeuristic pleasure does not last long, as the woman's companions spot the voyeur and chase him away with their shouting and yelling. Yet, this moment changes the young man's life drastically. He stops reading the Qur'an and the woman's image begins to haunt him in every part of the *imamzadeh*. Every candle and marble stone is transformed into the woman's body, but every time he tries to touch her, the object changes back into its original state. One day, the body of a dead woman is brought to the *imamzadeh*. As the corpse washer does her job, he hears how she continually repeats the saying, as demanded by custom, "*Natars man haharetam*" [Don't be afraid, I am your sister!]. Convinced that the dead woman is the same woman he saw bathing, his life becomes less and less important to him and he begins performing mourning rituals for the woman. In his imagination, the sight of her naked body made the woman his lawful spouse. One day during his mourning ceremonies, he suddenly hears an unusual noise that grows louder with every repetition. Again, a female voice says, "*Natars man haharetam*." Persuaded that the woman has called for him, he slowly removes the tombstone of the woman's grave, installed in the wall. Suddenly, he remembers that necrophilia is taboo and a sin. But, having pulled the body out of the wall, he loses control and rips the shroud off her body. Totally out of his mind, he embraces her ecstatically, laughing like a madman and growing even more hysterical. As he desecrates the dead body, he starts feeling sick, staggers, and falls over while embracing his beloved, the white body burying him like a marble tombstone.

Mortezza Hannaneh and New Music

In his article *"Musiqi"* (Music), the composer Mortezza Hannaneh (1923–1989) expresses his guidelines for a better understanding of European symphonies through Islamic and Sufi principles. He speaks about the Iranian people's lack of understanding and even backwardness regarding classical symphonic music. In his opinion, Iranians' lack of interests in European music comes from the lack of orchestras in their music. He also states that an Iranian audience has difficulties accessing European music because of how different it is from traditional Iranian music. The audience's enthusiasm for their national music is due to their familiarity with these musical traditions. He therefore demands better musical education that would teach Iranians the skills necessary to appreciate this music. To become familiar with classical music, Hannaneh advises, one should start with fairly simple music, like waltzes or rhapsodies, while drawing on information about the composer and their technique. Using the example of cinema, Hannaneh argues that the impact of the combination of music and image creates a new feeling of vitality. Visual imagination is, for him, the key to understanding symphonies. It is the image that conveys the message to the audience and has the potential to evoke different feelings. Hannaneh also observed this in Persian poetry, which creates inner pictures with colorful compositions that lead to the reader's emotional engagement with the topic. Thus, Hannaneh concludes, creating an image while listening to music enables the listener to be touched in a way similar to that experienced by readers of Hafez' poetry.[108]

Though Hannaneh deals with Western music in his article, he proposes to access these symphonies through Sufi principles. The idea of being moved by music to such a degree that one can enter another state

---

[108] Mortezza Hannaneh, 'Musiqi (Music),' *Fighting Rooster Magazine*, no. 1 (1948), 3–10.

of mind can be traced as far back as to the Indian poet Amir Khusrow (1253–1325), who wrote,

> Blessings upon he who, in a single moment, can move another
> To weeping, to laughter, to wakefulness, to slumber![109]

Generally, this idea refers to the Sufi concept of *'sama*, that is, listening to music and poetry. The Sufi master Abu Sa'id (d. 1049) theorized the practice of listening to music and poetry to include ecstatic dancing to love songs accompanied by drums and lutes for the purpose of altering the listener's state of being. Abu Sa'id's emphasis on musical performances brought forth harsh criticism from clerics in Nishapour and Baghdad and has continued to be discussed as a concept in the twentieth century. Ahmad Kasravi, for example, criticized this devotional Sufi practice because "they played the lute and flute, stamped their feet, clapped their hands, spun and jumped around in such a way that they foamed at the mouth, became dizzy and fell over."[110] He criticized them and their performance for not being an expression of their love of God but rather the result of being drunk or of an ecstatic memory of earthly love.[111]

For Hannaneh, however, the practice of *sama* was not intended as a critique of religious practices but rather served as a pedagogical means to reveal similarities between different music styles and to facilitate an understanding of classical music.

Ziapour's Writings on Painting

Parallel to Hannaneh's article about music, Ziapour published an article about painting in the same issue. His main point was that the true purpose of painting had not yet been recognized in Iran. Yet, Ziapour does not criticize the audience for their skepticism toward new modernist expression. Instead, he insists that it is part of the artist's responsibility to create an artistic scene and to educate audiences to access this new form of art. Like in his manifesto, he criticizes Iranian painting for remaining rooted in naturalistic expression, which, for him, is a sign of lacking innovation and, as a practice, a form of mere imitation. For Ziapour, the artist's task is to "gain a

---

[109] Khusrow, Amir. i'jaz-i Khusravī, 2:277, cited in Ahmed, *What Is Islam?* 426.
[110] Ridgeon, *Sufi Castigator*, 56.   [111] Ibid.

deeper insight into the reflections of nature, which are hidden to the normal population, so that he can foster his artistic expression and also be able to demonstrate his impressions through his own insight and through artistic expression with proficiency and perpetuation."[112]

As Ziapour saw it, naturalism's prevalence in Iran was rooted in the outdated concept of artistic creativity as a God-given talent. Ziapour proclaimed that "to become a good artist one has to work hard, show diligence, comprehend nature and to understand how one can use it for its own benefit, as well as to understand the objective of art."[113] Ziapour harshly criticizes artists still working in representational styles and declares their artistic lives "worthless." In particular, Ziapour attacked contemporary Iranian painters working in the miniature style of the schools of Reza Abbasi and Behzad because "they have no aim or purpose. Aesthetics has no significance or importance. They place no value on line, or drawing or use of colour."[114]

At the same time, however, Ziapour demands a modernization on Iranian terms and not an imitation of Western modernist painting styles, when he explains that,

We should be moving to link up with the world culture and we should try at the same time to preserve our identity. When I came back to Iran, I was in rebellious mood. I was asking myself, why are we not drawing upon all these good things that we have in our possession? I have seen how the Europeans reacted to their own past, how they were reacting to the present, what kind of forms they selected for their outpouring and rebellion, and how they handled their own development. My task and my message were to try to find in our own indigenous culture something that was still living and had some compatibility with the universal language of painting. I wanted to find such elements and nurture them and eventually to elevate the status of my country's art and culture.[115]

In his article, Ziapour formulates a new approach toward cultural heritage and its incorporation into art in general, as well as painting, because, as he states,

No one denies Iran is a land of art and talent and that it is actually amongst the leading countries. All these tiles and carpets that adorn our houses and

---

[112] Jalil Ziapour, 'Naqashi (Painting),' *Fighting Rooster Magazine*, no. 1 (1948), 12–15, 12.
[113] Ibid.   [114] Ibid., 14.   [115] Ibid., 12.

walls are the result of Iranian talent and direct attention of the public towards art and artists. But our artists have to learn how they can advance art towards perfection and authenticity. They must teach the public how they should observe art and what they should expect from each style of art.[116]

Revisiting the *Fighting Rooster's* artistic productions, one can see how transcultural processes of translation decisively shaped the development and formation of a local modernism in Iran. The formation of this local modernism can be attributed to the artistic encounter with modernist expression, which took place predominantly when Iranian artists went abroad to study in Europe. In particular, the individual agency of Jalil Ziapour, who became a spokesperson for modernism after his return from France, supported the dissemination of modernist expression. Throughout his career, Ziapour consistently emphasized that his stay in Paris and his encounter with Western art had spurred his artistic innovations and inspired him "to try to find in our own indigenous culture something that was still living and had some compatibility with the universal language of painting."[117] The preceding iconographic analysis of Ziapour's artistic works outlines the crucial role played by André Lhote and the political implications of French Cubism in the development of a politically engaged art in Iran in the late 1940s and into the 1950s. The analysis of Nima's poem represents another case study of how Iranian artists translated modernism into a local context through Persian metaphors. The adaptation of a European modernist language was by no means merely a formalist experiment with Western modernity but rather enabled local artistic innovation, which became a critical tool for reflection on the sociopolitical discourses of the time. Based on this, we can conclude that the *Fighting Rooster*'s cultural production was not only an aesthetic manifestation of modernism in Iran but also drew on Bergsonian thought as the basis for a political ideology for Iranian artists.

In summary, the foregoing analysis of the *Fighting Rooster's* artistic production has shown that the first generation of Iranian Modernist artists was already trying to answer the question of how to adopt Western modernity, while remaining Iranian. What we see in the *Fighting Rooster Association* is, in other words, that the debate about Iran's modernization and westernization did not begin under

[116] Ibid.   [117] Ibid.

Mohammad Reza Shah with the politicization of Islam in the 1960s that would eventually lead to the Islamic Revolution in 1978/79 but rather that the debates about the equality of the monarchy and the people in fact date back to the political discourse of Iran's constitutional period in the early twentieth century.

Conclusion

My field research for this study began in the summer of 2013 in Tehran, where I conducted interviews with artists, curators, and critics. After months of reading and studying Iran's modern history, I wanted to interview the artists and see how their works were connected to the specific sociocultural and sociopolitical contexts of their production. For one of my first interviews, I met the artist Sadegh Tabrizi, who, as an "official" member of *Saqqakhaneh*, holds a prominent place in Iranian art history. It was very enlightening to meet Tabrizi as a contemporary witness of Iran's vivid art scene before and after the Revolution and to learn more about his artistic practice. I was very surprised, however, that Tabrizi has not been keeping any record of the pieces he made in the years before the revolution, which were sold to museums and collectors. As we delved deeper into his artistic practice and discussed his artistic references to Iran's cultural heritage, Tabrizi explained that his inspiration came to him in dreams and reflected the visual impressions of his daily life in Iran.

At this early stage in my research and with the very classical training I received as an art historian in Germany, I found it challenging to be confronted with missing archives and to make sense of dreams and impressions as primary sources for artistic practice. With this in mind, I scheduled my next interview with an artist whose artworks from the 1970s were openly political and socially committed, to learn more about the relationship between art and politics in prerevolutionary Iran. Thus, a few days later, I met Koorosh Shishegaran, who had designed political posters that had been an effective tool for social mobilization before and during the revolution. In cooperation with his brothers, Koorosh, Behzad, and Ismail Shishegaran, he produced numerous political posters for the Iranian revolutionaries between 1978 and 1979.

Trained at the College of Decorative Arts, Shishegaran employed modernist aesthetic language in his artworks to express his political

Conclusion 257

Figure 5.1 Koorosh Shishegaran, *For Today*. Off-set print poster, 1978, 49 × 60 cm

messages and opposition to the government. These iconic posters consist of drawings and lines of text in English and Persian condemning state violence against political activists, demanding a free press, and calling on Iran to fight imperialism. To effectively communicate these political messages to the masses, the artists employed guns, fists, flowers, and peace doves as standardized symbols of the revolution in their designs. The poster *For Today* (1978) portrays the brothers from a frontal perspective as they hold red guns pointed into their wide-open mouths, as if they were going to commit suicide. The black bar under the faces and guns bears the title *For Today* and the date October 1978. The interplay of image and text communicates the powerful message that the current political status quo in Iran had become unbearable.

Due to inexpensive cost of reproduction and the powerful revolutionary iconography, Shishegaran's posters were widely disseminated and could be found on Tehran's city walls and in the streets at the demonstrations. Thus, Shishegaran's artistic practice illustrates the strong relationship between art and political activism in Iran before and during the revolution. Shishegaran's use of art as a means of political activism was based on his socialist understanding of art, which was an important foundation for the articulation of utopian aspirations for social and political transformation in Iran.[1]

With this background knowledge, I was very surprised that during our interview Koorosh Shishegaran distanced himself from any political aspirations in his artworks. Instead, he explained that his art should rather be seen in the broader discourse of a global humanity and as a means to promote peace and freedom among the nations. Shishegaran also distances himself from political themes in his artistic practice. After the revolution, Shishegaran's art was no longer compatible with the political interests "of the master narrative of the Islamic Republic." As Hamid Keshmirshekan explains, "the new state did not tolerate these Third Worldist revolutionary concerns and would not allow them to be practiced after the consolidation of the Islamic Republic."[2] Distancing himself from political issues in his artworks, Shishegaran began to further explore the dynamic lines and calligraphic traces, which can already be found in his posters from the 1970s, and turned them into autonomous pictorial elements to create abstract compositions. According to Keshmirshekan, this shift in Shishegaran's artistic practice points to the wider topic of Iran's complex cultural transformations in the twentieth century "from utopianism and avant-gardism to radicalism, and ultimately conservatism." According to Keshmirshekan, "the crisis of political and cultural legitimacy in Iran" over the past fifty years has resulted in the fact that,

> Utopianism, idealism, ideological radicalism and revolutionary fervor can no longer be received with enthusiasm. This reflects the skepticism of the generations of idealist romantics who feel that their utopian ideals have now been discarded.[3]

The social and political realities of the Islamic Republic, which did not fulfill the leftist goals of the revolution, led many artists to distance themselves from their earlier political activities, which had contributed to the fall of the Shah and the establishment of the Islamic Republic. In

---

[1] Hamid Keshmirshekan, 'The Trajectory of Koorosh Shishegaran's Artistic Phases: From Utopianism to Aestheticism,' in Keshmirshekan, *Koorosh Shishegaran: The Art of Altruism* (London: Saqi Books, 2016), 23–42, 34.
[2] Ibid., 37.   [3] Ibid., 39.

one conversation we had, the exiled artist Behruz Heshmat stated that many modernist artists were deeply engaged in the political discussion of the time. Heshmat characterized the retrospective concentration and emphasis on formalist qualities of modernist Iranian artworks as a coping mechanism and displacement strategy for dealing with the feeling of shame and disappointment at the consequences of the Iranian Revolution.[4]

Due to political restrictions and censorship, a critical reassessment of the Iranian Revolution and discussions of Iran's modern past cannot take place openly today in the Islamic Republic of Iran. Nor does the memorialization of the country's Pahlavi past play a significant role in the official discourse of state-promoted memory and identity politics. The reason for this is that the Iranian Revolution was based on opposition toward the Shah and pursued the goal of overthrowing the monarchy to establish an Islamic Republic. The Iranian Revolution replaced the Pahlavi monarchy with the Islamic Republic and set as its goal the destruction of the Pahlavi past and erasure of its memory.

In the "master narrative of the Islamic Republic," however, the revolution plays only a subordinate role because it "was too messy" and "included too many secularists, leftists, feminists, and nationalists to be neatly packaged as an 'Islamic Revolution.'"[5] Instead, it was mainly the subsequent Iran–Iraq war that strengthened the state and provided ideological justification and legitimacy for the newly established regime. As Narges Bajoghli explains,

> The war, which followed on the heels of the revolution, allowed the regime to imprison members of the opposition for reasons of "national security," to mobilize the population in defense of the revolution as the regime defined it, and to consolidate its power.[6]

This means that the official memory politics in today's Iran concentrate mostly on the commemoration of the victims of the Iran–Iraq war. The state's commemoration builds on the collective memory of the war but also supports the production of future memories through the

---

[4] Conversation with Behruz Heshmat and the author. Munich, 18 September 2014.
[5] Narges Bajoghli, *Iran Reframed: Anxieties of Power in the Islamic Republic* (Stanford: Stanford University Press, 2019), 28.
[6] Ibid.

aestheticization of politics by establishing and maintaining martyr museums, holding public events, and installing public wall paintings. In 2010, for example, one of Iran's largest museums opened its doors, the Museum of the Islamic Revolution and Holy Defense (*Muse-ye enqelab-e Islami va defa-ye moqadas*). As an official site and prestige object of the Islamic Republic, the museum's exhibition is a means to communicate the ideological justification of Iran's current politics. The museum exhibition confronts visitors with audiovisual material and reconstructed war scenes that allow them to experience scenes of the revolution and the war and thus presents postrevolutionary history through the ideological lens of the Islamic Republic.

In the broader context of memories and memorialization and the absence of the Pahlavi past in official historical discourses of the Islamic Republic, modernist art plays a key role in the memorialization of Iran's prerevolutionary times both inside and outside Iran. As this study has shown, modernist art can, however, also serve as an inclusive way of reconnecting with an Iranian identity. The government's focus on the Iran–Iraq war was, for instance, used in the process of nation-building and helped to redefine a national identity that excluded exiles or political opponents. In particular, for the Iranian diaspora community, modernist art often serves as visual manifestations and relic of a metaphorical return to Iran's prerevolutionary past. As was elaborated in this study, employing modernist art in the form of a collective national memory is a highly political act and every period tends to remodel memories for its own political ends. In other words, the "act of remembering is always in and of the present, while its reference is of the past and thus absent."[7] In the case of contemporary Iran, the Pahlavi times are remembered from within the political and social framework of today's Islamic Republic. This demonstrates just how influential the present is when it comes to the production of memories but also presents the pitfall that, as Andreas Huyssen writes, "every act of memory carries with it a dimension of betrayal, forgetting, and absence."[8]

These complex politics of memory are one of many reasons for the exclusion of Iranian modernist art's socialcultural and sociopolitical dimensions. The social construction of memory and processes of collective repetition, manifested in exhibitions and art history, helped

---

[7] Andreas Huyssen, *Present Pasts: Urban Palimpsets and the Politics of Memory* (Stanford: Stanford University Press, 2003), 3–4.
[8] Ibid., 4.

place modernist Iranian art in service of the Pahlavi monarchy, as a visual representation of the country's successful secularization and modernization. This strategy was particularly effective because the monarchy had created a suitable infrastructure to coopt of all fields of culture. A connection between patriotism and the aesthetics of an imagined Persian Empire led to an aestheticization of politics (in particular, in the architectural field), the construction of monuments, and the 2,500-year celebration of the Persian Empire. In particular, visual architectural references helped to communicate Mohammad Reza Pahlavi's imagined connection to Iran's ancient past and the eternal narrative of a secular Iranian identity. Yet, modernist art, which incorporated references to Iran's Islamic heritage, could also easily function as part of the state's official doctrine. This was mainly made possible by Western scholarship's validation of Orientalist spiritualism. As Hamid Yousefi explains, "Pope and Corbin offered metahistorical visions of Islam which granted Pahlavi's secular and military outlook a spiritual dimension."[9]

This study has illustrated that the image of modernist Iranian art as an expression of the monarchy's modernity was immensely powerful and remains effective today. This can be seen in recent exhibition projects, which were held outside Iran, as discussed in the first chapter of this study. The exhibition projects in New York and Berlin staged Iranian modernist artworks as evidence of the country's previous secularism and democracy. By doing so, the exhibitions analyzed in this work crafted their own histories of Iranian modernism and glorified an imaginary Persian past while ignoring contemporary discourses in Iran about the country's modernist heritage in Iran. Regarding modernism as evidence for Iran's westernization calls forth a permanent comparison and competition with Western artistic modernity. In this context, Iranian experiments with the visuality of Western modernity always appear as asynchronous and belated imitations of Western styles. One should not forget, however, that Iran's ideological proximity to Western nation-states was a side effect of imperial and colonial politics. A collective memory of Iranian modernist art as a symbol for the country's alleged Western progressiveness in exhibitions and art historiography not only reaffirms the westernized

---

[9] Hamed Yousefi, 'ART+ART: The Avant-Garde in the Streets,' *E-Flux Journal*, no. 82 (2017), www.e-flux.com/journal/82/133639/art-art-the-avant-garde-in-the-streets/, accessed 18 November 2020.

ideology of the Pahlavi state but also reduces the artistic production of this period to the status of inferior derivatives of Western modernity. Ultimately, this kind of interpretation runs the risk of confirming global power political structures and international hierarchies.

To liberate modernist Iranian art from its ideological instrumentalization as a mere visual manifestation of the Pahlavi past and as attempts to catch up with Western artistic achievements, it is necessary to take Iran's anticolonial response into account, which was powerfully articulated in terms of the discourse of westoxification in Iran. The second chapter of this study illustrated, that this discussion not only took place in intellectual and literary circles but was also mirrored in the field of contemporary art. Artists and critics were deeply engaged in negotiating new concepts of a possible Iranian modernity as a significant other to Western colonial modernity. In particular, aesthetic expression and art criticism proved to be a laboratory for an anticolonial concept of artistic modernity in Iran. In particular, al-e Ahmad's art criticism demonstrates that modernist Iranian art was not an apolitical leisure-time activity for the upper class. His texts show that modernist Iranian art was an integral part of the anticolonial discourse of *gharbzadegi*, which encouraged artists to use their artworks as a means of political expression.

At the time, art critics and artists demanded a hybrid merging of local visual traditions with modern means of expression to articulate a specific version of an Iranian modernity, which took into account the sociopolitical concerns of the period in which it originated. In fact, this idea was based on an analytical concept of modernity, which promised a creative artistic response to Iran's profound transformation and the country's political struggles for liberalization and democratic participation. In this regard, it is important to reflect critically upon the art-historical categories of canon and stylistic development and to discover how individual artworks addressed the contexts in which they were produced. Our analysis of the term *Saqqakhaneh* in the third chapter clearly demonstrated how powerful historiographical categories can become. In the case of *Saqqakhaneh*, which is often seen as a state-sponsored modernism, one can see how formalism contributed to a depoliticized understanding of modernist Iranian art. Clinging to *Saqqakhaneh* as a stylistic category not only prevents a deeper investigation of the artworks and their contents but also contributes to the concealment of a contextualized understanding of Iranian modernism. In the case of *Saqqakhaneh*, in particular, using the artworks as primary sources for art-historical analysis offers us an opportunity to rethink Iranian modernist artistic expression. Looking at works by Tanavoli and Zenderoudi, for instance, one can discern how modernist artists responded to the sociocultural and sociopolitical discourses of their time. Likewise, it also shows that Iran's modernist art was far more than mere experiments with modern forms. The artists' incorporation of Islamic iconography can also help us to question general assumptions about modernism's inherent characteristics, such as its secularity and status as a radical break with the past.

Contrary to the general assumption that *Saqqakhaneh* represents the first manifestation of an Iranian modernism that was successfully able to go beyond being an imitation of Western modernism, the *Fighting Rooster Association* is an earlier example of an artistic group in Iran that was already actively discussing the questions of how to become modern while preserving a specific Iranian identity in the 1950s. The *Fighting Rooster Association* has long been dismissed in art history for its belated experiments with Western modernity and has yet to receive the full attention it deserves. The last chapter demonstrated that the *Fighting Rooster's* artistic practice is a vivid example of how the adaptation of European modernity took place on aesthetic and substantive levels. In particular, modernity's transculturality and the influence of French philosophy enabled the artists to craft an alternative leftist discourse about a possible Iranian national identity. The *Fighting Roosters* were deeply engaged in Iran's political discourse and called for the equality of the monarchy and the people in their artistic productions. This debate dates back to Iran's constitutional era in the early twentieth century. In fact, this reconnection with earlier discussions about the country's modernization as well as Iran's position in Britain and Russia's imperial "Great Game" should provoke us to rethink established notions about Iran's modernity. In other words, an analysis of the context of artistic production can help us rethink concepts of modernity and see that Iran's modernization has a long and complex history, which had started well before Mohammad Reza Shah came to power. The *Fighting Rooster's* exclusion from the Pahlavi canon of modernist art also highlights the state's conceptualization of modernism as a means of soft power. Due to the group's leftist alignment and their ideological proximity to Iranian Communists, however, the Pahlavi monarchy, as a close ally of Western powers in the fight against Soviet socialism, did not recognize the *Fighting Rooster's* artistic activities in their official cultural politics.

Starting with individual artworks as primary sources for the study of modernist Iranian art history has a great potential for both revealing art's instrumentalization and dismantling imperial historiography as well as retracing alternative histories behind the artworks. As we have seen in the foregoing iconographic analysis, for many artists such as Bahman Mohassess, Hossein Zenderoudi, Parviz Tanavoli, and Jalil Ziapour, the events of the oil crisis of 1951–1953, which led to Mosaddeq's overthrow, had a decisive impact on their artistic practice. Motivated by commercial interests, British and US secret services orchestrated Mosaddeq's removal from office. The reinstatement of Mohammad Reza Shah as Iran's ruling monarch shattered the hope for national independence and the country's liberation from colonialist power politics. For the Iranian intelligentsia, the 1953 coup represented an unprecedented act of imperial and colonial interference in Iran's political affairs and fueled the anticolonial discourse, which in turn became highly influential in all fields of culture and eventually contributed to the success of the Islamic Revolution.

This book has illustrated that modernist Iranian art did not evolve within a sociopolitical vacuum, but, rather, that it was deeply rooted in contemporary sociopolitical discourses and also mirrored Iran's cultural and political transformations. The monarchy's instrumentalization of modernist artistic production as a symbol for the country's modernization and secularization, along with the complex politics of memorialization of prerevolutionary Iran, however, has established a depoliticized understanding of Iranian modernism. In particular, Western modes of knowledge production produced the formalist canon of modernist Iranian art based on linear narratives of stylistic development and artistic progress in Iranian modernist art. This formalist art canon has concealed the strong interconnection between art and politics in Iran and reduced rich artworks to mere aesthetic experiments. To gain a deeper understanding of the intellectual richness and aesthetic creativity of Iranian modernist art beyond formalist innovation, we must start to engage with and discover the many layers and hidden stories behind a given work. Freeing Iranian modernist artworks from the idea that they originated in a sociopolitical vacuum not only offers the opportunity to broaden this new, emerging field of research but might also provide an opportunity for the voices of Iranians to be heard in their century-long struggle for liberalization and democratization.

Select Bibliography

Abahsain, Muhammad Mansour. 'The Supra–Symbolic Moth in Arabic Religious Poetry from the Late Ottoman Period.' *Journal of Arabic Literature*, vol. 24, no. 1 (1993), 21–27.

Abrahamian, Ervand. *The Coup: 1953, the CIA and the Roots of Modern U.S.-Iranian Relations*. New York: New Press, 2013.

― *A History of Modern Iran*. Cambridge: Cambridge University Press, 2008.

Adib-Moghaddam, Arshin. *What Is Iran? Domestic Politics and International Relations in Five Musical Pieces*. Cambridge: Cambridge University Press, 2021.

Afary, Janet, and Kevin B. Anderson. *Foucault and the Iranian Revolution: Gender and the Seductions of Islamism*. Chicago: University of Chicago Press, 2005.

Afsarian, Iman. 'Chera ma nemitavanim honar-e moaser dashte bashim?' ['Why Can't We Have Contemporary Art?']. *Herfeh: Honarmand* (Autumn, 2015). 101–102.

― 'The Fortunate Adolescents (Part 1).' 2012. https://iran.britishcouncil.org/en/underline/visual-arts/fortunate-adolescents. Accessed 23 July 2018.

Aghaee, Ehsan. *A Retrospective Exhibition of Works of Saqqakhana Movement*. Exh.-Cat. Tehran: Museum of Contemporary Art Tehran, 2013.

Aghaie, Kamran Scot (ed.). *The Women of Karbala: Ritual Performance and Symbolic Discourses in Modern Shi'i Islam*. Austin: University of Texas Press, 2005.

Ahmed, Shahab. *What Is Islam? The Importance of Being Islamic*. Princeton: Princeton University Press, 2016.

Al-Din Rumi, Jalal. *The Masnavi*. Translated by Jawid Mojaddedi. Oxford: Oxford University Press, 2004.

Al-e Ahmad, Jalal. 'The Fifth Triple Yolk Egg' ['Tohme seh zarde panjom Tochme morgh']. In Mustafa Zamaninya (ed.), *Adab wa hunar-i imruz-i Īrān: Maǧmū'a-i maqālāt-I*. Tehran: Nashr-e Mitra, 1994. 1377–1385.

― 'For Mohassess and the Wall' ['Be Mohassess va baray-e divar']. In Mustafa Zamaninya (ed.), *Adab wa hunar-i imruz-i Īrān: Maǧmū'a-i maqālāt-I*. Tehran: Nashr-e Mitra, 1994. 1341–1355.

Occidentosis: A Plague from the West (Gharbzadegi). Translated by R. Campbell. Berkeley: Mizan Press, 1983.
'Painting Exhibition in "Apadana"' ['Namayesgah-ye naqashi dar "Apadana"']. In Mustafa Zamaninya (ed.), Adab wa hunar-i imruz-i Īrān: Mağmū'a-i maqālāt-I. Tehran: Nashr-e Mitra, 1994. 1286–1293.
Plagued by the West (Gharbzadegi). Translated by Paul Sprachman. Delmar, NY: Center for Iranian Studies Columbia University, 1981.
Weststruckness (Gharbzadegi). Translated by John Green and Ahmad Alizadeh. Costa Mesa, CA: Mazda Publisher, 1997.
Alavi, Bozorg. Geschichte und Entwicklung der modernen persischen Literatur. Berlin: Akademie Verlag, 1964.
Albrecht, Judith. '"How to Be an Iranian Woman in the 21st Century?" Female Identities in the Diaspora.' In Heinrich Böll Foundation in Cooperation with Transparency for Iran (eds.), Identity and Exile: The Iranian Diaspora between Solidarity and Difference, vol. 40 of the Publication Series on Democracy. Berlin: Heinrich Böll Foundation, 2016. 47–61.
Alinejad, Donya, and Halleh Ghorashi. 'From Bridging to Building: Discourses of Organizing Iranian Americans across Generations.' In Heinrich Böll Foundation in cooperation with Transparency for Iran (eds.), Identity and Exile: The Iranian Diaspora between Solidarity and Difference, vol. 40 of the Publication Series on Democracy. Berlin: Heinrich Böll Foundation, 2016. 62–75.
Alvandi, Roham, Nixon, Kissinger, and the Shah: The United States and Iran in the Cold War. Oxford: Oxford University Press, 2014.
Aminrazavi, Mehdi. The Wine of Wisdom: The Life, Poetry and Philosophy of Omar Khayyam. Oxford: Oneworld Publications, 2005.
Anderson, Benedict R. Imagined Communities: Reflections on the Origin and Spread of Nationalism. London: Verso, 1991.
Ansari, Ali M. Modern Iran: The Pahlavis and After. London: Routledge, 2007.
'The Myth of the White Revolution: Mohammad Reza Shah, "Modernization" and the Consolidation of Power.' Middle Eastern Studies, vol. 37, no. 3 (July 2001), 1–24.
Ansary Pettys, Rebecca. 'The Ta'zieh: Ritual Enactment of Persian Renewal.' Theatre Journal, vol. 33, no. 3 (October 1981), 341–354.
Antliff, Mark Robert. 'Bergson and Cubism: A Reassessment.' Art Journal, vol. 47, no. 4 'Revising Cubism' (Winter, 1988), 341–349.
Antliff, Mark, and Patricia Dee Leighten. Cubism and Culture. New York: Thames & Hudson, 2001.
Ardalan, Nader, and Laleh Bakhtiar. The Sense of Unity: The Sufi Tradition in Persian Architecture. Chicago: The University of Chicago Press, 1973.

Arjomand, Said Amir. *The Turban for the Crown: The Islamic Revolution in Iran*. New York: Oxford University Press, 1988.

Attar, Farid al-din. *The Conference of the Birds*. Translated by Dick Davis. London: Penguin Books, 2005.

Babaie, Sussan. 'Voices of Authority: Locating the "Modern" in "Islamic" Arts.' *Getty Research Journal*, no. 3 (2011), 133–149.

Babaie, Sussan, and Talinn Grigor (eds.). *Persian Kingship and Architecture: Strategies of Power in Iran from the Achaemenids to the Pahlavis*. London: Tauris, 2015.

Bajoghli, Narges. *Iran Reframed: Anxieties of Power in the Islamic Republic*. Stanford: Stanford University Press, 2019.

Balaghi, Shiva. 'Iranian Visual Arts in "The Century of Machinery, Speed, and the Atom": Rethinking Modernity.' In Shiva Balaghi and Lynn Gumpert (eds.), *Picturing Iran: Art, Society and Revolution*. London and New York: I. B. Tauris, 2002. 21–37.

Balaghi, Shiva, and Lynn Gumpert (eds.). *Picturing Iran: Art, Society and Revolution*. London and New York: I. B. Tauris, 2002.

Banai, Nuit. 'From Nation State to Border State.' *Third Text*, vol. 27, no. 4 (2013), 456–469.

Barnhisel, Greg. *Cold War Modernists: Art, Literature, and American Cultural Diplomacy*. New York: Columbia University Press, 2015.

Behdad, Ali. 'The Powerful Art of Qajar Photography: Orientalism and (Self)-Orientalizing in Nineteenth-Century Iran.' *Iranian Studies*, vol. 34, no. 1/4, 'Qajar Art and Society' (2001), 141–151.

Behpoor, Bavand. 'Introduction to "The Nightingale's Butcher's Manifesto" and "Volume and Environment II".' *ARTMargins*, vol. 3, no. 2 (June 2014), 118–128.

Belting, Hans, and Andrea Buddensieg (eds.). *The Global Art World: Audiences, Markets, and Museums*. Ostfildern: Hatje Cantz, 2009.

Benjamin, Rogers. *The Oriental Mirage, Orientalism: Delacroix to Klee*. Sydney: Art Gallery of New South Wales, 1997.

Bennett, Tony. *The Birth of the Museum: History, Theory, Politics*. London: Routledge, 2005.

Bergson, Henri. *An Introduction to Metaphysics*. Translated by T. E. Hulme. Indianapolis: Hackett Publishing Company, 1999.

Bhabha, Homi. *The Location of Culture*. London: Routledge, 1994.

Biswas, Shampa. *Nuclear Desire: Power and the Postcolonial Nuclear Order*. Minneapolis: University of Minnesota Press, 2014.

Blank, Richard. *Schah Reza – der letzte deutsche Kaiser. Dokumente aus der Regenbogenpresse*. Reinbek bei Hamburg: Rowohlt, 1977.

Bloch, Werner. 'Warten auf Farah.' *DIE ZEIT*. No. 49 (24 November 2016).

Bombardier, Alice. 'A Contemporary Illustrated Qur'an. Zenderoudi's Illustration of Grosjean's Translation (1972).' In Cancian Alessandro (ed.), *Approaches to the Qur'an in Contemporary Iran*. Oxford: Oxford University Press, 2019. 325–352.

Les pionniers de la Nouvelle peinture en Iran. Œuvres méconnues, activités novatrices et scandales au tournant des années 1940. Bern: Peter Lang, 2017.

Boroujerdi, Mehrzad. *Iranian Intellectuals and the West: The Tormented Triumph of Nativism*. New York: Syracuse University Press, 1996.

Bourdieu, Pierre. *Distinction: A Social Critique of the Judgement of Taste*. Cambridge, MA: Harvard University Press, 1984.

Bourdieu, Pierre, and Hans Haacke (eds.). *Free Exchange*. Cambridge: Polity Press, 1995.

Brill, Dorothée, Joachim Jäger, and Gabriel Montua (eds.). *The Tehran Modern: A Reader about Art in Iran since 1960*. Berlin: Nationalgalerie, Staatliche Museen zu Berlin, 2017.

Chelkowski, Peter J. 'Iconography of the Women of Karbala: Tiles, Murals, Stamps, and Posters.' In Kamran Scot Aghaie (ed.), *The Women of Karbala: Ritual Performance and Symbolic Discourses in Modern Shi'I Islam*. Austin: University of Texas Press, 2005. 119–138.

Mirror of the Invisible World: Tales from the Khamseh of Nizami. Exh.-Cat. New York: Metropolitan Museum of Art, 1975.

Chelkowski, Peter. 'Narrative Painting and Painting Recitation in Qajar Iran.' *Muqarnas*, vol. 6 (1989), 98–111.

Chelkowski, Peter, and Hamid Debashi. *Staging a Revolution: The Art of Persuasion in the Islamic Republic of Iran*. London: Booth-Clibborn, 1993.

Chichoki, Nina. 'Sculpted Poetry.' In Ruyin Pakbaz and Yaghoub Emdadian (eds.), *Pioneers of Modern Iranian Art: Parviz Tanavoli*. Tehran: Tehran Museum of Contemporary Art, 2003. 9–15.

Clifford, James. *The Predicament of Culture: Twentieth-Century Ethnography, Literature, and Art*. Cambridge, MA: Harvard University Press, 1998.

Routes: Travel and Translation in the Late Twentieth Century. Cambridge, MA: Harvard University Press, 1997.

Cockcroft, Eva. 'Abstract Expressionism: Weapon of the Cold War.' *Artforum*, vol. 15 (1974), 39–41.

Cronin, Stepanie (ed.). *Reformers and Revolutionaries in Modern Iran: New Perspectives on the Iranian Left*. London: Routledge, 2004.

Dabashi, Hamid. 'Ardeshir Mohassess, Etcetera.' In Nicky Nodjoumi and Shirin Neshat (eds.), *Ardeshir Mohassess: Art and Satire in Iran*. Exh.-Cat. New York: Asia Society Antique Collectors' Club, 2008. 17–29.

The Last Muslim Intellectual: The Life and Legacy of Jalal Al-e Ahmad. Edinburgh: Edinburgh University Press, 2021.

'Nima Yushij and Constitution of a National Subject.' In Davison Andrew and Himadeep Muppidi (eds.), *The World Is My Home: A Hamid Dabashi Reader.* London: Transaction, 2010. 147–185.

'Ta'ziyeh as Theatre of Protest.' *TDR*, vol. 49, no. 4 'Special Issue on Ta'ziyeh' (Winter 2005), 91–99.

Theology of Discontent: The Ideological Foundation of the Islamic Revolution in Iran. New York: New York University Press, 1996.

Daftari, Fereshteh. 'Another Modernism: An Iranian Perspective.' In Shiva Balaghi and Lynn Gumpert (eds.), *Picturing Iran: Art, Society and Revolution.* London and New York: I. B. Tauris, 2002. 39–82.

'Another Modernism: An Iranian Perspective.' In Lynn Gumpert (ed.), *Modernisms: Iranian, Turkish, and Indian Highlights from NYU's Abby Weed Grey Collection.* New York and Munich: Grey Art Gallery, New York University, 2019. 43–63.

Persia Reframed: Iranian Visions of Modern and Contemporary Art. London: I. B. Tauris, 2019.

'Redefining Modernism: Pluralist Art before the 1979 Revolution.' In Fereshteh Daftari and Layla S. Diba (eds.), *Iran Modern.* Exh. Cat. New York: Asia Society Museum in association with Yale University Press New Haven, 2013. 25–43.

Daneshmir, Reza, and Catherine Spiridonoff. 'Subterranean Landscape: The Far-Reaching Influence of the Underground Qanat Network in Ancient and Present-Day Iran.' *Architectural Design*, vol. 82, no. 3 (2012), 62–69.

Daneshvar, Simin. 'Painters' Roundtable Report' ['Gozaresh-e mizgerd-e naqashan']. In Mustafa Zamaninya (ed.), *Adab wa hunar-i imruz-i Īrān. Mağmū'a-i maqālāt-I.* Tehran: Nashr-e Mitra, 1994. 1297–1325.

Darabi, Helia. 'Tehran Museum of Contemporary Art as a Microcosm of the State's Cultural Agenda.' In Hamid Keshmirshekan (ed.), *Contemporary Art from the Middle East: Regional Interactions with Global Art Discourses.* London: I. B. Tauris, 2015. 221–245.

Deleuze, Gilles, and Félix Guattari. *Kafka: Toward a Minor Literature.* Minneapolis: University of Minnesota Press, 1986.

Deylami, Shirin S. 'In the Face of the Machine: Westoxification, Cultural Globalization, and the Making of an Alternative Global Modernity.' *Polity*, vol. 43, no. 2 (April 2011), 242–263.

Diba, Farah. Interview with Donna Stein. 'For the Love of her People: An Interview with Farah Diba about the Pahlavi Programs for the Arts in Iran.' In Staci Gem Scheiwiller (ed.), *Performing the Iranian State.* London: Anthem Press, 2013. 75–82.

Diba, Kamran. 'Iran.' In Wijdan Ali (ed.), *Contemporary Art from the Islamic World*. London: Scorpion Publication, 1989. 150–158.

'The Origins of TMoCA: A Personal Account.' In Dorothée Brill, Joachim Jäger, and Gabriel Montua (eds.), *The Tehran Modern: A Reader about Art in Iran since 1960*. Berlin: Nationalgalerie, Staatliche Museen zu Berlin, 2017. 24–37.

Diba, Layla S. 'The Formation of Modern Iranian Art: From Kamal al-Molk to Zenderoudi.' In Fereshteh Daftari and Layla S. Diba (eds.), *Iran Modern*. Exh. Cat. New York: Asia Society Museum in association with Yale University Press New Haven, 2013. 45–65.

Dixon, John Morris. 'Tehran Museum of Contemporary Art: A Cultural Hybrid.' *Progressive Architecture*, no. 5 (May 1978), 68–71.

Drucker, Johanna. 'Formalism's Other History.' *The Art Bulletin*, vol. 78, no. 4 (1996), 750–751.

Eiman, Alisa. 'Shaping and Portraying Identity at the Tehran Museum of Contemporary Art (1977–2005).' In Staci Gem Scheiwiller (ed.), *Performing the Iranian State: Visual Culture and Representations of Iranian Identity*. London: Anthem Press, 2013. 83–99.

Eisenstadt, Shmuel. 'Multiple Modernities.' *Daedalus*, vol. 129, no. 1 (Winter 2000), 1–29.

Elkins, James. *Is Art History Global?* New York: Routledge, 2007.

'Style.' Grove Art Online. Oxford Art Online. 2003. https://doi.org/10.1093/gao/9781884446054.article.T082129. Accessed 23 October 2019.

Elser, Oliver. 'Just What Is It That Makes Brutalism Today So Appealing? A New Definition from an International Perspective.' In Oliver Elser, Philip Kurz, and Peter Cachola Schmal (eds.), *SOS Brutalism: A Global Survey*. Exh.-Cat. German Architecture Museum, Frankfurt am Main. Zurich: Park Books, 2017. 15–19.

Emami, Karim. 'ART IN IRAN xi. POST-QAJAR.' *Encyclopædia Iranica*, Online edition, 2009. www.iranicaonline.org/articles/art-in-iran-xi-post-qajar. Accessed 23 October 2019

'Artists Must Be Able to Sell.' In Houra Yavari (ed.), *Karim Emami on Modern Iranian Culture, Literature & Art*. New York: Persian Heritage Foundation, 2014. 173–175.

'Making Reciprocity Stick: Artists Are Becoming Critics.' In Houra Yavari (ed.), *Karim Emami on Modern Iranian Culture, Literature & Art*. New York: Persian Heritage Foundation, 2014. 226–227.

'A New Iranian School.' In Houra Yavari (ed.), *Karim Emami on Modern Iranian Culture, Literature & Art*. New York: Persian Heritage Foundation, 2014. 160–162.

'Saqqa-khaneh Dominant.' In Houra Yavari (ed.), *Karim Emami on Modern Iranian Culture, Literature & Art* . New York: Persian Heritage Foundation, 2014. 170–172.

'Saqqakhaneh School Revisited.' In *Saqqakhaneh*, Exh.-Cat Tehran: Tehran Museum of Contemporary Art, 1977.

Engelhardt, Katrin. 'Die Ausstellung 'Entartete Kunst' in Berlin 1938.' In Uwe Fleckner (ed.), *Angriff auf die Avantgarde: Kunst und Kunstpolitik im Nationalsozialismus*. Berlin: Akademie Verlag, 2007. 94–98.

Enwezor, Okwui. 'Mega-Exhibitions and the Antinomies of a Transnational Global Form.' *Manifesta Journal: Journal of Contemporary Curatorship*, no. 2 (2003), 94–119.

Enwezor, Okwui, Nancy Condee, and Terry Smith (eds.). *Antinomies of Art and Culture: Modernity, Postmodernity, Contemporaneity*. Durham, NC: Duke University Press, 2008.

Enwezor, Okwui, Katy Siegel, and Ulrich Wilmes (eds.). *Postwar: Art between the Pacific and the Atlantic, 1945–1965*. London: Prestel Publishing, 2016.

Eshaghi, Peyman. 'Quietness beyond Political Power: Politics of Taking Sanctuary (Bast Neshini) in the Shi'ite Shrines of Iran.' *Iranian Studies*, vol. 49, no. 3 (2016), 493–514.

Etemadi, Parvaneh. '"In Order to Create, One Must First Destroy": An Interview with Parvaneh Etemadi.' Payvand, 2017. www.payvand.com/news/17/apr/1123.html. Accessed 23 October 2019.

Ettinghausen, Richard, and Ehsan Yarshater. *Highlights of Persian Art*. Boulder: Wittenborn Art Books, 1979.

Fanon, Frantz. *The Wretched of the Earth*. New York: Grove Press, 1963.

Farahi, Farshad. 'World of Similitude: The Metamorphosis of Iranian Architecture.' *Architectural Design*, vol. 82, no. 3 (1 May 2012), 52–61.

Farhad, Massumeh. 'Isfahan xi. SCHOOL OF PAINTING AND CALLIGRAPHY.' *Encyclopedia Iranica*, Online edition. 2007. www.iranicaonline.org/articles/art-in-iran-xi-post-qajar. Accessed 23 October 2019.

Ferdowsi, Abolqasem. *Shahnameh: The Persian Book of Kings*. New York: Mage, 1997.

Finbarr, Barry Flood. 'From Prophet to Postmodernism? New World Orders and the End of Islamic Art.' In Elisabeth Mansfield (ed.), *Making Art History: A Changing Discipline and Its Institutions*. London: Routledge, 2007. 31–53.

Fischer, Michael M. J. *Iran: From Religious Dispute to Revolution*. Madison: University of Wisconsin Press, 1989.

Flaskerud, Ingvild. *Visualizing Belief and Piety in Iranian Shiism*. London: Continuum, 2010.

Fock, Gisela. *Die iranische Moderne in der Bildenden Kunst: Der Bildhauer und Maler Parviz Tanavoli*. Vienna: Verlag der Österreichischen Akademie der Wissenschaften, 2011.

Foroutan, Aida. 'Why the Fighting Cock? The Significance of the Imagery of the Khorus Jangi and Its Manifesto "The Slaughterer of the Nightingale".' *Iran Namag*, no. 1 (Spring 2016), XXVIII–XLIX.

Fouladvand, Hengameh. 'Mohammed Ehsai's Modernist Explorations in Calligraphic Form and Content.' *Arte East*, 2008. https://arteeast.org/quarterly/mohammed-ehsais-modernist-explorations-in-calligraphic-form-and-content/?issues_season=summer&issues_year=2008. Accessed 11 June 2018.

Frampton, Kenneth. 'Towards a Critical Regionalism: Six Points of Architecture of Resistance.' In Hal Foster (ed.), *The Anti-Aesthetic: Essays on Postmodern Culture*. London: Pluto Press, 1983. 16–30.

Fraser, Andrea. 'From the Critique of Institutions to an Institution of Critique.' *Artforum*, vol. 44, no. 1 (2005), 100–106.

Galloway, David. *Parviz Tanavoli: Sculptor, Writer, and Collector*. Tehran: Iranian Art Publishing, 2000.

'Remembering TMoCA.' In Dorothée Brill, Joachim Jäger, and Gabriel Montua (eds.), *The Tehran Modern: A Reader about Art in Iran since 1960*. Berlin: Nationalgalerie, Staatliche Museen zu Berlin, 2017. 38–49.

Gertje R. Utlej. *Picasso, The Communist Years*. New Haven: Yale University Press, 2000.

Gharib, Gholam Hossein. 'Nabsh.' *Fighting Rooster Magazine*, no. 1 (Tehran, 1948), 16–30.

Goldzamt, Edmund. 'Das Erbe von William Morris und das Bauhaus [1].' *Hochschule für Architektur und Bauwesen, Weimar*, vol. 23, no. 5–6 (1976), 485–488.

Goudarzi, Mortezza. *Chostoochooy-e hoviat dar naghashi-e moaser-e Iran* [The Search for Identity in Iran's Modern Painting]. Tehran, 2002.

Grasskamp, Walter. *Die unbewältigte Moderne: Kunst und Öffentlichkeit*. München: Beck, 1994.

Green, Nile. 'Between Heidegger and the Hidden Imam: Reflections on Henry Corbin's Approaches to Mystical Islam.' *Method & Theory in the Study of Religion*, vol. 17, no. 3 (2005), 219–226.

Grenier, Catherine. *Modernités Plurielles 1905–1970 Dans Les Collections Du Musée National D'art Moderne*. Paris: Centre Pompidou, 2013.

Grigor, Talinn. *Building Iran: Modernism, Architecture, and National Heritage under the Pahlavi Monarchs*. New York: Periscope Pub, 2009.

Contemporary Iranian Art: From the Street to the Studio. London: Reaktion Books, 2014.

'Kingship Hybridized, Kingship Homogenized: Revivalism under the Qajar and the Pahlavi Dynasties.' In Sussan Babaie and Talinn Grigor (eds.), *Persian Kingship and Architecture: Strategies of Power in Iran from the Achaemenids to the Pahlavis*. London: Tauris, 2015. 219–254.

'Recultivating "Good Taste": The Early Pahlavi Modernists and Their Society for National Heritage.' *Iranian Studies*, vol. 37, no. 1 (2004), 17–45.

'Shifting Gaze: Irano-Persian Architecture from the Great Game to a Nation State.' In Rujivachkurul Vimalin (ed.), *Architecturalized Asia: Mapping a Continent through History*. Honolulu: University of Hawai'i Press, 2013. 217–230.

Grigorian, Marcos. 'Foreword.' In *Catalogue First Tehran Biennial*. Tehran: Ministry of Art and Culture Tehran, 1958. 2–8.

Gruber, Christiane. 'The Martyrs' Museum in Tehran: Visualizing Memory in Post-Revolutionary Iran.' *Visual Anthropology*, vol. 25, no. 1–2 (2012), 68–97.

Guilbaut, Serge. *How New York Stole the Idea of Modern Art: Abstract Expressionism, Freedom, and the Cold War*. Chicago: University of Chicago Press, 1983.

Gumpert, Lynn. *Modernisms; Iranian, Turkish, and Indian Highlights from NYU's Abby Weed Grey Collection*. New York and Munich: Grey Art Gallery, New York University, 2019.

Haghani, Fakhri. 'The City of Ray and the Holy Shrine of Shah/Hazrat Abdol Azim: History of the Sacred and Secular in Iran though the Dialectic of Space.' In Soheila Shahshahani (ed.), *Cities of Pilgrimage*. Berlin: Lit, 2009. 159–176.

Hakkak, Ahmad Karimi. 'Nima Jushij. A Life.' In Ahmad Karimi Hakkak and Kamran Talattof (eds.), *Essays on Nima Yushij: Animating Modernism in Persian Poetry*. Leiden: Brill, 2004. 11–68.

Recasting Persian Poetry: Scenarios of Poetic Modernity in Iran. Salt Lake City: University of Utah Press, 1996.

Hakkak, Ahmad Karimi, and Kamran Talattof. *Essays on Nima Yushij: Animating Modernism in Persian Poetry*. Leiden: Brill, 2004.

Hall, Stuart. 'Cultural Identity and Diaspora.' In Patrick Williams and Laura Chrisman (eds.), *Colonial Discourse and Post-colonial Theory: A Reader*. London: Routledge, 1994. 227–237.

Han, Byung-Chul. *Hyperkulturalität. Kultur und Globalisierung*. Berlin: Merve Verlag, 2005.

Hannaneh, Mortezza. 'Musiqi. (Music).' *Fighting Rooster Magazine*, no. 1 (Tehran, 1948), 3–10.

Harmanşah, Ömür. 'ISIS, Heritage, and the Spectacles of Destruction in the Global Media.' *Near Eastern Archaeology*, vol. 78, no. 3 'Special Issue: The Cultural Heritage Crisis in the Middle East' (September 2015).

Heidegger, Martin. 'Building Dwelling Thinking.' In Martin Heidegger (ed.), *Poetry, Language, Thought*. New York: Harper Colophon, 1976. 141–159.

Hillmann, Michael (ed.). *Iranian Society: An Anthology of Writings by Jalal Al-e Ahmad*. Lexington, KY: Mazda Publication, 1988.

Hobsbawm, Eric, and Terence Ranger. *The Invention of Tradition*. Cambridge: Cambridge University Press, 2012.

Hosseini-Rad, Abdolmajid. 'Iranian Contemporary Art.' In *Iranian Modern Art Movement: The Iranian Collection of the Tehran Museum of Contemporary Art*. Tehran: Tehran Museum of Contemporary Art, 2006.

Huntington, Samuel P. *The Clash of Civilizations and the Remaking of World Order*. London: Penguin Books, 1996.

Huyssen, Andreas. 'German Painting in the Cold War.' *New German Critique*, no. 110 (2010), 209–227.

Present Pasts: Urban Palimpsets and the Politics of Memory. Stanford: Stanford University Press, 2003

Hyder, Syed Akbar. 'Iqbal und Karbala: Re-reading the Episteme of Martyrdom for a Poetics of Appropriation.' *Cultural Dynamics*, vol. 13, no. 3 (November 2001), 339–362.

Iradj Moeini, Seyed Hossein, Mehran Arefian, Bahador Kashani, and Golnar Abbasi (eds.). *Urban Culture in Tehran: Urban Processes in Unofficial Cultural Spaces*. Cham: Springer, 2018.

Jackson, A. V. Williams. 'The Allegory of the Moths and the Flame. Translated from the Manṭiq aṭ-Tair of Farīdad-Dīn 'Attār.' *Journal of the American Oriental Society*, vol. 36 (1916), 345–347.

Jacobi, Hannah. *Stimmen aus Teheran: Interviews zur zeitgenössischen Kunst im Iran*. Frankfurt: Edition Faust, 2017.

Jafari, Parastoo. *New Word, Other Value: Artistic Modernism and Private Patronage: Associations and Galleries in Pre-Islamic Revolution Iran*. Munich: OPH Press, 2020.

Jalali, Bahman. *Days of Blood: Days of Fire, 1978–1979*. Tehran: Zamineh, 1979.

Juneja, Monica. 'Alternative, Peripheral or Cosmopolitan? Modernism as a Global Process.' In Juli Allerstorfer and M. Leisch-Kiesl (eds.), »*Global Art History«: Transkulturelle Verortungen von Kunst und Kunstwissenschaft*. Bielefeld: Transcript, 2018. 79–108.

Karjoo-Ravary, Ali. 'Shi'i Rituals in Pahlavi Iran: Audio Recordings from the Ajam Archive.' https://ajammc.com/2017/11/10/archive-iranian-islam-1979-shii-rituals-mohammad-reza-shah. Accessed 14 January 2020.

Keshmirshekan, Hamid (ed.). *Amidst Shadow and Light: Contemporary Iranian Art and Artists*. Hong Kong: Liaoning Creative Press, 2005.

(ed.). *Contemporary Art from the Middle East: Regional Interactions with Global Art Discourses.* London: I. B. Tauris, 2015

Contemporary Iranian Art. New Perspectives. London: Saqi Books, 2013.

Koorosh Shishegaran: The Art of Altruism. London: Saqi Books, 2016.

'Neo-Traditionalism and Modern Iranian Painting: The 'Saqqa-khaneh' School in the 1960s.' *Iranian Studies*, vol. 38, no. 4 (2005), 607–630.

'The Question of Identity vis-à-vis Exoticism in Contemporary Iranian Art.' *Iranian Studies*, vol. 43, no. 4 (2010), 489–512.

'Reclaiming Cultural Space: The Artist's Performativity versus the State's Expectations in Contemporary Iran.' In Staci Gem Scheiwiller (ed.), *Performing the Iranian State: Visual Culture and Representations of Iranian Identity.* London: Anthem Press, 2013. 145–155.

'SAQQĀ-KĀNA SCHOOL OF ART.' *Encyclopedia Iranica.* Online edition, 2009. www.iranicaonline.org/articles/saqqa-kana-ii-school-of-art. Accessed 4 July 2018.

Khalili, E. Nader. *Art and Architecture.* 'Iran Yesterday, Today, Tomorrow.' No. 18–19 (June–November 1973).

Khan, Saira. *Iran and Nuclear Weapons: Protracted Conflict and Proliferation.* London: Routledge, 2005.

Kohn, Margaret, and Keally McBride. *Political Theories of Decolonization: Postcolonialism and the Problem of the Foundation.* New York: Oxford University Press, 2011.

Korycki, Katarzyna, and Abouzar Nasirzade. 'Desire Recast: The Production of Gay Identity in Iran.' *Journal of Gender Studies*, vol. 25, no. 1 (2016), 50–65.

Kuban, Zeynab, and Wille Simone (eds.). *André Lhote and His International Students.* Innsbruck: Innsbruck University Press, 2020.

Künkler, Mirjam, John T. S Madeley, and Shylashri Shankar. *A Secular Age beyond the West: Religion, Law and the State in Asia, the Middle East and North Africa.* Cambridge: Cambridge University Press, 2019.

Lacan, Jacques. 'The Mirror Stage as Formative of the Function of the I as Revealed in Psychoanalytic Experience.' In Vincent B. Leitch, et al. (eds.), *The Norton Anthology of Theory and Criticism.* New York: W. W. Norton, 2001. 1163–1169.

Lampe, Franziska. 'Zum Holzschnitt als visuelle Strategie um 1918/19.' In Nils Grosch (ed.), *Novembergruppe 1918. Studien zu einer interdisziplinären Kunst für die Weimarer Republik.* Münster: Waxmann, 2018. 43–60.

Lashkari, Amir, and Mojde Kalantari. 'Pardeh Khani: A Dramatic Form of Storytelling in Iran.' *Asian Theatre Journal*, vol. 32, no. 1 (2015), 245–258.

Lenze, Franz. *Der Nativist Ǧalāl-e Āl-e Aḥmad und die Verwestlichung Irans im 20. Jahrhundert.* Berlin: Klaus Schwarz Verlag, 2008.

Mahlouji, Vali. 'Perspectives on the Shiraz Arts Festival: A Radical Third World Rewriting.' In Fereshteh Daftari and Layla S. Diba (eds.), *Iran Modern*. Exh. Cat. New York: Asia Society Museum in association with Yale University Press New Haven, 2013. 87–91.

Mansfield, Elisabeth (ed.). *Making Art History: A Changing Discipline and Its Institutions*. London: Routledge, 2007.

Marx, Karl, and Friedrich Engels. *The Communist Manifesto*. New York: International Publishers, 1948.

Mashhadizadeh, Abbas. 'Abbas Mashhadizadeh Talks History of Iranian Academic Art.' *Honaronline*, 2007. www.honaronline.ir/Section-visual-4/96791-abbas-mashhadizadeh-talks-history-of-iranian-academic-art. Accessed 23 October 2019.

'Honar dar zendegi va zendegi dar honar. Darbare-ye Lilit Teryan.' http://old.sharghdaily.ir/pdf/90-09-03/vijeh/22.pdf Accessed 21 October 2019.

Matin-Asgari, Afshin. 'From Social Democracy to Social Democracy: The Twentieth Century Odyssey of the Iranian Left.' In Stephanie Cronin (ed.), *Reformers and Revolutionaries in Modern Iran: New Perspectives on the Iranian Left*. London: Routledge, 2004. 37–64.

Michels, Eckard. *Schahbesuch 1967. Fanal für die Studentenbewegung*. Berlin: Ch. Links Verlag, 2017.

Mignolo, Walter D. *The Darker Side of Western Modernity: Global Futures. Decolonial Options*. Durham, NC: Duke University Press, 2011.

Mirsepassi, Ali. *Democracy in Iran: Islam, Culture, and Political Change*. New York: New York University Press, 2010.

Intellectual Discourse and the Politics of Modernization: Negotiating Modernity in Iran. Cambridge: Cambridge University Press, 2004.

Iran's Quiet Revolution: The Downfall of the Pahlavi State. Cambridge: Cambridge University Press, 2019.

Political Islam, Iran, and the Enlightenment: Philosophies of Hope and Despair. Cambridge: Cambridge University Press, 2010.

Transnationalism in Iranian Political Thought: The Life and Times of Ahmad Fardid. Cambridge: Cambridge University Press, 2017

Mirsepassi, Ali, and Hamed Yousefi. 'Abby Weed Grey's Journey to the East: Iranian Modernity during the Cold War.' In Lynn Gumpert (ed.), *Modernisms: Iranian, Turkish, and Indian Highlights from NYU's Abby Weed Grey Collection*. New York and Munich: Grey Art Gallery, New York University, 2019. 65–77.

Mitchell, Timothy. 'The Stage of Modernity.' In Timothy Mitchell (ed.), *Questions of Modernity*. Minneapolis: University of Minnesota Press, 2000. 1–34.

Mitter, Partha. *The Triumph of Modernism, India's Artists and the Avant-Garde 1922–1947*. London: Reaktion, 2007.
Mojabi, Javad. *Pioneers of Contemporary Persian Painting, First Generation*. Tehran: Iranian Art Publishing, 1996.
Saramdan-e Honar-e Noh [The Pioneers of New Art]. Tehran: Behnegar, 2015.
Mollanoroozi, Majid. *Selected Works of Tehran Museum of Contemporary Art: Berlin – Rome Travelers*. Exh.-Cat. Tehran: Tehran Museum of Contemporary Art, 2017.
Montazami, Morad, and Narmine Sadeg (eds.). *Behdjat Sadr: Traces*. Paris: Zaman Books, 2014.
Mouffe, Chantal. *Agonistics: Thinking the World Politically*. London: Verso, 2013.
Moussavi-Aghdam, Combiz. 'Art History, "National Art" and Iranian Intellectuals in the 1960s.' *British Journal of Middle Eastern Studies*, vol. 41, no. 1 (2014), 132–150.
Muhammad, Abdel Haleem. *The Qur'an*. New York: Oxford University Press, 2004.
Naef, Silvia, Irene Maffi, and Wendy Shaw. '"Other Modernities": Art, Visual Culture and Patrimony Outside the West. An Introduction.' *Artl@s Bulletin*, vol. 9, no. 1 (2020), Article 1.
Naficy, Hamid. *The Making of Exile Cultures: Iranian television in Los Angeles*. Minneapolis: University of Minnesota Press, 1993.
Nahidi, Katrin. *'How It Breaks My Heart to Leave You': Images of Women in Shirin Neshat's Video Works*. Exh.-Cat. Tübingen: Stiftung Kunsthalle Tübingen, 2017. 135–147.
Najmabadi, Afsaneh. 'The Erotic Vatan [Homeland] as Beloved and Mother: To Love, to Possess, and to Protect.' *Comparative Studies in Society and History*, no. 3 (1997), 442–467.
Nasr, Seyyed Hossein. *The Garden of Truth: The Vision and Promise of Sufism, Islam's Mystical Tradition*. New York: Harper Collins, 2007.
Nirumand, Bahman. *Persien, Modell eines Entwicklungslandes*. Reinbek b. Hamburg: Rowohlt, 1967.
Nodjoumi, Nicky, and Shirin Neshat (eds.). *Ardeshir Mohassess: Art and Satire in Iran*. Exh.-Cat. Asia Society. New York: Asia Society Antique Collectors' Club, 2008.
Nye, Joseph S. *Soft Power: The Means to Success in World Politics*. New York: Public Affairs, 2004.
Pahlavi, Mohammad Reza. *Toward the Great Civilization: A Dream Revisited*. London: Satrap Publishing, 1994.
Pakbaz, Ruyin. *Contemporary Iranian Painting and Sculpture*. Tehran: Ministry of Fine Arts and Culture, 1974.

'Dar jostiju-ye hoviyat' ['Seeking Identity']. *Herfeh: Honarmand.* Tehran: Herfch:Honarmand, 2007. 18.

Encyclopedia of Art. Tehran: Farhang-e Moaser, 1999.

Naqashi-ye Iran: Az diruz ta emruz [Iranian Painting: From Yesterday to Today]. Tehran: B Nashr-e Naristan, 2000.

Pakbaz, Ruyin, and Yaghoub Emdadian. *Massoud Arabshahi: Pioneers of Iranian Modern Art.* Exh.-Cat. Tehran: Tehran Museum of Contemporary Art, 2001.

Pioneers of Iranian Modern Art: Charles Hossein Zenderoudi. Exh.-Cat. Tehran: Tehran Museum of Contemporary Art, 2001.

Pakbaz, Ruyin, and Yaghoub Emdadian (eds.). *Pioneers of Modern Iranian Art: Parviz Tanavoli.* Exh.-Cat. Tehran: Tehran Museum of Contemporary Art, 2003.

Parsi, Trita. *Losing an Enemy: Obama, Iran, and the Triumph of Diplomacy.* Yale: Yale University Press, 2017.

Parsikia, Farshid, et al. *Horus-e changi, Pazuheshi darbare-ye anjoman-e honari* [The Fighting Rooster, Research about the Artistic Association]. Tehran: Poshtebaamag.ir, 2019

Parzinger, Helmut. 'On the Unifying Power of Art and an Unrealised Exhibition.' In Dorothée Brill, Joachim Jäger, and Gabriel Montua (eds.), *The Tehran Modern: A Reader about Art in Iran since 1960.* Berlin: Nationalgalerie, Staatliche Museen zu Berlin, 2017. 6–13.

Pfisterer, Ulrich (ed.). *Metzler Lexikon Kunstwissenschaft: Ideen, Methoden, Begriffe.* Stuttgart: Metzler, 2019.

Pickett, James. 'Soviet Civilization through a Persian Lens: Iranian Intellectuals, Cultural Diplomacy and Socialist Modernity 1941–55.' *Iranian Studies*, vol. 48, no. 5 (2015), 805–826.

Pope, Arthur Upham, and Phyllis Ackerman, *A Survey of Persian Art from Prehistoric Times to the Present.* London: Oxford University Press, 1938.

Popp, Roland. 'An Application of Modernization Theory during the Cold War? The Case of Pahlavi Iran.' *The International History Review*, vol. 30, no. 1 (2008), 76–98.

Pratt, Marie Louise. 'Arts of the Contact Zone.' *Profession* (1991), 33–40.

Prita, Meier. 'Authenticity and Its Modernist Discontents. The Colonial Encounter and African and Middle Eastern Art History.' *The Arab Studies Journal*, vol. 18, no. 1 (Spring 2010), 12–45.

Rancière, Jacques. *Aesthetics and Its Discontents.* Cambridge: Polity, 2009. 23.

Dissensus: On Politics and Aesthetics. London: Bloomsbury Academic, 2010. 21.

Ridgeon, Lloyd. *Morals and Mysticism in Persian Sufism: A History of Sufi-futuwwat in Iran*. London: Routledge, 2014.
Sufi Castigator, Ahmad Kasravi and the Iranian Mystical Tradition. London: Routledge, 2006.
Roaf, S. 'BĀDGĪR.' *Encyclopædia Iranica*, Online edition, 1988. www.iranicaonline.org/articles/badgir-traditional-structure-for-passive-air-conditioning. Accessed 4 February 2017.
Robbins, Daniel. *André Lhote, 1885–1962. Cubism*. Exh. Cat. New York: Leonard Hutton Galleries, 1976.
Rosalyn, Deutsche. 'Property Values: Hans Haacke, Real Estate and the Museum.' In R. Deutsche (ed.), *Evictions: Art and Spatial Politics*. Cambridge, MA: MIT Press, 1996. 159–192.
Rutherford, Jonathan. 'The Third Space: Interview with Homi Bhabha.' In J. Rutherford (ed.), *Identity, Community, Culture, Difference*. London: Lawrence and Wishart, 1990. 207–221.
Sadeghi-Boroujerdi, Eskandar. 'Gharbzadegi, Colonial Capitalism and the Racial State in Iran.' *Postcolonial Studies*, vol. 24, no. 2 (2021), 173–194.
Safran, William. 'Diasporas in Modern Societies: Myths of Homeland and Return.' *Diaspora: A Journal of Transnational Studies*, no. 1 (1991), 83–99.
Said, Edward. *Orientalism*. New York: Penguin Books, 1978.
Salemy, Mohammed, and Stefan Heidenreich. 'Vultures over TMOCA? What's behind the Cancellation of the Berlin Exhibition from the Collection of Tehran Museum of Contemporary Art.' *E-flux*, 2016.
Samadzadegan, Behrang, Behnam Kamrani, and Siamak Delzendeh. Etemad Newspaper, 9 April 2014. www.magiran.com/article/2926864. Accessed 23 October 2019.
Sandijian, Manuchehr. 'Temporality of "Home" and Spatiality of Market in Exile: Iranians in Germany.' *New German Critique*, no. 64 (Winter 1995), 3–36.
Sarshar, Houman. 'From Allegory to Symbol: Emblems of Nature in the Poetry of Nima Yushij.' In Ahmad Karimi Hakkak and Kamran Talattof (eds.), *Essays on Nima Yushij: Animating Modernism in Persian Poetry*. Leiden: Brill, 2004. 99–138.
Saunders Stonor, Frances. *Who Paid the Piper? CIA and the Cultural Cold War*. London: Granta, 1999.
Savoy, Bénédicte. *Die Provenienz der Kultur. Von der Trauer des Verlusts zum universalen Menschheitserbe*. Berlin: Matthes & Seitz Berlin, 2018.
Schimmel, Annemarie. *Mystical Dimensions of Islam*. Chapel Hill: University of North Carolina Press, 1975.

Severi, Hamid. 'Mapping Iranian Contemporary Publications and Knowledge-Production.' In Hamid Keshmirshekan (ed.), *Contemporary Art from the Middle East: Regional Interactions with Global Art Discourses*. London: I. B. Tauris, 2015. 69–88.

Shahshahani, Soheila (ed.). *Cities of Pilgrimage*. Berlin: Lit, 2009.

Shams, Alex. 'The Weaponization of Nostalgia: How Afghan Miniskirts Became the Latest Salvo in the War on Terror.' *Ajam Media Collective* 6. 2017. https://ajammc.com/2017/09/06/weaponization-nostalgia-afghan-miniskirts/. Accessed 4 July 2018.

Shariati, Ali. *Fatima Is Fatima*. Translated by Laleh Bakhtiar. Tehran: Shariati Foundation, 1981.

Shaw, Wendy M. K. *What Is 'Islamic' Art? Between Religion and Perception*. Cambridge: Cambridge University Press, 2019.

Sheybani, Manuchehr. Poem (Untitled). *Fighting Rooster Magazine*, no. 1 (Tehran, 1948), 43–45.

Shirazi, Reza M. *Contemporary Architecture and Urbanism in Iran: Tradition, Modernity, and the Production of 'Space-in-Between'*. Cham: Springer, 2018.

Shirvanloo, Firouz. 'Creative Return to Iran's Ancient Art.' Tehran, 1977. Cited in Ruyin Pakbaz and Yaghoub Emdadian (eds.). *Massoud Arabshahi: Pioneers of Iranian Modern Art*. Exh.-Cat. Tehran: Tehran Museum of Contemporary Art, 2001. 8–9.

Slobodian, Quinn. *Foreign Front: Third World Politics in Sixties West Germany*. Durham, NC: Duke University Press, 2012.

Spivak, Gayatri Chakravorty. 'The Rani of Sirmur: An Essay in Reading the Archives.' *History and Theory*, vol. 24, no. 3 (October 1985), 247–272.

———. 'Three Women's Texts and a Critique of Imperialism.' *Critical Inquiry*, vol. 12, no. 1 'Race, Writing, and Difference' (Autumn 1985), 243–261.

Stowasser, Barbara Freyer. *Women in the Qur'an, Traditions, and Interpretation*. New York: Oxford University Press, 1996

Tadjvidi, Akbar. *L'art moderne en Iran*. Tehran: Ministry of Fine Arts and Culture, 1967.

Talar-e Qandriz. Tehran: Herfeh Honarmand, 2016.

Talattof, Kamran. 'Ideology and Self-Portrayal in the Poetry of Nima Yushij.' In Ahmad Karimi Hakkak and Kamran Talattof (eds.), *Essays on Nima Yushij: Animating Modernism in Persian Poetry*. Leiden: Brill, 2004. 69–98.

Tanavoli, Parviz. 'Atelier Kaboud.' In David Galloway (ed.), *Parviz Tanavoli: Sculptor, Writer, and Collector*. Tehran: Iranian Art Publishing, 2000.

Taylor, Charles. *A Secular Age*. Cambridge, MA: Belknap Press of Harvard University Press, 2007.

Tekiner, Deniz. 'Formalist Art Criticism and the Politics of Meaning.' *Social Justice*, vol. 33, no. 2 'Art, Power, and Social Change' (2006), 31–44.
Tottoli, Roberto. 'At Cock-Crow: Some Muslim Traditions About the Rooster.' *Der Islam, Bd.*, vol. 76 (1999), 139–144.
Vahabi, Nader. *ATLAS de la diaspora Iranienne*. Paris: Ed. Karthala, 2012.
Van Hook, James C., and Adam M. Howard (eds.). *Foreign Relations of the United States, 1952–1954, Iran, 1951–1954*. Vol. XIX. Washington: Government Printing Office, 2017. https://static.history.state.gov/frus/frus1951–54Iran/pdf. Accessed 23 October 2017.
Wasserstrom, Steven M. *Religion after Religion: Gershom Scholem, Mircea Eliade and Henry Corbin at Eranos*. Princeton: Princeton University Press, 1997.
Wedekind, Gregor. 'Abstraktion und Abendland: Die Erfindung der documenta als Antwort auf 'unsere deutsche Lage.' In Nikola Doll (ed.), *Kunstgeschichte nach 1945: Kontinuität und Neubeginn in Deutschland*. Köln: Böhlau, 2006. 165–182.
Weibel, Peter. 'Globalization: The End of Modern Art?' *ZKM Magazine*, 2013. https://zkm.de/en/magazine/2013/02/globalization-the-end-of-modern-art. Accessed 25 October.
Weingarden, Lauren S. 'Aesthetics Politicized: William Morris to the Bauhaus.' *Journal of Architectural Education*, vol. 38, no. 3 (1985), 8–13.
Wilson, Peter Lamborn. '"The Saqqa–Khaneh" from Saqqakhaneh, 1977.' In Fereshteh Daftari and Layla S. Diba (eds.), *Iran Modern*. Exh. Cat. New York: Asia Society Museum in Association with Yale University Press New Haven, 2013. 231–233.
Winegar, Jessica. 'The Humanity Game: Art, Islam, and the War on Terror.' *Anthropological Quarterly*, vol. 81, no. 3 (2008), 651–681.
Wünsche, Isabel. 'Expressionist Networks, Cultural Debates, and Artistic Practices: A Conceptual Introduction.' In Isabel Wünsche (ed.), *The Routledge Companion to Expressionism in a Transnational Context*. New York: Routledge Taylor & Francis Group, 2019. 1–30.
Yarshater, Ehsan. 'Contemporary Persian Painting.' In Richard Ettinghausen and Ehsan Yarshater (eds.), *Highlights of Persian Art*. Boulder: Wittenborn Art Books, 1979. 363–377.
'Foreword' VIV. In Jalal Al-e Ahmad (ed.), *Plagued by the West (Gharbzadegi)*. Delmar, NY: Center for Iranian Studies Columbia University, 1981.
Yavari, Houra. *Karim Emami on Modern Iranian Culture, Literature & Art*. New York: Persian Heritage Foundation.
Young, Robert J. C. *Postcolonialism: An Historical Introduction*. Oxford: Blackwell, 2001.

Yousefi, Hamed. 'ART+ART: The Avant-Garde in the Streets.' *E–Flux Journal*, no. 82 (May 2017).
Yushij, Nima. 'About the City of the Morning.' *Fighting Rooster Magazine*, no. 1 (Tehran, 1948), 1–2.
Zia-Ebrahimi, Reza. 'Self-Orientalization and Dislocation: The Uses and Abuses of the "Aryan" Discourse in Iran.' *Iranian Studies*, vol. 4, no. 4 (July 2011), 445–472.
Ziapour, Jalil. 'Naqashi' (Painting). *Fighting Rooster Magazine*, no. 1 (Tehran, 1948), 12–15.
  Refute of the Theories of Past and Contemporary Ideologies from Primitive to Surrealism. 1948. www.ziapour.com/wp-content/uploads/2008/12/jalil_ziapour_theory.pdf. Accessed 4 April 2019.
Zolghadr, Tirdad. *Ethnic Marketing*. Zurich: JRP/Ringier, 2006.
Zolghadr, *Traction*. Berlin: Sternberg Press, 2016.

Index

2,500th-anniversary, 122, 165, 195, 261

Abbasi, Reza, 178, 253
Abdol-Azim, 160
Achaemenid Empire, 120
Action Française, 222
Afsarian, Iman, 7, 75, 205
Ahmadinejad, Mahmoud, 52, 78
Al-e Ahmad, Jalal, 97–107, 131–145, 171, 192
  Gharbzadegi, 97–107, 163
  Ziyarat, 159
Amanat, Hossein, 123, 125
Anglo-Iranian Oil Company, 141
anti-colonialism, 59, 92, 97, 99, 114, 139, 172–176, 193, 262
anti-modernism, 92, 164
Apadana Gallery, 133
Arabshahi, Massoud, 30, 183, 202
Arani, Taghi, 235
archaeology, 67, 119–121
architecture, 117–123
Ardalan, Nader, 123, 129
art historiography, 2, 3, 7, 9, 15, 28, 30, 89, 132, 134, 146, 158, 202, 220, 261
art history, 177–182, 189–207, 220–222, 260
Arts and Crafts Movement, 179
Ashura, 131, 149, 151, 175
Association of Iranian Painters, 79
Atelier Kaboud, 158
Attar, Farid al-din, 153, 238, 244

Bacon, Francis, 38, 76, 82
badgir, 127
Barr, Alfred, 29
bast, 160
Bauhaus, 179

Bergson, Henri, 18, 209, 222–225
Bhabha, Homi, 48, 57
bismillah, 236
Blaue Reiter, der, 156
Bode, Arnold, 54
Bourdieu, Pierre, 5, 88, 112
Brandt, Willy, 59
Braque, George, 221
Brücke, die, 156
brutalism, 126
Bush, George, 25

calligraphy, 186, 188, 237
Camus, Albert, 139
canon, 2, 182, 189, 200, 209, 262, 264
capitalism, 102, 174
Carpet Museum, 109
censorship, 40, 76, 106, 112, 231, 259
Chalipa, Kazem, 83
clergy, 104, 160, 174, 195, 248
coffeehouse painting, 44, 151, 154
Cold War, 4, 174, 196–198, 200, 232
College of Decorative Arts, 136, 158, 171, 178, 256
colonialism, 11, 15, 60, 92, 93, 96, 102, 234
Communist Manifesto, 102, 227
Constitutional Revolution, 95, 160, 215
Corbin, Henry, 162, 165–166
Cossack Brigade, 117
coup d'état, 4, 39, 71, 172, 174, 205
critique of modernization, 91
Cubism, 199, 209, 220–229

daftar-e makhsus-e shahbanu, 72, 109
Daneshvar, Simin, 27, 136–138
Delaunay, Robert, 221
democracy, 1, 4, 60, 68, 75, 95, 107, 164, 230

283

diaspora, 23–24, 26
Diba, Farah, 67, 80, 91–107, 147, 165, 194, 198
Diba, Kamran, 72, 86, 114, 125, 192, 200
documenta, 54–55
Dolatabadi, Parvin, 211
Dreyfus Affair, 222
Duchamp, Marcel, 221

École-des-Beaux-Arts, 2, 208
Ehsai, Mohammad, 32, 199
Elkins, James, 13, 182
Emami, Karim, 1, 30, 168–176, 184
Entartete Kunst (Degenerate Art),, 53
Enwezor, Okwui, 11
erfan, 32, 233
Ernst, Max, 82
ershad, 76, 79
Esfandiari, Ahmad, 134, 197
Esfandiari-Bakhtiari, Soraya, 61
Etemadi, Parvaneh, 82, 205
exile, 23–26, 131, 173, 259
exoticism, 18, 88, 138, 145, 182, 208
Expressionism, 3, 155

fana, 152, 185
Fanon, Frantz, 174
Fardid, Ahmad, 93–97, 165
Farmanfarmaian, Monir, 82
Fauvism, 199, 219
Fighting Rooster Association, 18, 208–254
formalism, 9–10, 134, 204, 262
Foucault, Michel, 93, 96
Fraser, Andrea, 88
Freedom Tower, 123
French Revolution, 110
Fuller, Buckminster, 123

Ganjavi, Nizami, 212
Gérôme, Jean Léon, 212
Ghandriz, Mansour, 30, 182
Gharib, Gholam Hossein, 208, 249–251
Gilgamesh Gallery, 169
Gleizes, Albert, 222
global art history, 14
Godard, André, 2, 120
Green Movement, 69, 78

Greenberg, Clement, 9
Grey, Abby Weed, 196–198
Grigorian, Marcos, 136, 154
Gropius, Walter, 179
Guggenheim Museum, 87

Haacke, Hans, 87
Hafez, 121, 233, 248, 251
Haftmann, Werner, 54
Hagigat, Nahid, 40
hamam, 211
Han, Byung-Chul, 58
Hannaneh, Morteza, 208
Hannaneh, Mortezza, 142, 251–252
Haraguchi, Noriyuki, 116
Hegel, Georg Wilhelm Friedrich, 181
hegemony, 95, 113
Heidegger, Martin, 57, 94, 166
Herfeh Honarmand, 204
heritage, 135, 154, 162, 165, 169, 253
Hertzfeld, Ernst, 119, 120
Heshmat, Behruz, 259
Hosseini, Mansoureh, 142
hostage crisis, 24
Hotel Darband, 121
Hovanessian, Vartan, 121
hybridity, 8, 57

iconography
 Shi'ite, 148, 157, 201
Imam Ali, 213
Imam Hussein, 131, 148, 149, 151, 175
imitation, 146, 219
immaturity, artistic, 219
Imperial Iranian Academy, 165
imperialism, 102, 135, 136, 137, 139, 173, 175, 257
 cultural, 134
Ingres, Dominique, 212
institutional critique, 87
institutionalization, 92, 206
instrumentalization, 206, 262
International Association for Energy Economics, 51
Ionesco, Eugène, 105
Iran Modern, 16, 20–21, 26–65
Iran-Iraq war, 22, 51, 70, 83, 259
Iranshahr, 118
Islamic art history, 14, 67

Index

Islamic Republic, 16, 20, 22, 35, 49, 56, 67, 69, 77, 86, 130, 258
Islamic State, 64

Jafari, Shaban, 42
Jalali, Bahman, 40, 65
Javadipour, Mahmoud, 133

Kahn, Louis, 123
Kahnweiler, Daniel-Henry, 221
Karbala, battle of, 83, 150, 169, 175, 192, 213
Kasravi, Ahmad, 234
Kazemi, Hossein, 133
ketab-e mah, 106, 136
Khatami, Seyyed Mohammad, 74
Khayyam, Omar, 153
Khomeini, Ayatollah, 51, 74, 175
Khosrow and Shirin, 212, 217
Kollwitz, Käthe, 157

l'art pour l'art, 225
Lacan, Jaques, 48
Laleh Park, 114
Léger, Fernand, 221
Lettrism, 30
Lhote, André, 18, 209, 221, 224, 254

Mafi, Reza, 34, 199
Maleki, Khalil, 142
manifesto, 176, 224–229, 252
Marini, Marino, 158
Martyr Museum, 71, 260
martyrs, 30, 71, 83, 149, 175
Marx, Karl, 98, 102
Marxism, 99, 103, 134, 145, 227
Massignon, Louis, 165
Matin Daftari, Leili, 82
memorialization, 259
memory, 259, 260
metal works, 30, 170, 190
Metzinger, Jean, 222
Migration, 21–23
miniature painting, 42, 83, 213, 236
Ministry of Fine Arts, 5, 136
minor literature, 194
mo'aser, 14
mobilization, 62, 100, 113, 231, 256

modernism, 45, 168, 172, 208, 225, 263
  calligraphic modernism, 31
  Iranian, 26–30, 131–145, 161, 162, 172, 173, 189, 196, 202, 204, 206, 262, 264
  local, 27, 170, 184, 254
  postcolonial, 131
  school of, 177, 189
  state-sponsored, 205, 262
modernities, 12, 15, 16, 28, 60
modernity, 1, 3, 7–13, 49, 219, 233, 235, 261
modernization, 92, 93, 99, 101, 108, 110, 113, 120, 131, 137, 215, 261
modernization theory, 93, 101
Mohassess, Ardeshir, 42
Mohassess, Bahman, 37, 139–143
Mollanoroozi, Majid, 49, 80
Morris, William, 179
Mosaddeq, Mohammad, 4, 99, 141, 205, 230
moth, 153
Moussavi, Mir Hossein, 78
Muharram, 131, 151, 169, 214
Muzaffar al-Din, Shah, 160
mysticism, 165, 234

Nasr, Seyed Hossein, 165
National Front, 69, 142, 231
National Gallery Berlin, 16, 49, 63
National Socialism, 53
nationalism, 25, 163, 209, 217, 231
nationalization, Iran's oil, 3, 39, 69, 141
nationalization, Iran's oil, 264
nativism, 104
Negarastan Museum, 109
neo-traditionalism, 170, 201
Neshat, Shirin, 89
Nirumand, Bahman, 62
Nodjoumy, Nicky, 40
November Revolution, 156
nuclear politics, 49, 50–53, 89
Nuclear-Non-Proliferation Treaty, 51

October Revolution, 156
Ohnesorg, Benno, 63
Orientalism, 18, 60, 94, 95, 96, 119, 134, 212, 234, 261

Orphic Cubism, 209, 221
Oveissi, Nasser, 34, 192

Pahlavi, Ashraf, 165
Pahlavi, Mohammad Reza Shah, 70, 97, 108, 117, 122, 125–128, 163–167, 230
Pahlavi, Reza Shah, 117, 230
Pakbaz, Ruyin, 6–7, 133, 197
parasite, 225
parcham, 151
pardeh, 150, 154
Parvaresh, Afshin, 84–88
Pechstein, Max, 156
Persepolis, 119
Pezeshkian, Houshang, 134
Picasso, Pablo, 218, 221
Pilaram, Faramarz, 30, 182
pilgrimage, 161, 167
pioneer, 218
poetry, 212, 230, 238
political Islam, 92, 106, 234
Pollock, Jackson, 47
Pope, Arthur Upham, 120, 261
preservation, 109
primitivism, 138, 154, 227
prohibition, image, 65
protest, 65, 68, 78, 84, 86, 99, 141
Puteaux Group, 221

qanat, 128
Qur'an, 105, 190

Rafsanjani, Ali Akbar, 74
Rancière, Jacques, 10
Ray, 159
regionalism, 126
rend, 246
return to the self, 113, 129, 205
Reza Abbasi Hall, 158
rotunda, 116
Roudaki Art and Culture Foundation, 78
Rouhani, Hassan, 52
Rouhbakhsh, Jafar, 83
Rumi, Jalal al-din, 185

Sadeghi, Ali Akbar, 83
Sadeghi, Habibollah, 83
Sadr, Behjat, 35, 142, 197
Said, Edward, 95

Sami-Azar, Alireza, 74
saqi, 246
Saqqakhaneh, 17, 26, 30–31, 146–148, 163, 167–207
  emergence, 158–162
  exhibition, 190–193
Saqqakhaneh fountain, 168
Sartre, Jean-Paul, 139, 143
SAVAK, 40, 62, 108
School, Isfahan, 177
Section d'Or, 221
secularism, 11, 16, 20, 22, 27, 38, 46, 89, 114, 128, 162, 195, 234, 261
secularization, 31, 114, 120, 148, 162, 261
Sepehri, Sohrab, 197
Shahnameh, 44
Shariati, Ali, 96, 113, 192, 214
Shayad Aryamehr, 122
Shaygan, Daryush, 165
sher-e klassik, 240
sher-e no, 240–246
Sheybani, Manouchehr, 230, 246–249
Shiraz Arts Festival, 149
Shirvanloo, Firooz, 183
Shishegaran, Koorosh, 256–258
shrines, 159
Simorgh, 244
Siroux, Maxime, 120
Society for National Heritage, 120
Soft power, 55–56
solidarity, 102
Soviet Socialism, 4, 230
spirituality, 94, 147, 162, 165, 185, 189, 226
Spivak, Gayatri, 172
Steinmeier, Frank-Walter, 46
style, 178, 181, 201
subjectivity, 45
Sufism, 185, 216, 233–235
Suhrawardi, Shahab, 165
Symbolism, 241

ta'ziyeh, 149, 150, 174, 214
Tabatabaie, Jazeh, 34
Tabrizi, Sadegh, 34, 183, 192, 256
Taghizadeh, Jinoos, 79
Tajvidi, Akbar, 5–6
Talar-e Qandriz, 182, 189
Taliban, 64
talismans, 170, 190

Index

Tanavoli, Parviz, 30, 158, 181, 184–189, 197, 202
  Heech, 184–189
Tandis, 204
Tehran Biennial, 136, 168, 176, 182, 197, 199, 210
The Tehran Modern, 16, 46–50, 56–61, 63–66
Tehran Museum of Contemporary Art, 69, 84, 109, 113–117, 123–131, 202
Third Force, 142
Third Reich, 53
Third World, 59, 62, 101, 173, 205, 258
tradition, 3, 6, 8, 13, 30, 125, 128, 201, 262
Tudeh, 99, 206, 230

Unanimism, 241
universalism, 46, 129, 190, 219
universality, 4
University of Tehran, 2, 42, 96, 220
urbanization, 227

Vaziri-Moghaddam, Mohsen, 142
Vishkaie, Mehdi, 134
VOKS, 232

Warhol, Andy, 67
westernization, 11, 36, 92, 103, 127, 147, 172, 188, 195, 201, 202, 254, 261
westoxification, 17, 92–107, 144, 147, 148, 159, 164, 168, 194, 262
White Revolution, 36, 72, 123, 163, 174
wine, 246
Wirtschaftswunder, 54
Wright, Frank Lloyd, 124

Yazd, 114, 127, 130
Yazid, 149, 175, 214
Yushij, Nima, 142, 230, 238–246

Zarif, Mohammad Javad, 52
Zaynab, 213, 214, 217
Zeitgeist, 181
Zenderoudi, Hossein Charles, 30, 148–158, 202
Ziapour, Jalil, 18, 134, 208–220
  Zaynab Khatoun, 82, 209–218
Zoroastrianism, 127, 159, 242
zurkhaneh, 43

Printed in the United States
by Baker & Taylor Publisher Services